Spiritist Review - 1858

Spiritist Review - 1858

Journal of Psychological Studies

Allan Kardec

Original Title - Revue Spirite – Allan Kardec

Translator: Luiz A.V. Cheim
Editors: John C. Maddeen and Jussara Korngold
Cover Design: Mauro de Souza Rodrigues

ISBN 9780985279325
Published through a partnership between the United States Spiritist Council and the
Spiritist Research Institute (IPEAK)

Copyright © 2015 by the United States Spiritist Council
Contact: info@spiritist.us (http://www.spiritist.us)

Manufactured in the United States
First print: April 2015
ISBN: 098527932X

Preface to the English Edition

The Spiritist Review was written and published by Allan Kardec from January 1858 to April 1869. Kardec died on March 31st, 1869. He had finished the April 1869 issue of the Review which was published after his death.

In total there are 136 monthly Issues of the Review, bundled in volumes of 12 issues per year, yielding 12 volumes. It is the largest spiritist production of Allan Kardec.

In The Mediums' Book, part I, chapter III, about *The Method*, the author makes the following observation about the Review: *"Diverse collection of facts, theoretical explanations and isolated sections, that complement the scope of what is found in the two preceding works (The Mediums' Book and The Spirits' Book), forming in a certain way their application."*

While complementing the two main books of the Spiritist Doctrine, and showing their most important applications, the Review is indispensable to all those willing to have an in-depth understanding of Kardec's thoughts.

It is the most comprehensive piece of work about the spiritist movement of the 19th century, containing the formation and modus operandi of the spiritist groups as well as statistics about the number and distribution of followers around the world.

In addition to the profound study of the spiritist theory and the explanations about several questions raised by the spiritists, the Review shows the evolution of Kardec's thought during the construction of the Spiritist Science.

It analyzes new phenomena, like for example the possessions. Some theoretical adjustments were proposed, showing the evolutionary character of the Spiritist Science.

It is the most adequate collection of texts, which demonstrate Allan Kardec's lucidity, equilibrium and common sense.

The Spiritist Review is all that and much more.

We have always cherished the desire of having the Review published in English.

The world needs to know that grandiose work of Kardec. English has become the official language of the whole world. English is also the most important vehicle of dissemination of any Science which have adopted this language as their main mode of communication in all corners of the world.

The Spiritist Science needed an English version of Kardec's largest production.

Thanks to the dedication of a dear friend, Dr. Luiz Americo Venturini Cheim, the Spiritist Research Institute – IPEAK can now see this dream come true, virtually allowing everybody around the world to have access to the Spiritist Review in English.

I met Dr. Luiz Cheim in the late 70's when both of us were young undergraduate students at the Federal University of Rio de Janeiro, Brazil. His major was Electrical Engineering, mine was Physics. Since those days we were united by Spiritism, creating a group of enthusiastic youngsters for the study of Spiritism in the hall of residence of that University. We shared that experience for about four years.

Time passed. Our professional lives led us to very different journeys and places. He continued his studies abroad, seeking his PhD at the University of Nottingham, in England. I stayed in Brazil and obtained my Doctor's Degree at Unicamp. We were then separated for some time by our careers and life commitments.

Our spiritist ideals and profound admiration for Kardec's work out-lived all that and maintained an invisible bond between us.

In 2010, together with a group of friends in Curitiba, Brazil, we created the IPEAK's website, aiming at promoting all works of Kardec, already achieved in Portuguese and French. We lacked the site in English. In order to achieve that it was necessary to have the Spiritist Review translated into English.

On hearing about the IPEAK project, our dear friend Dr. Luiz Cheim offered to translate all works of Kardec which were not yet available in English.

Spiritism united us once again through this new project of the IPEAK.

We now have the great satisfaction of offering to the public this current translation of the Spiritist Review carried out by Dr. Luiz Cheim.

His academic and professional experiences, as well as his knowledge of the required languages, although not a native English speaker, are testimonies of the quality work that he is developing. In his own words: *"I beg you and the spiritist community for your forgiveness with respect to my failures and limitations, at the time that I thank Jesus and Kardec for having given me such an undeserved opportunity..."*

Our IPEAK was born with the objective of promoting the works of Kardec to the whole world. We thank all members of this Institute for their dedication and tireless contribution.

Thank you my dear friend Dr. Luiz Cheim, for this current English translation.

Thank you so much dear master Allan Kardec for providing us with this remarkable doctrine which gives us the opportunity and privilege of learning and studying for our own betterment and for the progress of humanity. Thank you also for the expressions of true friendship and love which blossom around us thanks to our initial understanding of the underlying principles of this unique doctrine.

Dr. Cosme Massi - IPEAK

November 2013.

Table of Contents

January 1858

Introduction

The speed of propagation of the strange spiritist manifestations, all over the world, is a demonstration of the interest they attract. Starting as a simple object of curiosity they soon drew the attention of serious investigators who, since the beginning, perceived the inevitable influence they would have on the moral condition of society. The new ideas which stem from them become more popular daily and nothing can stop their progress as everybody, or almost everybody can reach out for these phenomena, and no human power will impede their manifestation. If muffled in one point, they appear in one hundred others. Those, therefore, who would find any given inconvenient in such manifestations, would be embarrassed to suffer their consequences by the force of the facts, as the same happens to new technologies which may hurt particular interests in the beginning but gets naturally accommodated with time.

What was not said and perpetrated against magnetism! However, every blow against it, every weapon which hurt it, including ridicule, collided with reality and only served to give magnetism more evidence. Magnetism is a natural force and facing natural forces man is like a pygmy, like these little dogs barking against everything that scares them away.

What happens to somnambulism also happens to the spiritist manifestations: if they do not take place in daylight and publicly, nobody will preclude them from happening in the intimacy, as each family may find a medium in the household, from the children to the elderly, as they can also find a somnambulist. Thus, what if the first to be found is a medium and a somnambulist? Who can preclude that? There is no doubt that the skeptics did not think about it. We insist that when a force is part of Nature, it can only be temporarily stopped but never eliminated! Its course, however, may be only deviated. Well, the force revealed in the phenomena of manifestations, whatever its cause may be, is part of Nature, and, like magnetism and its accompanying electric force, will also not be destroyed. It is therefore necessary that those manifestations be observed and studied in all their phases in order to realize their governing laws. If it is an error and an illusion, time will tell; if it is the truth, like compressed steam, will expand the more it is compressed. Is it a surprising fact that, in the Americas, only in the USA, there are seventeen journals dedicated to the subject, not counting a large number of non-periodical publications whereas in France, the European country where the ideas mostly found support, do not have one?[1] It would be unnecessary to dispute the utility of a special organization to make the public aware of this new science and prevent it against the excesses of credulity, as well as skepticism. This is the blank which we propose to fill out with the publication of this Review, aiming at providing a communication media to those interested in these questions and to connect, through a common bond, those who understand the Spiritist Doctrine, from its true moral point of view: practice of good and evangelical charity towards everyone.

If it were only a simple collection of data the task would be easy. These multiply everywhere with such a speed that it would yield endless subject matter but the facts, on their own, would become tedious by repetition and specially by similarity. What is necessary to the thoughtful person is something that resonates to their intelligence. It was only a few years ago that the first phenomena manifested themselves and already we are far away from the "turning and speaking" tables which represented

---

1 Up until now there is only one journal in Europe dedicated to the Spiritist Doctrine – the Journal de l'âme – published in Geneve by Dr. Boessinger. In the USA the only journal in French is the *Spiritualiste de la Nouvelle Orléans*, published by Mr. Barthès.

their infancy. Today it is a Science which uncovers a whole world and exposes the eternal truths that were already sensed within our own spirit. It is a sublime doctrine that shows the path of duty to mankind and uncovers the widest field never presented to the observation of the philosopher. Had we stayed inside the narrow limits of an anecdotal Review our work would be incomplete and sterile, as the interest would have soon passed.

It is possible that the denomination of Science which we gave to Spiritism will be contested. That Science would not have, without a doubt and in any case, the characteristics of an exact Science and it is precisely in this aspect that those who intend to judge and experiment are in error, as if they were dealing with a chemical analysis or a mathematical problem; The fact that it is a philosophical Science is already enough. Every Science must be based on facts but those, by themselves, do not constitute the Science which is born from the coordination and logic inference of the facts: it is the set of laws which govern those facts. Has Spiritism arrived at the state of Science? If that means a completed Science, no doubt it is premature to positively answer that question but the observations are already in large numbers today to allow, at least, the deduction of the general principles and where the Science begins.

The thoughtful examination of the facts and its resulting consequences is, thus, a complement, without which our publication would be of mediocre use and only offer a secondary interest to the thoughtful person and those who want to understand what they see. Nevertheless, as our aim is to get to the truth, we will welcome all observations directed to us and, as much as allowed by the acquired knowledge, we will try to resolve the doubts and clarify the still obscure points. Our Review will thus be a tribune where the discussion will never distance itself from the standards of the strictest conveniences. In one word, we will discuss but will not dispute. Language inconveniences have never being good arguments to the eyes of wise people: it is the weapon of those who do not have something better to offer and which turn against those who use it.

Although the phenomena with which we occupy ourselves have been more recently produced in a broader way, everything demonstrates that they have been occurring since the remotest ages. Natural phenomena do not follow the same path as the inventions which follow the progress of the human spirit, while those are in the order of all things, their cause is as old as the world and their effects must have been produced at all times. Therefore, what we witness today is not a modern discovery. It is the awakening of the ancient times; ancient times cleared from the mystic enclosure that generated superstition; ancient times enlightened by civilization and progress in the field of positive things.

The capital consequence arising from these phenomena is the communication that human beings can establish with the beings of the incorporeal world and, within certain limits, the knowledge which can be acquired regarding their future state. The communication with the invisible world is a fact, unequivocally found in the biblical books. The Bible, however, on one hand, is not sufficiently authoritative to some skeptics; on another hand, to the believers, these are supernatural facts, given by a special favor of Divinity. Had we not found those manifestations in a thousand of other diverse sources, they would not then represent a proof of generality to everyone. The existence of the spirits and their intervention in the corporeal world is attested and demonstrated, not as an exceptional fact but as a general principle, in St Augustine, St Jerome, St Chrysostome, St Gregory of Nazianzus, and in many other Fathers of the Church. That belief forms, moreover, the basis of all religious systems. The wisest philosophers of the ancient times admitted them: Plato, Zoroaster, Confucius, Apuleius, Pythagoras, Apollonius of Tyana, and many others. We find them in the mysteries and oracles, among Greeks, Egyptians, Hindus, Chaldeans, Romans, Persians, and the Chinese. We see them surviving all vicissitudes of the peoples, to all persecutions, challenging all physical and moral revolutions of humanity.

We find them later among the soothsayers and witches of the Middle Ages; in the Willis and Valquirias of the Scandinavians, the Elves of the Teutonic, the Leschios and Domeschnios Doughi of the Slavs, the

Ourisks and Brownies of the Scottish, the Poulpicans and Tersarpoulicts of the Bretons, the Cemis of the Caribbean; in one word: the whole phalanx of nymphs, good and evil geniuses, gnomes, fairies and elves with which all nations have filled the space.

We find the practice of evocation in the peoples of Siberia, Kamchatka, Iceland, among the native Indians of North America and aborigines of Mexico and Peru, Polynesia and even among the primitive savages of New Holland.[2]

The ignorance of a common principle, more or less modified, cannot be due to some absurdities which surrounded or enclosed that belief during various times and places. In truth, a doctrine does not turn universal, survive thousands of generations, implant from one corner of the planet to the next, among widely diverse peoples, from all degrees of the social scale, if it is not based on something positive. What should that be? This is what the recent manifestations show us. Searching for the possible relationships between those manifestations and all those beliefs is to search for the truth.

The history of the Spiritist Doctrine is, somehow, the history of the human spirit. We will have to study it from all angles, providing an inexhaustible source of observations, as much instructive as interesting, about facts that are generally not well known. This will give us the opportunity to explain a number of popular legends and beliefs, which have their part of truth, allegory and superstition.

Concerning the current manifestations, we will report all pertinent phenomena that we witness or those that come to our knowledge, whenever we recognize they deserve the attention of our readers. We will do the same in response to the spontaneous effects, sometimes produced among people ignorant of the spiritist practices from those who may reveal an occult power or the independence of the soul, such are the visions, apparitions, clairvoyance, premonition, intimate warnings, secret voices, etc.

To the reported facts we shall add the explanations, as highlighted from the set of principles. With that respect we shall reinforce the fact

---

2 Former name of Australia (NT)

that these principles are derived from the teachings of the spirits, always making abstraction of our own ideas. They do not come, therefore, from a personal theory but from what was communicated to us and of which we are simple interpreters.

Large space will also be reserved to the written or oral communications of the spirits, as long as they have a useful purpose, as with the evocations of past or current personalities, well known or unknown, without neglecting the intimate evocations which, many times, are not as instructive. In a word: we will encompass all phases of the material and intelligent manifestations of the incorporeal world. The Spiritist Doctrine finally offers us the possible and rational solution to a number of moral and anthropological phenomena that we witness daily, whose explanation we would uselessly search for in all other known doctrines. In that category we place, for example, the simultaneity of thoughts, the anomaly of certain characters, sympathies and antipathies, the intuitive knowledge, the aptitudes, the tendencies, the destinies which look like hallmarks of fatality and, in a broader picture, the distinctive character of the peoples, their progress or their degeneration, etc.

To the citation of the facts we will add the research on the possible causes which could have produced them. From the appreciation of the actions, useful teachings will naturally sprout regarding the line of conduct mostly in agreement with sound moral. In their instructions the superior spirits always have the objective of awakening in men the love for the good, for the practice of the evangelical precepts; hence they shall guide our thoughts that will preside over the writings of this collection.

Thus, the scope of our work comprehends everything related to the knowledge of the metaphysical side of the human being. We will study them in their present as well as future states, considering that studying the nature of the spirit is to study the human being, as the human being will one day participate of the world of the spirits. That is the reason why we will add to the main title the subtitle *"journal of psychological studies"*, allowing for the understanding of its comprehensive scope.

NOTE: Despite the abundance of our personal observations and the sources from where we collect the facts, we do not underestimate our difficulties for the task or our insufficiency. In order to supplement them we count on the benevolent support of all of those interested in such problems. We shall thus be thankful for the communications transmitted to us about the several subjects of our studies. With that respect we draw attention to the following ten points about which documents can be provided:

1. Material or intelligent manifestations obtained in meetings where the person was present;
2. Facts about lucid somnambulism or ecstasies;
3. Facts of clairvoyance, predictions, premonitions;
4. Facts relatively to the occult power attributed, with or without reason, to certain persons;
5. Legend and popular beliefs;
6. Facts of visions and apparitions;
7. Particular psychological phenomena that sometimes occur at the moment of death;
8. Moral and psychological problems to be solved;
9. Moral facts, notable acts of devotion and abnegation whose propagation may serve as useful example
10. Indications of past or modern publications, French or foreign, in which one can find facts relative to the manifestations of occult intelligences, with the designation and, if possible, citation of texts. The same regarding the issued opinions about the existence of the spirits and their relationships with human beings, from former or contemporary authors, whose names and wisdom give them authority

Different Forms of

Manifestation

The spirits attest their presence in multiple ways, according to their aptitude, will and higher or lower levels. All phenomena that we shall analyze are naturally connected to one or another of those forms of communication. In order to facilitate the understanding of the facts, we believe it is our duty to initiate the series of our articles with a broad description of the forms of communication. They can be summarized as the following:

1. Hidden action: nothing is evident. These are, for example, the inspirations or
2. suggested thoughts, intimate warnings, influence over events, etc.
3. Obvious action or manifestation: when it is of any demonstrable way.
4. Physical or material manifestations: those translated by noticeable phenomena such as noises, moving objects. Frequently, these manifestations do not carry any message, having the only objective of attracting the attention to anything and convince us of the presence of a super-human power.

5. Visual manifestations or apparitions: when the spirit shows itself under any form, without bearing any of the known properties of matter.

6. Intelligent manifestations: When the manifestations indicate an intelligent action that is revealed or exhibited through a thought process. Every manifestation which has a meaning, even a simple move or noise, indicating some freedom of action, corresponding to a thought or obeying a will, is an intelligent manifestation. They exist in all degrees.

7. The communications: these are intelligent manifestations aiming at an exchange of ideas between human beings and the spirits. The nature of these communications varies according to the superiority or inferiority of the manifesting spirit and the nature of the discussed subject. These can be frivolous, rude, serious or instructive.

The frivolous communications are given by mischievous, frisky, and frolicsome spirits that are more rascal than wicked. With these types of communications we give no importance to what they say.

The rude communications are translated by expressions that shock decorum. They derive from inferior spirits or spirits not yet stripped from the impurities of matter.

The serious communications are grave with respect to the subject and how they are formulated. The language of the superior spirits is always dignified and free of triviality. Every communication that excludes frivolity, rudeness and has a useful objective, even if of particular interest, is therefore serious.

The instructive communications are the serious communications that have the objective of some sort of teaching, given by the spirit about Sciences, Moral, Philosophy, etc. These are the more or less profound and more or less truthful in accordance to the degree of elevation and dematerialization of the spirit. In order to take real advantage of these communications, they must be regular and followed with perseverance.

The serious spirits associate themselves with those who want instruction and help. They leave to the frivolous spirits the task of engaging with those individuals who do not see in these manifestations as anything but a pastime. Only through regularity and frequency of communications can one appreciate the moral and intellectual value of the spirits with whom we entertain ourselves, as well as the degree of trust they deserve. If it is necessary to have experience to be able to judge the human beings, it is even more so to judge the spirits.

Different Types of Communication

The intelligent communications between spirits and the human beings may happen through signs, writings and/or verbal words. The signs consist of significant movement of certain objects and, more frequently, of noises and vibrating raps. When these phenomena have some meaning there is no doubt about the intervention of an occult intelligence thus, if every effect has a cause, then every intelligent effect must have an intelligent cause.

Under the influence of certain persons, designated by the name of *mediums*, and sometimes spontaneously, any given object may execute agreed movements, strike a number of times and thus respond as yes, no or by a pre-established letter of the alphabet. The raps may be heard without any apparent movement and without a visible cause, on the surface, in the tissues of the inert bodies, on a wall, on a stone, on a piece of furniture or in any other object. From all these objects and for being more comfortable, given its mobility and the facility with which we accommodate around it, the tables are those most frequently utilized, therefore the generic designation of the phenomenon by trivial expressions such as "talking tables", "dance of the tables", expressions which should be conveniently banned, first for its ridicule and finally for the possibility of inducing into error, leading to belief that the tables may have any special influence with this respect.

We shall give to this type of communication the name *spiritist sematology* which is an expression that provides a perfect idea and encompasses all varieties of communications by signs, moving objects, and raps. One of our members proposed that we should designate, especially this last type of communication, by the word *typtology*.

The second mode of communication is the writing. We shall designate it by the name *psychography*, also proposed by a member.

In order to communicate through writing, the spirits employ, as intermediaries, certain endowed persons having the ability to write under the influence of the occult force which guides them, obeying a power evidently strange to their control, as they cannot stop neither proceed and, in the majority of the cases, have no clue about their own writings. An involuntary movement, almost febrile, agitates the hand; they take and dispose of the pencil, irrespective of their own intention. Neither their will nor the desire can force them to continue, in case they were supposed to stop. That is the *direct psychography*.

Writing is also obtained by the sole superimposition of the hands over an object, conveniently attached to a pencil or any other writing tool. The objects more generally employed are the baskets or planchettes, adequately arranged. The occult force acting on the person transmits itself to the object, which becomes an extension of the hand, yielding a necessary movement to produce the characters. That is the *indirect psychography*.

The communications transmitted through *psychography* are more or less extensive, according to the degree of the mediumistic faculty. Some obtain only words; with others the faculty is developed through exercise yielding complete written phrases and, sometimes, essays that are developed about proposed subjects or spontaneously produced by the spirits, without the need of any previous enquiry. On occasions the handwriting is clear and legible; some other times it can only be deciphered by the medium who then reads it through a kind of intuition or *second-vision (remote viewing)*. Through the hand of the same person the writing sometimes changes, in general completely, with the occult manifesting intelligence, and the type of writing always replicates for the same communicating entity. This is not, however, absolute.

From time to time the spirits transmit certain written communications without direct intervention. In this case the characters are spontaneously sketched by a super human power, visible or not. As it is useful that all things are properly named, we will call this mode of written communication by the name *pneumatography*, to distinguish it from *psychography* or handwriting obtained by a medium. The difference between these two words is easy to understand. In the *psychography* the medium's soul performs, necessarily, a role, at least as an intermediary, whereas in the pneumatography it is the spirit who acts directly, on its own.

The third mode of communication is the oral word. Certain persons suffer the influence of an occult power in their vocal cords, similarly to what is felt on the hands of those who write. They transmit by the spoken word everything that others do through the writings. As with the written communications, the oral ones sometimes take place without a corporeal mediation. Spoken words and phrases may reach our ears and brains without an apparent physical cause. The spirits can also show themselves in our dreams or even while awaken and speak to us in order to give us warnings and instructions.

Following the same nomenclature system adopted to the written communications, we should call the voiced word transmitted by the medium by the name "psychology" and those given directly by the spirits by the name "pneumatophony"[3]. However, the word psychology already has a well-known use which we cannot change. We will then name all verbal communications *pneumatophony:* the first ones constitute the mediated pneumatophony[4] while the last ones form the direct pneumatophony.

The most incomplete type of communication, from all kinds, is sematology. It is too slow and can only be used in a painstaking process of

---

3 At first Kardec called this phenomenon, Spiritology. (NT)
4 Later called by Kardec: Psychophony. (NT)

communication. The superior spirits would not willingly employ them due to its slowness or even due to the incompleteness of the "yes" or "no" answers that are subject to error. For the teachings, they prefer the quickest ones: written and oral word. These are certainly the most complete media for the transmission of the spirits' thoughts due to its precision of answers and the extension of the treated developments.

The writings clearly have the advantage of leaving material traces, being one of the most adequate modes to fight disbelief. Nevertheless, we do not have the freedom of choice: the spirits communicate through the modes they find more adequate and that depends on the aptitudes.

Spirits' Answers to

a Few Questions

Q – How can the spirits act upon matter? This seems contradictory to everything we think about the very nature of the spirits.

A – Based on your assumptions, a spirit does not consist of anything materially based. This assumption is not correct. We have already told you that the spirit is something and therefore can act on its own. Because your world is materially dense to allow it to communicate without an intermediary. It is this intermediary that serves as the link that attaches the spirit to matter.

OBSERVATION: Considering that the link uniting the spirit to matter is immaterial or at least intangible this answer would not have addressed the issue if we did not have the example of other equally intangible forces that act upon matter: take the case of our thoughts, the primary cause of every voluntary movements and electricity that lifts up, knocks down and transports inert matter. Just because the cause is unknown it is illogical to conclude that it does not exist. The spirit may have levers unknown to us. Nature demonstrates every day that its power is not limited to what is witnessed by our senses. The immediate cause, in the spiritist phenomena, is inarguably a physical agent but the primary cause is intelligence acting upon this agent as our thought acts upon our members. When we want to knock something it is our arm that knocks; it is not our thought that hits, but it is the thought that guides the arm.

Q – Among the spirits who produce the material effects, there are those we commonly call the "rapping-spirits". Are these spirits from a special class or are they the same who produce the movements and noises?

A – Certainly the same spirit may produce multiple effects but there are those associated more particularly with certain things, like among you there are the blacksmiths and the couriers.

Q – Does the spirit who acts upon a solid object, in order to move or rap, penetrates inside the substance of the body or acts from the outside?

A – One and the other. We have already said that matter is no obstacle to the spirits as they can penetrate everything.

Q – Do the material manifestations, such as noises, movements of objects and all other phenomena, which we provoke, indistinctly produced by superior as well as inferior spirits?

A – It is only the inferior spirits who occupy themselves with such manifestations. The superior spirits, sometimes, employ them, as you would do with a courier, in order to attract attention. Would you believe that spirits of a superior category are at your service to please you with their tricks? This is the same as asking if, in your world, the serious and wise people are the ones who play the role of clowns and jesters.

Observation: The spirits who reveal themselves through material effects are, generally, of inferior order. These spirits amuse or scare away those individuals who are attracted to these visual spectacles as opposed to those who desire to learn and practice intelligent exercises. Sometimes, however, they act spontaneously, on other occasions, under the orders of superior spirits. If the communications of the superior spirits offer a more serious interest, the physical manifestations also have utility to the observer; they reveal unknown forces of nature and provide us with means of studying the character and, so to speak, the customs of all classes of the spiritual population.

Q – How can one prove that the occult power, acting in the spiritist manifestations, is outside of the human being? Couldn't we think that they reside in ourselves, that is, we act under the impulse of our own spirit?

R – When something is done against your will and desire it means that it is not you who is producing it, although many times you are the lever used by the spirit to act and your will would come to help. In this case, you can serve as a convenient tool to the spirit.

Observation: It is, above all, the intelligent communications that marks the intervention of a strange power. When spontaneous and alien to our own thoughts and control and when answering questions to which a solution that is unknown to the audience, we have to search outside ourselves for the cause of such communications. This becomes evident to whoever wants to observe the facts with attention and perseverance. The nuances of details escape the superficial observer.

Q – Are all spirits capable of giving intelligent manifestations?

A – Yes, as all of them are intelligent. However, because there are spirits of all degrees, as among you, some say senseless or stupid things and others shrewd things.

Q – Are all spirits capable of understanding the questions addressed to them?

R – No. The inferior spirits are incapable of understanding certain questions, which does not impede them from answering right or wrong. It is still the same among you.

Observation: Consequently one can see how essential it is to be alert against the belief in the endless knowledge of the spirits. They are like human beings and it is not enough to question the first that shows up to obtain a wise answer. It is necessary to know to whom we are directing our attention. Someone interested in knowing the customs of a people has to study them from one extreme to the other side of the scale. Investigating only one class is to have a false idea, as judging the whole by the part. The spiritual population is like ours; there is everything; the good, the evil, the sublime, the trivial, the knowledgeable and the ignorant. Those who have not observed them seriously, on all levels, cannot boast of knowing them. The physical manifestations reveal to us the spirits of lower levels; these are the street and the shanty. The instructive and wise communications bring us in contact with the superior spirits; they are the social elite: the upper class and the working class.

Physical

Manifestations

We read the following in the *"Le Spiritualiste de la Nouvelle-Orléans"*, from February 1857:

"Lately we asked if all spirits, irrespective of their level,, make the tables move, produce noises, etc, and grab the hand of a lady, serious enough not to joke with these things. In response, they violently sketched these words: 'Who makes the monkeys dance in the streets? Would that be the superior individuals?'"

"A spiritualist friend, of Spanish origin, who died last summer, gave us several communications, having one of those the following passage: The manifestations you are looking for are not among those more pleasant to the serious and elevated spirits. Nevertheless, we agree that they have their utility, as they can perhaps serve more than any other to convince contemporary people.'

"In order to obtain such manifestations it is absolutely necessary to develop certain mediums whose physical constitution is in harmony with the spirits who produce them. We do not doubt that you will see them developing among us, then, they will not be these little knocks which you hear but noises similarly to the shot of the musket intertwined by the roar of the cannon."

"In a corner of the city there is a house inhabited by a German family. One can hear strange noises in the house, while certain objects are displaced. This is what we were told as we did not verify it. Thinking that the owner of the house might be able to clarify it to us, we invited him to participate in some sessions dedicated to this kind of manifestations and, later, the wife of this honorable gentleman did not want him around us, he said, as the noise had increased in his house. About this subject this is what was written by the hand of Mrs......:"

"We cannot deter imperfect spirits from making noise or other upsetting or even scary things; the fact that they are in contact with us, who have good intent, does not diminish the influence they exert on the medium in question."

We call your attention to the perfect agreement between what the spirits in New Orleans, regarding the source of physical manifestations, said and what was said to us. With effect, nothing would color this origin with more vigor than this answer, at the same time spiritual and profound: "Who make the monkeys dance in the streets? Would that be the superior individuals?"

We will have the occasion to transcribe numerous examples of that type of manifestations from American journals, even more extraordinary than those we have just cited. No doubt we shall be responded with the proverb: "The good lie comes from far away". When such marvelous things come to us from 2,000 leagues away but that we cannot verify them, the doubt is admissible; however, these phenomena have crossed the oceans with Mr. Home, who gave us proof of them. It is true that Mr. Home did not go to a theater to show his prodigies and not everybody, having paid for a ticket, could see them. Hence, many see him as a clever conjuror, not considering that the top notch of society, who witnessed these phenomena, would not willingly serve him as partners. If Mr. Home were a charlatan, he would not have refused the magnificent offers from many public playhouses and would have accumulated fortunes. His disinterest is the strongest answer that one can give to his detractors. An uninterested charlatanism would be unwise and a monstrosity. Later we will talk in detail about Mr. Home and the mission that brought him to France. Meanwhile here is a fact of spontaneous manifestation, reported to us by a trustworthy and distinct physician, even more authentic as he was the personal witness to those manifestations.

A distinct family had a fourteen-year-old orphan maid whose character, naturally good and delicate, granted her the affection of her masters. In the same neighborhood lived a family whose lady of the house, nobody knows why, had created aversion against the young maid, turning her into an object of all sorts of harassments. One day, as she was getting home, the neighbor lady showed up infuriated at her doorstep, holding a broom in her hands, wanting to spank her. Terrified the young maid ran to the door, trying to ring the doorbell but, unfortunately, the bell cord was broken so that she could not reach it.

Behold that the doorbell rang by itself and people came from inside to attend the door. In the heat of the situation she did not realize what had happened but later the bell continued to ring, from time to time, without a known cause, during the day as well as at night. When someone attended the door, there was nobody there. The next-door neighbors were accused of perpetrating bad taste frolics. The complaint was taken to the police commissioner who opened an inquiry and tried to establish if a secret cord would communicate with the exterior, but nothing was found. However, things continued to happen more insistently, interfering with everyone's rest and particularly with the young maid who was accused of generating the noise. Having being advised, the employers laid her off, moving her into a friend's house, in the countryside. Since that happened the doorbell went quiet and nothing similar happened in the new home of the young orphan.

This, as many other facts that we have to report, did not happen at the Missouri river banks or in Ohio, but in Paris, at "*Passage des Panoramas*". An explanation is now suitable. The young lady, of course, was not ringing the bell. She was terrified with the facts to think about a joke where she would be the first victim. No less positive is the fact that the bell ringing was due to her presence, as the effect ceased when she left. The doctor who witnessed the fact explains it as a powerful magnetic force unconsciously exerted by the young lady. This explanation by no means seems conclusive to us: why would she have lost such a power after leaving the house?

He argues that the terror generated by the neighbor produced a super excitation on the young maid and that the effect would have ceased with the cause when these two connections were severed. We confess that the argument is not convincing to us. If the intervention of an occult power is not clearly demonstrated, at least it is likely, according to similar cases of that we have experienced. Thus, admitting such an intervention, we will say that under the circumstances of the facts, since its first occurrence, a protector spirit wanted to probably protect the young lady from harm's way. As such, by leaving the house, despite the affection granted by her employers, could perhaps have been in her own interest. Once the lady had left, the spirit protecting this young orphan was no longer required to continue with the noise.

The Goblins

The intervention of incorporeal beings in people's private interests has been part of popular beliefs through the ages. Wise people will certainly not accept, literally, all these legends, all diabolical stories and ridiculous tales that are pleasantly repeated by the fireplace. However, these phenomena, witnessed by us, prove that those tales are based on something, as the facts, which take place today, must also have happened at other times. Remove every marvelous and fantastic aspect which made them superstitious and we are left with the characters, facts and gestures of our modern spirits: some good, benefactors, courteous, pleased by serving others, like the good *Brownies*; others, more or less malicious, jokers, capricious and even malevolent, like the *Goblins* of Normandy, the *Boggles* in Scotland, the *Bogherts* in England, the *Cluricaunes* in Ireland and the *Pucks* in Germany.

According to each popular tradition, these Goblins enter into people's homes to prank them with their bad taste jests. "Knock on doors, displaced furniture, taps on barrels, hammered floors and ceilings, whispering whistles, loud sighs, pulling the drapes and bed sheets of people in bed, etc."

The English *Boghert* exercises its perversities mostly against children who they seem to hate. "They frequently seize their bread and butter or bowl of milk; agitate the bed sheets at night; move up and down the stairs with great noise; throw dishes and cause damages to the houses."

In certain areas of France, the Goblins are considered to be like species of family demons, which are carefully fed with the most appreciable delicacies as they bring to their masters stolen wheat from someone else's granaries. It is really curious to find this old tradition from the ancient Gaul among the Borussians of the 10th Century (today's Prussians). Their *Koltkys*, or family demons, would also steal wheat from other granaries and bring that to their affectionate associates. Who does not recognize in these devilish tricks – leaving aside the unkindness of the stolen wheat, which the dishonest would use as excuse on transferring the blame to the bad reputation of the spirits – who, we were saying, cannot recognize the rapping spirits and those that, without harm, can be called disturbers? similar fact to the one described above, about the young orphan maid of *"Passage des Panoramas"*, if it had happened in the country side, no doubt, it would be attributed to the Goblin of the region, later amplified by the gossipers fertile imagination; someone would have even seen the Goblin hanging on the doorbell, laughing, making fun of the fool who would open the door.

Private Evocations:

"Mom, I am here!"

Mrs.…. had just lost her only fourteen years old daughter a few months ago. The daughter was the object of great affection and tenderness, very worthy of the mother's regrets for the qualities which would certainly have turned the girl into a perfect lady. The girl died of a long lasting and painful disease. Inconsolable with her loss, the mother saw her own health debilitating daily, endlessly repeating that she would soon meet her daughter.

Informed about the possibility of communicating with the beings from beyond the grave, Mrs. … decided to look for some relief to her own misery by talking to her daughter. She was acquainted with another lady whom she knew was a medium but both were not much in favor of such evocations, particularly considering the seriousness of the circumstances, so they then asked for my assistance. It was only the three of us: the mother, the medium and I. Here is the result of this first session:

Mother: In the name of the All Mighty God, spirit of Julia, my beloved daughter, I ask you to come, if God thus allows.

Julia: Mom, I am here!

Mother: Is that you my daughter, who answers me? How can I know it is you?

Julia: Lili.

OBSERVATION: This was her family childhood nickname; neither the medium nor I knew about it, as she was only known, for many years, by the name Julia. With this sign her identity was evident. Not withholding her emotions, the mother wept.

Julia: Mother, why such affliction? I am happy, very happy. I no longer suffer and always see you.

Mother: But I cannot see you! Where are you?

Julia: I am here, just beside you, with my hand over Mrs. X (the medium) so that she can write what I tell you. See my writing (the writing was really hers).

Mother: You say: my hand. Then, you have a body?

Julia: I no longer have the body which had me suffer so much but I have its appearance. Aren't you happy for I no longer suffer and can talk to you?

Mother: If I saw you I would then be able to recognize you?

Julia: Yes, no doubt; and you have already seen me many times in your dreams.

Mother: I have, indeed, seen you many times in my dreams, but I thought it was just the effect of memories and imagination.

Julia: No. It is me, I am always with you and I try to give you consolation; It was I who inspired you the idea of the evocation. I have so many things to tell you. Do not trust Mr. Z… He is not sincere.

OBSERVATION: This gentleman, only known by the mother, cited in such a spontaneous mode, was even another proof of identity of the manifesting spirit.

Mother: What can Mr. Z do against me?

Julia: This I cannot tell you. It is forbidden to me. I can only warn you not to trust him.

Mother: Are you among angels?

Julia: Oh! Not yet. I am not perfect enough.

Mother: However, I never knew any fault in you. You were good, kind, loving and benevolent to everyone. Then this is not enough?

Julia: To you, my dear, I did not have defects and I believed it as you told me so many times! But now I see how much else I need to be perfect.

Mother: How will you acquire these missing qualities?

Julia: In new existences which will be happier and happier.

Mother: Will your new existences be on earth?

Julia: I know nothing about it.

Mother: Since you have done nothing wrong in your life, why you had to suffer so much?

Julia: Trial! Trial! I withstood it with patience, as from my trust in God. Today I am very happy for that. So long, dear mother!

Facing facts like this, who would dare to talk about the emptiness of the grave, when the future life reveals itself to us in such a touchable way, so to speak? This mother, undermined by her sorrow, experiences today an indescribable happiness on talking to her daughter; between them no more separation; their souls are interconnected in a spiritual intimacy, by the exchanges of thoughts.

Despite the discretion surrounding this fact, we would not have published it had we not had the formal permission to do so. That mother told us: May all those who lost their earthly loved ones experience the same consolation that I do!

We will add only one word to those who deny the existence of the good spirits. How can they demonstrate that the spirit of this young lady was a malevolent demon?

Private Evocations –

A Conversion

The following evocation will not be of lower interest, although from a different point of view.

A gentleman, here named Georges, a pharmacist from a southern city, had lost his father some time ago, to whom he was tenderly affectionate and to whom he devoted profound veneration. The late Mr. Georges – the father – added to his higher education, all qualities of a good man, although he embraced materialistic views. With that regard, his son shared the same ideas, if not even beyond those of his father; he doubted everything: God, soul, future life. Spiritism did not adapt to those thoughts. On reading "The Spirits' Book", however, he felt a certain reaction, reinforced by a direct conversation we had with him. He would say: "If my father could answer me, I would no longer doubt." It was then that the following evocation was carried out, in which we encounter numerous lessons.

1. In the name of the All Mighty, spirit of my father, I request that you manifest yourself. Are you by my side?
   - Yes.

2. Why don't you manifest directly to me, considering our mutual love?
   - Later.
3. Can we meet one day?
   - Yes, soon.
4. Shall we love each other as in this life?
   - More.
5. In which condition you find yourself?
   - I am happy.
6. Have you reincarnated or are you wandering (errant)?
   - Wandering for a short time
7. What was your sensation on leaving the corporeal involucre (wrapping)?
   - A perturbation.
8. How long did the perturbation last?
   - Ten years for you, ten minutes for me.
9. But it was not long ago that I lost you. Was not that only four months ago?
   - If you, as a living being, were in my place, you would have felt that time.
10. Do you now believe in a good and fair God?
    - Yes
11. When living on earth did you also believe?
    - I had the prior knowledge but did not believe.
12. Is God All Mighty?
    - I have not gone up to him to know his power. It is only God who knows the limits of his power as it is only God who is his equal.
13. Is God occupied with human beings?
    - Yes.
14. Shall we be punished or rewarded according to our actions?
    - If you do bad things, you will suffer.

15. If I act in the right way, will I be rewarded?
    - You will advance in your path.
16. Am I in the right path?
    - Do the good things and you will be.
17. I believe I am good but it would be better if I could find you one day, as a reward.
    - May this thought sustain you and give you courage.
18. Will my son be good as his grandfather?
    - Develop his virtues and eliminate his wickedness.
19. This is so wonderful that it is hard for me to believe that we are communicating now.
    - Where does the doubt come from?
20. On sharing your philosophical ideas, I was led to believe that everything can be attributed to matter.
    - Do you see at night what you do at daytime?
21. Oh my father! Then am I in the dark?
    - Yes.
22. What do you see today that is exceedingly marvelous?
    - Explain yourself better.
23. Have you met my mother, my sister and Ana, the good Ana?
    - I saw them.
24. Do you see them again whenever you want?
    - Yes.
25. Is my communication with you painful or enjoyable?
    - It is happiness to me if I can lead you to the right path.
26. What can I do to communicate with you, on returning home, given that it gives me real pleasure? This help would serve to guide me better and help me to educate my children.
    - Every time something leads you to do the right thing, follow it. I will inspire you.
27. I am quiet now as I am afraid I can bother you.
    - Speak still if you so wish.

28. Given that you allow, I shall make a few more questions. Which disease killed you?

- My trial had come to an end.

29. Where did you acquire the manifested pulmonary disorder?

- Never mind. The body is nothing. The spirit is everything.

30. What is the nature of the disease that so often wakes me up at night?

- You will know later.

31. I consider my disease serious and wanted to live longer for my children.

- It is not. Man's heart is a life engine. Let nature follow its course.

32. Considering that you are present here, under which form do you show yourself?

- The same appearance as my corporeal form.

33. Are you in a determined spot?

- Yes: behind Ermance (the medium).

34. Could you make yourself visible?

- It is not worth it. You would be frightened.

35. Do you have an opinion about each one of us present here?

- Yes.

36. Would you like to say something to each one of us?

- In which sense do you ask me this?

37. From the moral point of view.

- Another time. Let us call it a day.

The effect that this communication had on Mr. Georges was immense and an entirely new light seemed to clarify his ideas. In a session, which he attended the next day, in the home of Mrs. Roger, a somnambulist, he ended up eliminating the few doubts he would still have. Here is a summary of the letter he sent us:

"That lady spontaneously shared with me such precise details about my father, my mother, my children and my health; she described all circumstances of my life with such accuracy, even reminding me about facts that I had long forgotten; in one word, gave me patent proof of this marvelous faculty which the lucid somnambulists have that, since then, I had undergone a complete change of ideas. In the evocation, my father had revealed his presence. In the session of somnambulism I was, so to speak, the visual witness of the extra corporeal life, the life of the soul."

In order to describe, with such details, two hundred leagues away, something that only I knew, it was necessary to be able to physically see. Well, as it was not possible with the eyes of the body, there was then a mysterious link, invisible, connecting the somnambulist to the absent people who she had never met! There was, thus, something outside matter. What could that be other than what is called soul, the intelligent being to which the body is only an involucre, but whose action goes much beyond our sphere of activities? Currently Mr. Georges not only is no longer materialist but he is also one of the strongest and most dedicated adepts of Spiritism, what makes him doubly happy by the confidence he now has in the future and by the pleasure he experiments with the practice of good. This evocation, very simple in the beginning, is not less notable from several aspects. The character of the old Mr. Georges reflects well in his brief and sentenced answers, according to his habits. He was a man of few words. Never spoke a useless word. But it was no longer the skeptical speaking. He acknowledges his error; his spirit is freer, more clairvoyant, and portrays the unity and power of God by these admirable words: "Only he is his equal". He, who in his life, used to attribute everything to matter, now says: "The body is nothing. The spirit is everything." And another sublime phrase: "Do you see at night what you do at daytime?"

To the diligent observer everything has an extension and this is how, step by step, he finds confirmation of the immense truths taught by the spirits.

The Medium's Trial[5]

The critics of the Spiritist Doctrine eagerly pointed to an article published by Scientific America[6] in July 11th of last year under the title "The Tried Mediums". Several French newspapers replicated the article as an irrefutable argument. We have, ourselves, reproduced it, adding some observation which shows its value.

"Some time ago, through the Boston Courier, an offer of $500 dollars was made to any person who, in the presence of and according to the will of a group of Professors from the University of Cambridge, reproduced some of these mysterious phenomena which, the spiritualists say, frequently take place in the presence of agents named mediums."

"The challenge was accepted by Dr. Gardner and several other people who would brag about being in contact with the spirits. The contestants met in the Albion building, in Boston, in the last week of June, ready to test their super natural powers. Among them were the Fox sisters who were prominent for such events. The examining committee was composed of the Cambridge Professors Pierce, Agassiz, Gould and Horsford, all well-known experts. The spiritualists' trials lasted several days. The mediums had never before seen such a great occasion to evidence their talent and inspiration. However, as the priests of Baal, in the

---

5   The original French title is equivalent to "The tried mediums". See below.(NT)

6   The actual title that shows in the Scientific American, July 11th 1857 is: *Cambridge Professors and the Spiritualists* - Kardec may have used the expression "tried mediums" because that is how it has likely appeared in the French press of those days (NT)

days of Elijah, in vain they evoked their divinities, as demonstrated by the following passage from the committee's report:

"The committee declares that Dr. Gardner, not having been able to present an agent or medium who, from the room next door, would reveal a word requested to the spirits; who could read the English word written inside a book or on a folded piece of paper; who could answer one question which only superior minds could answer; who could vibrate the piano strings without touching it or even move a small table without the help of hands; as he was unable to give to the committee a testimony of a phenomenon which, even with the most elastic interpretation and greatest good will, could be considered as equivalent to the required proofs; of a phenomenon requiring the intervention of a spirit to be produced, supposing or at least implying such an intervention; of a phenomenon up until now unknown to Science or whose cause was not touchable and immediately recognized by the committee, he has no right to claim from the Courier of Boston the payment of $500 dollars as offered."

This experiment reminds us of another one, which took place in France ten years ago, concerning the *pro or con* lucid somnambulists, who can generate a magnetic field. The Science Academy had the task of awarding 2,500 francs to the magnetized somnambulist who could read blindfolded. Usually all somnambulists did this on stages or playhouses. They would read from closed books and deciphered letters which were seated upon or well sealed and folded and placed on their chests. In front of the Academy, however, they read absolutely nothing and the award was not given to anyone.

These attempts demonstrate again the absolute ignorance on the part of our critics, with respect to the principles on which the spiritist manifestations are based. They have the idea that such phenomena must obey the will and repeat itself with a mechanical precision. They forget or do not know that the cause of such phenomena is entirely ethical and that the spirits, who are the immediate agents, do not obey anybody's caprice – medium or otherwise.

The spirits act when they wish to do so and before whom they please. At times, when least expected, their manifestations take place with more energy and, whenever requested, they do not occur.

The spirits behave in ways unknown to us. What is outside matter cannot be controlled by matter. Assessing them from our point of view is to be fooled. If they find it useful to manifest through particular signs, they will do that but never under our command or to satisfy our useless curiosity.

Besides, one must take into account a very well-known cause which pushes spirits away, namely their dislike for certain people who want to submit their discernment to a trial, framing questions about known things. We assume that when something does exist then the spirits have to know it. Just because it is something known to us or that we have means of knowing it would the spirits bother to answer. Such suspicion irritates the spirits and it turns the serious spirits away who, out of their own will, speak to those who trust them, without ulterior motive.

Do we not have a daily example among us? Superior people, who are conscious of their worth, do not like to respond to naïve questions aimed at testing them on elementary things. How would they react if we argued: "But if you do not answer is that you do not know!" They would turn their back to us. This is what the spirits do.

Then you will say: If that is the case, how can you convince us? Considering the interest of the Spiritist Doctrine, shouldn't the spirits want to make their presence known? We will answer that it is too much pride in someone to consider oneself indispensable to the success of the cause. Well, the spirits do not like arrogant people. They convince whomever they wish and to those who believe in their own importance they show their dislike by not listening to them.

In summary, let us see their answers given to two questions about the subject:

Q – Can one ask the spirits to give us material proof of their existence and power?

A – No doubt certain manifestations can be provoked but not everyone is able to do that and, many times, what is demanded is not obtained. They do not bend to the caprices of the human beings.

Q – But when someone requests proof in order to be convinced, would not be convenient to have this proof so as to have one more example?

A – The spirits only do what they want and what is allowed to them. Talking to us and answering your questions, this attests their presence: this should be enough to the serious persons, who seek the truth in the word.

The Scribes and Pharisees told Jesus: "Master, we would like to see you make some prodigy" to which Jesus answered: "A wicked and adulterous generation asks for miraculous signs! But none will be given except the sign of the prophet Jonah." (Matthew 12:39)

We shall even add that it is a great degree of ignorance as to the nature and causes of the manifestations to consider provoking them for any reward. The spirits despise greed as much as pride and selfishness. This only condition can be a reason for them not manifesting themselves. Know this, therefore, that you will obtain one hundred times more from an uninterested medium than from one moved by profit and glamour and that one million would not stop him from doing what he should not do. If there is something strange is the fact of finding mediums capable of submitting themselves to such trials with the purpose of obtaining money.

The Visions

We read in the *Courier de Lyon*:

In the evening of 27th to 28th of August 1857, a singular case of intuitive vision took place in *Croix-Rouse*, under the following conditions:

"Some three months ago the couple B…, dignified weavers, touched by kind commiseration, took to their home, as a maid, a mentally challenged young lady, who lived near Bourgoing."

"Last Sunday the couple was woken up by the lancinating screams of the maid who was asleep in a loft adjacent to their bedroom. Mrs. B… went upstairs, put the lights on and found the maid bursting into tears, her spirit in an indescribable state of excitement, twisting her arms in terrible convulsions, calling for her mother who she had just seen dying, she said, before her eyes."

"After giving the little maid the best consolation she could, Mrs. B… returned to her bedroom. The incident had been almost forgotten when yesterday, Tuesday, in the afternoon, the mail man brought Mrs. B… a letter from the little maid's tutor, informing her that in the early hours from Sunday to Monday, between 2 and 3 am, her mother had died as a consequence of a fall from the top of a flight of stairs."

"The poor mentally challenged lady left yesterday, in the morning, for Bourgoing, followed by Mr. B…, her boss, in order to receive the inheritance of her mother, whose deplorable end she had sadly seen in her dreams."

Facts of such a nature are not rare and we will have frequent opportunities to review some of these with incontestable authenticity. These occurrences are sometimes produced during the sleep, as in a dream. This is understandable as dreams are nothing more than an incomplete and natural somnambulistic state. We will designate the visions that take place during that state as "somnambulistic visions" to distinguish them from those which take place while awake called double or second vision or remote viewing. Finally we will call "ecstatic visions" those who take place in ecstasy. These generally recognized by thematic facts and things of the incorporeal world. The following fact belongs to the second category.

A ship-owner of our acquaintance, residing in Paris, told us the following story a few days ago:

"In the last month of April, feeling unwell, I went for a stroll to the Tuileries, with a friend of mine. It was a magnificent day; the gardens were vibrant with people. Suddenly the crowd disappears before my eyes; I no longer feel my body and it is as if I was transported and I distinctly see a ship entering the port of *Havre*. I recognize it as the "*Clémence*" which we were waiting for in the Antilles. It approached the wharf and I could clearly identify the mast, sails, sailors, the minimum details, as if I were there. Then I told my partner: "Behold, the *Clémence* has arrived. We will have news still today. It was a happy trip."

On returning home a telegram message was then given to me. Before I read it I declared: "It is the news of the arrival of the *Clémence*, which arrived at the port of Havre at 3 o'clock. The message did really confirm the arrival, exactly at the time we were at the Tuileries."

When the visions have beings of the incorporeal world, as subjects, one could take them as the result of imagination, classifying them as hallucinations, since nothing that occurred could demonstrate their legitimacy. But in both cases described above there is a material and positive link to reality. We challenge all physiologists and philosophers to explain them based on the ordinary systems. Only the Spiritist Doctrine can do that through the emancipation of the soul which, momentarily escaping from the material harnesses, is transported beyond the sphere of corporeal activities.

In the first case it is likely that the mother's soul had come to visit the daughter and warned her about her death but in the second case it is certain that the ship did not come to meet the owner in the Tuileries. One must agree that it was his soul that went to meet the ship at the Havre.

Acknowledgement of the Existence and Manifestation of the Spirits

Just as the initial manifestations made numerous followers, they also found significant disbelief from aggressive critics and, many times, even people interested in their discredit. Today the facts have spoken so astonishingly that it is now inevitable to acknowledge the evidence. If, however, there is still systematic, incredulous disbelief, we can assure them that in a few years the same thing that happened to all discoveries will happen to the spirits manifestations, namely that good judgment should have made them less skeptical to all things related to progress.

Among those who did not want to investigate these strange phenomena any further we can already see many agreeing that our century is so rooted in extraordinary things and that nature has so many unknown reserves that it would be more than levity to deny things that we cannot understand. Those give proof of wisdom.

Here is an authority against which we could not raise any suspicion of accepting a mystification: it is one of the main ecclesiastic's journals of Rome, the *Civiltà Cattolica*. We reprint below an article published by this journal last March, where one can see that it would be difficult to demonstrate the existence and manifestation of spirits by more trustworthy arguments. It is true that we diverge with respect to the nature of the spirits as the article only recognizes the manifestation of the bad ones, whereas we admit the good and the bad.

This is a point that we shall analyze later with all the necessary developments. The acknowledgement of the spiritist manifestations by such a respectable and grave authority is of capital importance. What remains, therefore, is the need for assessment. This is what we will do in the next issue. Reproducing the article "*L'Universe*" which is preceded by the following judicious reflections:

"With the publication of an article, in Ferrara, about the practice of animal magnetism, we referred our readers to the shrewd publications available in the *Civiltà Cattolica,* in Rome, about the modern necromancy, keeping us from providing broader explanations. We give today the last of these articles that contains, in a few pages, the conclusions of the Roman Review. Besides the interest, naturally associated to the subject, and the trust inspired by a piece of work found in the *Civiltà,* the special opportunity of the subject, at this point in time, spares us from calling the attention to an issue which many people, in theory, as well as in practice, have treated so lightheartedly, despite the vulgar rule of prudence which recommends that those facts be examined with more circumspection the more extraordinary they are."

Here is the article:

"From all issued theories to *naturally* explain the multiple phenomena known as American Spiritualism, none reaches the objective and, even less, explains the reason of all those phenomena. If one or another of these hypotheses is enough to explain some, many will remain inexplicable. The deception, the lie, the excess, the hallucinations must, no doubt, have a great participation in those referred facts; but, after making this statement, there is still such a quantity of events that in order to negate their reality it would be necessary to negate faith to the authority of the senses and to the human testimony."

"Among these facts a certain number can be explained by the mechanical theory or mechanic-physiologic; one part remains, however – and much more considerable – which could never be explained by those theories. To this order of facts one associates all those in which, they say, the resulting effect evidently surpasses the intensity of the generating force, which should produce them. These are:

1.   The movements, the violent displacements of heavy and well balanced loads, to the simple pressure or superimposition of hands;
2.   The effects and displacements produced without any contact, consequently without any mediated or immediate mechanical impulse;
3.   Other manifesting intelligent effects, whose intelligence and will are distinct from the experimenters and from those who produce them."

"In order to make sense of these three orders of multiple facts, we still have the theory of magnetism. But, however extensive the concessions we are prepared to make, and even blindfolded admitting all free hypotheses on which they are based; all errors and absurdities which they contain, as well as the miraculous faculties attributed by them to the human will, to the nervous fluid or any other magnetic agents, this theory will never, with the support of its principles, explain how can a table, magnetized by a medium, manifest by its own movements intelligence and willpower, which are distinct from the medium and, sometimes, contrary and superior to the medium's intelligence and will."

"How can one determine the reason for the occurrence of those phenomena? We want also to look for some unknown occult causes; to some still unknown forces of nature; to the new explanations of certain faculties, to certain laws, up until now, maintained in a state of inertia, latent in the heart of Creation. This would be equivalent to openly confess our ignorance and increase the number of mysteries that the poor human spirit cannot decipher today or ever. By the way, we do not hesitate to confess our ignorance regarding many of those phenomena whose nature is so obscure that the most appropriate attitude, as it seems to us, is not to try to explain them. As compensation, there are others that we do not find so difficult to uncover the explanations, as we can find them in natural causes. Why then would we resort to causes belonging to the supernatural order? We would be, perhaps, deviated by the objections counter offered by the skeptical and by those who, negating this supernatural order, tell us that it is impossible to define the limits of the natural order so as to indicate with precision where one ends and where the other begins."

"The answer to such an objection seems easy to us: admitting that one cannot precisely determine the dividing point of these two opposing orders, the natural and the supernatural, it does not follow that one cannot define, with certainty, if a given effect belongs to this or to that other.

Who can distinguish in the rainbow the exact point where one color ends and the other starts? Who can precisely determine the exact moment when the day ends and the night begins? Nevertheless, nobody is naive enough not to know if the color of a given region of the rainbow is yellow or red, or if at a given time it is day or night. Who does not perceive that in order to know the nature of a fact, by no means it is necessary to determine the delimiting regions of the category to which it belongs, and that it is enough to certify that the effect has the peculiar characters of that category?"

"Let us apply such a simple observation to the following assertion: we cannot say where the limits of the natural forces are; nonetheless, given a fact, many times we can, pending on its characters, tell with certainty that it belongs to a supernatural class. And in order not to run away from our problem, among the phenomena of the talking tables there exist those that, in our opinion, most evidently manifest these characters; such are those in which the agent who move the table acts as a free and intelligent cause, at the same time showing its own will and intelligence, that is superior or contrary to the intelligence and will of the mediums, experimenters, of the assistants; in one word, distinct from those, whatever the means of indicating those distinctions. In such cases, however, we are forced to recognize that the agent is a spirit and it is not a human spirit; and thus it is outside of the causes that we typically call natural, those that we say go beyond poeple's forces."

"These are precisely the phenomena that, as said before, resisted to any theory based on purely natural principles, while in our theory the explanation is easier and clearer, as everyone knows that the power of the spirit over matter goes much beyond human beings' forces and that there aren't marvelous effects, among those cited by modern necromancy, which cannot be attributed to its action."

"We know very well that some readers, on noticing that we brought the spirits to the explanation, will smile with disbelief? Not to mention those that, as good materialists, do not believe in the existence of the spirits and consider fake all that is not tangible matter, as well as those who admitting the spirits deny any influence or intervention with respect to our world."

"There are, these days, many people who, conceding to the spirits what no catholic could refuse, that is the existence and the ability to interfere with the facts of human life, in an occult or patent way, ordinary or extraordinary, they seem, in practice, to negate their faith, on considering as shameful, as excess of credulity, as superstitions of old women, the recognition of such actions of spirits, in certain special cases, being satisfied by not denying them, in thesis."

"In actual fact, one century ago, the simplicity of the middle ages was object of mockery when witches and wicked spirits were observed all over the place, and it was such the upheaval around the subject that it is not surprising that so many weak minds, wishing to show otherwise, have since then a sort of disgust and shame for believing in the spirits' intervention. However, this excess of incredulity is not less astonishing than the contrary attitude of other times; and if the excess of credulity drags people towards vain superstitions, on another hand the refusal to admit anything directly leads to the impiety of naturalism. The individual of wisdom, the prudent Christian must thus avoid both extremes, steadily staying on the median, since that is where virtue and truth reside. Now, regarding the talking tables, where would a prudent faith incline us to?"

"The first and wisest rule from those imposed by such prudence tells us that, in order to explain the phenomena which show a character of extraordinary nature, we should not resort to supernatural causes, unless those of natural order are not sufficient to explain them. On the other hand, and as a consequence, there is the obligation of admitting the former when the latter are not sufficient. This is exactly our case. With effect, among the phenomena we discuss, there are some for which no theory, no purely natural cause would be sufficient to fully explain them. Thus, it is not only prudent but necessary to look for the explanation in the supernatural order or, put differently, attribute them to pure spirits, considering that outside and above nature there is no other possible cause."

"Here is a second rule, an infallible criterion to tell, regarding a given fact, if it belongs to the natural or supernatural order: this is to examine well its characters and, according to them, determine its causes. Well, the most marvelous facts of such nature, which nothing else can explain, offer characters that not only demonstrate a free and intelligent cause but also show a will and intelligence that can be nothing but human. In this case, such a cause cannot be anything else other than a pure spirit."

Therefore we can arrive to the same conclusion via an indirect and negative path, by exclusion, and another direct and positive, based on the very nature of the facts. That is, among the phenomena of modern necromancy there is at least one category of facts that, without any doubt, are produced by the spirits. We are led to that conclusion by such a simple and natural reasoning that, on accepting it, away from the fear of giving in to an imprudent credulity, we would judge, on the contrary, refusing to admit it, to be giving proofs of an unjustifiable incoherence and weakness. There are no missing arguments to confirm our statement; what is missing, however, is space and time to develop them. What we have said so far is enough and can be summarized in the following four propositions:

1. Among the discussed phenomena, letting aside those that can be reasonably explained by hallucinations, exaggerations and imposture, there are others, in large number, impossible to shed any

doubt about their existence, without violating the laws of healthy criticism.

2. All natural theories discussed and exposed above are insufficient to satisfactorily explain all these phenomena. If they explain some, they leave the largest number – and those are the most difficult ones - absolutely unexplained and inexplicable.

3. Implying the action of an intelligent cause, the phenomena of this last order can only be explained by the intervention of the spirits, whatever the character of these spirits may be, a subject to be handled below.

4. All these facts can be divided in four categories: several must be rejected for being false or fraudulent. As to the others, the easier and simpler to understand, such as the turning tables, on certain occasions these admit a purely natural explanation, for example, such as in the mechanical impulse. A third class form those phenomena of more extraordinary and mysterious appearance whose nature is doubtful since they seem to go beyond natural forces, although do not present characters which evidently require supernatural causes to explain. Finally, we group in the fourth category the facts that evidently offer those characters, which must be attributed to pure spirits."

"But how are these spirits? Good or bad? Angels or demons? The answer to this question cannot offer doubts, although insufficiently considered, the nature of the spirits, on the one side, and the character of their manifestations, on the other. This is what remains to be shown."

Joan of Arc's Story Dictated by Herself to Ms. Ermance Dufaux

A recurrent question frequently addressed to us is related to the spirits who answer the questions directed to them, with more or less precision, when people would like to know whether the spirits could write a lengthier piece of work. The proof is in the story, like this one, that does not handle a series of questions and answers but is a complete and ordered narrative, similarly to what a historian would do, containing a huge amount of details, more or less already known, with respect to the hero lady's life.

Those who might believe that Ms. Dufaux was inspired by her personal knowledge of the subject, we answer that she was only fourteen years old when she wrote the book. In addition and not withstanding her stable family background and education, she would not have been able to find intimate documents, hardly found in the archives of those days. We are aware that the doubters will have thousands of objections but for us, who saw the medium in action, the origin of the book is unquestionable.

Given that Ms. Dufaux's faculty attains to the evocation of any spirit, which we have ourselves demonstrated through personal communications transmitted to us, her specialty is history. She equally wrote the story of

Louis XI and Charles VIII that, as with that of Joan of Arc, will also be published. A curious phenomenon happened to her. In the beginning she was a good psychograph medium, writing with facility. Slowly she turned into pneumatophony[7] and along with the development of this faculty, the first one diminished. Today she hardly writes and does with difficulty. When speaking, however, and this is original, she feels the need to have a pencil in her hand and pretends to be writing. Another person is needed to register her words, similarly to those of Sibyl. As with every medium favored by the good spirits, she has never received communications that are not of an elevated order. We shall return to the story of Joan of Arc to explain the facts of her life, related to the invisible world; we will then cite what she had dictated to her most notable interpreter.

---

7   1 vol, in-12, 3 francs, Dentu, Palais-Royal

The Spirits' Book

Containing the principles of the Spiritist Doctrine
About the nature of the incorporeal world, their manifestations and
relationships with human beings; the moral laws, present life, future life
and the future of humanity.
WRITTEN IN ACCORDANCE WITH THE DICTATION AND
PUBLISHED BY THE AUTHORITY OF THE SUPERIOR SPIRITS
By Allan Kardec

As indicated in the title, this work is not a personal doctrine: it is the result of the direct teachings of the spirits themselves about the mysteries of the world where we will be one day and about all questions which concern humanity; they somehow give us a life code, outlining the route to our forthcoming happiness. As this book is not the result of our own ideas, since we had a diverse way of seeing things about many important points, our modesty had nothing to suffer with the praises. We prefer, however, to give the word to those who are completely disinterested of such questions.

The *Courrier de Paris*, June 11th, 1857 published the following article about the book: "The Spiritist Doctrine".

Not long ago the editor Dentu has published a really notable book, even curious so to speak, if it weren't for things that cause repugnance to any banal classification.

The Spirits' Book, by Mr. Allan Kardec, is a new page of the great book of infinity and, we are persuaded, a mark shall be placed on that page. It would be deplorable to think that we are here to promote bibliographic propaganda: it would be preferred to have our pen broken, had that been admitted. We don't absolutely know the author of the book but we proclaim out loudly that we would like to know him. Whoever wrote that introduction which forwards *The Spirits' Book* must be a soul open to all dignified feelings.

By the way, so as to avoid any doubt with respect to our good faith and the accusation of partisanship, we must say, with all honesty, that we have never carried out a profound study of the supernatural things. If the observed facts caused us admiration, they have not made us shrug them off. We somehow belong to the so-called "dreamers" category, since we do not think as everybody else does. Twenty leagues away from Paris, under the trees, at sunset, surrounded by a few sparse cottages, we naturally think about things very different from the Stock Exchange, the macadamias of the boulevards, the races of Long Champ. Many times we asked ourselves, and for a long time, before having heard about mediums, what happened in the regions conventionally called Heaven. Not long ago we even proposed a theory about the invisible worlds, consciously keeping it to ourselves, thus feeling very happy to have found it, almost entirely, in Mr. Allan Kardec's book.

To all the hopeless of this world; to all those who walk and wash with tears the soil of their fallen paths, we say: Read The Spirits' Book. It will make you stronger. We also say to the happy ones, to those who have only found applause and fortune: study it and it will make you better.

The body of the work, says Mr. Allan Kardec, must be entirely attributed to the spirits who dictated it. It is admirably divided in a system of questions and answers. These are, sometimes, sublime facts which does not surprise us. However, what should we say about the merit of someone who knew how to provoke them? We challenge the most incredulous to laugh at this work when reading it in silence and solitude. Everyone should honor the one who wrote its preface.

The doctrine is summarized in a simple phrase: do not do to others what you wouldn't have them do to you. We regret that Mr. Allan Kardec did not add: do to others what you would have them do to you. By the way, the book clearly states that, without it the doctrine would not be complete. It is not enough not to do evil things but it is necessary to do the good ones. If you are only a good person you will have completed half of the task. You are an imperceptible atom of this huge engine called world, where nothing is useless. Do not tell us that it is possible to be useful without doing good deeds. We would be forced to write a book to answer that. Reading the admirable answers of the spirits to Mr. Kardec, we told ourselves that there was a beautiful book to be written. We soon noticed, however, our own mistake. The book has already been written. We would only spoil it had we tried to complete it.

You are an educated person and have the good will of those who only need instruction? Then read the *Book First*, about the *Spiritist Doctrine*.

You belong to the class of those who are only concerned with themselves and, as they say, take their time to do their business and cannot see beyond their own interests? Read the *Moral Laws*.

You are ruthlessly hunted by disgrace and, from time to time, tortured by uncertainty embracing you with its cold arms? Study the third book: *Hopes and Consolations*.

Everyone who entertains noble thoughts in their hearts and believe in the good read the book from start to finish.

Those who only found subject for prank, our lament.

G. DU CHALARD

From the many letters addressed to us, since the publication of *The Spirits' Book*, we will mention only two as they somehow summarize the impression produced by the book and the essentially moral principles contained in it.

Bordeaux, *25th April 1857.*
Dear Sir,

You have submitted my patience to a great test by the delay in the publication of The Spirits' Book, announced long ago. Fortunately I did not lose it with the wait as the book goes beyond any idea I might had, based on the prospects. Impossible to describe the effect it had on me. I feel like someone coming out of the darkness. It feels like a door, closed until now, suddenly opened to me and my ideas amplified in a few hours. Oh, how much humanity and those miserable concerns seem greedy and puerile sided by this future, which I envisaged but which was so much masked by prejudice that I could only imagine. Thanks to the teachings of the spirits, now that very future seems defined, perceptible, but immense, beautiful and in harmony with the Creator's majesty.

Those who, on reading this book, meditate, as I did, will find an endless treasure of consolations as it encompasses all phases of the existence. I have suffered, along my life, losses which vividly affected me; today they do not cause me any distress and my only concern is to usefully employ my time and capabilities to accelerate my own progress hence now, for me, good has an objective and I understand that a useless life is an egoistic one, which will not help us to progress in our future life.

If everyone else, who thinks like you and myself, and there are many, I hope, for the glory of humanity, could understand each other, unite and work together, which power wouldn't that be to speed up the announced regeneration!

When I am in Paris I will have the honor to look for you and, if not an inconvenience, I will request some explanations about certain parts of the book, and a few advices about the application of the moral laws under certain personal circumstances.

You may have, Sir, the expression of my whole gratitude, since you have done me enormous good, showing me the only path to real happiness in this world and thus, hopefully, a better place in the other one.
Yours...

D...

Lyon, 4ᵗʰ July 1857.

Sir,

I do not know how to express my gratitude for the publication of The Spirits' Book, which I have just read. How much consolation in your teachings to our poor humanity! As for myself, I confess, I feel stronger and more encouraged to withstand the penalties and annoyances of my poor existence.

I have shared the acquired convictions, during the study of your work, with many friends. All feel very happy; they now understand the inequalities of social positions and no longer complain against the Divine Providence; hope, supported by a happier future, as long as behaving accordingly, give them comfort and courage.

I wish, Sir, I could be useful to you. I am a simple person of the people, raised on an insignificant position through work, lacking instruction, as I was obliged to work since childhood. Nevertheless, I have always loved God and done my utmost to be useful to my neighbors. That is why I always look for things that can make them happier. Let us unite, all scattered adepts, and make every effort to help you. You have raised the flag and it is our duty to follow you. We count on your support and advice.

Respectfully, Sir, if you allow me to call you my comrade, your dedicated…. C

We have many times been asked about the modes of communications that constituted The Spirits' Book. We thus summarize here, with pleasure, the answers we have given to such questions. It is an opportunity to pay tribute of gratitude to so many people who had the good will of supporting us.

As explained, the communications given through raps, earlier called typtology, are too slow and incomplete for a lengthy work; hence such resource was never employed. Everything was obtained in writing by the intermediary of several psychograph mediums. We have, ourselves, prepared the questions and coordinated the work in its entirety. The answers are those literally given by the spirits. The majority of those written answers were witnessed by us, others were obtained from communications sent to us by comrades or collected by us here and there, wherever we had been carrying out studies. It seems that for that matter the spirits multiply, in front of us, the reasons for observation.

The first mediums who contributed to our work were Ms. B… whose good will never failed us. The book was almost completely written by their mediation, in the presence of a large audience who attended the sessions in which they had the most vivid interest. Later the spirits recommended a complete revision in private sessions, when all additions and corrections were then implemented, according to their assessment. This essential part of the work had the support of Ms. Japhet [8] who showed enormous good will and disinterest to all demands from the spirits, as they were the ones who precisely scheduled the sessions.

The disinterested would not be here a special merit, since the spirits disapprove of any traffic of interest regarding their presence, but Ms. Japhet, who is also a somnambulist medium, and had her time committed with utility, understood that it would also be a useful application to dedicate it to the propagation of the Doctrine. As for ourselves, we have already declared, since the beginning, and we have the satisfaction of reinforcing now, that we have never thought of making The Spirits' Book an object of speculation. Its product will be applied to those things of general interest. That is why we shall be always grateful to those who, from their heart and for the love of good, associated to the work we have dedicated ourselves.

ALLAN KARDEC [9]

---

8 Rue Tiquetonne, 14
9 Paris. Typography Cosson & Co. Rue de Four-Saint-Germain, 43

February 1858

Different Orders of Spirits

A central point in the Spiritist Doctrine is the difference among the spirits, be it intellectual or moral. Their teachings never changed regarding this subject. Nevertheless, it is essential to know that they do not eternally belong to the same order and that, as a consequence, these orders do not constitute distinct species: they indicate different degrees of development. The spirits follow the progressive march of nature. Those of the inferior orders are still imperfects; later, after depuration, they reach the superior orders; they move along the hierarchy while acquiring qualities, experience and knowledge which they still lack. The breast-feeding child is not similar to what it shall be at a mature age; however it is always the same being.

The classification of the spirits is based on their degree of progress, their acquired qualities and their imperfections that need to be stripped off. By the way, such classification has nothing of absolute. Each category only shows one key feature but from one degree to the next the transition is soft, the nuance fades away towards the extremes, like it does in nature, in the colors of the rainbow or in the several stages of human life. It is then possible to form a higher or lower number of classes, according to the point of view used to consider the subject. The same happens to all forms of scientific classification: they can be more or less complete, more or less rational, more or less accommodating to the intelligence but, whatever they may be, they can never change the fundamentals of the Science.

Once questioned about this subject the spirits may have given different answers with respect to the number of categories but this is not important. Critics take this apparent contradiction not considering that the spirits themselves do not give importance to what is purely conventional. To them, thought is everything. They leave to us the choice of format, expressions and classification – in one word, the systems.

We shall still add the following consideration: one should never forget that, among the spirits, as with human beings, there are those that are highly ignorant and we must resist our tendency to think that the spirits must all know everything just because they are spirits. Every classification requires method, analysis and profound knowledge of the subject. Well, in the spiritual world, those who have limited knowledge, like the ignorant among us, are incapable of an ample view of the broad picture and to establish a system; and those who are capable may vary in the details, according to their viewpoint, especially when a division has nothing of absolute. Linnée, Jussieu and Tournefort have each followed a different method. Nonetheless, the Science of Botany has not changed. They have neither invented the plants nor their features. They observed the analogies and formed the groups or classes based on that.

That was how we proceeded. We did neither invent the spirits nor their characters. We saw and observed; we judged them based on their words and acts, then we classified them based on their similarities. This is what anybody else would have done in such a case.

However we cannot claim authorship of the whole work. If, on one hand, the classification given below was not entirely outlined by the spirits and if it is of our own initiative, on the other hand it contains all elements acquired from their teachings. The remaining work was to formulate a physical arrangement of the material.

The spirits generally admit three main categories or large divisions. At the end, on the bottom of the scale, lies the imperfect spirits, those who still need to go through all or almost all stages: these are categorized by the prevalence of matter over the spirit and by their inclination towards evil. Those at the second level are categorized by the prevalence of the spirit over matter and by the desire of good deeds: these are the good spirits. The first category thus comprehends the pure spirits, those who have reached the supreme degree of perfection.

Such a division seems perfectly rational to us and presents well defined characters. What was still missing to distinguish, in sufficient number, was the nuances of each group. This is what we did with the help of the spirits, whose benevolent instructions have never failed us.

With the support of that classification table it will be easy to determine the category and the degree of superiority or inferiority of the spirits with whom we may entertain ourselves and, as a consequence, the degree of confidence and regard they deserve. Besides this is of our personal interest as we ourselves, by our souls, belong to the spiritual world in which we shall enter as soon as we leave our mortal covering (wrapping), indicating to us what we need to do in order to achieve perfection and the supreme good.

Nevertheless, we will observe that the spirits do not always and exclusively belong to this or that class. Their progress only gradually takes place and many times more in one direction than in another, being thus able to have characters of several categories, which is easy to observe from their language and acts.

Spirits' Scale

THIRD ORDER – IMPERFECT SPIRITS

General characteristics: Prevalence of matter over the spirit. Have tendency towards evil. Show ignorance, arrogance, egotism and all their consequent passions.

Have the intuition of God but do not understand God.

Not all of them are essentially bad; some show more levity, inconsequence and wickedness than evilness. Others neither practice good nor evil but by simply not being good they reveal inferiority. Others still rejoice with iniquity and are delighted by the very opportunity of practicing it. These can associate their intelligence to meanness or malevolence but whatever their intellectual development may be, their ideas are not much elevated and their feelings more or less abject.

Their comprehension about the spiritual world is limited and their little knowledge is mixed with their preconceived ideas from their corporeal life. They can only give us false and incomplete notions but the thoughtful observer many times discovers in their communications, though imperfect, the confirmation of the immense truths taught by the superior spirits.

Their character is revealed by their language. Every spirit who, in the communications, betrays one thought may be classified in the third order; thus every bad thought which is suggested to us comes from a spirit of that order.

They see the happiness of the good spirits and this is an inexorable distress to them, as they experience all anguishes produced by envy and jealousy.

These spirits keep the memory and perception of the sufferings of their corporeal life and those perceptions are sometimes harder than reality. They really suffer by the ill deeds they had to endure and by those they had imposed to others. As they suffer for a long time they judge their suffering as eternal. God allows them to think so in order to help them seek a better way.

These spirits may be divided in four main groups:

NINTH CLASS: IMPURE SPIRITS

They are inclined towards evil, object of their concerns. As spirits their advices are perfidious, spread discord and mistrust and use all masks to better deceive others. They associate themselves to those persons of sufficiently weak character to give in to their suggestions in order to take them to perdition, happy if able to delay progress, leading others to succumb in their trials.

Their language can be recognized in the manifestations. The triviality and gross expressions, with the spirits as with human beings, are always indications of moral, if not intellectual inferiority. Their communications reveal the baseness of their tendencies. When trying to deceive, speaking in a sensible way, they soon reveal their origin as they cannot sustain such role for long.

Certain peoples made them malevolent divinities; others designated them by demons, genies or evil spirits.

When incarnated the bodies they animate are inclined to all kinds of vices as well as their consequent vile and degrading passions: sensuality, cruelty, forgery, hypocrisy, cupidity and sordid greed. They do evil things for the pleasure of it, most of the time without motive and, by their hatred of good, usually electing their victims among good people. They are a scourge to humanity, whatever the class they belong and the varnish of civilization does not spare them from the opprobrium and ignominy.

EIGHTH CLASS: FRIVOLOUS SPIRITS

These spirits are ignorant, malevolent, inconsequent and scorner. Get involved in all things, responding to anything with no regard whatsoever to the truth. As they enjoy provoking small upsets as well as little happiness, the spirits like to produce discord and maliciously induce error by mystifications and naughtiness. Spirits in this class are typically designated as elves, goblins, trasgos and gnomes. They depend on the superior spirits by whom they are frequently employed just as we do with our servants and workers.

They seem, more than the others, attached to matter, having an active role as agents of the vicissitude of global elements, living in the air, water, fire, in the solid bodies or even in the entrails of the earth. Several times they manifest their presence through sensitive effects such as raps, movements, abnormal displacements of solid bodies, air agitation, etc. which gave them the name "boisterous spirits". It is acknowledged that those phenomena are not due to a fortuitous and natural cause when they present an intentional and intelligent character. All spirits can produce these effects but the superior spirits, generally, leave that to the inferior spirits, more apt to material than intelligent actions.

When communicating, their language sometimes shows wit and happiness but almost always without depth. Their sarcastic and satiric expressions contain caprices and ridicule. They sometimes assume fictitious names for malice rather than malevolence.

SEVENTH CLASS: PSEUDO-WISE SPIRITS

Having extensive knowledge, these spirits assume to know more than they actually do. They show some progress from several points of view. Their language has a serious character, which may lead to mistakes regarding their capacity and illumination, but, very frequently, it is simply a reaction of their prejudices and systematic ideas carried over from their earthly life. Their words are a mixture of some truths and some absurdities, which stem presumption, pride, envy and stubbornness that they have not yet stripped.

SIXTH CLASS: NEUTRAL SPIRITS

These are not good enough to do good deeds or bad enough to do evil ones. They incline towards one or the other and do not rise above the vulgar of humanity, with respect to morality as well as intelligence. These spirits attach themselves to earthly things whose gross pleasures they miss.

SECOND ORDER – GOOD SPIRITS

General characteristics: Prevalence of spirit over matter; desire of good. Their qualities and capacities for the practice of good are proportional to the level they have reached: some have science, others wisdom and goodness; the most advanced unite knowledge to moral qualities. As they are not completely de-materialized, they more or less maintain, according to their classes, traces of the corporeal existence, both in their language as well as in their habits, where we can even identify certain customs, without which they would be perfect spirits.

They understand God and the infinity and already enjoy the happiness of the good ones. They feel happy for the good they spread as well as the evil they avoid. Love is a bonding source of ineffable happiness, unaltered by envy, or sorrow, or remorse, or by any other bad passion which torment the imperfect spirits; nevertheless all still have to endure trials before reaching absolute perfection.

As spirits, they give rise to good thoughts deviating human beings from tortuous paths; during life they protect those who are worthy of their protection and neutralize the influence of the imperfect spirits over those who are not pleased to submit to them.

When incarnated, these are good and benevolent to all their neighbors. They are not moved by pride or selfishness, or even by ambition. Do not experiment hate, resentment, envy or jealousy and practice good for the good.

These are the commonly designated good geniuses or protector geniuses, spirits of good in the vulgar beliefs. Over the times of superstition and ignorance, they were transformed into beneficent divinities.

They can also be divided into four main groups:

FIFTH CLASS: BENEVOLENT SPIRITS

Goodness is their prevalent quality. Enjoy protecting and serving people but their knowledge is limited: they have progressed more in the moral than in the intellectual sense.

FOURTH CLASS: SPIRITS OF SCIENCE

The extension of their knowledge is what distinguishes them. Less concerned with the moral questions than with the scientific ones, for which have more aptitude but only see science from its utility point of view, not blending that with any passion characteristic of the imperfect spirits.

THIRD CLASS: WISE SPIRITS

Moral qualities of the highest order are what distinguish them. Their knowledge is not unlimited but they have such a high intellectual capability that it allows them to make a shrewd judgment of human beings and all things.

SECOND CLASS: SUPERIOR SPIRITS

Unite science, wisdom and benevolence. Their language, permanently dignified and elevated, breathes generosity and, sometimes, it is sublime. Their superiority enable them, more than the others, with the ability to give us the most rightful notions of the incorporeal world, within the limits allowed to humans. Show good will in the communications with those who, in good faith, look for the truth and whose souls are released enough from the earthly harnesses to understand it, but stay away from those animated by curiosity or those deviated from the righteous path due to the influence of matter.

When exceptionally reincarnate on earth it is to accomplish a mission of progress. It is when they offer us the type of perfection that humanity may aspire in this world.

FIRST ORDER – PURE SPIRITS

General characteristics: Influence of matter is non-existent. Possess absolute intellectual and moral superiority over the spirits of the other orders.

FIRST CLASS: PURE SPIRITS

Have passed through all degrees of the scale and are cleansed from all impurities of matter. Having achieved supreme perfection attainable by the creature, they do not have to go through trials and atonements. No longer subjected to incarnation in perishable bodies, enjoy the eternal life by God's side.

Live an unaltered happiness as they no longer are subjected to the needs and vicissitudes of the material life, but such a happy state is not a monotonous idleness in a perpetual state of contemplation. They are the messengers and ministers of God whose orders execute in order to maintain universal harmony. Command all spirits below them, attributing missions and helping in their progression. Show contentment in supporting the individual with their anguishes, stimulating them towards the practice of good, encouraging them with the expiation of their faults which keep them away from the supreme happiness. These are sometimes called angels, archangels or seraphim.

Human beings can communicate with them but anyone who intended to have them at their service would be presumptuous.

Errant or Incarnated Spirits

Regarding their intimate qualities, the spirits belong to different orders, which they successively go through as they depurate. With respect to their *state*, the spirits can be incarnated, that is united to the body in any world, or errant, that is, disconnected from a material body and waiting for a new incarnation, so as to improve.

The errant spirits do not form a special category. It refers to one of the states in which they can be found.

The errant state, or erraticity, does not mean inferiority to the spirits, since they can be found in all degrees in such a state. Every spirit who is not incarnated is, as a consequence, errant, with the exception of the pure spirits who, for not having to go through other incarnations, are in a definitive state.

Since the incarnation is a transient state, erraticity is really the normal state of the spirits, and such a state is not forcibly expiation. In the state of erraticity they are happy or unfortunate, according to their degree of elevation, and the good or the bad that they might have practiced.

Mademoiselle Clairon

and the Phantom

This story caused uproar in its time, by the position of the hero lady and by the large number of persons who witnessed it. Despite its singularity, it would have been probably forgotten had Mademoiselle Clairon not published it in her memoirs. This is where we extracted the report below. The analogy it has, with some of the current facts, gives it a natural place in this collection.

Mademoiselle Clairon was not only known for her beauty but also for her talent as a singer and actress in tragic roles. She had inspired a young Breton, Mr. S..., in one of these passions, understanding that he did not possess the necessary talents to fully succeed in his passion. Mademoiselle Clairon only corresponded with her friendship. Nevertheless Mr. S... presence had become such an annoyance that she decided to break up their relationship for good. Heartbroken he experienced a long lasting illness, which killed him in 1743. Here is how Mademoiselle Clairon described it.

"It was two and a half years since the day we met and the day he died. He sent for me, asking for my kind acceptance of seeing him over his last moments. My relationships did not allow me to do that. He did die having only servants around him and an old lady who was his only companion for a long time. He lived in Rempart, near Chaussée d'Antin, where they had started to build. I lived at Rue de Bussy, near the Rue du Seine and Saint-German Abbey. I was with my mother and several friends having just finished dinner. I had just sung beautiful pastoral songs which delighted my friends when, at eleven o'clock sharp, we heard a piercing scream. Its somber modulation and duration shocked everyone. I felt like passing out and indeed I was unconscious for about fifteen minutes."

"My whole family, friends, neighbors, and the police would hear the same scream, always at the same time, coming from the bottom of my window as if it vaguely came through the air. I rarely had dinner in the city but during those days nothing would be heard and, many times, when asking my servants and my mother for any news, on returning to my room, the scream would blast right in the middle of the group."

"On one occasion I had dinner with the president of B..., who wanted to kindly follow me home to ensure that I would be safe. When we got to the house, by the door, he was saying goodbye to me when the scream blew between the two of us. Just as the whole of Paris was aware, he knew about the screams but he still had to be helped to his carriage, looking more dead than alive."

"Still on another occasion I asked my good friend Rosely to join me on a shopping tour to Rue Saint-Honore, looking for fabrics. The only subject of our conversation was my "phantom" as he was called. This very talented young man would not believe in any of those things but was impressed by my adventure. He requested that I should evoke the phantom, saying that he would then believe if the phantom responded. Be it by weakness or audacity I did what he asked me. The scream was heard three times, and it was horrifying for its loudness and speed. On returning home we needed the support of several people to remove us from the carriage, as both of us were unconscious. After this event I heard nothing for some months. I thought the situation was definitely over. What a mistake."

"Every spectacle had been transferred to Versailles for the wedding of the Dauphin. A room was organized for me at Saint-Cloud Avenue, which I shared with Mrs. Grandval. At 3 am I said to her: it is the end of the world; it would be really difficult that the scream would find us here. It then blasted! Mrs. Grandval thought that our room was in hell. Dressed in evening gown, she ran away from top to bottom of the stairs; nobody could sleep that night. At least it was the last time we heard it."

"Seven or eight days later, on talking to people to whom I was acquainted, the eleven o'clock tick tock was followed by a musket gunshot, from one of my windows. We all heard the noise and saw the fire but the window was intact. We concluded that I was the missed target and that we should then take better precautions in the future. Mr. Marvillen, then a police commissioner, requested that all houses near the street from my own house should be searched. The street was full of all types of spies but, regardless of how much care was taken, for three consecutive months those shots were seen and heard, always at the same hour of the day, at the same spot of the window, without anybody being able to identify its real origin. The fact was duly registered by the police."

"Once, already accustomed to my phantom, who I considered a poor devil limited to his own wickedness, I did not take notice of the time. As it was a hot day, I opened the deplorable window, talking to the officer at the balcony. At eleven o'clock sharp a gunshot was heard and both of us were thrown on the floor, in the middle of the room, where we fell like the dead. On recovering our senses we noticed that both of us had had the faces unbelievably slapped, him on the left face and me on the right one – we laughed like crazy."

"Two days later I was invited by Mademoiselle Dumesnil to attend an evening party at her house; I took a carriage at eleven o'clock with my chambermaid. The moonlight was beautiful and we were taken through boulevards lined by houses. The maid said:

"Wasn't it here that Mr. S... died?"

"According to the information I was given, yes it must have been here", I answered, pointing towards one of the two houses across from where we were."

"A gunshot was fired from one of the houses. It went through our carriage; the scared coachman drove fast ahead, thinking that some thieves were assaulting us."

"We arrived at our destination just recovered from the incident as, I must confess, for a long time I had that look of horror in my face; however, that event was the last with a firearm."

"Those explosions were followed by the clapping of hands, with certain rhythm and repetition. This noise, to which the kindness of my audiences had me accustomed to, went undetected for some time but my friends noticed them. They said: we have been watching. It is at eleven o'clock, near your door that it happens. We hear but do not see anybody. It can only be the continuation of those events. As the noise was not so bad, I did not keep track of its duration. I did not give attention either to the harmonious sounds that were heard later. It sounded like a celestial voice giving the accords of an aria, about to be sung. That voice would start at the Bussy quarters and stop at my door. As it happened before with all the other noises, it was heard but nothing could be seen. Just over two and a half years later everything stopped, at last."

Sometime later Mademoiselle Clairon had, through the old lady who was the only companion of Mr. S... the following report about his last moments.

"He was counting the minutes, she said, when at about ten thirty the servant came to tell him that you would not come. After a moment of silence he took my hand, on a desperate impulse that scared me, and said: What a cruelty! She will not gain anything from that. I will hound her as much in death as in life! I tried to calm him down but he was already dead."

In the edition we have in hand, the following note, without signature, precedes this story:

"This is a very singular anecdote which has provoked and will provoke the most diverse opinions. We love the marvelous even when we do not believe in it. Mademoiselle Clairon seems convinced of the facts that she describes. We shall satisfy ourselves with the observation that at the time she was or thought she was tormented by her phantom she was twenty two and a half to twenty five years old, which is the age of inspiration whose faculty she constantly exercised and exalted through her life style, in and out of the theatre. It is also necessary to remember that in the beginning of her memoirs she said that in her infancy she was entertained by adventures of apparitions and witches that, as she was told, were all real stories."

We only know the facts from the descriptions of Mademoiselle Clairon. Thus we can only judge by induction. Well, this is our thought: Described by Mademoiselle Clairon herself the fact has more authenticity than if it were reported by others. Besides, when she wrote the letter where these facts are described she was sixty years old hence she was beyond the age of credulity mentioned by the author of the note. That author does not question the good faith of Mademoiselle Clairon with respect to her adventure: only admits that she might have been victim of an illusion. Had it had happened once there is nothing of extraordinary in it but as it happened for two and a half years then it seems more difficult to us. Even more difficult is to suppose that such an illusion might have been shared by so many people, audible and visual witnesses of the facts, including the police itself.

Knowing what can happen in spiritist manifestations, as we do, the adventure has nothing of surprising and we accept it as likely. With that hypothesis we do not hesitate to admit that the author of all those malevolent acts is nobody else but Mr. S..., particularly if we notice the coincidence of her words with the duration of the phenomena. He had said: "I will hound her as much in death as in life!" Well, his relationship with Mademoiselle Clairon had lasted two and a half years, which was the same time period of the produced manifestations.

Continuing with the nature of this spirit, he is not bad and it is with reason that Mademoiselle Clairon classifies him as a poor devil but one cannot classify him as the personified benevolence. The violent passion that he experienced as a man proves that the earthly ideas prevail on him. The profound traces of that passion, which survived the destruction of his body, prove that as spirit he was still under the influence of matter. His vengeance, as harmless at it appeared, denotes non-elevated feelings. If we then refer to our table of classification of the spirits, it will not be difficult to determine his class: the absence of real meanness separate him from the last class of the impure spirits but he evidently had much of the other classes of the same order as nothing in him could justify a superior position.

Noticeable is also the succession of modes through which he manifested his presence. On the very day and exact moment of his death he made himself heard for the first time, in the middle of a pleasant dinner. When alive, he used to see Mademoiselle Clairon with an imaginary aura involving the object of his keen passion. However, since the separation of his soul from the material covering, the illusion gave rise to reality. There he is, by her side, seeing her surrounded by friends, everything firing up his jealousy. Her singing and happiness sound like an insult to his desperation which is translated as a scream of hatred repeated every day at the same time, as if to blame her for having refused to bring him some consolation in his last moments. The screams are succeeded by the gunshots, certainly harmless, but not less capable of showing his powerless hate and desire to disturb her rest. Later his desperation takes a more tranquil format evolving, no doubt, to healthier ideas, seemingly having taken sides: what remains are his memories of the applause directed to her thus he repeats it. Even later he seems to say farewell when those harmonious sounds were like an echo of the melodious voice that had him so much enchanted.

Isolation of Heavy Bodies

The motion imposed by the will on inert bodies is so much known today that it would be almost puerile to report facts of such a kind. The same does not apply when the movement is followed by less obvious phenomena, for example, like its levitation into air. Although the Annals of Spiritism cite numerous examples, this phenomenon presents such an exception to the gravitational laws that the doubt on those who witness them is extremely natural. We confess ourselves that no matter how much familiar we are with the things of extraordinary nature, we are happy for being able to verify its reality.

The fact we are going to report repeated many times before our eyes in meetings held in the residence of Mr. B..., at Rue Lamartine and we know that they have also occurred many times in other places. Hence, we can attest it as a fact. Here is an example of such a case:

Eight or ten people, among them some bestowed by a special power, although they were not recognized as mediums, sat around a heavy and massive dinner table, with their hands at the edge, all united by intention and will. After a period of time, between ten or fifteen minutes, depending on the more or less favorable conditions of the ambient, the table would be moving, despite its one hundred kilograms of weight; it slid to the right or to the left on the floor; it would be directed to any designated part of the room; then it would stand sometimes on one foot, sometimes on the other, until it formed a 45° angle and rapidly swung imitating the pitch and roll of a ship. If in that position the audience doubled their will power, the table would completely rise from the floor, staying at about ten to twenty centimeters high, sustained in the air without any support for a few seconds, and then completely falling on its full weight.

The motion of the table, the lifting on one foot and the swing, occurred almost at will. It happened often and several times in the session and frequently without any hand contact; will power alone was enough for the table to move sideways, as indicated. The complete isolation was more difficult to obtain, but it was repeated often enough that it could not be considered as an exceptional event. Now this would not only happen in the presence of experts who could be too accessible to the illusion, but in front of twenty or thirty people, among them at times some very unsympathetic who would not fail to raise the hypothesis of secret preparation, without any consideration for the home owners, whose honest character should rule out any suspicion of fraud and to whom it would be a strange pleasure to spend some hours a week mystifying an assembly of people without any benefit.

We reported the fact in all its simplicity, without limitation or exaggeration. We do not say we saw the table flying through the air like a feather, but as it is, the fact is not a lesser demonstration of the possibility of isolation of heavy bodies without support, by means of a hitherto unknown power. We will not say either that it was sufficient to extend the hand or make any sign so that the table would move or rise as if magically.

We say, instead, to be faithful to the truth, that the first movements were always somewhat slow, and only gradually acquired its maximum intensity. The complete lifting would only take place after several preparatory attempts that worked as tests in a kind of throwing exercise. The effective power seemed to redouble their efforts by the encouragement of the spectators, as a man or a horse that carries a heavy burden, and who is excited by voices and gestures. Once the effect was produced everything would return to calm normality and for a few moments nothing else was obtained, as if that same power had to take a breather.

We shall often have the opportunity to cite such phenomena, either spontaneous or induced, and produced in quantities and under circumstances far more extraordinary. But having witnessed them, we shall always report in such a way to avoid any false or exaggerated interpretation. If to the description above we had been satisfied to say that we saw a table of 100 kilograms come off the ground by the touch of some hands, no doubt that many people would have figured out that the table went up to the ceiling with the speed of the blink of an eye. That is how by the proportions given by imagination the simplest things become prodigies. What shall it be when the facts have gone through the centuries and passed through the mouth of the poets! Had we said that superstition is the daughter of reality, the concept would be taken as a paradox. However, nothing is truer: there is no superstition that is not based on a somewhat real fact. The essential is to discern where one ends and the other begins. The best way to fight superstition is not by challenging it in absolute terms. In the minds of some people there are ideas that do not uproot easily, because there are always facts that can be mentioned to support their ideas. On the contrary it is necessary to reveal what is real. Then there still remains the ridiculous exaggeration to which common sense will do justice.

The Forest of Dodona and

the Statue of Memnon

To get to the forest of Dodona we took Rue Lamartine and stopped for a moment at Mr. B... house where we saw a docile piece of furniture challenging us with a new problem of static. Assistants in numbers sat around the table in question, in any order, hence there was neither number nor cabalistic places; the hands resting on the edge of the table; mentally or in loud voice they appeal to the spirits who are used to attend to their invitation. Our opinion about this kind of spirits is well known which is why we treat them somewhat unceremoniously. Four or five minutes are hardly passed and a clear sound of knock-knock is heard at the table, often strong enough to be heard from the adjacent room, and repeats as long and as often as desired. The vibration is felt in the fingers, and when applying the ear against the table – which should not be forgotten – one unmistakably recognizes that the noise is originated from the very substance of the wood as the whole table vibrates, from the feet to the top.

What is causing this noise? Is it the wood that raps or is it, as they say, a spirit? Let us dismiss, to begin with, any idea of hoax as we are in the house of serious people, in good company, incapable of having fun at the expenses of those who, with good will, they admit to their homes. Indeed this house is not privileged. The same events occur in many others equally honorable. Allow us however a small digression before giving the answer.

A young bachelor's degree student was in his room, busy studying for his examination when he hears a knock on his door. I do believe that everyone admits that it is possible to distinguish the nature of the noise, and especially with respect to its repetition, if it is caused by a crack in the wood, agitation of the wind or any other accidental cause, or if it is someone who is actually knocking, requesting entry. In the latter case the noise has an intentional character that cannot be misunderstood. That is what our student thinks. However, in order not to be unnecessarily disturbed, he wanted to make sure, by testing the visitor. If it's someone, he says, hit one, two, three, four, five, six times, hit the top, bottom, right, left, hit like the musical accord, play the military call, etc.., and to every one of these requests the noise obeys with the utmost accuracy. Surely, he thought, this may not be a burst in the wood, nor the wind, nor even a cat, however intelligent it may be. Here's a fact. Let us see where the syllogistic arguments take us to, as a consequence.

He then used the following train of thought: I hear noise thus there is something that produces it. That noise obeys my commands, so the cause that produces it understands me. Well, something that understands has intelligence thus the cause of the noise is intelligent. If the cause is intelligent then it is neither the wood nor the wind; if it is neither the wood nor the wind, so it's someone. He then opens the door. We see that it is not necessary to be a doctor to draw such a conclusion; and we trust that our future bachelor is sufficiently versed in his principles to achieve the following conclusions: Suppose that by opening the door he finds nobody, and that the noise continues exactly as before. He will continue his sorites[10]: "I have just unarguably demonstrated to myself that the noise is produced by an intelligent being, since it responds to my thoughts. I always hear this sound before me, and it is certain that it is not I who

---

10   The *sorites paradox* is the name given to a class of paradoxical arguments, also known as little-by-little arguments, which arise as a result of the indeterminacy surrounding limits of application of the involved predicates (N.T.)

knocks, thus it is someone else. Well, if I do not see it then it is invisible. Corporeal beings belonging to humanity are perfectly visible. Whoever knocks, being invisible, are not a corporeal human being. Indeed since we call spirits the incorporeal beings, the one who knocks, not being corporeal, is then a spirit."

We judge the conclusions of our student rigorously logical. What we had as an assumption is a fact, regarding the experiences that were taking place in Mr. B... house. We'll add that there was no need for the imposition of hands, all the phenomena occurring equally well while the table was free from any contact. Thus, according to the wish, the raps occurred in the table, on the wall, at the door, and any other verbally or mentally designated place. They indicated the time, the number of people present; the military rhythms, the harmony of a familiar tune, they imitated the sounds of a barrow worker, the grinding of the saw, echo, police patrol sirens or platoons and many other effects which would take us too long to describe. We were told that in some circles they heard the whistling wind, the rustling of leaves, the burst of thunder, the splashing of the waves, which is not surprising at all. The intelligence of the cause became obvious when, through those same raps, we got categorical answers to certain questions. In reality it is this intelligent cause that we called, or rather, which it has called itself spirit. When this spirit wanted to give a more developed communication, he indicated by any particular sign that he wanted to write; then the writing medium would take the pencil and transmit his thoughts in writing.

Among those present, not including those who were around the table, but everyone who filled the room, there were some authentic skeptical, half-believers and fervent followers, which form, as we all know, a truly unfavorable mix. We let the first group to be our guest, hoping that they would see the light. We respect all beliefs, even incredulity which is some sort of belief, when that is respectful enough not to shock any contrary opinion. Thus we do not consider their observations useless.

Their reasoning, much less prolonged than our student above, may be summarized as this: I do not believe in spirits hence it cannot be spirits and since it is not spirits than it is a trick. Such a supposition leads them to believe that the table would have some type of engine, much like Robert Houdin. Our answer to that is very simple: first, it would be necessary that all tables and all pieces of furniture had such mechanism, as none can be privileged; second, there isn't any known mechanism sufficiently ingenious to produce all the effects we have just described, at will; third it would be necessary that Mrs. B... had prepared walls and doors of her apartment, on purpose, which is very unlikely; fourth, at last, it would have been still necessary to prepare the tables, doors and walls of all houses where similar events take place daily, which cannot be presumed either since the skillful constructor of such wonders would be known. The half-believers accept all phenomena, but they are undecided with respect to their causes. We refer to the arguments of our future Bachelor above. The believers have three well-defined nuances: those who see it nothing more than a fun game and a pastime in the experiments and those whose admiration can be translated by the expressions: It's amazing! This is strange! This is funny! But do not go beyond that. Then come the serious ones, the educated, the observers, the ones whom no detail escapes. Then comes, finally, the ultra-believers, if we may say so, or rather, the blind believers, those that can be criticized by an excess of credulity; since their faith is not enlightened enough, show such a confidence in the spirits that they admit their thorough knowledge and, above all, their prescience. Thus it is in good faith that they ask questions about every single subject, not thinking that they might have gotten the same answers had they have paid the first fortuneteller. For these, the "talking table" is not an object of study and observation; it is an oracle. Against this there is only the trivial form and its vulgar uses. If the wood that makes the table, instead of being cut for the domestic activities, were standing, we would have a "talking tree"; if it were carved as a statue, we would have an idol before which the credulous would prostrate.

Now we transpose the seas and twenty-five centuries and transport ourselves to the foothill of Mount Taurus in Epirus. There we will find the sacred forest whose oak trees provided oracles; add the prestige of worship and the splendor of religious ceremonies, and we easily have the explanation about the veneration of an ignorant and credulous people, unable to see reality through so many means of fascination.

Wood is not the only substance that can serve as a vehicle for the manifestation of the rapping spirits. We have seen them happen in a wall, thus in stone. We thus have the talking stones. If these stones represent a sacred figure, we have the statue of Memnon or that of Jupiter Ammon as oracles similar to the trees of Dodona.

It is true that history, indeed, does not tell us that these oracles were rendered by raps, as we see today. In the forest of Dodona, it was the wind whistling through the trees, the rustling leaves, or the murmur of the fountain that sprung at the foot of the sacred oak of Jupiter. The statue of Memnon issued, they say, melodic sounds, at the first rays of sunlight. But history also tells us, as we shall have the occasion to demonstrate, that the ancients knew perfectly well the phenomena attributed to the rapping spirits. Make no mistake that the very principle of their belief rests in the existence of animated beings on trees, rocks, water, etc... But since this kind of event was exploited, the raps were no longer enough; the visitors were too numerous to offer each person a particular session; by the way, it would have been very simple: it was necessary the prestige, and since they enriched the temple with their offerings, the costs would have been covered. The essential was to look to the object as sacred, inhabited by a divinity. Under those conditions it was possible to produce whatever they wanted and without the need for so many precautions. The priests of Memnon, they say, used trickeries: the statue was hollow, and the sounds she made were produced by acoustic processes. This is possible and even probable. The rapping spirits themselves, who generally are less scrupulous than others, are not always, as we have already said, at the service of the first to show up. They have their will, their occupations, their susceptibilities, and neither one nor the other likes to be exploited by greed. What a discredit to the high priests if their idol did not speak conveniently! It was necessary to make up for his silence and, if needed, to give a hand. It was in fact more comfortable to avoid much trouble by providing the answers according to the circumstances. What we see today proves that, despite all that, the old beliefs had the knowledge of the spiritist manifestations by principle, being this the reason we say that modern spiritualism is the revival of antiquity, but antiquity illuminated by the lights of civilization and reality.

Greed

Moral Dissertation

Dictated by the spirit of St. Louis to Ms. Ermance Dufaux,
on January 6th, 1858

I

Thou hast, and listen to me. One day two children of the same father received a bushel[11] of wheat each. The older brother locked his wheat in a remote place. The younger found a poor man in his way, begging for money; he swiftly gave him half of the wheat he received, pouring it on the man's mantle. Then he moved on, sowing the remaining seeds about his father's field.

Over that time there was a terrible hunger and the birds from the sky were found dead on the pathways. The older brother rushed to his hiding place only to find dust. The younger one was sadly contemplating his dry wheat when he noticed the poor man who he had once helped. Brother, said the beggar, I was dying and you helped me; now that hope has dried in your heart, follow me. Your half-bushel has yielded five times more in my hands. I will give you food and you will live in abundance.

---

11   In French: "boisseau" – old measure of capacity for grain, equivalent to approximately 36 liters (NT)

II

Listen to me you who are miser! Do you know happiness? Yes, don't you? Your eyes shine with dark reflections in the orbits deeply carved by greed; your lips clasp, your nostrils dilate and your ears are attentive. Yes, I hear: it is the jingle of gold that your hand caresses, by pouring in your box. You say: what a supreme ecstasy! Silence, someone is coming! Quickly shut it up! Oh! How pale you are! Your whole body shakes. Control yourself! The footsteps move away. Open it! Look once more, it is your gold. Open it! Do not be afraid. You are quite alone. Do you hear? It's nothing. It's the wind moaning through the cracks. Look! How much gold! Plunge your hands, sound the metal. You are happy.

Happy you! But you cannot rest at night and ghosts invade your sleep.

You are cold! Get closer to the fireplace. The fire that crackles so happily warms you up. Snow falls. The cold traveler involves himself in his coat; the poor is shivering under the rags. The flame of the fire diminishes; throw on more wood. No, stop! It's your gold blazing with that wood; it is your gold that you burn!

You are hungry! Look, take it, satisfy yourself. All this is yours. You paid with your gold. With your gold! This abundance disgusts you; will this superfluous be needed to maintain life? No, this piece of bread will be enough; too much, still. Your clothes fall in tatters; your house cracks and threatens to ruin; you will suffer cold and hunger, but who cares! You have gold!

Miserable! Death will separate you from this gold. You will leave it by the edge of your grave, as the dust shaken by the traveler at the door, where the loving family awaits to celebrate the expected return.

Your weakened blood, aged by your voluntary misery, has frozen in your veins. Eager heirs throw your body into a corner of the cemetery; behold you are now face to face with eternity. Miserable! What have you done to the gold that has been entrusted to you to relieve the poor? You hear these blasphemies? You see these tears? You see this blood? These are the blasphemies of the sufferings that you could have alleviated; these are the tears you caused, the blood you shed. You horrify yourself; you wish you could escape but you cannot. You suffer, desperately! Your suffering contorts you. Suffer! There will be no mercy for you! You had no compassion on your unhappy brother. Who would have for you? Suffer! Suffer always! Your punishment will never end. To punish you, God wants you to believe so.

OBSERVATION: Listening to the end of these eloquent and poetic words, we were surprised to hear St. Louis talking about the eternity of suffering, when all the superior spirits are in agreement to combat this belief, when the last words: "to punish you, God so wants you to believe so" explains it all. We reproduced them in the general characteristics of the spirits of the third order. Indeed, the more imperfect the spirits the more restricted and circumscribed their ideas. For them the future is vague, and they do not understand it. They suffer, their suffering is long, and for those who suffer for a long time, it is like suffering forever. This thought, alone, is a punishment.

In a next article we will cite facts of manifestations that might enlighten us regarding the nature of suffering beyond the grave.

Conversations From

Beyond the Grave

Evocation – Ms. Clary D....

NOTE: Ms. Clary D... was an interesting girl, who died in 1850 at age 13, who has since then become the genie of the family, where she is frequently evoked and where she gives a large number of communications of the highest interest. The conversation we reproduce below occurred between us on January 12th, 1857 through her brother, who is a medium.

1. Do you have precise memories of your corporeal existence?
 - The spirit sees the present, the past and some of the future, according to their perfection and their proximity to God.
2. The condition of perfection is relative only to the future, or it also refers to the present and the past?
 - The spirit sees the future more clearly as they get closer to God. After death, the soul sees and embraces, at a glance, all past lives, but cannot see what God prepares.
For that we need to be fully in God, there are many existences.
3. Do you know when your reincarnation will be?
 - In 10 or 100 years.
4. On Earth or another world?
 - On another.

5. The world where you will be, compared to Earth, will have better conditions, same as on Earth or inferior?

- Much better than on Earth. One is happy over there.

6. Since you are here among us, are you in a particular place? Where?

- I'm ethereal in appearance. I can say that my spirit itself extends much further. I see many things and I transport myself far from here with the speed of thought.

My appearance is right by my brother's side and guides his arm.

7. This ethereal body that dresses you up allows you to experience physical sensations, such as heat and cold?

- When I remember much of my body I feel a sort of impression, as when a blanket is removed from you and, for some time, you still keep the sensation that you have it on.

8. You said you can move with the speed of thought. Isn't the thought the soul itself, which detaches from its covering?

- Yes

9. When your thoughts move to a given region, how does the separation of the soul take place?

- The appearance vanishes. The thought goes alone.

10. Is it therefore a faculty that stands out, the actual "being" stays put?

- The form is not the being.

11. But how does this thought act? Is it not always through matter?

- No.

12. When your thinking faculty stands out, don't you act then by means of matter?

- The shadow fades away and reproduces wherever the thought may guide it.

13. Considering that you were only 13 years old when your body died, how can you give us answers beyond the reach of a child of that age, about such abstract questions?

- My soul is very old!

14. Among your previous existences can you mention one in which you had raised your knowledge most?

- I was in the body of a man who I made a virtuoso. After his death I was in the body of a girl whose face stamped my own soul. God rewards me.

15. Could we be allowed to see you here as you are now?

- You could.

16. How could that be? It depends on us, on you or on those closest to you?

- On you.

17. Which conditions should we satisfy to obtain that?

- You need to be secluded for some time, with faith and fervor; you need to be in a small group; you need some isolation and a medium like Home.

Mr. Home

The phenomena produced by Mr. Home caused so much sensation as it is certain that they confirm the wonderful reports from overseas, whose truthfulness comes attached to some distrust. He showed us that, letting aside the widest margin due to exaggeration, there was still enough to attest to the reality of the events which took place outside of all known laws.

Much was said and in multiple ways about Mr. Home, and we confess that he was far from captivating the sympathy of everybody, in some due to the spirit of system, in others to ignorance. For the last ones we want even to admit a conscientious opinion, if they could not verify the facts by themselves: but if in such a case there is space for doubt, a systematic and passionate hostility is always out of place. In every causal relationship, judgment without knowledge is lack of logic and slander without proof is the same as to forget good manners.

Let us forget for a moment the intervention of spirits and do not see in the reported facts anything beyond physical phenomena. The stranger they seem the more attention they deserve. They may explain the phenomena as they will, but not with a preconceived idea, if they do not want such a judgment to be put in doubt. What seems astonishing, and even more abnormal than the phenomena in question, is to see those same people who incessantly rant against the opposition of certain scientific groups to the new ideas; that continually throw on their faces - and this with a less restrained language - the troubles experienced by the authors of the most important discoveries; who mention Fulton, Galileo and Jenner all the time, slipping themselves into similar error, which they say, and rightly so, that not long ago anyone who had talked about communication from one extreme to the other of our planet, in a few seconds, would have been considered foolish. If they do believe in progress to which they claim to be apostles, they should then be consistent with themselves, not enticing the reproach they throw onto others, by denying what they do not understand.

But let us go back to Mr. Home. Coming to Paris in October 1855, he was thrown, on his arrival, into the world of high society, a circumstance that should have imposed more discretion in the judgment made of him, as the higher and more educated that world is, the lesser suspicious it is of graciously falling in the hands of an adventurer, as a toy.

That same position has prompted comments. Who is Mr. Home, they ask! To live in this society and make expensive trips, they say, one needs fortune. If that is not the case then powerful people must support him. A thousand hypotheses were raised with that regard, each more ridiculous than the other. What was not said about his sister who he brought with him about a year ago! It was said that she was a medium even more powerful than him, that the two should perform wonders that would blanch those of Moses. Questions were addressed to us, more than once, with that respect. Here is our answer.

Coming to France, Mr. Home was not directed to the public. He does not like or seek publicity. Had he come with the purpose of speculation, he would have traveled the country making propaganda; he would have sought every opportunity for manifestation; however, he avoids them; he would have established a price for the events, but he asks nothing of anybody. Despite his reputation Mr. Home is not what one might call a public man. His private life belongs only to him. Since he asks for nothing, no one has the right to question how he makes his living, without committing an indiscretion. Is he maintained by powerful people? This is not of our concern. All we can say is that in this elitist society he has conquered sympathy and made devoted friends, whereas with a playful conjuror, we pay, have fun and that is all that is.

In Mr. Home, we see only a man with an outstanding faculty. The study of that ability is all that we are interested in and all that should interest those who are not only driven by curiosity. History has not yet opened the book of his secrets. Until then he belongs to science.

As for his sister, here is the truth. She is an eleven-year-old girl, brought to Paris for her education, assigned to an illustrious figure. She hardly knows about her brother's faculty. Hence that is all too simplistic and prosaic to the lovers of wonders.

Now, why would Mr. Home have come to France? It was not to seek fortune, as we just demonstrated. Would that be to get to know the country? But he does not travel; he rarely goes out and has absolutely no touristic habits. The actual reason being his doctors' advice, who considers the climate in Europe necessary for his health, but the natural facts are sometimes providential. We therefore think that if he has come it is because he should have done so.

France, still in doubt about the spiritual manifestations, needed a big blow; it was Mr. Home who had that mission; the bigger the blow, the greater its impact. The position, credit, the lights of those who welcomed him and were convinced by the evidence of the facts, shook the convictions of many people, even among those who were not eyewitnesses.

The presence of Mr. Home was thus a powerful aid in the propagation of the spiritist ideas. If it did not convince everyone, it threw the seeds that will be more fruitful as the number of mediums multiplies. That faculty, as we have said elsewhere, is not an exclusive privilege; it exists in a latent state and in various degrees in a lot of people, just waiting for the opportunity to develop. The principle lies within us, effect of our own organization. It is part of nature thus it is present in a germinal state in all of us. It is not far the day when we shall see mediums emerging from all sides, in our environment, our families, among the poor as well as the rich, so that truth may be known by all, because, as it has been announced, it is a new era, a new phase that begins for humanity. The evidence and the popularization of the spiritist phenomena will provide a new path to the moral ideas as steam has done to the industries.

If the private life of Mr. Home should be closed to the investigations of an indiscreet curiosity, there are certain details which, rightfully so, may be of interest to the public and the assessment of the facts, so that its knowledge may be even useful.

Mr. Daniel Dunglas Home was born on March 15th, 1833, near Edinburgh. He is now therefore 24 years old. He descends from the ancient and noble Scottish family of Dunglas, formerly sovereign. He is a blond young man of medium height, whose melancholic looks has nothing of eccentric; he has a very delicate body structure, showing kind and simple habits, amiable and benevolent character, from which his contact with wealth did not produce arrogance or ostentation. Gifted with excessive modesty, never shows off his wonderful faculty, never speaks of himself and, even if in an intimate expansion he tells personal stories, he does that with simplicity and never with the emphasis typical of the creatures with whom the malevolence seeks to compare him. Many intimate facts of our personal knowledge prove his noble feelings as well as the elevation of his soul. We attest with such more pleasure the more it is known about the influence of the moral dispositions over the nature of the manifestations.

Zealous friends with an exaggerated enthusiasm, conveniently used by malevolence, have sometimes told of the phenomena to which Mr. Home is an involuntary instrument. Being as they are, these do not require further amplification, which bring more harm than help to the cause. As our purpose is the serious study of everything related to the Spiritist Science, we will strictly attain to the reality of the facts attested by ourselves or by trustworthy eyewitnesses. We can therefore comment on them, knowing that we are not speculating about fantastic things.

Mr. Home is a kind of medium that produces ostensive manifestations, not excluding the intelligent communications, but his natural predispositions give him a special aptitude to the first ones. Under his influence the strangest sounds can be heard, the air agitates; solid bodies move, stand up, displace from one side to another in the air; musical instruments produce melodious sounds; beings from the extracorporeal world materialize, speak, write and sometimes embrace us, to the point of pain. Several times, in the presence of witnesses, he found himself lifted in the air, without support, several meters high.

From what we have been taught about the class of spirits who usually produce such manifestations, one should not conclude that Mr. Home has only been in contact with the lowest class of the spiritual world. His character and distinguished moral qualities, on the contrary, should attract the sympathies of superior spirits. For the inferior spirits, he is merely an instrument to energetically open the eyes of the blind, without subtracting him from communications of a higher order. It is a mission that he has accepted, mission not exempt of trials nor dangers, but which he performs with resignation and patience, under the aegis of the spirit of his mother, his genuine guardian angel.

The causes of Mr. Home's manifestations are innate to him, his soul seems to hold to the body only by weak bonds; he has more affinity with the spiritual world than with the corporeal world. This is why he unties them so effortlessly, and more easily than others enters into communication with the invisible beings.

His faculty was revealed at an early age. He was six month old when his cradle rocked alone, in the absence of the nanny, and changed its place. In his early years he was still so fragile that he could barely stand; sitting on the carpet, his toys would come to him when he could not reach them. At the age of three he had his first visions whose memory he has not retained. He was nine years old when the family moved to the United States; there the phenomena proceeded with increasing intensity as the years passed, but his reputation as a medium was only established in 1855, at a time when the spiritist manifestations began to popularize in that country. In 1854 he came to Italy, as we said, for health reasons. He amazed Florence and Rome with his prodigies.

Converted to Catholicism in the latter city, he pledged to break relations with the world of spirits. Indeed, for a whole year he seemed to have been abandoned by his occult power, but as such power is beyond his will, at the end of that time, as announced by the spirit of his mother, the manifestations resurfaced with renewed strength. His mission was assigned; he should stand out among those who the Providence had chosen to reveal, though patent signs, the power that overshadows all human greatness. If Mr. Home were, as intended by those who judge without seeing, only a skilled conjurer, he would always have, no doubt, hidden tricks in his bag. However, he cannot produce them at will. It would be impossible to promote regular sessions since many times, just when he had necessity of his faculty that could fail him. Sometimes the phenomena manifest spontaneously, when they are least expected, while on other occasions they cannot be provoked, which is an unfavorable circumstance for those wanting to make scheduled exhibitions.

We have proof of the following fact, taken from hundreds of others. It was over fifteen days that Mr. Home was not having any manifestation when, having lunch at a friend's house with two or three acquaintances, they suddenly heard knocks on the walls, furniture and ceiling. It seems that they are back, he said. At this time Mr. Home was sitting on a sofa with a friend. A servant brought a tray of tea, getting ready to place it on the table in the middle of the room. Although heavy, the table suddenly rose from the floor, lifting to about 20 to 30 cm in the air, as if attracted by the tray. Terrified, the servant dropped the tray down. In one leap, the table moved towards the sofa, coming to a rest in front of Mr. Home and his friend, not disarranging anything that was on its top. Unquestionably, this fact is not the most curious of so many we have heard, but it has this peculiarity which is worth mentioning: it was spontaneously produced, without provocation, in an inner circle, where none of the assistants, having witnessed identical facts one hundred times, needed new evidences. It was certainly not the case for Mr. Home to show his skills, if skills do exist.

In a next article we will describe other events.

Spiritist Manifestations,

by Paul Auguez[12]

Answer to Mr. Viennet, by Paul Auguez

Mr. Paul Auguez is a sincere and informed follower of the Spiritist Doctrine. In his work, which we read with great interest, it is possible to recognize the elegant style of the author of "*Elus de l'avenir*". It is a wise and logical demonstration of the doctrine's fundamentals, which are the existence of spirits, their relationships with human beings, the immortality of the soul and its individuality after death. The article's main purpose is to respond to the sarcastic aggressions from Mr. Viennet. He only covers the main points, with limited fatual evidence, using reasoning and respectable authorities, that this belief is not founded on systematic ideas or vulgar prejudices. On the contrary, it rests on solid foundations.

Mr. Viennet's weapon is ridicule; Mr. Auguez' is science. By numerous citations that demonstrate a serious study and profound knowledge, he proves that if today's supporters, despite their ever-increasing number, and the enlightened people from all countries who join them, are physically unbalanced individuals, as claimed by the distinguished scholar, such disease is shared by them with most of the geniuses who honor humanity.

---

12   Brochure in-12, 2.50 francs. Dentu, Palais-Royal and Germer Baillière, Rua de l'École de Médicine, 4

In his rebuttals, Mr. Auguez always kept the dignity of language, whose merit will never be praised enough. In his rebuttal, those rude diatribes cannot be found anywhere, those arguments which became a common place of bad taste, proving nothing but a lack of urbanity. Everything that he says is grave, serious, and deep, even up to the wise person he addresses. Has he managed to convince him? We do not know; we frankly doubt it. But as his book is definitely written to all, the seeds it spreads will not be lost. More than once we shall have the occasion to quote passages from his book, in the course of this publication, whenever we are dragged by the nature of the subject. The theory developed by Mr. Auguez, except perhaps in some secondary points, is the same as we profess. Thus, we will not criticize his remarkable work, which will be read with benefit. We would wish for one thing only: a little bit more clarity in the demonstrations and method for sorting the matters. Mr. Auguez dealt with the subject scientifically; because he was addressing a wise person that can certainly understand more abstract things, but he should have known that he wrote less to an individual than to an audience that always reads with more pleasure and more benefit what they can understand without much effort.

ALLAN KARDEC

March 1858

To the Readers

of the Spiritist Review

Many of our readers wanted to respond to the appeal we made in our first monthly issue regarding the information to be sent to us. A large collection of facts has been acknowledged, among which some of great importance, for which we are eternally grateful. We are no less grateful to the reflections that sometimes follow them, even when they reveal an incomplete understanding of the subject. These will allow clarifications about points that may not have been well understood. If we do not immediately acknowledge receiving the documents sent to us it does not mean that have gone unnoticed. We always take good care of them so that sooner or later they will be used.

Lack of space is not the only cause that may delay publication, but also the opportunity of the circumstances and the need to connect them to the articles so that they may serve as useful complements.

The multiplicity of our tasks, added to an extensive correspondence, leave us sometimes physically incapable of responding, as we would wish to do so and as it is our duty to do, to all of those who honor us with their letters. We thus beg you to please do not misinterpret our silence, independently of our wishes. We do hope that your motivation does not weaken and your correspondence continues. As such, we once again call your attention to the footnote at the end of the introduction of our first monthly issue, regarding the information we kindly ask you to provide, requesting that you do not forget to let us know when we can mention people and places without causing any issues.

The observations above are also equally applicable to the questions that are addressed to us, about the several points of the doctrine. When they need more extensive development it is even less possible to answer in writing since, many times, the same thing must be responded to many people. As our Review is destined to serve as a medium of correspondence, those responses will have a natural place here, whenever the discussed matters give us that opportunity. This will be a benefit and advantage to all as we will be able to provide a more complete answer.

The Plurality of Worlds

Who has not yet wondered, on considering the moon and other celestial bodies, if those globes are inhabited? Doubt was possible before science had initiated us into the nature of those globes; with the current state of our knowledge, at least there is the likelihood, but some objections to this really seductive idea are drawn from science itself. It is said that the moon, as it seems, has no atmosphere, and possibly no water. In Mercury the average temperature should be that of the melting lead, in view of its proximity to the Sun, so that if there is any lead there it should run like the water in our rivers. In Saturn the opposite happens; we lack a term of comparison for the cold that must exist there; sunlight must be very weak, despite the reflection of its seven moons and its rings; as for that distance, the Sun may only appear as a star of first magnitude. Under such circumstances, the question is whether life is then possible.

It is incomprehensible that serious people can make such an objection. If the atmosphere of the Moon was not perceived, is it reasonable to infer that it does not exist? Couldn't it be that it is comprised of unknown elements or of such a low density that do not produce appreciable refraction? We say the same about the water and liquid that may exist there.

As with respect to living beings, wouldn't that be a denial of the Divine power to judge impossible an organization different from what we know, when before our eyes the Providence of nature extends with such an admirable solicitude up to the smallest insect and provides all

103

beings with the appropriate organs for the ambient where they live, be it in water, air or land, or submerged in darkness or exposed to sunlight? Had we never seen a fish, we could not have conceived beings living in water; we would have no idea of their structure. Until recently, who would have believed that an animal could live indefinitely inside a stone? But, not mentioning these extremes, could the beings that live under the fire of our torrid zone exist in the polar caps? Yet, in the ice zones there are beings organized to live in such a condition that could not withstand the scorching heat of a vertical sun.

Why then can one not admit that certain beings can be built in order to live in other globes and in a medium completely different from ours? Certainly, without a deep knowledge of the physical constitution of the Moon, we know enough to ensure that we could not live there, given the way we are made, as we cannot live in the company of the fish, in the middle of the ocean. For the same reason, the inhabitants of the Moon, if they could one day come to Earth, once they have been organized to live without air or with a very singular air, perhaps completely different from ours, they would be asphyxiated in our thick atmosphere, like us in the water.

Again, if we have no visual and material proof of the presence of beings that live in other worlds, nothing demonstrates that life forms appropriate to any other medium or atmosphere may not exist. On the contrary, the simple common sense tells us that this is how it should be, since the belief that these immeasurable globes that circulate in space are simple unproductive and inert masses is just unacceptable to reason. The observation shows irregular surfaces, like on Earth, as there are mountains, valleys, and cliffs, extinct and active volcanoes. Why then there would not be organic beings? Be it, they will say; there may be plants and even animals; humans, however, civilized people like us, knowing God, cultivating the arts, sciences, is that possible?

It is certain that nothing mathematically proves that the beings that inhabit other worlds are human beings like us, or which are more or less advanced than us, from a moral point of view. But when the savages of

America saw the arriving Spaniards, they had no doubt that there was another world overseas, cultivating arts unknown to them. Earth is spotted by a countless quantity of islands, large and small, and everything that is inhabitable is inhabited. Whenever a rock surfaces from the sea, there we have people, sticking their flags. What would we say if the inhabitants of one of the smallest of these islands, perfectly knowing the existence of other islands and continents, but never having had relationship with those who inhabit them, considered themselves the only living beings on the planet? We would tell them: How can you believe that God made the world only for you? By which strange singularity your little island, lost in the solitude of the ocean, would have the privilege of being the only inhabited one? The same can be said about the other spheres. Why Earth, small globe, imperceptible in the vastness of the universe, which is indistinguishable from other planets by its position, by its volume, by its structure, which is neither the largest nor the smallest, which is not in the center nor in the extreme, why, I was saying, among many others, Earth would be the only residence of rational and thinking beings? Which person of wisdom would think that these millions of stars that shine over our heads were made to entertain our eyes? What would then be the usefulness of those other millions of globes, invisible to the naked eye and which do not even serve to illuminate us? Would it not be pride and wickedness to think so? We say that it is not logical to those to whom impiety does not matter at all. We have then arrived to the conclusion of the plurality of the worlds, by a simple reasoning, the same employed by many others before us. Such reasoning is confirmed by the revelation of the spirits. Indeed they teach us that all these worlds are inhabited by corporeal beings, appropriate to the physical constitution of each globe; that among the inhabitants of those globes, some are more, others less advanced than us, from an intellectual, moral and even physical point of view. Even more: we now know that it is possible to enter into communication with them and obtain information regarding their current state; we also know that not only all the globes are inhabited by corporeal beings, but that the space is populated by intelligent beings, invisible to us because of the material veil cast over our soul, and that they reveal their existence by hidden or patent means.

So everything in the universe is populated. Life and intelligence are everywhere: in solid globes, in the air, in the depths of Earth, and even in the ethereal. Is there anything in such a doctrine that is repulsive to reason? Isn't that, at the same time, great and sublime? It lifts us from our own inferiority, much to the contrary of this selfish and greedy thinking which places us as the only beings worthy of occupying God's mind.

Jupiter And a Few
Other Worlds

Before going into details about the revelations made to us by the spirits, with respect to the state of different worlds, let us see the logical consequence that we can reach by ourselves and simple reasoning. Let us refer to the spirits' scale we gave in the previous issue. Those willing to seriously dive into this new science, we recommend a careful in depth study of that scale, as it contain the key to many mysteries.

The spiritual world is composed of souls of all humans on this Earth and other spheres, released from the corporeal connections; by the same way, all humans are animated by incarnated spirits. There is therefore solidarity between these two worlds: human beings will have the same qualities and imperfections of the spirits to whom they are united; the spirits will be more or less good or bad, depending on the progress they have made during their corporeal existence. These few words summarize the whole Spiritist Doctrine. As the acts of human beings are the product of their free will, they retain the stamp of perfection or imperfection of the spirit that animate them. It will be, therefore, easy for us to have an idea about the moral state of any given world, according to the nature of its inhabiting spirits; somehow we can describe its legislation, draw a picture of their customs, habits, and social relationships.

Let us then suppose a world solely inhabited by spirits of the ninth class, impure spirits, and let us travel there in our thoughts. We will see all passions unleashed and unrestrained; the moral state in its lowest degree of savageness; animal life in all its brutality; lack of social ties, as each person lives and acts only for themselves and to the satisfaction of their gross appetites; egotism reigns there as supreme and absolute, dragging in its wake hatred, envy, jealousy, envy and murder.

We turn now to another sphere where there are spirits of all classes of the third order: impure spirits, frivolous, pseudo-wise, neutral. We know that evil prevails in all classes of that order, but without having the idea of good, the idea of evil diminishes as they move away from the last class. Selfishness is always the leading cause of action, but customs are softer, intelligence more developed, evil presents itself somewhat disguised, dressed up, masked.

These same qualities engineer another defect □ pride, as the higher classes are sufficiently educated to be aware of their superiority but not enough to understand what they lack. Hence their tendency to enslave inferior or weaker races, maintained under their control. As they do not have the feeling of good, having only the instinct of the self, they put their intelligence at the service of satisfying their own passions. In such a society the impure element, if dominating, crushes the other; otherwise the least evil one will try to destroy their enemies; in any case there will be struggle, bloody fight of extermination, because these are two elements that have opposing interests. To protect property and people there will be the need for laws, but these will be dictated by personal interests and not by justice; they shall be made by the strong to the disadvantage of the weak.

Suppose now a world where, between the bad elements we have just seen, there is some of the second order. In this order, in the midst of evil, we shall see some emerging virtues. If the good ones are a minority, they will fall victims of the evil ones; however, as their dominance progressively prevails, legislation becomes more human, more equitable and Christian charity is no longer a dead letter for everyone. Out of this goodness another vice will rise. Despite the war that the bad ones incessantly declare to the good ones, they cannot help it but to intimately admire them. Observing the rise of virtue over vice and not having the strength or will to do so, they try to parody and hide it. Hence the large number of hypocrites in every society where civilization is still imperfect.

Let us continue our journey through the worlds to the one that will give us some rest from the sad spectacle we have just watched. It is only inhabited by spirits of the second order. What a difference! The degree of purification achieved among them excludes any immoral thought and this is enough to give us an idea of its moral state. The legislation is very simple, as human beings do not need to defend themselves against each other; nobody wants to harm their neighbor; no one takes what does not belong to them; no one seeks to live at the expense of their fellow citizens. Everything breathes benevolence and love; human beings do not seek to mutually harm each other; there is absolutely no hatred; selfishness is unknown and hypocrisy would have no objective. Absolute equality does not reign there, as it would presume a perfect identity of intellectual and moral development. Well we see from the spirits' scale that the second order comprises several degrees of development, thus there will be inequalities in this world, as some are more advanced than others, but as there is only good thoughts among them all, the most advanced will never conceive anything out of pride or the others out of envy. The inferior understands the ascendancy of the superior and submits to that since such an ascendency is purely moral and nobody uses that to oppress others.

The consequences we extracted from this picture, although presented in a hypothetical way, are not any less rational. Everyone can infer the social state of a world by the proportion of the moral elements that we suppose constitutes it.

We have seen, through the above abstraction made of the revelation of the spirits, the odds are in favor in the explanation of the plurality of worlds. Well, it is no less rational to think that not all of them are in the same degree of perfection and, therefore, our assumptions may well be the expression of reality.

In a positive way, we only know our own world. Which position does it occupy in this hierarchy? Behold! Just consider what takes place in this world to conclude that it is far from deserving the first class and we are convinced that by reading these lines you have already spotted its position. When the spirits say that, "if it is not the last; it is one of the last," unfortunately, simple common sense says that they are not mistaken. We have much to do to elevate it to the category we last described, and we needed that Christ had come to show us the path.

With respect to the reference we can give as to our reasoning about the several globes of our planetary maelstrom, all we have is the teaching of the spirits. Now, for those who will only admit this existence from its tangible evidence, the fact is that, with that respect to their assertion, we do not have the stamp of direct experimentation. However, don't we everyday accept with confidence other travelers' descriptions of regions we have never seen? If we are only to believe in what we see, we will believe in a few things only. What in this case gives some value to what the spirits say is the agreement among them, at least on the capital points. For us who have witnessed such communications hundreds of times; who appreciated them in their minimum details; who probed their weak and strong points, who observed the similarities and contradictions, we find in them all the characters of the likelihood. However, we offer them as nothing more than information and teachings, to which everyone is free to attribute the importance that best suits their opinion.

According to the spirits, Mars would be even less advanced than Earth. Spirits incarnated there seem to belong almost exclusively to the ninth class, of the impure spirits, so that the first picture given above would be a description of that world. Several other smaller globes are, with some nuances, in the same category. Earth would come next. The majority of its inhabitants belong undeniably to all classes of the third order and a reduced proportion to the last classes of the second order. The superior spirits, from the second and third classes, here sometimes execute missions of civilization and progress, but these are exceptions. Mercury and Saturn come after Earth. The numerical superiority of the good spirits gives them predominance over the inferior spirits, resulting in a more perfect social order, less selfish relationships and therefore happier living conditions. The Moon and

Venus are more or less at the same level, and in all aspects, more advanced than Mercury and Saturn. Uranus and Neptune would be even above the latter ones. It is supposed that the moral elements of these two planets are formed by the first class of the third order and the great majority by spirits of the second order. Human beings are infinitely happier there than on Earth, since they do not have to sustain the same struggles nor suffer the same tribulations, as they are not exposed to the same physical and moral vicissitudes either.

Of all planets, the most advanced by all means is Jupiter. It is the exclusive realm of goodness and justice, since it only has good spirits. One can have an idea of the happy state of its inhabitants by the description we gave of a world inhabited by spirits of the second order.

The superiority of Jupiter is not only in the moral state of its inhabitants; it is also in its physical structure. Here is the description we were given about this privileged world, where the majority of the good individuals who have honored our Earth with their virtue and talent live.

The conformation of the body is more or less the same as those of Earth's inhabitants, but it is less material, less dense and with a very low specific weight. While we painfully crawl on Earth, the inhabitants of Jupiter transport themselves from one place to another by sliding on the surface of the soil, almost tirelessly, like the bird in the air or the fish in the water. As the matter that forms the body is more refined, it dissipates after death, without being subjected to putrid decomposition. Most of the diseases that afflict us are unknown there, especially those originating from the excesses of all kinds and the debauchery of passions. Subsistence is in concert with that ethereal organization; it would not be sufficient enough for our coarse stomachs, and ours would be too heavy for them. It consists of fruits and plants which, in fact, they somehow harvest, for the most part, from the environment, whose nutritious emanations they inhale. Life span is proportionally much longer than that on earth. The average is equivalent to about five of our centuries. The development is also very fast and childhood lasts only a few of our months.

Under this light covering, the spirits easily unleash and communicate with each other only through their thoughts, which do not exclude the articulated language. Second sight (remote viewing) is a permanent faculty to them. Their normal state can be compared to our lucid somnambulists. That is why they manifest to us more easily than those incarnated in grosser and more material worlds. The intuition they have of their future; the security given by a conscience exempt of remorse, are the reasons why death does not cause them any concern. They see its arrival without fear and as a simple transformation.

The animals are not excluded from this progressive state, although not similar to that of human being, even relatively to the physical. Their body, more materialized, is attached to the ground, like ours on Earth. Their intelligence is more developed than that of our animals. The structure of their limbs adapts to all requirements of the work. They are responsible for the execution of manual jobs. They are the servants and foremen. Human beings' occupations are purely intellectual. For them the human being is a god, but a protective deity, who never abuses his or her power to oppress them.

The spirits, who inhabit Jupiter, when they want to communicate with us, are usually delighted to describe their planet. When asked why, they reply that they do it in order to inspire the love of good in us, with the hope that we will get there one day. It was with that purpose that one of them, who lived on earth with the name of Bernard Palissy, the famous potter of the XVI century, spontaneously tried, without any request, a series of drawings, remarkable for its originality as for the talent of execution, intended to let us know, in their smallest details, this world so strange and so new to us. Some of them portray characters, animals, scenes of the private life; the most admirable, however, are those that represent houses, true masterpieces that nothing on Earth could give us an idea as they do not resemble anything we know.

It is an indescribable kind of architecture, so original and yet so harmonious, ornamentation so rich and so graceful, that it challenges the most fertile imagination. Victorien Sardou, a young scholar of our circle of friends, full of talent and future, but with no drawing skills, served him as an intermediary. Palissy promised us a series which somehow will be an illustrated essay about this wonderful world. We hope that this original and interesting collection which we will talk about in a special article devoted to drawing mediums, can one day be delivered to the public.

Planet Jupiter, despite the inviting picture given to us, is not, however, the most perfect of the worlds. There are others, unknown to us, which are far superior, both physically and morally, and whose inhabitants enjoy even more perfect happiness: they are the resting place of the superior spirits, whose ethereal covering has nothing else of the known properties of matter.

We have been asked, many times, if we think that human's condition here would be an absolute obstacle for him to pass, without an intermediary, from Earth to Jupiter. To all questions regarding the Spiritist Doctrine we have never answered with our own ideas, against which we are always on guard. We simply pass the teachings given to us, which we do not accept lightheartedly and with a thoughtless enthusiasm. We clearly answer the above question as this is the formal sense of our instructions and the result of our own observations: YES, on leaving Earth, human beings can immediately go to Jupiter, or an analogous world, because it is not unique in its category. There can be certainty about this? NO. However, he can go, as there are on Earth, though in a very small number, very good spirits and quite dematerialized not to feel awkward in a world where wickedness has no access. However, he cannot be sure about this, as he can be deceived regarding his personal merit and, moreover, may have another mission to accomplish elsewhere. Those who can expect this favor are certainly neither the selfish nor the ambitious, nor the greedy, nor the ungrateful, nor the envious, nor the proud, nor the futile, nor the hypocrites, nor the sensual, nor any of those dominated by their attachment to Earthly things.

To those, long and tough trials may still be necessary. That depends on their will.

Confessions of

Louis XI

Story of his life, dictated by himself to Ms. Ermance Dufaux

When talking about the story of Joan of Arc, dictated by her, proposing to cite several passages, we said that Ms. Dufaux had also written the story of Louis XI. This work, one of the most precious of its kind, contains valuable documents from a historical point of view. In that work, Louis XI shows himself as the profound politician that we know. Besides, he gives us the key to several so far inexplicable facts. From the spiritist point of view, it is one of the most curious presentations of lengthy works produced by the spirits. Two things are remarkable with that regard: the speed of execution, as it took only fifteen days to dictate the subject of a thick volume, and the precise memory that a spirit may keep of his Earthly life. To those who doubted the origin of this work, and wanted to attribute it to the memory of Ms. Dufaux, we would say that it would be necessary that a fourteen year old child had a phenomenal memory, and a not less extraordinary precocity in order to be able to write, in a surge, the work of such a nature. However, admitting that it was so, we ask where such a child would have obtained the new explanations about the somber politics of Louis XI, and if it would not be more interesting that her parents had attributed the merit to her. From all stories written through her, Joan of Arc was the only one published. We hope the others will follow soon, and we anticipate a greater success, the more spread out the spiritist ideas are today.

We extracted, from the story of Louis XI, a passage about the death of Count Charolais.

Facing the historical fact that Louis XI had given the general government of Normandy to the Count of Charolais; historians confess that they cannot understand a King, who was such a great politician, making such a mistake.[13]

The explanations given by Louis XI are difficult to contest, since confirmed by three facts known to all: the conspiracy of Constain; Count Charolais' trip following the execution of the culprit and, finally, the assignment of the general government of the Normandy to this prince, province which united the states of the Dukes of Burgundy and Brittany, enemies always allied against Louis XI.

Louis XI thus writes:

"The Count of Charolais was awarded with the general government of Normandy and a pension of thirty six thousand pounds. It was a great imprudence to increase the power of the Burgundy house in such a way. Although this explanation keeps us away from the link of England's businesses, I think it is my duty to explain here the motives which lead me to so proceed."

"Soon after his return from the Netherlands, the Duke of Burgundy had fallen seriously ill. The Count of Charolais did love his father, despite the displeasures imposed on him. It is certain that his impulsive and impetuous character and, above all, my perfidious insinuations, could excuse him. He treated him with perfect filial love, day and night, not moving away from his bed."

"The old Duke crisis made me reflect seriously. I hated the Count and thought I had everything to fear from him. Nevertheless, he had only one daughter at a young age, circumstance which after the Duke's death, who did not give indications that would live long, had originated a minority which the Flemish, always turbulent, had made extremely stormy. I

---

13   History of France, by Velly and followers

could have then easily taken over, if not all the properties of the Burgundy house, at least part of it, by masking this usurpation with an alliance or by leaving everything that power would yield as hateful. There were more than necessary reasons to poison the Count of Charolais. Besides, the idea of a crime would no longer scare me."

"I managed to seduce the prince's sommelier, Jean Constain. Italy was a kind of poisoner's laboratory: it was there that Constain sent Jean d'Ivy, who he had corrupted by a considerable amount of money to be paid on his return. D'Ivy wanted to know the target of the poison. The sommelier committed the imprudence of revealing that it was Count Charolais."

"After accomplishing his task, d'Ivy showed up to receive the agreed amount but, instead of paying, Constain covered him with indignity. Furious with the reception, d'Ivy swore vengeance. He went to Count Charolais and told him everything he knew. Constain was arrested and taken to Rippemonde Castle. Afraid of torture, he confessed to everything but my complicity, hoping perhaps that I would intercede in his favor. He was already at the top of the tower, place destined to the execution, and everything was prepared to behead him when he manifested his desire to speak to the Count. He then told the Count about the role I played in the attempt murder."

"Despite his amazement and rage he did not speak. As a result, those present could only make vague conjectures based on the surprising events created by the reports. Yet, despite the importance of such a revelation, Constain was decapitated and his properties confiscated but delivered to the Duke of Burgundy's family. His informer had the same fate, partially due to an answer given to the prince of Burgundy. The latter asked if the promised amount had been paid if he would have denounced the plot. With an unconceivable recklessness he said no."

"When the Count came to Tours he requested a private audience. He showed all his fury and covered me with condemnation. I calmed him down giving him the general government of Normandy and the pension of thirty six thousand pounds. The general government was a decorative title and from the pension he received only the first part.

Fatality and Premonition

Instructions given by St. Louis

One of our corresponding members wrote the following:

"Last September a fast boat, crossing from Dunkirk to Ostend, was caught by surprise by a nightly storm. The boat capsized having four of the eight crew members perished. The remaining four, in which group I was, were able to hold onto the keel. We spent the whole night in such a horrible position, without any other perspective but death, which seemed inevitable to us who could feel it in all its anguish. At dawn the wind blew us to the coast hence we were able to swim our way to the land."

"Why, in such a dangerous situation, applicable to all, only four have succumbed? Notice that in my case it is the sixth or seventh time which I escape from such an imminent danger and more or less in the same conditions. I am really led to believe that an invisible hand protects me. What have I done to deserve it? I do not know much; I am a worthless and useless creature in this world and I do not brag about having more value than others; on the contrary: among the victims of the disaster there was a dignified cleric, model of evangelical virtue, and a venerable nun from the congregation of St. Vincent de Paul, who was about to accomplish a sanctified mission of Christian charity. It seems that fatality has a very important role in my destiny. Wouldn't the spirits be there for something? Would that be possible to obtain an explanation from them with that respect enquiring, for example, if they are the ones who provoke or avoid the dangers which threaten us?"

According to the wishes of our correspondent, we addressed the following questions to the spirit of St. Louis who, out of good will, always communicates when there is a useful instruction to be provided:

1. When there is an imminent danger threatening someone, is it a spirit who guides the danger and, when avoided, is it another spirit who deviates them?
    -   On incarnating, the spirit chooses a trial; once chosen, a kind of destiny is created which cannot be conjured, once the spirit is submitted to that. I speak about the physical trials. The spirit, keeping his free will regarding good and bad, is always free to withstand or reject the trial. When seeing someone abating, a good spirit may come to help but cannot influence so as to dominate their will. A malevolent spirit, that is inferior, showing and exaggerating about the physical dangers, may shock and scare but yet the will of the incarnated spirit is not less free of any hurdle.
2. When a person is faced by an imminent accident it seems to me that the free will is worth nothing. I then ask if it is an evil spirit who provokes such an accident, to which he is some sort of cause and, in case the danger is avoided, if a good spirit came to help him.
    -   Good or bad spirits may not suggest anything other than good or bad thoughts, according to their nature. The accident is marked on the individual's destiny. When your life is endangered it is a sign that you desired that, so that you can deviate from bad and become better. When you escape from danger, still under its influence, you think more or less strongly, pending on the more or less strong action of the good spirits, about becoming a better person. Under the influence of bad

spirits (I say bad referring to the wickedness which still exists in them) you equally think that you will escape other dangers and again you will give in to the unstoppable passions.

3. Fatality, which seems to preside over the material destinies of our life, would then be an effect of our free will?

    -   You yourself have chosen your trial; the tougher it is and the better you support it, the more you elevate. Those who spend life in abundance and human happiness are the weak spirits, who remain stationary. Thus, the unfortunate by far outnumbers the happy ones in this world; hence the spirit generally chooses the trial which produces more fruits. They see very well the futility of your greatness and your pleasures. Besides, even the happiest life is always agitated, always perturbed even if it is not by pain.

4. We fully understand this doctrine, but this does not explain whether certain spirits have a direct action over the material cause of the accident. Suppose that at the time a man goes through a bridge, the bridge collapses. Who led the man to go through that bridge?

    -   When a man goes through a bridge that must fall it is not a spirit that impels. It is the instinct of his destiny that leads him to that.

5. Who makes the bridge collapse?

    -   The natural circumstances. The matter has in itself the causes of destruction. In this case, if the spirit has to resort to an element foreign to his nature to move the material forces, he will preferably appeal to the spiritual intuition. Thus, should that bridge collapse having the water disarranged the stones which compose it or the rust eroded the chains that support it, the spirit will, say, suggest that the man passes through this bridge instead of breaking one or another at the time he passes through it. In fact, you have physical evidence of what I say: whatever the accident, it always occurs naturally, that is the causes are linked to each other and callously produce them.

6.   Let us take another case in which the destruction of matter is not the cause of the accident. A badly intentioned man shoots at me; the bullet hardly scratches me. Was it deviated by a good spirit?
     -   No.

7.   Can the spirits directly warn us about a danger? Here is a fact that seems to confirm it: A lady leaves her house and goes down the avenue. An inner voice tells her: go home. She hesitates. The same voice is heard several times. She then goes back but, on re-covering, she says: But... what am I doing at home? I will go out. This is just the effect of my imagination. Then she goes back her way. A few steps ahead a column, which was being removed from a house, hits her on the head and she falls, unconscious. Which voice was that? Was it not a premonition of what was about to happen to her?
     -   It was the instinct. No presentiment has these characteristics: they are always vague.

8.   What do you understand by the voice of instinct?
     -   I understand that before incarnating, the spirit has knowl-edge of all phases of its existence. When these phases have an essential character, the spirit retains a sort of impression in their intimate self and such impression, awakening when the moment comes, turns into premonition.

NOTE: The explanations above refer to the fatality of material events. The moral fatality is comprehensively treated in The Spirits' Book.

Utility of Certain

Private Evocations

The communications obtained from highly elevated spirits or who animated the great characters of the antiquity is precious for its highly educational content. These spirits have acquired a degree of perfection that allows them to cover a more extensive sphere of ideas; to penetrate mysteries beyond the reach of common humanity and therefore, better than others, initiate us on certain things. It does not follow that communications from spirits of lower orders are useless. Far from it: the observer collects many teachings from them. To learn about the customs of a people we must study it in all degrees of the scale.

Those who only had seen one face would hardly know it. The story of a people is not the story of their kings and social luminaries. To judge the people it is necessary to see them in their private life, in their particular habits. However, the superior spirits are the celebrities of the spiritual world. Their own elevation puts them at such a height above us that we are amazed by the distance that separates us. Spirits more bourgeois – kindly allow us to use the expression – describe the condition in their new existence in a more tangible way. In them, the connection between bodily life and the spirit's life is more intimate; we understand it better, because it touches us more closely. Learning from them about what they became, what they think, what people of all conditions and all characters experience, both good people and the vicious ones, great and small, the happy as the unhappy ones of the century, in a word, people who lived among us, who we have seen and known, whose real life is known to us, as their virtues and caprices, understanding their joys and their sufferings; we associate with them and harvest a moral teaching which is so more useful the more intimate are the relationships between them and us.

We put ourselves in place of the one who was like us more easily than in place of those who we only see through the mirage of a heavenly glory. Vulgar spirits show us the practical application of the great and sublime truths, whose theory the superior spirits teach us. Moreover, there is nothing useless in the study of a science. Newton found the law of the forces of the universe in an extremely simple phenomenon.

Such communications have another advantage: to verify the identity of the spirits in a more precise manner. When a spirit tells us that he was Socrates or Plato, we are compelled to believe his word because he has no identity card. We can see in his words if he confirms or not the origin he assigns to himself: we judge him an elevated spirit - that is all. If he was really Socrates or Plato, it does not matter. But when the spirit of our relatives, our friends or those who we know manifest to us, there are a thousand circumstances of intimate details that the identity could not be mistaken. Thus we obtain, in a certain way, the material evidence. We therefore think that it will be appreciated if we carry out, from time to time, some of these intimate evocations: it is the romance of the spiritual life without fiction.

Family Conversations

From Beyond the Grave:

Lemaire, the Murderer

Sentenced to maximum penalty by the Court of Aisne,
and executed on December 31st, 1857

Spirit evoked on January 29th, 1858.

1. I ask Almighty God to allow Lemaire the murderer, executed on December 31st, 1857 to come to us.
   - I am here.
2. How could you so promptly attend our appeal?
   - Raquel said so.[14]

---

14 Ms. Raquel, evoked a few days earlier, through the same medium, manifested instantly. The following questions were addressed to her with respect to this subject:

Q – How could you come so promptly, at the very instant of your evocation? One would say that you were ready?

A – When Ermance (medium) calls us, we come immediately.

Q – You thus have a lot of sympathy for Ms. Ermance?

A – There is a link between us. She would come to us. We come to her.

Q – Is there a similarity of characters between you? How come there is sympathy?

A – She has never entirely left the spiritual world.

3. What do you feel in our presence?
    -   Shame.
4. How can a young lady, kind like a lamb, serve as intermediary to you, a slaughterer?
    -   God allows so.
5. Were you lucid up to the last moment?
    -   Yes.
6. Immediately after your execution, were you aware of your new existence?
    -   I was immersed in great perturbation, which I have not left yet. I felt a great pain; it seems that my heart felt it. I saw something rolling at the bottom of the gallows. I saw the blood running and my pain was pungent.
7. Was it a physical pain, similarly to that caused by a serious injury, like for example the amputation of a limb?
    -   No. Imagine remorse, a great moral pain.
8. When have you started to feel that pain?
    -   Since I became free.
9. The physical pain caused by the execution was felt by the body or by the spirit?
    -   The moral pain was in my spirit. The body felt the physical pain but, separated, the spirit still resented.
10. Did you see the mutilated body?
    -   I saw something formless, which I had apparently left, however I felt whole. I was myself.
11. Which impression has such a sight caused on you?
    -   I felt too much pain. I was dominated by it.
12. Is it true that a few moments after decapitation the body still lives and that the executed is conscious of their ideas?
    -   The spirit leaves gradually. The tighter the ties with matter, the longer the separation.
13. How long does it take?
    -   It varies. (see previous answer)

14. They say that an expression of rage, beyond the movements, has been noticed in the face of certain executed people, as if they wanted to speak. Is it the effect of a nervous contraction or there is participation of the will?

    - The will because the spirit had not left yet.

15. What was the first feeling that you experienced on entering the new existence?

    - An intolerable suffering. A kind of pungent remorse whose cause I ignored.

16. Are you with your accomplices with whom you were simultaneously executed?

    - Most unfortunately. Seeing each other is a continuous suffering. Each condemns the other's crimes.

17. Do you meet your victims?

    - I see them... They are happy... Their eyes pursue me and I feel them in the depth of my being... I hopelessly try to escape.

18. What is your feeling in their presence?

    - Shame and remorse. I elevated them with my own hands and still hate them.

19. What is the feeling they have when they see you?

    - Pity!

20. Do they show hate or the desire of vengeance?

    - No. Their prayers attract reparation to me. You cannot imagine the suffering one has by owing everything to those that one hates.

21. Do you regret your Earthly life?

    - I only regret my crimes. If the fact still depended on me I would not have succumbed.

22. How were you led to such a criminal life?

    - Listen! I thought I was strong; I chose a tough trial and gave in to evil temptations.

23. Was the tendency towards crime in your nature or were you dragged by the environment in which you lived?
    - The tendency towards crime was in my nature as I was an inferior spirit. I wanted to rise rapidly but I requested more than proportioned to my strengths.
24. Had you been given good educational principles could you have deviated from the life of crime?
    - Yes, but I chose the position in which I was born.
25. Could you have acted as a good man?
    - As a weak man, as incapable of good as of evil. I could have slowed down, during my existence, the progress of evil, which was in my nature but I could not have elevated to a point as to practice good.
26. When alive, did you believe in God?
    - No.
27. It is said that you repented at the moment of your death. Is it true?
    - I believed in a vindictive God... and feared God's justice.
28. Is your regret more sincere now?
    - Ah! I see what I have done!
29. What do you think about God now?
    - I feel God but do not understand him.
30. Do you find it fair, the punishment inflicted on you when on Earth?
    - Yes.
31. Do you hope for forgiveness of your crimes?
    - I don't know.
32. How do you intend to redeem your crimes?
    - By new trials but it seems that eternity is between us.
33. How could you atone for your faults in a new existence if you do not keep memory of those?
    - I will have their intuition.
34. Are those trials experienced on Earth or on another world?
    - I don't know.

35. Where are you now?
    - In my suffering.
36. I ask about the place where you are now…
    - Near Ermance.
37. Are you incarnate or errant (see note 6)?
    - Errant. If I were incarnate I would have hope. As I said: it seems that eternity is between the reparation and me.
38. Considering that you are here, if we were able to see you, how would you present yourself?
    - Under my corporeal form, with the head separated from the body.
39. Can you show up to us?
    - No. Leave me!
40. Can you tell us how you escaped from Montdidier prison?
    - I no longer know… I suffer so much that only the memory of the crime remains… Leave me!
41. Can we provide any relief to your suffering?
    - Vow that I reach atonement.

Family Conversations

From Beyond the Grave:

The Queen of Oude

Note: From now on we shall remove the formula of evocation from these conversations which is always the same, unless its answer presents any particularity.

1. Which sensations did you experience on leaving this Earthly life?
   - I couldn't tell. I still experience a perturbation.
2. Are you happy?
   - No.
3. Why aren't you happy?
   - I miss life... I don't know. I experience a pungent pain. Life would have released me from this... I wish my body would rise from the grave.
4. Do you regret not have been buried in your country, but among the Christians?
   - Yes. Indian soil would weigh less over my body.

5. What do you think about the eulogies given to your mortal remains?
   - They were too stingy: I was the Queen and not everyone bent their knees before me... Leave me... I am forced to speak... I do not want you to know what I became... Behold, I was Queen.
6. We respect your hierarchy and ask you to respond to instruct us. Do you think that one day your son will recover the paternal domains?
   - My blood will certainly reign as it is worthy of that.
7. Do you give the same importance to the reintegration of your son to the throne of Oude as when you were alive?
   - My blood cannot be confused with the crowd.
8. What is your opinion about the true cause of the Indian uprise?
   - The Indian was made to be the master in their house.
9. What do you think about the future of that country?
   - India will be great among the nations.
10. It was not possible to attest your place of birth in the death certificate. Can you say it now?
    - I was born out of the noblest blood in India. I believe I was born in Delhi.
11. You who always lived in the splendors of luxury and surrounded by honors, what are your thoughts now?
    - They were owned to me.
12. Does your Earthly position confer you a more elevated position in the world where you are today?
    - I am always Queen.... May they send me slaves to serve me! I don't know, it seems that they are not concerned with me here... Nevertheless, I am always myself.
13. Were you an adept of the Muslim religion or an Indian religion?
    - Muslim; but I was too great to worry about God.
14. Which difference you observe between your religion and the Christian religion, regarding human beings's future happiness?
    - Christian religion is absurd as it considers all men brothers.

15. What is your opinion about Mohamed?
    - He was not the son of a King.
16. Did he have a divine mission?
    - Why would I care?
17. What is your opinion about Christ?
    - The son of the carpenter is not worthy of occupying my thoughts.
18. What do you think about the Muslim custom of subtracting women from men's eyes?
    - I believe women were made to dominate. I was a woman.
19. Have you ever been jealous of the freedom women enjoy in Europe?
    - No. Why should I bother with their freedom? Are their servants on their knees?
20. What is your opinion about woman's condition, in general, in the human species?
    - Why bother with women? If you talked about Queens!
21. Do you remember any other existence on Earth, prior to the one you just left?
    - I must have always been Queen.
22. Why did you respond so promptly to our appeal?
    - I did not want to come; I was forced... Do you think I would bother to answer? Who do you think you are before me?
23. Who forced you to come?
    - I don't know.... However, there may not be anybody greater than me here.
24. Where are you located?
    - Near Ermance.
25. Under which form are you here?
    - I am always Queen... Do you think I am no more? You are not much respectful... Know this that one should address Queens differently.
26. Why can't we see you?
    - I don't want you to.

27. If we could see you would that be with your dresses, ornaments and jewelry?
    - Certainly!
28. How can that be that having left all that behind, your spirit has kept the appearance, especially with your clothes and jewelry?
    - They have not left me... I am always as beautiful as I was.... I don't know the idea you make of me! It is true that you never saw me.
29. Which impression you experience among us?
    - If I could I would not be here. You treat me with such little respect! I don't want to be treated like this... Call me Majesty; otherwise I will respond no more.
30. Your Majesty knew the French language?
    - Why not? I knew everything.
31. Would your Majesty prefer to answer in English?
    - No... Won't you leave me alone? ... I want to leave... Leave me. Do you think I am submitted to your caprices? ... I am a Queen, not a slave.
32. We kindly ask you to answer two or three more questions.

St. Louis' response, who was present:

Leave the poor astray lady! Have pity on her blindness. May she serve you as an example! You do not know how much her pride suffers.

NOTE: This conversation offers several lessons. Evoking this fallen greatness, now in the grave, we did not expect very profound answers, given the type of education women have in that country. We thought we could find in this spirit, if not philosophy, at least a truer sense of reality and healthier ideas about the vanities and earthly greatness. Far from it, her earthly ideas preserved all their strengths: it is pride, which loses nothing of its illusions, struggling against its own weakness and that, indeed, must suffer a lot from its impotence. Having foreseen responses of an entirely different nature, we had prepared several questions that have lost their meaning. The answers were so different from what we expected, as also the other persons present, that we could not find in them the influence of a strange thought. They have, however, such a characteristic hallmark of personality, which clearly demonstrate the identity of the manifested spirit. We are impressed, and rightly so, to see Lemaire, the man degraded and sullied by all crimes, manifest in his language, from beyond the grave, feelings which denote a certain elevation and a very accurate assessment of the situation, while the Queen of Oude, whose social position could have developed the moral sense in her, worldly ideas have not suffered any change. It seems easy to explain the reason for this anomaly. For more degraded he could be, Lemaire lived in the midst of a civilized and enlightened society, which had reacted over his rude nature; without realizing it, he had absorbed some rays of light which surrounded him and it was that very light that brought up in him thoughts which were muffled by his abjection, but whose germ, nonetheless, subsisted. The situation is completely different with the Queen of Oude: the environment in which she lived, the habits, the absolute lack of intellectual culture, everything should have contributed to maintain the ideas that she acquired since her childhood in all their vigor. Nothing could change that primitive nature maintained by her empire of prejudice.

Family Conversations From Beyond the Grave: Dr. Xavier

A very talented doctor who we shall call Xavier, who died a few months ago, was heavily involved with magnetism, leaving a manuscript which he thought would change Science. Before he died he had read The Spirits' Book, wishing he could have had a contact with its author. The illness which killed him would not allow it. His evocation followed a request from his family and the eminently instructive answers it contains led us to insert it in this collection, subtracting however everything which was of particular interest.

1. Do you remember the manuscript you left?
   - I give little importance to that.
2. What is your current opinion about it?
   - Vain work of a being who ignored himself
3. Nevertheless you thought that work would revolutionize Science.
   - Now I see very clearly.
4. As a spirit could you correct and finalize the work?
   - I started from a point which I hardly knew. I would have perhaps to redo everything.
5. Are you happy or unhappy?
   - I wait and suffer.

6. What do you wait for?
   - New trials.
7. What is the cause of your suffering?
   - The evil things I have done.
8. However, you have not done evil intentionally.
   - Do you know human heart well?
9. Are you errant[15] or incarnate?
   - Errant
10. When you were alive, what was your opinion about Divinity?
    - I did not believe it.
11. And now?
    - I don't believe enough.
12. You wanted to contact me, do you remember that?
    - Yes.
13. Do you see me and recognize the person with whom you wanted to establish a relationship?
    - Yes.
14. Which impression The Spirits' Book had on you?
    - It unsettled me.
15. What do you think about it now?
    - It is a great piece of work.
16. What do you think about the future of the Spiritist Doctrine?
    - It is great but certain disciples cause it harm.
17. Who cause it harm?
    - Those who attack real things: the religions, the first and simplest beliefs of human beings.
18. As a doctor and considering your own studies, no doubt you can answer the following questions: Can the body preserve, for a few moments, its organic life after the separation of the soul?
    - Yes.

---

15 The spirit is said to be errant when in a kind of wandering state, between incarnations. The spirit is then said to be in the state of erraticity. Only pure spirits do not need to reincarnate thus they are not in the state of erraticity but in their permanent condition. (NT)

19. For how long?
    - There isn't a time.
20. I ask you to please clarify.
    - This only lasts a few moments.
21. How does the separation between soul and body happen?
    - Like a fluid which escapes from any container.
22. Is there a real line separating life and death?
    - Both states touch and confuse each other. Thus, the spirit gradually loosens its ties, but does not break them.
23. This loosening of the soul, does it happen more promptly on some people than on others?
    - Yes, on those who elevated above matter when alive, as their souls belong more to the spiritual world than to the Earthly one.
24. When the union between the soul and the body of a child takes place?
    - When the child breathes, as if receiving the soul with the exterior air.

    OBSERVATION: This opinion is a consequence of the Catholic dogma. In fact, church teaches that the soul will only be saved by baptism; well, as the intrauterine death is very frequent, what would then happen to that soul who, according to the church, was subtracted from the only mean of salvation, in case it existed in the body before birth? To be consistent it would be necessary that baptism took place, if not in fact, at least intentionally, at the very moment of conception.

25. How do you then explain intrauterine life?
    - Like the plant which vegetates. The child lives the animal life.

26. Is there a crime in subtracting life before birth, considering that in such occasions the child has no soul, thus it is not a human being?
    - The mother or any other person who would take the life of a child before birth would commit a crime as it would impede the soul from withstanding the trials to which the body would be an instrument.
27. Nevertheless the atonement which the reincarnating soul would have to suffer would take place?
    - Yes but God knew that the soul would not bond to that body. Thus, no soul should bond to that corporeal covering: it was the mother's trial.
28. In case the mother's life was at risk due to the child's birth, would it be a crime to sacrifice the latter to save the former?
    - No. It is preferable to sacrifice the non-existent being than the existing one.
29. Does the union between the soul and the body take place instantly or gradually, that is, there would be the need for an appreciable time for such a union to be complete?
    - The spirit does not suddenly enter the body. To measure that time imagine that the first breath that the child receives is the soul entering the body: the time for the chest to move up and down.
30. Is the union between the soul and this or that body predestined or does the choice only take place at the moment of birth?
    - God marked it. This question requires more developments. Choosing their trials, the spirit requests to incarnate. Thus, God who knows and sees everything, previously knew that a given soul would unit to a given body. When a spirit is born in the low social classes, he knows that his life will be of hardship and suffering. The child who will be born has an existence which results, up to a certain degree, from the position of her parents.

31. Why do good and virtuous parents have children of perverse nature? Put differently, why the good qualities of the parents do not always attract, by sympathy, a good spirit to animate their child?
    - A bad spirit requests good parents hoping that their good advices guide them through a better path.
32. Can the parents, through their thoughts and prayers, attract to the body of the child a good spirit instead of an inferior one?
    - No. They can, however, improve the spirit of the child to which they gave birth. It is their duty. Bad children are a trial to the parents.
33. The maternal love for the preservation of the child's life is understood but, taking into account that such a love is natural, why there are mothers who hate their children, and many times since birth?
    - Bad spirits who try to obstruct the spirit of the child, so that the child succumb the desired trials.
34. We thank you for the explanations you gave us.
    - I will do everything to instruct you.

> NOTE: The theory given by this spirit about the union between soul and body is not that accurate. The union begins since conception, that is, since the moment when the spirit, not yet incarnated, attaches to the body by a fluidic tie which progressively reinforces, up until birth. The incarnation only completes when the child breathes. (See The Spirits' Book, Q 344 and next).

Mr. Home, Second Article

(see February 1858 issue)

As said before, Mr. Home is a medium of the kind that physical phenomena are more readily produced under his influence, not excluding, however, the more intelligent manifestations. Every effect which manifests the action of a free will is, as a consequence, intelligent, that is, it is no longer mechanical and could not be attributed to an exclusively material agent. From this to the more instructive communications of an elevated moral and philosophical reach, however, there is a great distance and it is not of our knowledge that Mr. Home obtains those of such a nature. As he is not a writing medium, the majority of the answers given through him are produced by vibrating raps, indicating the letter of the alphabet, always an imperfect and slow means which hardly serves the developments of certain extension. Nevertheless, he can also write by a process which we will discuss soon.

Let us say, from starters and general principle that the ostensive manifestations, those which shock our senses, can be spontaneous or provoked. The first ones are independent of the will, many times they even happen against the will of the one who is their object and to whom they are not always pleasant. Facts of such a nature are frequent and without resorting to the reports more or less authentic of the remote eras, contemporary history offers us numerous examples whose cause, ignored in principle, is perfectly known today: these are, for example, the remarkable noises, the disordered displacements of objects, the drawing of curtains, the removal of blankets, certain apparitions, etc.

Certain persons are gifted with a special faculty which gives them the power to provoke those phenomena, so to speak, at least partially, at will. That faculty is not so rare and in a hundred people at least fifty have it, on a higher or lower degree.

What distinguishes Mr. Home is that this faculty is developed in him, as in the mediums of his kind, say, in an exceptional way. Some people do not achieve more than light raps or an insignificant displacement of a table, whereas under the influence of Mr. Home one can hear the most striking noises and all pieces of furniture of a room can be scrambled and stacked on top of each other. However extraordinary these phenomena may be, the enthusiasm of some eager admirers still found a way of amplifying them through pure and imaginative invention. On another hand, the detractors did not remain inactive: they told all sorts of stories which only took place in their imagination.

Here is an example:

The Marquis of..., one of the figures who mostly showed interest on Mr. Home, and in whose residence he was received in the intimacy, was with him one day at the Opera. Mr. P.... one of our members who personally knows both of them, was also in the audience. His neighbor establishes a conversation with him. The subject is Mr. Home.

- Would you believe, he says, that the pretentious witch, that charlatan, found ways to penetrate into the Marquis of ... house? But his trickery was discovered and he was kicked and thrown out into the streets, as a vile schemer?
- Are you sure? Asks Mr. P... Do you know the Marquis?
- Certainly, responded the other.
- In that case, replied Mr. P..., look over to that parterre balcony box. You will be able to see the Marquis, accompanied by Mr. Home himself, who he does not seem to wish to kick out.

After this, our unfortunate gossiper, considering more appropriate not to continue the conversation, grabbed his hat and left.

From this one can assess the value of certain statements. For sure, if some facts which are promoted by slander were true, many doors would have been closed to him. However, as the most respectable houses were always open to him, one has to conclude that he has always and everywhere behaved like a gentleman. By the way, it was enough to have had a brief conversation with Mr. Home to realize that with his shyness and simplicity of character, he would be an awkward impostor. We insist on this point for the morality of the cause.

Let us go back to the manifestations.

Since our objective is to make the truth known, in the interest of Science, all that we report was collected from such authentic sources that we can ensure the most scrupulous accuracy: we got them from very serious eyewitnesses, so much enlightened and highly placed that their honesty cannot be in doubt. If it was said that these people could have been, in good faith, victims of an illusion, we would reply that there are circumstances that dismiss any assumption of that nature. Incidentally, these people were very interested in knowing the truth, thus they would hardly not be prepared against any false appearance.

Mr. Home usually begins his sessions by the known events: raps on a table, or anywhere else in the apartment, by the ways we have already described. It is then followed by the movement of the table, which operates, in principle, by the laying of his hands only, or from several gathered people, then at a distance and without physical contact: it is a kind of warming up test. Very often he does not obtain more than that. It depends on his current disposition and, sometimes, of that of the assistants. There are people before whom he has never produced anything, even friendly people. We will not stay long on this subject which is so much known nowadays and that only changes in speed and energy. Many times, after several swings and oscillations, the table rises from the floor and gradually moves up, slowly, by small impulses, not even a few centimeters, but then it moves up to the ceiling and beyond the reach of hands. After having been suspended in space for a few seconds, it moves down as it had climbed, slowly, gradually.

The suspension of an inert body having a specific weight incomparably higher than that of the air is a known fact and therefore it is understood that the same can happen to an animated body. We are not aware of any occurrence in which Mr. Home had acted upon anybody else other than himself; yet the fact has not occurred only in Paris but in several places, both in Florence and in France, especially in Bordeaux, in the presence of the most respectable witnesses whose names we would cite if needed.

> As with the table, his body was elevated to the ceiling and taken back down in the same way. What is bizarre in this phenomenon is the fact that it is not produced by an act of his will. He has said himself that he does not notice the fact and always thinks he is on the ground except when he looks downward. The witnesses are the ones who see him rising. According to him, at those moments he experiences the sensation produced by the rocking of the ship over the waves. Indeed, this fact is not absolutely peculiar to Mr. Home. History records many authentic examples which we will report later.

Of all the manifestations produced by Mr. Home, the most extraordinary is, no doubt, the apparitions, which is the reason why we insist on them in view of the serious resulting consequences and the light they shed on a number of other facts. The same applies to the sounds produced in the air; musical instruments that play by themselves, etc. We will examine these phenomena in detail in the next issue.

Back from a trip to Holland, where he has produced a profound effect in the court and in the high society, Mr. Home has just left for Italy. Having his health seriously altered, he needed a milder climate.

We acknowledge with pleasure the news given by some newspapers, of an inheritance of 6,000 francs that was given to him by an English lady that he has converted to the Spiritist Doctrine and in recognition for the satisfaction that she experienced. By all accounts, Mr. Home deserved such a proof of consideration. From the donor's side, the act is a precedent that will have the applause of all those who share our convictions. Hopefully one day the Doctrine will have its Maecenas: posterity will inscribe his name among the benefactors of humanity.

Religion teaches us the existence of the soul and its immortality; Spiritism gives us their living and tangible proof, no longer by reasoning but by facts.

Materialism is one of the vices of today's society because it favors selfishness. What is there, really, out of the self, to someone who only cares about matter and the present life?

The Spiritist Doctrine, intimately connected with religious ideas, explaining about our nature, shows us happiness in the practice of the evangelical virtues; it reminds human beings of their duties to God, to society and to themselves. Assisting in its propagation is to strike a mortal blow to the scourge of skepticism that invades us like a contagious disease. Honor, therefore, to those who employ on Earth their God's favored gifts to that duty!

Magnetism and Spiritism

When the first spiritist phenomena appeared, some people thought that this discovery, if one can use this word, would strike a mortal blow against magnetism, and that the same that happens with the inventions would happen to it: the most perfect determines the oblivion of its predecessor. It did not take long for such an error to dissipate and the close relationship between the two Sciences was readily recognized. As they are both indeed based on the existence and manifestation of the soul, far from fighting each other, they can and should provide mutual support, as they complement and mutually explain one another. However, their respective supporters disagree on some points: certain magnetists[16] do not admit yet the existence or at least the manifestation of the spirits. They think they can explain everything only by the action of the magnetic fluid, an opinion that we just observe, reserving to discuss it later. We also shared that in principle but, as many others, we had to surrender to the evidence of the facts.

Contrary to that, the adepts of Spiritism are all in agreement with magnetism. All admit their actions and recognize a manifestation of the soul in the somnambulistic phenomena. That opposition, by the way, weakens daily, and is easy to predict that it is not far the day when there will be no distinction. Such divergence of views is not surprising. At the

---

16 Magnetizer is the one who practices magnetism. Magnetist is the one who adopts its principles. It is then possible to be a magnetist without being a magnetizer, but not otherwise

beginning of a Science it is still so new that it is very easy to anybody, looking at things from their own point of view, to form a different idea about it. Those more positive Sciences have always had, and still have, their schools, which fervently hold opposing theories. Scientists have raised school against school; flag against flag and, many times to their dignity, the controversy became irritating and harmful to the offended self-esteem and exceeded the limits of a wise discussion. Hopefully the sectarians of magnetism and Spiritism, better inspired, do not give the world the scandal of such low level discussions, always fatal to the propagation of the truth, whatever side they take.

We may have our opinion, sustain it and discuss it, but shredding each other is not a means of self-enlightenment, an unworthy process to the serious people, that becomes ignoble when personal interest is at stake.

Magnetism paved the way to Spiritism, and the rapid progress of the latter Doctrine is unquestionably due to the vulgarization of the ideas about the former. From the magnetic phenomena of somnambulism and ecstasy to the spiritist manifestations there is only one step. It is such a connection that, as a matter of fact, it is impossible to speak of one without speaking of the other. If we have to stay out of the Science of magnetism, then our picture will be incomplete and we may be compared to a Physics professor who abstains from talking about light. However, as the magnetism already has, among us, special institutes fairly accredited, it would be superfluous to insist on a subject treated with a superiority of talent and experience. We will thus only marginally refer to it but in such a way to sufficiently show the intimate relationship between the two Sciences which, in the end, are nothing but one.

We owed our readers this profession of faith which we finalize with a tribute to the people of conviction who, facing ridicule, sarcasm and unpleasantness, courageously dedicated themselves to the defense of such a humanitarian cause.

Whatever the opinion of the contemporaries regarding their personal interest, a view which is always more or less a reflection of lively passions, posterity will make them justice: it will place the names of Baron Du

Potet, director of the *"Journal du Magnetism"*; Mr. Millet, director of the *"Union Magnétique"*, side by side to their illustrious pioneers, the Marquis de Puysegur and Deleuze, the wise man. Thanks to their adamant efforts, popularized magnetism plunged its foot in the official Science, where it is already talked about in whispers. The word *"magnetism"* has turned into common language: it no longer scares people away, and when someone declares to be a magnetizer, they are no longer ridiculed.

April 1858

Psychological Period

As much as the spiritist manifestations had happened at all times, it is incontestable that they are exceptionally produced these days. The spirits, when questioned about this subject, were unanimous in their answer: "The times, chosen by the Providence for a universal manifestation, have come. Their duty is to dissipate the darkness of ignorance and prejudice. It is the beginning of a new era which prepares the regeneration of humanity." This thought is found notably developed in a letter we have received from one of our members, from which we extract the following excerpt:

"Everything has its time. The period that has just finished seems to have been specially destined by the Almighty to the progress of Physics and Mathematics and it is probably with the objective of disposing people to the knowledge of the exact Sciences which opposed them, for such a long time, to the manifestation of the spirits, as if that manifestation could be harmful to the positivism required by the study of Sciences. In one word, God wanted human beings to turn into a habit the search for the explanation of every phenomenon which could be produced before their eyes, in the Sciences of observation."

"It seems that the scientific period is now over. After the immense progress which took place over that period, it would not be impossible that the new period, which must succeed the other, would be destined, by the Creator, to the initiations of psychological order. In the immutable law of perfectibility established to the humankind, what can God do after having initiated human beings in the physical laws of motion and revealed the engine with which human beings change the face of the globe?"

"The human being has probed the most distant depths of space; the march of the globes and the general movement of the Universe are no longer secrets; human beings read the history of formation of our own planet in the geological layers; light is transformed, at will, into lasting images; the individual dominates lightning; with steam and electricity suppresses distances and the individual's thought travels across the space with the speed of light. Arriving at this summit, to which history of humankind offers no similar, whatever the degree of advancement may have been reached in the remote eras, it seems reasonable to me to think that the psychological order opens up a new road in the path of progress to man. It is at least what would be deduced from the facts that are produced in our days and multiply everywhere. Let us then wait for the moment to approach – if it has not yet done so – in which the Almighty will initiate us in new, great and sublime truths. It is up to us to understand it and support the Creator in the duty of regeneration."

This letter is from Mr. Georges who we spoke about in our first issue. We have only to congratulate him for his progress in the Doctrine. The eminent points of view he develops demonstrate that he understands it under its truthful prism. To him the Doctrine is not summarized by the belief in the spirits and their manifestations: it is a whole philosophy. As Mr. Georges, we believed that we have entered into a psychological period. The motives he presents are perfectly rational, as we do not think that the scientific period has given the final word; on the contrary, we suppose that it still reserves many more prodigies. We are in a transition period in which the characters of both periods blend.

The knowledge acquired by the antiquity about the spiritist manifestations did not serve as argument against the idea of the psychological period, which is in preparation. In fact, let us notice that in the antiquity such knowledge was limited to a strict circle of wise people. The people had only some idea about them, flawed by prejudice and disfigured by the charlatanism of the priests, who used them as a means of domination. As we have said elsewhere, such knowledge has never been lost; they remained as isolated facts, certainly because the time was not right for them to be understood. What happens today has a completely different character: the manifestations are general; shock society from top to bottom. The spirits no longer teach in the mysterious circles of the temple, inaccessible to the common ones. These facts happen in day light. They speak a language understandable by all.

Everything thus announce, from a moral point of view, a new phase to humanity.

Spiritism Among the Druids

Under the title *"Le vieux neuf"* Mr. Edouard Fournier published in the *Le Siècle,* a series of articles ten years ago, as much outstanding as interesting, from the erudition point of view, with respect to history. When commenting all modern inventions and discoveries the author proves that if this century has the merit of application and development, it does not have – at least in its majority – that one of precedence. Over the time that Mr. Fournier wrote this magnificent series, there was no understanding of spirits, not noticing that the events that take place today are a mere repetition of what was equally or better known by our ancestors. This is unfortunate, as his profound investigations would have allowed him to expose the old mystic just as he has exposed the ancient industry. We wish one day his extensive research may be directed to that spiritual side as well.

As for us, the personal observations do not leave any doubt relative to the ancient times and to the universality of the Doctrine taught by the spirits. The coincidence between what they tell us today and the beliefs of the remotest eras is a very important fact. We shall note, however, that if we find traces of the Spiritist Doctrine everywhere, we don't see it completed anywhere else. It seems that the task of coordinating these sparse fragments among all peoples has been reserved for our times, so that we can arrive at the unity of principles, through a more thorough, and above all, more general set of manifestations which, as it seems, give reason to the author mentioned in the preceding article, about the psychological period in which humanity gradually enters.

Ignorance and prejudice have disfigured this doctrine almost everywhere as these fundamental principles blend with the superstitious practices of all times, exploited with the objective of subduing reason. Nevertheless, under this stack of absurdities the most sublime ideas have germinated like precious seeds hidden under the burning bushes, waiting for the vivifying sunlight to develop. Our generation, more universally informed, brushes aside the burning bushes. Such a cleansing, however, cannot be accomplished without transition. Let us then allow the necessary time for the good seeds to develop and the weeds to be eliminated.

The Druidic Doctrine offers a curious example of what we have just said. This doctrine, which we only know the exterior practices, rises to the most sublime truths on certain aspects. But these truths were only known to the initiated ones: frightened by the human sacrifices, the public harvested the sacred agarics of the oak with a sanctified respect and only saw the phantasmagoria. We will be able to assess it by the following text, extracted from a document as much precious as unknown, which sheds a completely new light onto the truthful theology of our ancestors.

We offer a Celtic text to the reflection of our readers, published not long ago, whose appearance has caused certain commotion in the educated world. It is impossible to be certain about its authorship as well as to which century it belongs. It is, however, incontestable that it belongs to the tradition of the Bardic Welsh and that its origin is sufficient to award it the highest value.

It is known, indeed, that Wales was, and still is in our days, the most faithful asylum to the Gallic nationality which has suffered, among us, profound modifications. It has been just touched by the weak and short roman domination; preserved from the barbaric invasions by the strength of its inhabitants and by the natural difficulties of its territory; submitted later to the Normand Dynasty which felt impelled to allow it a certain level of independence, retaining the name Wales as an always distinctive mark connecting it to ancient times.

The Welsh (Cymraeg or Gymraeg) language, once spoken all over the northern part of the Gaul, has never ceased to be used as many customs are equally still Gallic.

From all foreign influences, Christianity was the only one completely successful. But that was not achieved without difficulties, relatively to the supremacy of the Roman Church whose reform in the XVI century did not do more than determining its fall, articulated long before in those regions full of an indefectible independence.

One can even say that on converting to Christianity the Druids were not extinct in the Gaul, as they were in our Brittany and in other regions of Gallic blood. They had, as an immediate consequence, a very solidly constituted society, mainly dedicated, apparently, to the cult of national poetry but which, under the poetic blanket, preserved a notable fidelity to the intellectual heritage of the old Gaul: the Bardic society of Wales, after been kept as a secret society during the whole Middle Ages, by oral transmission of its literary monuments and doctrine, similarly to what the Druids used to do, then decided around the XVI and XVII centuries to confide the most essential parts of their inheritance to the writings.

It is from that collection, whose authenticity is attested by an uninterrupted chain of traditions, that the text we mentioned proceeds and its value, given those circumstances and as mentioned before, does not depend on the hand which had the merit of writing it, neither on the period when the writing was given a definite format. It is the spirit of the medieval Bards that transpire from it, Bards who were in turn the last disciples of a wise and religious corporation which, under the name of Druids, dominated the Gaul during the first period of its history; more or less like the Latin clergy did during the Middle Ages.

Even if we were removed from all clues regarding the origin of the analyzed text, we would surely be on the right path, given its agreement with the Greek and Latin authors who left us their teachings about the Druids' religious doctrine. That agreement is reached out of indubitable points of solidarity as they are supported by the reasoning extracted from the very substance of those texts. Thus the demonstrated solidarity regarding the fundamental articles – the only ones we heard about from our ancestors – naturally extends to the secondary developments. Indeed, these developments, imbued with the same spirit, necessarily derive from the same source; they are part of the whole and cannot be explained by anything else but that way. At the same time that they refer to the primitive archives of the Druidic religion, by such a logic deduction, it is impossible to assign any other starting point to them. This is because, other than the Druidic influence, the region from where they originate has not suffered any other influence but the Christian that was totally strange to those doctrines.

The themes developed in the triads are so strange to Christianity that the rare Christian influences found here and there in the body of the text, at first sight, already distinguish them from the primitive structure. That influence, naively originated from the conscience of the Bardic Christians, could hardly interleave with the interstices of the Druidic tradition, if one can say so, incapable of blending with all that. Thus, the analysis of the text is as simple as rigorous, hence it can be simplified by leaving aside everything that contains the seal of Christianity and, once filtered, by considering as of Druidic origin all the rest, visibly characterized by a religion which is different from that of the Gospel or from the Catholic Councils.

Thus, in order to mention only what is essential, let us begin by the well-known principle that the dogma of charity to God and the individual is so peculiar to Christianity as the migration of the souls is to Druidism; a certain number of triads in which a spirit of love breathes, immediately revealing as indicators of a comparatively modern character, never known to the primitive Gaul, whereas the other triads, animated by a completely different breath, reveal even more markedly the distinguished character of the antiquity. Finally, one does not need to observe much to understand that the form of the teachings contained in the triads is of Druidic origin. It is a well-known fact that the Druids had a particular preference for the number three and used it in their lessons. This is additionally demonstrated through the Gallic monuments that contain the number three.

Diogenes Laertius has preserved one of those triads which succinctly summarize the duties of people to the Divinity, to their neighbors and to themselves. "Honor the superior beings, do not commit injustice and do cultivate ones virile virtue." The bard's literature propagated aphorisms of the same kind, relatively to all fields of human knowledge: Science, History, Moral, Law, Poetry. One cannot find a more interesting or adequate work to inspire great thoughts than that of the text published below, according to the French version by Mr. Adolphe Pictet.

From that series of triads the first eleven ones are dedicated to the exposition of the characteristic attributes of the Divinity. It is this segment that had the greatest Christian influence, as it was easy to predict. If one cannot deny that the Druidism incorporated the principle of God's unity, they had also conceived, in a confusing way, perhaps due to their disposition for the number three, something like the Divine Trinity. It is, nevertheless, incontestable that what complements such a high theological conception – that is, a distinction of the persons and particularly the third one – became completely strange to this old religion. All that contributes to prove that its former adepts were much more concerned with the establishment of the individual's freedom than with charity. It was precisely a consequence of this false starting point that made it perish. It seems also reasonable to associate the whole prologue to a more or less determined Christian influence, particularly from the fifth triad.

Following the general principles, relatively to the nature of God, the text continues to expose the constitution of the Universe. The body of this constitution is authoritatively formulated in three triads which, showing the particular beings in an order absolutely different from that of God, complete the idea that has to be made of a unique and immutable Being. Under more explicit formulas, the triads just reproduce what was already known, by the witnesses of the ancient times, about the circulation of the souls, alternatively passing from life to death and from death to life. We can consider them like in a famous Farsalia verse, in which the poet exclaims, upon addressing the priests of Gaul, that if what they teach is certain, then death is nothing more than the median of a long life: "*Longae vitae mors media est.*"

"GOD AND THE UNIVERSE

I – There are three primitive unities and from each one of those there could not be more than one: a God, a truth and a point of freedom which is the point where the balance of the whole opposition resides.

II – There things proceed from the three primitive unities: the whole life, the whole good and the whole power.

III – God is necessarily three things: the greatest part of life, the greatest part of science and the greatest part of power. From each thing there could not be a greater part.

IV – God cannot stop being three things: what has to constitute the perfect good, what has to desire the perfect good and what has to practice the perfect good.

V – Three guarantees of what God does and will do: God's infinite power, God's infinite wisdom and God's infinite love, as there is nothing that cannot be done, that cannot become truthful and that cannot be desired as an attribute.

VI – Three main objectives of God's work, as the Creator of all things: diminish evil, reinforce good and clarify the whole difference, so as to know what should be or, on the contrary, what should not be.

VII – Three things God cannot stop conceding: what there is of more advantageous, of more necessary and of more beautiful for each thing.

VIII – Three forces of existence: it cannot be different; it cannot be necessarily another one and cannot be able to be better since its conception. This contains the perfection of all things.

IX – Three things will necessarily prevail: the supreme power, the supreme intelligence and the supreme love of God.

X – The three greatness of God: perfect life, perfect science, perfect power.

XI – Three original causes of the living beings: divine love, according to the supreme intelligence; the supreme wisdom, by the perfect knowledge of all means; the divine power, according to the will, love and wisdom of God."

"THE THREE CIRCLES"

XII – There are three circles of existence: the circle of the empty region (*ceugant*) where, with the exception of God, there is nothing alive nor dead and no being that God cannot penetrate; the circle of migration (*abred*) where every animated being proceeds from death, where the individual has lived; and the circle of happiness (*gwynfyd*), where every animated being proceeds from life and that the individual will live in heaven.

XIII – Three successive states of the animated beings: the state of humiliation in the abyss (*annoufn*); the state of freedom in humanity and the state of happiness in heaven.

XIV – Three necessary phases of every existence regarding life: the beginning in *annoufn*; the transmigration in *abred* and the plenitude in *gwynfyd*. Without these three things nothing else can exist but God."

Thus, as a summary, about the capital point of the theology that God, as their Creator, takes the souls from the "emptiness", the triads do not precisely enunciate. After showing God in an inaccessible and eternal sphere, they simply show the souls originating in the last layers of the Universe, in the abyss (*annoufn*); from there these souls pass to the migration circle (*abred*), where their destiny is determined through a series of existences, according to the good or bad use of their freedom; finally, they elevate to the supreme circle (*gwynfyd*) where the migrations stop, where there is no more death, where life takes place in happiness, preserving a perpetual activity and total consciousness of their individuality.

Truthfully, Druidism does not follow the same mistakes as Eastern theologies, which lead the individual to be finally absorbed into the centre of an immutable Divinity since, on the contrary, it distinguishes a special circle, a circle of the emptiness or infinite (*ceugant*), which forms the incommunicable privilege of the supreme Being and in which no creature, whatever the degree of holiness, will ever penetrate. It is the highest point of the religion because it establishes the milestone for everyone's progress.

The most significant hallmark of that theology, given that it is a purely negative mark, consists in the absence of a particular circle, such as the

Tartar of the pagan antiquity, destined to the endless punishment of the criminal souls. To the Druids there isn't properly a hell. The distribution of penalties, to their eyes, occurs in the circle of the migrations, in more or less happy condition where always owner of their own freedom they atone their faults through the suffering and prepare for a better future, by the reformulation of their vices. In certain cases it is even possible that the souls degenerate to the *annoufn* region where they are born and to which no other meaning can be given but the animality. By this dangerous side of the degeneration, which nothing justifies, as the diversity of conditions in the circle of humanity is perfectly sufficient to the penalties of all degrees, Druidism would have then slipped to the metempsychosis. But such an unpleasant extreme, to which no requirement of the development of the soul through the migrations leads, as it will be seen by the series of triads relatively to the regimen of the *abred* circle, it seems to have occupied a secondary place in the religious system.

Apart from some obscurities due perhaps to the difficulties of a language whose profound metaphysical origin has not yet been well understood, the declaration of the triads with respect to the circle of *abred* spread the most vivid lights over the body of the Druidic religion. One feels a slight breath of superior originality. The mystery which offers the spectacle of our current existence to the intelligence, acquires there a singular feature not found anywhere else. One would say that a great veil, tearing off before and beyond life, allows the soul to suddenly swim with an unexpected power, through an undefined extension, never suspected before in their prison, among the thick walls of birth and death.

Whatever the judgment we pass on the truthfulness of that doctrine, it should be profound. Thinking of the effect that these principles about the origin and destine of the soul should have on simple creatures, it is easy to understand the huge influence the Druids had over the spirit of our ancestors. Amidst the darkness of antiquity, those sacred ministers could not appear to be, to the eyes of the people, anything but revealers of Heaven and Earth.

Here the remarkable text under scrutiny:

"CIRCLE OF ABRED"

XV – Three necessary things in the circle of *abred*: the least possible degree of the whole life, and from that its beginning; the matter of all things, and from there the progressive growth which only takes place in the state of need; the formation of all things of death, and from there the debility of the existences.

XVI – Three things that all living beings necessarily participate, through God's justice: God's help in *abred*, because without that nobody could know anything; the privilege of participating into God's love; and the agreement with God who is fair and merciful regarding the realization of God's power.

XVII – Three causes of the need in the circle of *abred*: the development of the material substance of every animated being; the development of the knowledge of all things; and the development of the moral force to overcome every *Cythraul* (evil spirit) opposition and to free the *Droug* (the evil). Without such a transition, per each state of life, there could not be the realization of any being.

XVIII – Three primitive calamities of *abred*: the need, the absence of memory and death.

XIX – Three necessary conditions to get to the plenitude of Science: transmigrate in *abred*, transmigrate in *gwynfyd* and remember the past things, up until *annoufn*.

XX – Three indispensable things in the circle of *abred*: transgression of the law, as it cannot be different; redemption through death before *Droug* and *Cythraul*; the development of life and the good through the separation from *Droug,* in the redemption of death and that by the love of God, who embraces everything.

XXI – Three efficient ways of God in *abred* to dominate *Droug* and *Cythraul* and to overcome one's position relatively to the circle of *gwynfyd*: the need, the loss of memory and death.

XXII – Three things are primitively contemporary: the individual, freedom and light.

XXIII – Three things are needed for the victory of the individual over evil: strength against pain, change and freedom of choice. Having the power of choice, the individual cannot have the prior certainty about the place where he or she is going to be.

XXIV – Three alternatives offered to the individual: *abred* and *gwynfyd*; need and freedom; good and evil. Having the whole in equilibrium, the individual can connect to one or another, at will.

XXV – By three things the individual fall in the need of *abred*: by the absence of efforts towards knowledge; by his or hers detachment from good and by his or hers attachment to wickedness. As a consequence of these things, he or she fall into *abred* until he or she analogous, and restarts the course of his or hers transmigration.

XXVI – By three things the individual necessarily returns to *abred*, although in other senses he or she is connected to what is good: by pride he or she falls down to *annoufn*; by deceitfulness, down to the equivalent point of demerit; by cruelty, down to the corresponding degree of animality. From there he or she transmigrates again to humanity, as before.

XXVII – The three main things to obtain in the state of humanity: science, love and the moral strength, in the highest possible state of development, before death. This cannot be achieved prior to the state of humanity and can only be achieved through the privilege of freedom and choice. These three things are called the three victories.

XXVIII – There are three victories over *Droug* and *Cythraul*: science, love and moral strength and as the knowledge, the wish and the power, realize whatever needed in their connection with things. These three victories start in the condition of humanity and develop eternally.

XXIX – Three privileges of the condition of the human being: the balance between good and bad and from that the ability to compare; the freedom of choice and from that the judgment and preference; the development of the moral strength as a consequence of the judgment and from that the preference. These three things are necessary to the realization of anything."

In summary, the beginning of the beings in the heart of the Universe happens at the lowest point of the scale of life. Without stretching the consequences of the declaration contained in the twenty-seventh triad, one can assume that in the Druids doctrine this initial point was in the mysterious and confusing abyss of animality. It does result, as a consequence, in the logic need of progress, as God has not destined the beings to remain in such a low and obscure condition since the origin of the soul's history. However, in the inferior zones of the Universe, such a progress does not develop according to a continuous line. That long life, being born in such a low level and having so much to improve, breaks into segments, which are connected to each other at the basis of its succession, but whose mysterious solidarity escapes the individual consciousness, thanks to the lack of memory, at least for some time. Those periodic interruptions, in the secular course of life, form what we call death; hence death and birth, from a superficial consideration, make such distinct events, in reality being nothing more than the two faces of the same phenomenon: one related to the period that ends, and the other to the one that begins.

That is why death itself is not a real calamity but a benefit from God. Breaking the narrowest links that we had established with our present life, it transports us to new conditions, thus giving place to a freer elevation, to new progresses.

Thus, as with death, the loss of memory which follows it should not be taken as anything other than a benefit. It is a consequence of the first point because if the soul clearly kept the memories from one period to the other, in the course of this long life, the interruption would be merely accidental and there would not be death, as such, neither birth, as these events would then loose the absolute character which distinguish and give them strength.

Even from the point of view of that theology it is not difficult to directly notice, with respect to the previous periods, how the loss of memory could be considered a benefit relatively to human beings in their present condition, if in those previous periods, as with the current position of people in a world of suffering and trials, they were unfortunately stained by crime and mistakes, today's primary cause of misery and atonement. It is evidently a great advantage to the soul to be free from the vision of so many faults and, at the same time, of the most distressing remorse which would then originate. As it does not oblige a formal repentance other than those relatively to the guilt of the present life, God really concedes an enormous grace, thus showing compassion for their weaknesses.

Finally, according to this mode of considering the mystery of life, the needs of all nature that we are submitted to and that since birth, by a fatal destiny, so to speak, determine the form of our existence in the present period, constitute a last benefit, as sensible as the other two. The most convenient character of our physical atonements is definitely given by those needs and our trials and, consequently, our moral development. It is still those same needs, as much with our physical organization as with the exterior circumstances, in whose environment we are placed, that forcibly drag us to death then dragging us, by the same reason, to our supreme liberation. In summary, as the triads imply in their energetic concision, one finds in them the three primitive calamities as the three efficient means of God in *abred*.

Which conduct allows the soul to really elevate in this life, deserving to achieve a superior state of existence after death?

The answer given by Christianity to this fundamental question is known by all: it is the condition of destroying pride and selfishness in oneself; developing in ones' intimate substance the forces of humility and charity, the only efficient and meritorious to God's eyes. Blessed are the humble!

Druidism's answer is way different and clearly contrasts with the latest one. As from their teachings, the soul elevates on the scale of existences with the condition of, by working on itself, fortifying its own personality. This result is naturally obtained by the development of the strength of character, added to the development of knowledge. This is what the twenty-fifth triad says, stating that the souls fall on the need of transmigrations, that is, in the confusing and mortal lives, not only for feeding the evil passions but also by neglecting the realization of the fair actions; by the lack of strength to stick to what is prescribed by the consciousness; in one word, by the weakness of character. Besides this lack of moral virtue, the soul is still halted in its progress towards heaven by the lack of perfection of the spirit. Intellectual illumination, which is necessary to the plenitude of happiness, does not happen in the happy soul by a simple and absolutely gracious irradiation from heaven. It only happens in the celestial life if the soul endeavors, since this life, to achieve it. Thus, the triad does not only mention the lack of knowledge but also the lack of efforts to acquire knowledge, which in the end, as with the preceding virtue, is a precept of activity and movement.

In fact, in the following triads, charity is recommended as much as Science and moral strength. But in this, still regarding the Divine power, it is sensitive to the influence of Christianity. It is to Christianity that the preaching and enthroning of the law of charity in God and human beings, in this world, belong and not to the strong and tough religion of our ancestors.

If such a law shines over the triads it is the effect of an alliance with the Gospel, or even better, of a happy improvement of the theology of the Druids by the action of the theology of the Apostles and not by a primitive tradition. Just subtract that Divine ray and there we have the Gallic moral, in its rude greatness, moral which was capable of producing powerful personalities, in the fields of heroism and Science, but which could not unite them, neither among them nor with the crowds of the simple ones.[17]

The Spiritist Doctrine does not consist only in the belief of the manifestations of the spirits but rather in everything they teach us about the nature and destiny of the souls. If we then refer to the precepts contained in The Spirits' Book, where we will find their complete teachings, we will be surprised by the identity of some fundamental principles with the Druidic doctrine, among which, one of the most notable, incontestably, is the reincarnation. In the three circles, in the three successive states of the animated beings, we find all phases of our spirits' scale. What is in fact

---

17   Extracted from Magasin Pitoresque, 1857

the circle of *abred* or the migration, other than the orders of spirits which depurate through successive existences? In the *gwynfyd* circle human beings no longer transmigrates; they enjoy supreme happiness. Isn't that the first order of the scale, of the pure spirits who having passed through all trials no longer need the reincarnation and enjoy eternal life? Notice still that, according to the Spiritist Doctrine, human beings preserve the free will; which they gradually elevates by their will, by their progressive perfecting and by the trials they endured, from the *annoufn* or abyss to the perfect happiness in *gwynfyd*, with the difference, however, that the Druidism admits the possible return to the inferior layers, whereas according to Spiritism, the spirit may remain stationary but cannot degenerate. In order to complete the analogy it would be sufficient to add to our scale, below the third order, the *annoufn* circle, which characterizes the abyss or the unknown origin of the souls, and above the first order the *ceugant* circle, or God's dwelling, inaccessible to the creatures. The table below will clarify the comparison.

Spirits' Scale			Druidic Scale
			Ceugant. God's dwelling.
1st Order	1st Class	Pure spirits. Will no longer incarnate.	*Gwynfyd. Home of the blessed ones. Eternal life.*
2nd Order	2nd Class	Superior spirits*	*Abred. Circle of the migrations or multiple corporeal existences, which the souls pass from annoufn to gwynfyd.*
2nd Order	3rd Class	Spirits of wisdom*	*Abred. Circle of the migrations or multiple corporeal existences, which the souls pass from annoufn to gwynfyd.*
2nd Order	4th Class	Spirits of Science*	*Abred. Circle of the migrations or multiple corporeal existences, which the souls pass from annoufn to gwynfyd.*
2nd Order	5th Class	Benevolent spirits*	*Abred. Circle of the migrations or multiple corporeal existences, which the souls pass from annoufn to gwynfyd.*
3rd Order	6th Class	Neutral spirits*	---------------------------
3rd Order	7th Class	Pseudo-wise spirits*	*Annoufn. Abyss, starting point of the souls*
3rd Order	8th Class	Frivolous spirits*	*Annoufn. Abyss, starting point of the souls*
3rd Order	9th Class	Impure spirits*	*Annoufn. Abyss, starting point of the souls*

* Depurating and elevating through the trials of reincarnation

Evocation of Spirits

in Abyssinia

In the *"Voyage aux sources du Nil"*, in 1768, James Bruce tells the story we reproduce below, regarding Gingiro, a small Kingdom located south of Ethiopia, east of the Kingdom of Adel. The story is about two Ambassadors sent to the Pope around 1625, by Susenyos, King of the Ethiopia (Abyssinia), having the Ambassadors to cross the Kingdom of Gingiro.

"Then, says Bruce, it was necessary to notify the King of Gingiro about the arrival of the entourage and request an audience with him. But at that time he was occupied with an important operation of witchcraft, without which the sovereign would not dare doing anything else."

"The Kingdom of Gingiro can be considered as the first, on this side of Africa, where the strange practice of predicting the future through the evocation of the spirits and via a direct communication with the devil has been established."

"The King thought convenient to wait for eight days before conceding an audience to the Ambassador and his companion, the Jesuit Fernandez. Consequently, on the ninth day they got permission to visit the court, which they did in the same afternoon."

"In Gingiro nothing gets done without resorting to magic. It can thus be seen how much human reason is degraded, a few leagues away. Do not tell us that such a weakness is due to ignorance or the heat of the region. Why would heat induce people to become wizards, which would not happen in a cold climate? Why would ignorance stretch the individual's power to the point of making him or her transpose the limits of ordinary intelligence and giving him or her the faculty of communicating with a new order of beings, inhabitants of another world? The Ethiopians, who embrace almost all Ethiopia, are blacker than the Gingironeans. Their land is hotter and as the latter, they are indigenous to the lands they inhabit, since the beginning of the centuries. However, they neither worship the devil nor pretend to have any communication with him; they do not sacrifice humans in their altars; finally, one cannot find, among them, any trace of similar atrocity."

"On those parts of Africa which have open communication with the sea, slave trading has been in place since the remotest centuries but the King of Gingiro, whose domains are almost entirely confined to the center of the continent, sacrifices to the devil the slaves he cannot sell to man. It is there that this horrific costume, of shedding human blood in all ceremonies, begins."

"I ignore", says Mr. Bruce, "its reach towards southern Africa, but I consider Gingiro as the geographic limit of the devil's Kingdom, on the northern part of the peninsula."

Had Mr. Bruce seen what we witness today, he would not have found anything frightening in those practices employed in Gingiro. He only sees a superstitious belief in them whereas we see their cause in the fact of falsely interpreted manifestations, which could be produced there, as anywhere else.

The role that the devil plays in their culture is not surprising. Firstly, it is necessary to observe that all barbaric peoples have attributed to a malefic power everything that they could not explain. Second, a sufficiently ignorant people, capable of sacrificing human beings, certainly could not attract superior spirits to their environment. By their nature, those spirits who visit them can only confirm them in their beliefs. Besides, one has to consider that the peoples of certain regions of Africa have preserved a large number of Jewish traditions, later mixed with some formless ideas of Christianity where they adopted the doctrine of the devil and the demons, as a result of their own ignorance.

Family Conversations
From Beyond the Grave:
Description of Jupiter

Bernard Pallissy
(March 9th, 1858)

NOTE: From previous evocations we knew that Bernard Palissy, a famous potter of the XVI century, lives in Jupiter. The following answers confirm, in all points, what we were told about that planet, in multiple occasions, by other spirits and through different mediums. We thought they would be read with interest as a complement to the classification we gave in our last issue. The identification of these descriptions, as with the previous ones, is a remarkable fact that serves as a presumption of accuracy.

1. Where did you go after leaving Earth?
   - I still remained here.
2. What was your condition here?
   - Under the aspect of a lovely and dedicated woman. It was a simple mission.
3. Did that mission last long?
   - Thirty years.

4. Do you remember the name of that woman?
   - It was obscure.
5. Does the importance given to your work please you? Does it compensate the sufferings you had to endure?
   - Why would I care about the material work of my hands? What is important to me is the suffering that has elevated me.
6. What was the aim of the admirable drawings you have produced about planet Jupiter, through the hand of Mr. Victorien Sardou?
   - The aim was to inspire in you the desire to become better.
7. Considering that you frequently come to this Earth, which you inhabited many times, you must know very well its physical and moral states in order to establish a comparison between Earth and Jupiter. We would ask you to enlighten us about those points.
   - I come to your globe only as a spirit. The spirit has no longer material sensations.

PHYSICAL STATE OF THE GLOBE

8. Is it possible to compare Jupiter's temperature to that one of our latitudes?
   - No. It is smooth and temperate; it is always the same whereas yours vary. Think of the Elysian Fields, whose description has already been given to you.
9. The picture given to us by the antiques about the Elysian Fields would be the result of an intuitive knowledge which they had of a superior world, such as Jupiter, for example?
   - From the positive knowledge. The evocation was in the hands of the priests.
10. Does the temperature, like here, vary according to the latitude?
    - No.

11. According to our calculations, the Sun must be seen by Jupiter's inhabitants as very small and, consequently, provide very little light. Can you tell us if the light intensity is like that on Earth or much weaker?
    - Jupiter is surrounded by a kind of spiritual light, related to the essence of its inhabitants. The gross light of your Sun was not made for them.
12. Is there an atmosphere?
    - Yes.
13. Is Jupiter's atmosphere formed by the same elements as of Earth's atmosphere?
    - No. People are not the same. Their needs change.
14. Are there water and seas in Jupiter?
    - Yes.
15. Is water formed by the same elements as ours?
    - More ethereal.
16. Are there volcanoes?
    - No. Our globe is not tormented like yours. Nature there did not have its great crises. It is the dwelling of the blessed ones. Matter almost does not exist there.
17. Do the plants have analogy with ours?
    - Yes, but they are more beautiful.

PHYSICAL STATE OF THE INHABITANTS

18. Has the conformation of the bodies of its inhabitants a relationship with ours?
    - Yes, it is the same.
19. Can you give us an idea of their height, as compared to the inhabitants of Earth?
    - Large and well proportioned. Larger than your largest people. The human being's body is like the form of his spirit: beautiful when he is good. The covering is worthy of the spirit: it is no longer a prison.

20. Are the bodies opaque, diaphanous or translucent there?
    - Some have a given property; others have another, according to their purpose.
21. We understand that, with respect to the inert bodies. But our question refers to the human bodies.
    - The body surrounds the spirit without hiding it, like a translucent veil which covers a statue. In the inferior worlds the gross covering hides the spirit from its neighbors. But the good ones have nothing else to hide: each and everyone can read from the heart of the others. What would happen if it were like that here?
22. Is there a difference of sex over there?
    - Yes, that is always the case where there is matter; it is a law of matter.
23. What is the basis of nourishment of its inhabitants? Is it animal and vegetal like here?
    - Purely vegetal. The human being is the protector of the animals.
24. We were told that part of their feeding is extracted from the environment, whose emanations they inhale. Is that true?
    - Yes.
25. Compared to ours, is life duration longer or shorter?
    - Longer.
26. What is the average life span?
    - How to measure time?
27. Could we take one of our centuries by comparison?
    - I believe it is more or less five centuries.
28. Is the development of the infancy proportionally faster than ours?
    - The human being preserves his superiority: his infancy does not compress the intelligence neither does aging extinguish it.
29. Are people subjected to diseases?
    - They are not subjected to your illnesses.
30. Is life divided between sleep and wake?
    - Between action and rest.

31. Can you give us an idea about the several occupations of people?
    - I would have to speak a lot. Their main function is to encourage the spirits who inhabit the inferior worlds, so that they can persevere on the good path. Not having misfortunes to alleviate within their own element, they look for them where they do exist: they are the good spirits who support you and attract you to the good path.
32. Do they cultivate some arts there?
    - They are useful there. Your arts are toys which distract your pains.
33. The specific density of the human body allows the human being to transport oneself from one point to another, without staying attached to the ground, like here?
    - Yes.
34. Is there the boredom and displeasure with life?
    - No. The displeasure with life originates from the disregard of oneself.
35. Being the bodies of Jupiter's inhabitants less dense than ours, are they formed by compact and condensed or airy matter?
    - Compact to us but not to you. It is less condensed.
36. Is the body impenetrable, considering that it is made of matter?
    - Yes.
37. Do the inhabitants have, like us, an articulated language?
    - No. There is communication through thought among them.
38. Is the second sight or remote viewing, as we were informed, a normal faculty which stays among you?
    - Yes. The spirits do not have hindrance. Nothing is hidden from them.
39. If nothing is hidden to the spirits do they know the future? (We refer to the spirits incarnated in Jupiter).
    - The knowledge about the future depends on the degree of perfection of the spirit: this has less inconvenient to us than to you; it is even necessary to us, up to a certain degree, for

the accomplishment of the missions we are given. But to say that we know the future without restrictions would be the same as to level us to God.

40. Can you reveal to us everything you know about the future?
    - No. Wait until you have deserved to know it.

41. Do you communicate with the other spirits, more easily than us?
    - Yes, always. There is no longer matter between them and us.

42. Does death inspire the same horror and fear as with us?
    - Why would it be frightening? Among us evil no longer exists. Only evil fears the last moment. It fears its judge.

43. What do the inhabitants of Jupiter become after death?
    - Always growing towards perfection, without going through more trials.

44. Wouldn't there be on Jupiter spirits who submit themselves to trials in order to accomplish a mission?
    - Yes but it is not a trial. Only the love of good takes them to the suffering.

45. Can they fail in their missions?
    - No because they are good. There is weakness only where there are defects.

46. Could you name a few spirits, inhabitants of Jupiter, who have accomplished a great mission on Earth?
    - St. Louis.

47. Couldn't you name others?
    - Why does it matter? There are unknown missions whose objective is the happiness of only one. At times, these are the greatest and most painful ones.

ABOUT THE ANIMALS

48. Is the body of the animals more material than that of people?
    - Yes. The human being is king, the god of the planet.

49. Are there carnivorous animals?
    - The animals do not shred mutually. They all live submitted to the human being and love one another.

50. Are there, however, animals which escape the control of humans, like the insects, fishes and birds?
    - No. They are all useful to the human being.

51. We were told that the animals are the workers and the foremen who execute the material tasks, build the houses, etc. Is that exact?
    - Yes. The human being no longer lowers to serve his or her neighbor.

52. Are the animal servers connected to one person or a family or are they taken and exchanged at will, like here?
    - They are all associated to a particular family. You change them looking for the best.

53. Do the serving animals live in slavery or in the state of freedom? Are they a property or can they change their masters, at will?
    - They are in the state of submission.

54. Do the serving animals receive any compensation for their work?
    - No.

55. Are the faculties of the animals developed by some sort of education?
    - They develop by themselves.

56. Do the animals have a more precise and characteristic language than those of the Earthly animals?
    - Certainly.

MORAL STATE OF THE INHABITANTS

57. The dwellings you gave us as a sample in your drawings, are they arranged in cities like here?
    - Yes. Those who love one another come together. Only the passions may establish solitude around people. If the bad

individual looks for his or her neighbor, who is an instrument of pain, why would a pure and virtuous individual run away from his or her brother?

58. The spirits are the same or of several degrees?
    - Several degrees but of the same order.
59. We ask you to refer to the spirits' scale we provided in the second number of the Review and tell us to which order those spirits incarnated in Jupiter belong.
    - All good, all superior. Sometimes good comes down to the evil but the evil can never blend with the good.
60. Do the inhabitants form different peoples, like here on Earth?
    - Yes, but all united by the bonds of love.
61. Thus, the wars are unknown?
    - Useless question.
62. Will people on Earth be able to arrive to such a degree of perfection, so that war would be unnecessary?
    - They will arrive to that, no doubt. The war will disappear with the egotism of the peoples, at the same time as fraternity becomes better understood.
63. Are the peoples governed by rulers?
    - Yes.
64. What is the consistency of the ruler's authority?
    - His superior degree of perfection.
65. What is the meaning of the superiority and inferiority of the spirits in Jupiter, considering that they are all good?
    - They have a greater or smaller sum of knowledge and experience; they become free of impurities as they enlighten.
66. Similarly to Earth, are there more advanced peoples than others in Jupiter?
    - No, but among the peoples there are several degrees.
67. If the most advanced people from Earth were transported to Jupiter which position would they occupy?
    - The one occupied by the monkeys among you.

68. Are the peoples ruled by laws?
    - Yes.
69. Are there criminal laws?
    - There is no more crime.
70. Who makes the laws?
    - God made them.
71. Is there rich and poor? In other words, are there people who live in abundance and others who lack the necessary?
    - No. They are all brothers and sisters. If one had more than the other the former would share with the latter; they would not be happy when their brother was in need.
72. According to this all fortunes would be the same?
    - I did not say that all are equally rich. You asked if there would be people with the superfluous while others would lack the necessary.
73. The two answers seem contradictory to us. We ask you to establish the agreement.
    - Nobody lacks the necessary; nobody has the superfluous. In other words, each person's fortune is related to their condition. Are you happy?
74. We understand now. But we asked, however, if the one who has less is unhappy with respect to the one that has more?
    - He cannot feel unhappy if he is neither jealous nor envious. Envy and jealousy produce more unhappiness than misery.
75. What is the consistency of wealth in Jupiter?
    - Why does it matter to you?
76. Are there social inequalities?
    - Yes.
77. What are they founded in?
    - In the laws of society. Some are more advanced than others in perfection. The superior have a kind of authority over the others, like the father over the children.
78. Are people's faculties developed by education?
    - Yes.

79. Can the individual acquire enough perfection on Earth to deserve to immediately pass to Jupiter?
    - Yes, but people are submitted to imperfections on Earth in order to be related to their neighbors.
80. When a spirit leaves Earth and must reincarnate in Jupiter, does it remain errant for some time, until it finds the body to which it should unite?
    - Remains errant for some time until it frees itself from the Earthly imperfections.
81. Are there multiple religions?
    - No. All profess the good and all adore one only God.
82. Are there temples and a cult?
    - By temple there is the person's heart; by cult, the good one does.

Family Conversations From Beyond the Grave: Mehemet Ali, Former Pasha of Egypt

March 16th, 1858

1. What has provoked you to attend our appeal?
   - I came to instruct you.
2. Are you upset for having come to us and for having to answer our questions?
   - No. I actually wish to answer those questions intended to instruct you.
3. Which proofs can we have of your identity? How can we know that it is not another spirit who took your name?
   - What would be the advantage?
4. We know from experience that inferior spirits, many times, use hypothetical names. That is why we have addressed you with that question.
   - They also take the elements of proof. But the spirit who wears a mask also reveals itself by its own words.
5. Under which form and in which place are you among us?
   - Under that of Mehemet Ali. Near Ermance (the medium).

6. Would you like us to give you a special place?
    -   Yes. The empty chair.

    Note: there was an empty chair that nobody had noticed.

7. Do you have a clear memory of your last corporeal existence?
    -   It is not clear since death has left some anxiety and lack of clarity.
8. Are you happy?
    -   No. I am unfortunate.
9. Are you errant or reincarnated?
    -   Errant.
10. Do you remember what you were before the last existence on Earth?
    -   I was poor on Earth. I was the envy of Earthly greatnesses and was moved up to suffer.
11. If you can be reborn on Earth, which position will you preferably choose?
    -   The obscure: the duties are lesser.
12. What do you think now about the position you have lately occupied on Earth?
    -   Pure vanity! I wanted to command people. Did I know how to command myself?
13. It was said that your reason was altered for some time already. Was it true?
    -   No.
14. Public opinion appreciates what you have done for the Egyptian civilization and places you among the great princes. Does it make you happy?
    -   Why would I care? People's opinion is like the wind in the desert blowing the dust.
15. Are you satisfied that your descendants are following the same path you did? Do their efforts interest you?
    -   Yes, as their objective is a benefit of all.

16. However, you are accused of acts of great cruelty. Do you regret them now?
    - I atone for them.
17. Do you see those who you ordered to be massacred?
    - Yes.
18. Which feelings do they experience towards you?
    - Hatred and pity.
19. Since you left this life have you ever seen Sultan Mahmud again?
    - Yes. We run away from each other in vain.
20. Which mutual feeling do you experience?
    - Aversion.
21. What is your opinion about the penalties and rewards that await us after death?
    - The atonement is fair.
22. What was the greatest hurdle you had to overcome to continue to progress towards your spiritual development?
    - I reigned over slaves.
23. Do you think that if the people you governed were Christian it would have facilitated their advancement?
    - Yes. The Christian religion elevates the soul. Muhammad's religion only speaks to matter.
24. When alive, was your faith in the Muslim religion absolute?
    - No. I considered God greater.
25. What do you think now about that religion?
    - It does not form people.
26. In your opinion, had Muhammad a Divine mission?
    - Yes but he misinterpreted that.
27. How did he misinterpret that?
    - He wanted to reign.
28. What do you think about Jesus?
    - That he came from God.
29. In your opinion who did more for human happiness: Jesus or Muhammad?

- Why do you ask this? Which people did Muhammad regenerate? Christian religion was pure since leaving God's hands. Muhammad's religion is the work of a man.

30. Do you believe that one of these two religions is destined to disappear from Earth?
    - People always progresses. The best will remain.

31. What do you think about the polygamy in the Muslim religion?
    - It is one of the links to barbarism for those who profess it.

32. Do you believe that women slavery is in accordance with God's wishes?
    - No. Woman and man are the same since the spirit has no sex.

33. Some say that the Arabs can be conducted only by the rigor. Don't you think that treating them badly instead of submitting them can only make them brutal?
    - Yes. That is people's destiny. They are degraded when enslaved.

34. Can you go back in time and tell us, when Egypt was flourishing, what were the causes of the moral decadence?
    - The corruption of the customs.

35. It seems that you do not give much importance to the monuments which cover the soil of Egypt. We cannot understand such indifference from a prince who was a friend of progress.
    - Who cares about the past? The present would not replace it.

36. Can you explain yourself more clearly?
    - Yes. It was unnecessary to remind the oppressed Egyptian of a brilliant past, as he would not understand it. I showed disdain for something that seemed useless to me. Couldn't I be wrong?

37. Did the priests of the old Egypt know the Spiritist Doctrine?
    - It was theirs.

38. Did they receive manifestations?
    - Yes.

39. Did the manifestations received by the Egyptian priests have the same source as those received by Moses?
    - Yes. He was initiated by them.

40. Why then did the manifestations received by Moses were more powerful than those received by the priests?
    - Moses wanted to reveal them whereas the priests wanted to hide them.
41. Do you think that the doctrine of the Egyptian priests had some connection with that of the Indians?
    - Yes. Almost invisible ties interconnect all mother-religions. They proceed from the same source.
42. From those two religions, the Egyptian and the Indian, which one is the original?
    - They are sisters.
43. How can you who in life were so little educated on these subjects, respond with such a depth now?
    - Other existences taught me.
44. In the erratic state in which you are now, do you have complete knowledge of your previous existences?
    - Yes, except the last one.
45. Have you then lived in the times of the pharaohs?
    - Yes. I lived in the Egyptian land three times: as a priest, as a beggar, and as a prince.
46. Under which dynasty were you a priest?
    - It was long ago! The prince was your Sesostris.
47. Therefore it seems that you have not progressed since you still atone the errors of your last existence.
    - Yes but I progressed slowly. Would I be perfect just because I was a priest?
48. Is it because you were a priest over that time that you could speak to us with such inside knowledge about the old religion of the Egyptians?
    - Yes but I am not sufficiently perfect to know everything. Others can read the past like from an open book.
49. Can you explain to us the motive for the construction of the pyramids?
    - It is too late.

Note: It was almost eleven o'clock in the evening.

50. We shall not ask you anything else but this. We kindly ask you to answer.
    - No. It is too late. This question would bring others.
51. Can you do us a favor and respond on a different occasion?
    - I cannot commit to that.
52. Nevertheless we thank the benevolence with which you responded to the other questions.
    - It is fine. I will come back.

Mr. Home, Third Article

(see February and March issues)

To the best of our knowledge, Mr. Home has not made appear any other body parts besides the hands. It has been reported, however, that a general who had died in Crimea appeared to his widow, visible only to her. We have not been able to confirm the authenticity of that report, since Mr. Home was involved with this case. As such, we limit ourselves only to what we can prove.

Why hands, instead of feet or head? This is what we ignore, as does Mr. Home.

Questioned about that, the spirits answered that other mediums could make the whole body appear. By the way, this is not the most important aspect: if the hands show up the other parts of the body are not less important, as we shall have the opportunity to see below.

Generally, the appearance of the hand happens initially under the table cloth, by ripples which run over the whole surface. Then it shows on the edges of the cloth which is raised by the hand; at times it comes to rest on the cloth, at the center of the table. On other occasions it grabs an object and takes it under the cloth. This hand, visible to all, is neither airy nor translucent. It has the natural color and opacity; it shows an indefinite termination towards the fist. If someone touches it with precaution, confidence and without a hostile second intention, it offers the resistance, solidity and impression of a live hand; it produces a soft heat comparable to that of a pigeon which may have died about thirty minutes ago. It is not absolutely inert, as it acts, produces movements which are imposed to them or resists, strokes or grabs us. If, on the contrary, we abruptly and by surprise try to grab it, we only find the emptiness.

A visual witness told us the following fact that happened to him:

He held a hand-bell between his fingers; an invisible hand, in the beginning, and visible later, came to try to take it away; as it was unsuccessful, it tried to pull it to make it slip through the fingers. The traction effort was noticeable, as it would be the one of any human hand. Having tried to violently grab that hand, his hand only found air; on opening the fingers, the hand-bell remained suspended in the air, slowing going down to rest on the floor.

Sometimes there are multiple hands.

The same witness described the following fact to us:

Several people are sitting down around one of the folding dining tables. Some raps are heard; the table agitates, opens up by itself and through the crease of the table three hands show up: one of normal size, another very large and a third very hairy. They touch and poke each other, shake hands with those around the table and then dissolve.

In the house of one of our friends who had lost a child at an early age, a hand of a newly born baby shows up. Everyone can see and touch it. That child sits on her mom's lap who distinctly feels the impression of the whole body on her knees.

The hand frequently comes to rest on you. Then you see it and if not, it feels the pressure of the fingers. At times it strokes you; on other occasions it pinches you to the point of pain. In the presence of several people, Mr. Home felt that his fist was grabbed and the audience could see that his skin was stretched. An instant later, he felt someone biting him; the impression of the teeth remained for over an hour.

The hand that shows up can also write. Sometimes it stops at the center of the table, takes up a pencil and writes on a piece of paper previously prepared. Most of the time, however, it takes the paper under the table and returns it completely written. If the hand turns invisible the text seems to be produced by itself. Answers to multiple questions can be obtained in such a way.

Another not less notable kind of manifestation, explained by what we have just described, is that of the musical instruments which play by themselves. These are, in general, pianos or accordions. In such cases one can see the keyboard as well as the bellows moving. The hand that plays is sometimes visible, sometimes invisible. The aria that is played can be known and even requested. If the invisible artist is left alone, he produces harmonious tunes which resemble the smooth melody of a wind harp.

In the house of one of our members, where these phenomena were produced many times, the manifesting spirit was that of a young man who died some time ago, a friend of the family, who revealed an outstanding musical talent when alive. The nature of the arias he used to play left no doubt about his identity in all of those who knew him.

The most extraordinary fact, in such kind of manifestation, is not, in our opinion, the apparition. If it were always airy it would be compatible with the nature we attribute to the spirits. Well, nothing would oppose to the idea of having that kind of matter perceptible to our sight, by some sort of condensation, without losing its airy property. What is really strange is the solidification of that very matter, sufficiently resistant to leave a visible impression in our organs. In the next issue we will give an explanation about this singular phenomenon, according to the teachings of the spirits. Today we shall limit ourselves to the deduction of a consequence relatively to the spontaneous playing of musical instruments. In fact, since the eventual tangibility of that ethereal matter is an attested fact and, since the hand, visible or not, offers sufficient resistance to exert pressure over the solid bodies, it is not surprising that it can apply sufficient pressure to touch the keyboard of a musical instrument. Besides, not less positive facts demonstrate that the hand belongs to an intelligent being. It is not strange than the fact that such an intelligence manifest itself by the means of musical notes, since it can manifest by writing or drawing.

Once entering into such an order of ideas, the raps, the motion of the objects and all spiritist phenomena of the material type, are explained very naturally.

Varieties

Malice has no limits in some individuals. Slander is always a poison against anyone who rises above the crowd. Mr. Home's adversaries thought that ridicule was a very weak weapon: it should have turned against the respectable names that surround him with their protection. Since they could not make fun of him, they tried to denigrate him. They spread the rumor with the objective which we understand well – and the evil tongues repeat – that Mr. Home did not travel to Italy, as announced, but that he was in prison in Mazas, under grave accusations, which they use as anecdotes, to satisfy the enthusiasm of the lazy and friends of scandals.

We can assure that there is no truth in all those malicious machinations. We have before us several letters from Mr. Home, stamped from Pisa, Rome and Naples, where he currently is located. We can then prove our statements.

The spirits are correct when they say that the real demons are among people.

A newspaper states: "According to the *Gazette des Hopitaux*[18], at this very moment a group of 25 people were taken to the hospital of the "alienated" in Zurich, for losing their minds, thanks to the turning tables and the

---

18 Gazette of the Hospitals

rapping spirits". First, we question if it has been well established that all 25 alienated have lost their minds thanks to the rapping spirits, what is contestable, at least until authentic proofs are provided. Admitting that these strange phenomena have been able to negatively influence certain weak characters, we then ask if, on another hand, the fear of devil has not created more madness than the belief in the spirits. Well, considering that one cannot prevent the spirits from rapping, the danger is in the belief that all those who manifest are demons. Eliminating this idea, by showing the truth, there will no longer be any more fear than that of the fireflies. The idea that one is beset by the devil is perfectly cut to disturb reason.

Contrary to that we have different news from another newspaper which says: "There is a curious statistical document about the dismal consequences that follows the habit of intemperance and heavy drinking among the English.

Out of 100 individuals taken to the Hamwel hospitals of the effected individuals, 72 have mental disorders associated to drunkenness."

We have received numerous reports of very interesting facts from our members that we will promptly publish in our forthcoming issues, since lack of space does not allow us to do that in the current issue.

Allan Kardec[19]

---

19 In this issue there was no indication of the printing company

May, 1858

Theory of the Physical Manifestations - First Article

I t is easy to conceive the moral influence of the spirits and the relationship they may have with our soul or with the incarnate spirit. It is understandable that two beings of the same nature may communicate with each other through thought which is one of their attributes, without the support of the organs responsible for the oral communication. It is, however, more difficult to figure out the material effect that they produce, such as the raps, the motion of the solid bodies, the apparitions and, above all, the tangible apparitions.

Let us try to provide the explanation, according to the spirits themselves and according to the observation of the facts.

The idea that we have about the very nature of the spirits makes these phenomena, at first sight, incomprehensible. It is believed that the spirit is the complete absence of matter and as such it cannot act materially. This is, however, wrong.

When questioned about the fact of being immaterial, here is how the spirits responded: *"Immaterial is not exactly the term as the spirit is something; otherwise it would be nothing. It is material, if you like, but of such an ethereal matter that it is as if it did not exist to you."* Thus, the spirit is not an abstraction as thought by some; it is a being whose intimate nature escapes our gross senses.

The spirit constitutes the soul that is incarnated in the body. When it leaves the body, with death, it is not deprived from the whole covering. They all tell us that they preserve the shape they used to have when alive; in fact, when they show up to us it is in the form we knew them.

Let us closely observe them at the very moment they depart from life: they are in a state of perturbation, everything is confusing around them; they see their own body, whole or mutilated, depending on the type of death. On another hand, they see themselves and feel alive; something tells them that what they see is their body but they cannot understand how come they are now separated. Thus, the tie that connected them is not completely broken.

Once this first moment of perturbation dissipates, the body becomes an old shell to them from which they were stripped without notice, but are still capable of seeing themselves in their primitive form. Well, this is not a system: it is the result of observations carried out with several mediums.

We can now report what we were told about certain manifestations produced by Mr. Home and by other mediums of the same kind: apparitions of hands, which have all properties of live hands, that we touch, grab and that suddenly disappears.

What can we conclude about this? That the soul does not leave everything in the coffin: it takes something. Therefore, there should be two types of matter in us: a dense matter which forms the external covering and another faint and indestructible matter. Death is the destruction, or even better, the dissolution of the first one, which is left by the soul; the other one detaches and follows the soul, which then always continues to have a covering. That covering is what we call "perispirit". This subtle matter, so to speak, which was connected to all parts of the body during life, preserves its shape and form. That is how all spirits are seen and why they appear to us, bearing the same appearance as they were in life.

But such a faint matter does not have the tenacity neither the rigidity of the compact matter of the body: it is, if we can say so, flexible and expansive. This is why the assumed shape is not absolute, although based on the appearance of the body: it shapes up according to the spirit's will who gives it, as he wishes, this or that appearance, whereas the solid covering offers an impenetrable resistance. Disengaging from these compressing obstacles, the perispirit extends or contracts; it transforms and, in one word, allows all changes to take place, in accordance with the will of the spirit who acts upon it.

Observation proves — and we insist about the word observation, as our whole theory is a consequence of the studied facts — that subtle matter, which constitutes the second body of the spirit, only step by step disconnects from the body, rather than instantly. Thus, the ties which connect the soul to the body do not suddenly break with death. Well, the state of perturbation that we observe lasts the whole time in which the rupture of the ties takes place. It is only when that rupture is complete that the spirit recovers the entire freedom of its faculties and the clear consciousness of itself.

Experience still proves that the duration of that detachment varies according to the individuals. With some it takes three or four days, whereas with others it does not complete in less than several months. Therefore, the destruction of the body, and its putrid decomposition, is not sufficient to produce the separation. That is the reason why some spirits tell us: *I feel the worms corroding me.*

With some people the separation starts before death: these are the ones who in life elevated themselves by their thoughts and purity of feelings, above the material things. In those, death only finds weak links between the body and the soul that break almost instantly. The more materialized a person's life has been and the more absorbed in the pleasures and concerns of personality, the stronger those links. It seems that the faint matter identifies itself with the dense matter and that a molecular cohesion is established between them. That is why they only separate slowly and with difficulty.

In the first instants following death, when there is still a union between the body and the perispirit, this better preserves the impression of the corporeal form from which, so as to say, reflects all nuances and even all alterations. That is why an executed person would tell us a few days after his execution: *If you could see me you would see me with my head separated from the body.* A man who was murdered told us: *See the injury that was inflicted into my heart.* He thought we could see him.

Those considerations would conduct us to the examination of the interesting question regarding the sensation and sufferings of the spirits. We shall do that in another article so that here we can restrain ourselves to the discussion of the physical manifestations.

Let us thus imagine the spirit dressed by its semi-material covering (wrapping), or perispirit, having the same form or appearance which he had when alive. Some even use that expression to describe themselves; they say: *my appearance is in a given place.* Evidently these are the gods of the ancients. The matter of that covering is sufficiently faint to escape our sight in its natural state, but it is not completely invisible. To begin with we see it through the eyes of the soul, in the visions produced during the dreams. But this is not what we want to discuss. In this ethereal matter there can be a modification; the spirit itself can make it pass through a kind of condensation which makes it visible to the bodily eyes. This is what happens in the airy apparitions. The subtleness of that matter allows it to pass through solid bodies, which explains why those apparitions do not encounter obstacles and why so many times they disappear through the walls.

The condensation can reach the point of producing resistance and tangibility. It is the case of hands that we can see and touch. But that condensation – and this is the only word we can use to give an idea, although imperfect, of our thought – or even, that solidification of the ethereal matter is only temporary or accidental, since it is not its natural state. This is why, in a given moment, the tangible apparitions escape us like a shadow. Therefore, by the same mode that a body can present itself in the solid, liquid or gaseous state, according to its degree of condensation, also the ethereal matter of the perispirit may appear in the solid, airy visible or airy invisible state. Next we shall see how that modification takes place.

The apparent, tangible hand, offers a resistance: it exerts pressure, leaves impressions, executes traction on objects that we hold. That hand then has a force. Well, these facts, which are not hypotheses, may take us to the explanation of the physical manifestations.

We must notice, before anything, that this hand obeys an intelligence, as it acts spontaneously; it gives unequivocal signs of a will and obedience to a thought; it thus belongs to a whole being who only shows us that part of itself; the proof is the fact that it produces impressions with the invisible parts; the teeth leave marks on the skin and produce pain.

Among the multiple manifestations, one of the most interesting is, no doubt, the spontaneous playing of musical instruments. The pianos and accordions are, apparently, the favorite instruments. This phenomenon is naturally explained by the above. The hand that is capable of holding an object can also exert pressure on the keyboard and produce the sound. In fact, many times we saw the fingers in action and, when the hand is not seen, the movement of the keys is seen as the bellows of the accordion extend and contract. The keys can only be pressed by invisible hands which show intelligence, playing perfectly rhythmical arias rather than incoherent sounds.

Since that hand can stick its nails in our flesh, pinch us, take whatever we hold in our hands; since we see it grabbing and moving an object, by the same way we would do it, they can also hit us, lift or knock a table down, ring the bell, draw a curtain, and even invisibly slap us in the face.

Some will raise the question of how that hand, in the airy invisible state, can have the same strength as in the visible tangible state. Why not? Don't we see the air knocking buildings down, gas thrusting projectiles, electricity transmitting signals, the magnetic fluid lifting masses? Why should the ethereal matter of the perispirit be less powerful?

But we should not want to submit it to our laboratory experiences and to our algebraic equations. Particularly because we have taken the gases by term of comparison, let us not attribute identical properties nor compute its strength by the same way we do with the steam. So far it escapes all of our instruments. It is a new order of ideas, outside the competence of the exact Sciences. That is why those Sciences do not offer us with the necessary special aptitude to appreciate those ideas.

We provide this theory about the motion of the solid bodies under the influence of the spirits just to show the problem on all its aspects and to demonstrate that, without distancing too much from the ideas we received, it is possible to figure out the action of the spirits over the inert matter. There is, however, another one of the highest philosophical reach, given by the spirits themselves, which sheds an entirely new light onto this problem. It will be better understood once it has been read. In fact, it is useful to get to know all systems so that they can be compared.

The explanation about the changes in the ethereal substance of the perispirit still remains to be given; by which process the spirit operates and, as a consequence, the role of the mediums of physical influence in those phenomena; what happens to them under those circumstances; the cause and the nature of their faculties, etc.

This is what we shall discuss in the next article.

The Rapping
Spirit of Bergzabern
Part I

We had already heard about certain spiritist phenomena, which in 1852 caused enormous uproar around Speyer, in Bavaria. We even knew that a brochure had been published in German, containing an authentic report. After long and unsuccessful searches, one lady from Alsace, subscriber of our Review, showing great interest and perseverance, for which we are mostly grateful, was able to find and offer us one volume of that brochure.

We provide here its full translation, hoping that it may be read with great interest since it demonstrates once more that these kind of manifestations are from all times and places, considering that the ones given here occurred d when discussions about the spirits were only in the beginning.

FOREWORD

"For the last several months a singular event is part of all conversations in our city and its surroundings. We refer to the Rapper, as it is known, from the tailor Peter Sänger's house.

So far we have abstained from any report in our daily – Journal of Bergzabern – about the manifestations which since January 1st, 1852 have been taking place in that house. As they have, however, drawn the general attention, to the point of having the authorities requested Dr. Bentner to provide an explanation to the case, and Dr. Drupping from Speyer had even visited the place, in order to observe the facts, we can no longer avoid the duty of publishing them.

We would feel really embarrassed if the readers expected us to pronounce about the facts: we leave that task to those who, by the direction of their studies and their positions, are more equipped to judge, which they will do without difficulties, if they find out the origin of those phenomena.

As for us, we shall limit ourselves to reporting the facts, mainly of those which we have witnessed or heard from trustworthy persons. The readers may decide by themselves.

F. A. Blanck

Editor, Journal of Bergzabern

May 1852

On January 1ˢᵗ, this year, in Bergzabern, at the house where the family of Peter Sänger lived, in the room adjacent to the living room, a sound like that from a hammer was heard, in the beginning, as if muffled and coming from far away, then becoming progressively stronger and more distinct. Those knocks seemed to be happening on the wall, near the bed of his twelve year old daughter.

The noise was customarily heard between nine thirty and ten thirty. In the beginning the couple did not give it importance; however, as that singularity repeated every night, they thought it could be coming from the neighbor's house, where perhaps a trickster could be trying to have some fun by knocking on the wall. They soon realized that there was no one playing tricks. The floor of the house was broken apart and the bed was moved to the opposite side of the room: then, remarkable thing, the noise changed its place and was noticed every time the girl was asleep.

It was obvious that the girl somehow took part in the manifestation of that noise. After unsuccessful searches by the police, people started to think that the noise should be attributed to some sort of disease or some particularity in the anatomy of her body. However, nothing so far has confirmed such a hypothesis. It is still a mystery to the doctors.

The event progressed with time: the noise prolonged for over an hour and the raps vibrated with more intensity. The girl changed bed and bedroom, but the rapper manifested in the other room; under the bed, on the bed and on the wall. The knocks were not identical: sometimes stronger, sometimes weaker and isolated, and finally succeeded rapidly, following the rhythm of the military marches and dances.

The girl was already occupying the room for some time when it was noticed that, during her sleep, she would produce short and incoherent words. The words soon became more distinct and more intelligible; it seemed that the child spoke to another person over whom she had authority. Among the facts produced by the author of this brochure reports one that he witnessed himself:

The child was in bed, lying on her left side. She had just fallen asleep when the noises started and this is how she began to speak: *"You, you! Knock a march!"* And the rapper played something which resembled a Bavarian march. The rapper stopped when a command to stop was given by the girl. Then she ordered: *"Knock three, six, nine times"*. The rapper executed the orders. After giving a new order for 19 knocks, 20 were produced, which made the girl rebut: *"This is not right: it was 20 knocks."* This was followed by the count of 19 knocks. She then requested 30 knocks and 30 were heard. Then to the order of 100 knocks only 40 were counted, given the speed which they were produced. Once the 100th knock was heard the girl said: *"Well done! Now I want 110."* We could only count up to 50. After the last knock the sleepyhead said: *"It is not right. You only did 106"*. This was soon followed by another 4 knocks to complete the 110. Then she asked: "One thousand!" Only 15 knocks were heard. "Come on!" She said. The rapper still knocked 5 times and stopped.

Then those who were present had the idea of giving orders directly to the rapper, who executed them. He stopped on hearing the command: "Halt! Silence! Enough!" Then, on his own and without a command, he restarted to knock. One of the individuals present said in a low voice, in one corner of the room, that he would like to command only by his thought, and his wish was 6 knocks. Then the experimenter positioned himself near the bed and did not say a word. The six knocks were heard. Still through his thought 4 knocks were requested and heard. The same experiment was carried out by others, but not always successfully.

The girl soon woke up, stretched, pushed the bed sheets away and stood up.

Once asked about what had happened she said that she had seen a large, scary faced man by her bed, and that he would have squeezed her knees! She fell asleep again and the manifestations proceeded until eleven o'clock. Suddenly the rapper stopped, the girl regained her normal sleep, recognized by the regularity of her breathing, and nothing else was heard that night.

We observed the fact that the rapper obeyed the order to produce military marches. Several people acknowledged the accuracy that the Russian, Austrian and French marches were produced.

On February 25th, in her sleep, the girl said: "*Now you no longer want to knock. You want to scratch. Okay, let us see how you are going to do that.*" In fact, on the very next day, instead of knocks it was possible to hear something like scraping, coming from the bed, which still happens today. The knocks were mixed with the scratches, sometimes alternately sometimes simultaneously, so that on playing marches and dance rhythms, the scratches would spot the strong times and the knocks the weak ones. According to the requests, the time of the day or people's ages, they were indicated by dry knocks or scratches. With respect to people's ages sometimes there were mistakes, soon corrected in the second or third attempt, as long as someone said that the number was wrong. Sometimes, instead of indicating the requested age, the rapper would execute a march.

Day by day the child's language becomes clearer, during her sleep. What was, in the beginning, only words or rapid commands to the rapper, with time transformed into a meaningful conversation with her parents. Therefore, one day she would entertain a conversation with her older sister, speaking in a directive, lecture-like voice, saying that her sister should go to the Church's mass, pray every day and show submission and obedience to their parents. Later at night she returned to the subject. Her teachings had nothing to do with theology but simply had some of those notions that one learns in school.

Knocks and scratches were heard for about at least an hour before the conversations, not only during the girls' sleep, but even while she was awake. We saw her eating and drinking while the knocks and scratches were heard as we also heard orders given to the rapper, who executed them, while she was not sleeping.

On the evening of Saturday, March 6th, several people gathered at Mr. Sänger's house as the girl, who was wide awake, had predicted that the rapper would show up at nine o'clock.

At 9 o'clock sharp, four violent knocks were heard on the wall, scaring those around them. Soon and for the first time, the knocks happened in and around the wood of the bed. The bed was completely shaken. Those bangs took place on all sides of the bed, first in one place, then in another. Knocks and scratches alternated. Following the girl's and the participants' orders, the knocks were heard from the inside of the bed, or from the outside. Suddenly the bed was lifted, moving in different directions, while strong knocks were made. About five people unsuccessfully tried to return the bed to its original place; as they had given up the bed still swung for a few moments before returning to the original position. This event had already happened once before this public occurrence.

Every night the girl would give a kind of speech, which we shall succinctly comment.

First of all it is necessary to note that as soon as the girl lowered her head, she would immediately fall asleep and the knocks and scratches would start. She would moan and get agitated with the knocks and seemed to feel unwell. This did not happen with the scratches. When she was about to speak, she would lie down, belly up, showing a pale face, as was her hands and arms. She would wave her right hand and say: *"Come on! Come close to the bed and join your hands. I will talk about the Savior of the world."* Then, the knocks and scratches would go silent and everybody would respectfully listen to the speech of the sleeping girl.

She would speak slowly, in a very intelligible way, in pure German, a surprising fact as everybody knew that she was behind in school, which certainly was related to a problem with her eyes which caused great difficulty in her learning. Her speech was about Jesus' life and his actions, since he was twelve years old; his presence in the temple, among the Scribes; his miracles and benefits to humanity. Then she would describe his sufferings and sternly censored the Jews for having crucified him, despite his good deeds and blessings.

At the end the girl would say a passionate prayer to God, asking him to give her the *"grace to withstand the sufferings He had sent her with resignation, as He had chosen her to enter into communication with the spirit"*. She would say that she did not want to die yet as she was still a child and she did not want to go down to the dark grave. Finishing her prayers she would solemnly recite the *"pater noster"* and then say: *"Now you can come"*. The knocks and scratches would then immediately restart. She still spoke twice to the spirit and in each of them the rapper stopped. She would say a few words and add: *"Now you can go, in the name of God"*. She would then wake up.

During those lectures the girl's eyes remained tightly closed but her lips moved. Those closer to the bed could observe her gestures. Her voice was pure and harmonious. Once awaken, she was asked about what she had seen and what had happened. She said:

- G: It is the man who comes to see me.
- Q: Where is he?
- G: Close to my bed with the other persons.
- Q: Did you see the other persons?
- G: I saw everyone who was close to my bed.

It is easy to understand that such manifestations have found many skeptical. Some even thought that this story was a pure mystification. But her father was incapable of any buffoonery, particularly of the type that requires the professional skills of a conjurer. He enjoys the reputation of a serious and honest man.

In order to address the issue and stop the suspicion, the girl was taken to a different house. As soon as she arrived there the knocks and scratches were heard again. Besides, a few days earlier she had gone with her mom to Mrs. Klein's house, a widow who lived half a league away, in a village by the name of Capela. Since she was tired, she was offered to rest on a sofa when the same phenomenon immediately started. Several witnesses can attest to this fact.

Considering that the child showed a healthy appearance, she should then be taken by an illness which affected her nerves and involuntary muscles, in case the phenomenon could not be explained by the manifestations described above. Finally, we shall mention that a few weeks ago the girl was taken to Dr. Bentner with whom she stayed in order to have those phenomena more closely studied by the wise doctor. Since then the noises that had by now completely stopped in Mr. Sanger's house, were now happening in the house of Dr. Bentner.

These are the facts that happened, with all their authenticity. We deliver them to the public without passing any judgment. We hope that the people of Medicine soon provide a satisfactory explanation.

Blanck

CONSIDERATIONS ABOUT THE RAPPING SPIRIT OF BERGZABERN

It is easy to provide the explanation requested by the reporter who we have just mentioned: There is only one, the one given by the Spiritist Doctrine. These phenomena have nothing of extraordinary to people familiarized with those to whom the spirits have acquainted us. The role given to the imagination of some people is also known. Had the girl only had visions, no doubt the partisans of hallucination would have celebrated the fact. But in this case there were material effects of unequivocal nature with a large number of witnesses. It would be necessary to admit that everyone was hallucinated to the point of having heard what they actually did not and seen motions of things that were stationary. Well, this would be an even more extraordinary phenomenon. To the skeptical there is only one resource: denial. It is easier and exempts reason.

From the spiritist point of view it becomes evident that the manifesting spirit was inferior to that of the girl, as he obeyed her; he subordinated even to the audience who gave him orders. If we did not know, from the Spiritist Doctrine, that the rapping spirits are at the bottom of the spirits' scale, the event itself would be a proof to us. In fact one could not conceive an elevated spirit who, as our wise individuals and philosophers, would have fun on rapping marches and waltzes and, in one word, act like a jester or submit themselves to human caprices. He shows himself with the looks of a scary man, circumstance which only reinforces that opinion. In general, the moral state reflects on the covering. It is then demonstrated to us that the rapper of Bergzabern is an inferior spirit, from the spirits of levity class, who has manifested much like others have done so and still do in our days. But what was the purpose of the manifestations? The news does not mention evocation. Today, that we are more experienced on those things, one would not allow such a strange visitor in, had he not informed about his objectives. We can only make conjectures. It is true that he did nothing revealing evilness or ill intention, as the girl had not suffered any physical or moral damage. Only men could have shocked her moral, harming her imagination with ridicule tales. Luckily they did not.

Then, this spirit, however inferior he might be, was neither evil nor malevolent. It was only one of those many spirits who, many times and despite our will, surround us. He could have acted on his own or been instigated by elevated spirits, with the objective of awakening men's attention and convince them about the reality of a superior power, outside the corporeal world.

As for the child, it is certain that she was one of those mediums of physical influence, gifted by such a faculty, despite her will, and who are related to the other mediums as the natural somnambulists are to the magnetic somnambulists. Prudently guided by an experienced person in this new Science, that faculty could have produced even more extraordinary things, capable of shedding new light onto these phenomena, which are only considered extraordinary because they are not understood.

Pride

Moral dissertation dictated by St. Louis to Ms. Ermance Dufaux
(19th and 26th January, 1858)

I

An arrogant man had a few acres of good land. He was proud of the heavy ears of corn that covered his field as he looked with pity to the empty field of a humble peasant. This man used to get up at the crack of dawn, spend the whole day working the ungrateful soil, patiently collect the stones to clear the land, and till the earth to remove the weeds. Well, in his eyes, his hard work fertilized the field and he harvested the best corn.

However, the chaff still grew in the field of the arrogant man and choked the corn as the owner bragged about the purity of his land and looked with disdain to the silent efforts of the humble person.

This I tell you that pride is analogous to the chaff that smothers the good grain. The one among you who judges oneself better than one's brothers and brags about it is senseless. Wise is the one who works by oneself, like the simple person in one's field, showing no vanity for one's work.

II

There was a rich and powerful man who enjoyed the prince's favor. He lived in palaces and had several servants willing to serve his desires.

One day while hunting, having his pack of dogs surrounding a deer in the deepest forest, he saw a woodcutter carrying a sheaf of firewood. He called the man and said:

- Vile slave! How can you pass by without bowing before me? I am like the Lord: my voice decides between war and peace in the Councils, and the greatest of the kingdom bow in my presence. Know this that I am a wise among the wisest and powerful amongst the most powerful, great among the greatest and that my elevation is the works of my own hands.

- "Sir! – Replied the poor man – I was afraid that my humble greetings would sound offensive to you. I am a poor man having only my arms by property but I do not envy your deceitful greatness. I sleep my sleep and I am not afraid, like you, that the Lord's pleasure may knock me down into my obscurity.

Well, the prince was upset by his pride and arrogance. The most humiliated ones rose against him, who was knocked down from the pinnacle of his power, like a dry leaf swept away by the wind, from the summit of a mountain. But the humble one peacefully continued his tough work, not worrying about tomorrow.

III

Those who are arrogant, humble yourself, as the Lord's hand shall bend your pride to the dust!

Listen! You were born where destiny left you; you came weak and naked from your mother's womb, like the last man. How come you raise your nose higher than your brother's, you who were born to pain and death like the others?

Listen! Your richness and your greatness, vanities of vanities, will escape your hands when the great day comes, like the fickle waters of the torrent, evaporated by the sun. You will not take your richness beyond the lumber of your coffin and the titles engraved on your gravestone, empty words.

Listen! The gravedigger's dog will play with your bones, which will then mix with the beggar's; your dust will muddle up with his, since one day both shall be only dust. Then, when you see the beggar dressed in your glory, you will curse the gifts you were given and you shall cry your own pride.

Humble yourself, arrogant, as the Lord's hand shall bend your pride to the dust.

1. Why does St. Louis speak in parables?
   - The human spirit likes mystery. The teachings are better incorporated into our hearts when we search.
2. It seems that the teachings should be more direct these days, without resourcing to allegory.
   - You will find it in the developments. I want to be read and moral needs a disguise under the attractiveness of pleasure.

Moral Issues

QUESTIONS ADDRESSED TO ST. LOUIS

1. Out of two rich men, the first one was born into opulence and never experienced need; the second one owes his fortune to his own work. Both employ them exclusively to satisfy their personal interests. Who is the one mostly to blame?
   - The one who met suffering. He knows what suffering means.
2. The one who continuously accumulates, not doing any good to anybody, will he have an acceptable excuse in the idea of saving enough for their children?
   - It is a compromise with evil consciousness.
3. Out of two greedy persons, the first one deprives himself from the necessary, dying of deprivation over his treasure; the second one is only stingy with the others: he is excessive with himself. While he runs away before the first opportunity to help or of doing something useful, he does not see limits to his personal pleasures. He gets upset when a favor is asked; he wants to surrender to his caprices, which never end. Who is the one mostly to blame and which one will have the worst place in the spiritual world?
   - The one who enjoys. The other one has already been punished.

4. The person who has not usefully employed his fortune while alive finds any relief in doing good deeds after death, by the destination given to his fortune?

   - No. The good that someone does is worth its cost.

Eternal Halves

The text below is an excerpt from a letter of one of our subscribers.

"A few years ago I lost a good and virtuous wife and, despite the six children she left me with, I felt completely isolated, when I then heard about the spiritist manifestations. I was soon part of a group of good friends who would engage this subject every evening. I then learned, from the communications received, that the true life is not on Earth but in the spiritual world; that my Clemency was happy there, working, like others, for the happiness of those who she had met here."

"Well, there is a point about which I eagerly wish you can clarify."

"One evening I said to my Clemency: my dear friend, despite our love, as it happened, we did not always have the same opinion in many things during our life. Why then did we have to make so many reciprocal concessions in order to live a harmonious life?"

"She then answered:"

"My friend, we were good and honest; we lived together and we can say, in the best possible way on this Earth of trials but, *we were not our eternal halves*. Such unions are rare on Earth. Yet they can be found and do represent a great favor from God. Those who enjoy such happiness experience a delight that you ignore."

"Can you tell me if you see your eternal half?"

"- Yes, she said. He is a poor man living in Asia; we will be only able to unite in 175 years, according to the way you count."

"Will the union be on Earth or in another planet?"

"- On Earth! But, listen: I cannot describe well enough the happiness of those united in such a way. I will ask Heloise and Abelard to come to explain to you."

"Then, Sir, those happy creatures came to talk to us about such an unspeakable happiness."

"- Attending our will, they said, two don't do more than one. We travel through space; we enjoy everything; we love each other with an endless love, above which there is only God's love and that of the perfect beings. Your greatest joys are not worth one of our glances and our handshakes."

"The thought of the eternal halves pleases me. It seems that God, on creating humanity, made it double, and separating the two halves of the same soul, he said: Go through this world and look for incarnations. If you do good, the trip will be short and I will allow your union. On the contrary, centuries will pass before you can enjoy such happiness. Such is, as it seems to me, the primary cause of the instinctive movement that drags humanity towards happiness, the happiness which we do not understand and do not strive to understand."

"I eagerly wish, Sir, a clarification about that theory of the eternal halves, and would feel very happy if I had the explanation about this subject in one of the next issues..."

Questioned about the subject, Abelard and Heloise gave us the following answers:

1. Were the souls created as a pair?
    -   Had they been created as a pair, they would be imperfect as single.
2. Is it possible that two souls may unite in eternity, forming one whole?
    -   No.

3. You and your Heloise make, since the origin, two perfectly distinct souls?
   - Yes.
4. Still now are you two distinct souls?
   - Yes, but always united.
5. Are all people in the same condition?
   - It depends if they are more or less perfect.
6. Are all souls destined to unite one day to another soul?
   - Each spirit tends to look for another similar spirit. It is what you call sympathy.
7. In such union is there a condition of sex?
   - The souls have no sex.

As much to satisfy our correspondent as to our own instruction, we addressed the following questions to the spirit of St. Louis:

1. Are the souls, who must unite, predestined since their origin, to such a union and each one of us has, in any part of the Universe, their *half*, to which will fatally unite one day?
   - No. There is no fatal and particular union of two souls. There is the union of all spirits but at different degrees, according to the position they occupy, that is, according to the acquired perfection: the more perfect, the more united. It is from discord that all human evils originate; complete happiness results from concord.
2. How can we understand the word *half*, sometimes used by the spirits to designate sympathetic spirits?
   - The expression is inaccurate. If a spirit were the half of another, once separated they would be incomplete.
3. Once united, do two perfectly sympathetic spirits remain united throughout eternity or can they separate and unite to other spirits?
   - All spirits are united among themselves. I speak about those who achieved perfection. In the inferior spheres, when one

spirit elevates, they are no longer sympathetic to those they left.

4. Are two sympathetic spirits the complement of one another or is that sympathy the result of a perfect identity?

   - The sympathy that attracts one spirit to the other results from the perfect agreement of their instincts and inclinations. If one had to complement the other they would lose their identity.

5. The necessary identity to the perfect sympathy, would it only consist of the similarity of thoughts and feelings or also of uniformity of acquired knowledge?

   - In the equality of the degree of elevation.

6. The spirits who are not sympathetic today, can they be later?

   - Yes, they will all be. Thus, the spirit who is in an inferior sphere today will reach, by perfecting, the sphere where another one resides. Their union will happen more promptly if the more elevated spirit, hardly withstanding the trials of their choice, stays in the same state.

7. Can two spirits who are sympathetic no longer be?

   - Certainly if one of them is lazy.

Those answers perfectly resolve the question.

The theory of eternal halves is a figure relative to the union of two sympathetic spirits; it is an expression even used in the common language, referring to a couple, and that should not be taken literally. The spirits who have used them certainly do not belong to the highest order. The scope of their knowledge is necessarily limited. They have expressed their thoughts with the words they would have used in their corporeal life. It is then necessary to reject such an idea that two spirits, created one to the other, should one day unite in eternity, after a more or less lengthy separation.

Family Conversations From

Beyond the Grave: Mozart

One of our subscribers sent us the following two interviews with the spirit of Mozart. When and how they happened is unknown to us; we do not know neither the interviewer nor the medium; we are completely unaware of all of this. It is remarkable, however, the perfect agreement between the answers thus obtained and those given by other spirits about several principal points of the Doctrine, in completely different circumstances, relative to us or to other people, which we have duly transcribed in previous issues and in The Spirits' Book.

It is about such similarities that we draw our readers' attention, and they should then arrive to the conclusion that seems most adequate to them. Those who could still think that the answers to our questions are the result of our own personal opinion will see if, in this case, we were able to have any influence over their answers.

We congratulate those individuals who maintained these conversations by the mode in which the questions were framed. Despite certain faults that demonstrates the inexperience of the interviewers, the questions are generally formulated in order, with clarity and accuracy, and do not move away from the line of seriousness. This framework produce the necessary conditions required to obtain good communications.

FIRST CONVERSATION

1. In God's name, spirit of Mozart, are you here?
   - Yes.
2. Why are you Mozart and not another spirit?
   - You evoked me: then I came.
3. What is a medium?
   - The agent who links my spirit to yours.
4. What are the physiological and soul related changes that the medium unwittingly suffers in order to act as an intermediary?
   - His body feels nothing but his spirit, partially released from matter, is in communication with mine, bonding myself to him.
5. What happens at this very moment?
   - Nothing with the body; only part of his spirit is attracted to me; I make his hand act by the power my spirit exerts over it.
6. Thus, the medium enters into communication with individualities different from theirs?
   - Certainly. You too, without being a medium, you are in touch with me.
7. What are the elements that contribute to this phenomenon?
   - The attraction of the spirits, with the objective of instructing human beings; physical laws of electricity.
8. What are the indispensable conditions?
   - It is a faculty given by God.
9. What is the determining principle?
   - I cannot say.
10. Can you reveal the laws?
    - No, no, not for now. Later you will know everything.
11. In which positive terms one could announce the synthetic formula of such a wonderful phenomenon?
    - Unknown laws that you could not understand.

12. Could the medium communicate with the soul of a living person? In which conditions?
    - Easily, if the person is asleep[20].

13. How do you understand the word *soul*?
    - Divine spark.

14. And the word *spirit*?
    - Spirit and soul are one in the same thing.

15. As immortal spirit, has the soul consciousness of the instant of death, consciousness of itself or of the *self* immediately after death?
    - The soul knows nothing about the past and ignores the future, unless after the death of the body. Then the soul sees its past life and its last trials; chooses its new atonement on a new existence, as the forthcoming trials. Thus, no one should regret their sufferings on Earth, but withstand them with courage.

16. Is the soul disconnected from all elements after death, from all Earthly ties?
    - Not from all elements. The soul has a proper fluid, extracted from the atmosphere of its planet, showing the appearance of its last incarnation. The earthly ties are nothing to the soul.

17. Does the soul know where it came from and where it is going to?
    - The answer to question 15 above solves that.

18. Does the soul carry anything from Earth?
    - Nothing other than the memories of the good deeds, the regret for the faults and the desire to move to a better world.

19. Does the soul embrace, in a retrospective glimpse, its entire past life?
    - Yes, to serve its future life.

---

20 If a person who is alive were evoked in the waking state, he can fall asleep at the time of the evocation or, at least, suffer numbness and a suspension of the sensitive faculties. Many times, however, the evocation does not produce anything if it is not done, above all, with a serious and benevolent intention.

20. Does the soul perceive the objective of the Earthly life and its meaning; the importance of what is done here with respect to a future life?

    - Yes, the soul understands the need for depuration to get to the infinite; wishes to purify in order to achieve the blessed worlds. I am happy but I am not yet in the worlds from where one enjoys the vision of God.

21. Is there a hierarchy of spirits in the future life? What is the law?

    - Yes. It is the degree of depuration that characterizes it. Goodness and virtues are the titles of glory.

22. Is the intelligence that determines the ascending march, as a progressive power?

    - Mostly the virtues, by loving thy neighbor.

23. A hierarchy of spirits presumes a hierarchy of residences. Does it exist? How?

    - The intelligence, which is God's gift, is always the reward of the virtues of charity and love to the neighbor. The spirits inhabit different planets, according to their degree of perfection. They enjoy greater or lesser happiness on those planets.

24. What should we understand by superior spirits?

    - The purified spirits.

25. Is our planet Earth the first of those steps, the starting point, or have we come from an even inferior point?

    - There are two globes before yours, which is one of the least perfect.

26. In which world do you live? Are you happy there?

    - Jupiter. I enjoy a great calm there; I love everyone around me. There is no hatred.

27. If you have memory of your earthly life then you should remember the couple A… from Vienna. Have you seen them both after your death? In which world and under which condition?

    - I do not know where they are. I cannot tell you. One is happier than the other. Why do you ask me about them?

28. Due to one unique word, indicative of a capital fact of your life and which you could not have forgotten; can you provide a positive proof of that memory? I request that you tell me that word.
    - Love, appreciation.

SECOND CONVERSATION

The interviewer is no longer the same. By the nature of the conversation, it seems to be a musician, happy for meeting a master. After several questions that we found useless to reproduce, Mozart says:

1. Let us finish G... issues. I will talk to you. I will tell you what we understand by melody in our world. Why haven't you evoked me earlier? I would have answered.

2. What is melody?
    - To you, many times it is like a memory from a past life; your spirit remembers what he has seen in a better world. In Jupiter, where I live, there is melody everywhere: in the murmur of the waters, in the whisper of the leaves, in the song of the winds; the flowers mutter and sing; everything produces melodious sounds. Be good and reach that planet by your virtues. By singing God's music you have chosen well. Religious music helps in the elevation of the soul. How much would I like to inspire in you the desire to see this world where we are so happy! We are all very charitable here; everything is beautiful! Nature is so admirable! All things inspire in us the desire to be with God. Courage! Courage! Believe in my spiritist communication. It is really I here, with you. I enjoy the power of telling you what we experience. I wish I could inspire you enough to the love of good, so that you could become worthy of such a reward, which is nothing compared to the ones I seek!

3. Is our music the same in other worlds?
    - No. No music can give you an idea of what we have here. It is Divine! Oh happiness! Strive to deserve the enjoyment of

such harmonies; fight, have courage! We do not have instruments here: the plants and the birds are the members of the choir. The thought composes and the audience enjoys, without a material hearing, without the help of the word, and all that from an incommensurable distance. That is still more sublime in the superior worlds.

4. What is the life span of an incarnated spirit in another planet other than ours?

    -   Short in the inferior planets; longer in worlds like in the one I am lucky to be. In Jupiter the average is about three hundred to five hundred years.

5. Would there be great advantage on returning to live on Earth?

    -   No, unless we are on a mission since we then advance.

6. Shouldn't we be happier remaining as spirits?

    -   No, no! We would stay stationary. We ask for the reincarnation in order to progress towards God.

7. Is it the first time I am on Earth?

    -   No. But I cannot talk about your spiritual past.

8. Could I see you in dreams?

    -   If God allows so, I will take you to my residence in your dreams, of which you shall keep the memory.

9. Where are you here?

    -   Between you and your daughter. I see you. I have the appearance I had when alive.

10. Could I see you?

    -   Yes. Believe it and you shall see. If you had a greater faith we could tell you why. Your own profession is a link between us.

11. How did you come inside here?

    -   The spirit penetrates everything.

12. Are you still too far away from God?

    -   Oh! Yes!

13. Do you understand eternity better than us?

    -   Yes, yes. You cannot understand it in the body.

14. What do you understand by Universe? Was there a beginning and will there be an end?
    - According to your thoughts the Universe is your land. Senseless! The Universe did not have a beginning nor will it have an end. Understand that it is entirely God's work. The Universe is the infinite.
15. What should I do to calm down?
    - Do not worry so much about the body. Your spirit is perturbed. Resist to that tendency.
16. Which perturbation is this?
    - You fear death.
17. What should I do to not fear?
    - Believe in God. Above all, believe that God does not deprive the family from a useful father.
18. How can I reach such a state?
    - By the will.
19. Where should I find such a will?
    - Move your thoughts away from that by your work.
20. What should I do to improve my skills?
    - You can evoke me. I got the permission to inspire you.
21. When I am working?
    - Certainly! Whenever you wish to work I will be sometimes by your side.
22. You will hear my work (a musical piece from the interviewer)?
    - You are the first musician to evoke me. I come to you with pleasure and listen to your works.
23. How come you were not evoked?
    - I was evoked but not by musicians.
24. By whom?
    - By several ladies and amateurs in Marseille.
25. Why does the Ave Maria take me to tears?
    - Your spirit detaches, unites to mine and Pergolese's, who has inspired me that piece of work, but I forgot that part.

26. How could you forget the music that you composed?
    - The one I have here is so beautiful! How should I remember what was only material?
27. Do you see my mother?
    - She is incarnated on Earth.
28. In which body?
    - I cannot tell you anything about it.
29. How about my father?
    - He is errant, helping with the good deeds. He will make your mom progress. They will reincarnate together and will be happy.
30. Does he come to see me?
    - Many times. You owe him your charitable impulses.
31. Was it my mother who has asked to reincarnate?
    - Yes. She really wanted to reincarnate to initiate a new trial to be able to go to a superior world. She has already covered a huge step.
32. What do you mean by that?
    - She has resisted all temptations. Her life on Earth was sublime when compared to her past, which was of an inferior spirit. She has thus climbed several steps.
33. She had then chose a trial beyond her strength?
    - Yes, that is right.
34. When I see her in my dreams, is that her herself that I see?
    - Yes, yes.
35. Had Bichat been evoked on the very day of the inauguration of his statue, would he have responded? Was he there?
    - Yes, he was; and I was too.
36. Why were you there?
    - As several other spirits who appreciate the good and feel happy when you glorify those concerned with the sufferings of humanity.

37. Thank you Mozart. Good-bye.

  - Believe me; believe that I am here... I am happy... Believe that there are worlds above yours... Believe in God... Evoke me more frequently, in the company of other musicians. I will be happy to instruct you, contributing to your progress, helping you to elevate to God. Evoke me. Good-bye.

Family Conversations

From Beyond the Grave -

The Spirit And the Heirs

One of our subscribers, from The Hague, Holland, reports to us the following fact that took place with a group of friends who were carrying out spiritist manifestations. This demonstrates, he says, once more, and without possible denial, the existence of an intelligent and invisible element, acting individually and directly upon us.

"The spirits announce themselves by the movement of a heavy table and by rapping. We asked their names: these are the deceased Mr. and Mrs. G...., very wealthy during their existence. The husband, who actually had the fortune, did not have children, having disinherited his relatives in favor of his wife's relatives, since she died not long before him. Among the nine people present in this session, there were two of the disinherited persons, as well as the husband of one of them.

Mr. G... was always a poor man and a humble servant to his wife. After her death, her family moved into his house to take care of him. The will was written with a medical testimony, declaring that the moribund man was perfectly aware of his actions.

The husband of the disinherited lady, who we shall call Mr. R... spoke in the following terms: "How dare you show up here, after the scandalous will you left?" Later, exacerbating even further, he ended up swearing at them. The table was then raised and the lamp thrown at the man's head with impact. He then apologized, asking for the reason of their presence at that session.

We came to explain to you the reasons of our conduct. The answers were given by means of hits on specific letters of the alphabet. Knowing the ineptitude of the husband, Mr. R... abruptly asked him to leave, allowing his wife to speak, who he would then listen.

Then the spirit of Mrs. G... said that Mrs. R... and her sister were rich enough and could go without their part in the inheritance; that others were evil and others, in the end, should suffer that trial; that due to those reasons the fortune was more adequate to her own family. Mr. R... was not satisfied with the explanation and threw up his rage with scolding slander. Then the table was violently agitated, jumped, heavily stomped on the floor and once again the lamp was thrown at Mr. R... head.

The spirit calmed down and tried to persuade the others that after her death she was informed that a superior spirit had dictated the last will and testament. Mr. R... and the ladies, realizing the futility of arguing any further, forgave one another. Soon the table rose near Mr. R... and smoothly landed on his chest, as if embracing him. The two ladies received the same demonstration of appreciation. The table then presented a strong vibration. Once the understanding was established the spirit said she was sorry for the actual heir, saying that she would end up crazy anyway.

Still, Mr. R... kindly reprimanded her for not having done any good in life, when she was gifted by such a great fortune, adding that she was not missed by anybody. "Yes, said the spirit; there is a poor widow residing at …. street who sometimes thinks of me, as I have from time to time given her food, clothes and heat."

Since the spirit had not provided the name of the poor woman, one of those present looked for the indicated address. And what is still worthwhile noticing is the fact that after the death of Mrs. G..., the poor lady had changed address. The latest was the one indicated by the spirit."

Death of Louis XI –

Second Article

(From the manuscript dictated by Louis XI to Ms. Ermance Dufaux)

NOTE: We draw the readers' attention to the observations made about these remarkable communications in our latest March issue.

Not feeling strong enough to hear the word "death", I had many times recommended to my officers that they should only ask me "not to speak much" whenever they saw me in any danger, and I would then know the meaning of that signal.

When there was no hope, Olivier le Daim harshly said to me, in the presence of Francisco de Paula and Coitier: *Your majesty, it is our duty to tell you. Do not have any hope on this saint man, or on anybody else, as this is the end. Think of your conscience. There is no more remedy.*

Following those cruel words, a complete revolution took place inside me. I no longer felt like the same man and actually surprised myself. The past rapidly unveiled before my eyes and I saw things in a new perspective. Something strange happened to me. The steel like stare of Olivier le Daim's eyes seemed to question me. I responded with apparent calm, trying to avoid that cold and inquisitive look: *I hope God helps me. It is possible, perhaps, that I am not as bad as you think.*

I then dictated my last wishes and sent all of those who surrounded me to be near the young King. I was left alone, only having my confessor, Francisco de Paula, le Daim and Coitier with me. Francisco gave me a touching exhortation. It seemed that each of his words erased my vices and that nature would have reestablished its course. I felt relieved, starting to reestablish some hope in God's clemency.

I was given the last sacraments with a resigned and firm piety. I would repeat every time: "*Our good Lady of Embrun, my good Lady, help me!*" On Tuesday, August 30th I fell ill again. Everybody left me for dead. Olivier le Daim and Coitier, feeling the public execration, remained by my deathbed, since they had no alternative.

Soon I completely recovered consciousness. I raised, sat down on the bed and looked around. Nobody from my family was there. No friendly hand to hold mine at such a supreme moment, to lessen my agony in a final contact. At that very moment my children might be playing while their father was dying. Nobody thought that the guilty one could still count on an understanding heart. I tried to hear a muffled sobbing but I only heard the laughs of the two miserable ones, still by my side.

In one of the corners of the room I saw my favorite greyhound dog, dying of age. My heart accelerated in happiness as I still had a friend, a being that loved me.

I signaled with my hand. The old hunter dog dragged herself towards my bed, licking my agonizing hand. Olivier noticed the move; he suddenly stood up, cursing and hitting the unfortunate dog with a baton, to see her dead. At death, my only friend gave me a long and painful look.

Olivier violently pushed me back to bed. I let go of my body and delivered my guilty soul to God.

Varieties - The False Mr. Home

S ome time ago we read the following article in the papers from Lyon, which was also posted on the city walls: *"Mr. Home, the notable medium who had the honor of carrying out experiments before H.M. the Emperor, from Thursday April 1ˢᵗ, will be giving sessions of spiritualism in the great Lyon theater. He will produce apparitions, etc... Special seats will be available to doctors and scholars, so that those can certify that nothing has been prepared. The sessions will vary, containing acts of the notable clairvoyant Mrs. ..., very lucid somnambulist, who will reproduce all feelings, one by one, according to the desires of the spectators. Tickets cost 5 francs first class, 3 francs second class."*

Mr. Home's antagonist (some people say Hume) did not wish to miss the occasion of exposing him to ridicule. In their passionate intent of finding something to bite, they took this gross mystification with such an enthusiasm that it speaks against their balance and their respect towards the truth, because before throwing stones at others it is necessary to verify if those stones will not hit another target. But passion is blind, does not think and many times, on trying to damage others, it is wrong. "Look at this, they joyfully said, "this so much praised man, now reduced to play on stages, giving spectacles at a price per head!" And their papers giving credit to the fact, without investigation. Unfortunately to them, their happiness did not last long.

We were soon asked to provide enough information to unmask the fraud, which was not difficult, particularly thanks to the large number of people proficient in Spiritism in that city.

As soon as the theater director knew what was going on, he immediately addressed the following letter to the newspapers: *"Mr. Editor, I promptly inform you that the announced spectacle in the great theater, due on April 1ˢᵗ will no longer happen. I thought the theatre would be occupied by Mr. Home and not by Mr. Lambert Laroche, so called Hume. Those who have anticipated the acquisition of their tickets can come to the theater's box office in order to be duly reimbursed."*

On another hand, the cited Lambert Laroche, from Langres, once questioned about his identity, was obliged to answer in the terms that we reproduce in its entirety, as we do not want to be accused of having introduced the smallest alteration.

Text in very poor French[21], as indicated by the original at the end of this article (E.T)

"You have submitted several excerpts of your correspondence from Paris, indicating that Mr. Home who gives sessions in a given theater of the capital, is now traveling to Italy and cannot, as a consequence, be in Lyon. Sir I ignore 1. Knowledge of this Mr. Home, 2. I do not know what his skills are, 3. I had never had anything in common with this Mr. Home, 4. I have worked and still work with a pseudo name Hume, justifying this name by the local and foreign newspapers cuttings that I submit to you 5. I travel with two companions, my

---

21 The original text in French: "Vous m'avez soumis diverse extre de vos correspondance de Paris, desquelles il résulterez que un M. Home qui donne des séance dans quelque salon de la capítalle se trauve en ce moment en Itali et ne peut par conséquent se trauvair à Lyon. Monsieur ignore 1.º la connaissance de ce M. Home, 2.º je ne sait quell ais son talent 3.º je n'ais jamais rien vue de commun àveque ce M. Home, 4º jait tavaillez et tavaille sout mon nom de gaire qui est Hume et dont je vous justi par les article de journaux étrangers et français que je vous est soumis 5º je voyage à vecque deux sugais mon genre d'experriance consiste en spiritualisme au évocation vision, et en un mot reproduction des idais du spectateur par un sugais, ma cepécialité est d'opere par c'est procedere sur les personnes étrangere comme on la pue le voir dans les journaux je vien despagne et d'afrique. Seci M. le rédacteur vous démontre que je n'ais poin voulu prendre le nom de ce prétendu Home que vous dites en réputation, le min est sufisant connu par sagrande notoriété et par les expérience que je produi. Agreez M. le redacteur mes salutation empressait".

type of experience contains spiritualism or evocation, vision and in one word, reproduction of the ideas of the spectator, my specialty is to operate that type of process in people, as seen in the papers from Spain and Africa. With this my Editor, I demonstrate here that I never wanted to take the place of any supposed Mr. Home who you say has a reputation, mine is sufficiently known by its great notoriety and experience I have. Receive, Mr. Editor, my cordial greetings."

It is useless to say that Mr. Lambert Laroche left Lyon with his head up. He will certainly go to other places looking for fools to easily deceive. I wish to say one word still to express our sadness about the deplorable avidity with which certain creatures, who consider themselves serious, use anything that may serve their animosity. Spiritism is very much accredited today and should fear nothing from the buffooneries; it is not more disgraced by the charlatans than the medical science is by the witch doctors of the streets; it finds everywhere – but notably among the enlightened people – zealous and innumerous defenders who know how to face mockery. Far from harming it, the Lyon case only serves its propagation, attracting the attention of the indecisive to the reality. Who knows it was not even provoked by a superior power with that objective? Who can brag about probing Providence's wishes?

As for the systematic adversaries, they can laugh but not slander. A few years more and we will see who will have the final word. If it is logical to doubt about something unknown, it is always imprudent to falsely manifest against the new ideas that, sooner or later, may oppose a humiliating denial to our perspicacity. History is there to prove it. Those, in their pride, who show disdain to the adepts of the Spiritist Doctrine, would they be as superior as they judge themselves? These spirits that they try to ridicule recommend the good and forbid the evil, even against the enemies; they tell us that we lower ourselves by desiring the evil. Who is then the most elevated: the one who tries to do the evil thing or the one who has neither hatred nor resentment in their heart?

Not long ago Mr. Home returned to Paris but he will soon leave to Scotland and from there to St. Petersburg.

DEMONSTRATIONS IN THE HOSPITAL OF SAINTES

The newspaper *L'Independant de la Charente-Inférieure* reported, last March, the following fact that would have taken place in the Civil Hospital of the Saints22.

The most marvelous stories have been told in this town, for eight days, everyone talking about the singular noises that are heard, sometimes imitating a trotting horse, sometimes the walks of a dog or a cat. Bottles placed on top of the fireplace are moved to another place in the room. On a given morning pieces of ragged cloth were found contorted and full of knots, impossible to untie. A piece of paper was once left on top of the fireplace where one could read: "What do you want? What are you asking for?" Next morning there was an answer, written with unknown, indecipherable characters. Matches left on the table would disappear as with magic.

Finally, every object changes place and spreads about all corners of the room. Such sortileges only happen in the obscurity of the night. Once the light is on, it is all silence; once the light is off the noises restart immediately. It is a spirit who is friendly with the darkness. Several people, among them some clergy and retired military, lied down in that bewitched room, unable to explain or discover the origin of the sounds.

A hospital employee, a suspect of being the author of those jokes, has just been fired. Some say, however, that he not only was not the culprit but, on the contrary, was also many times the victim of those phenomena.

It seems that this story has started more than a month ago. For a long time nothing was said as everyone was suspicious of their own senses, afraid of being ridiculed. The comments appeared only a few days later.

OBSERVATION: We have not had time yet to verify the authenticity of the facts shown above. We publish them with the due reservations. Notice, however, that if they are invented, they are not less possible and have nothing of more extraordinary than many others of the same type that were duly attested.

---

22 "The independent of the inferior Clarent", title of a newspaper taken from the name of one of the French Departments, by the Garonne river banks. This river crosses the Angouleme region.

Parisian Society of Spiritist Studies

Founded in Paris, April 1ˢᵗ, 1858

And authorized by the order of the Mayor of Police, on the advice of S. Exc. the Minister of the Interior and Public Safety, dated April 13ᵗʰ, 1858

The universal reach, so as to say, which is daily achieved by the spiritist beliefs, was vividly missing the creation of a center for regular observations. Such blank has just been filled out. The Society, whose formation we have the pleasure to announce, exclusively formed by serious persons, free from prevention and animated by the sincere desire of enlightenment, has counted, among its associates and since the beginning, on eminent people by their knowledge and social positions. We are certain that the society is called upon to realize countless services towards the authentication of truth. Its organic law ensures a homogeneity without which there will be no possible vitality. It is based on the experiences of men and things and on the knowledge of the necessary conditions to the observations that are the object of its investigations. On coming to Paris, the foreigners who are interested in the Spiritist Doctrine will then find a center where they can visit to obtain information and where they will also be able to report their observations[23].

---

23 For information relatively to the Society send to Mr. Allan Kardec, rue Sainte-Anne, 59 from 3 to 5 pm; or to Mr. Ledoyen, book seller, Galery d'Orleans, 31, Palais-Royal.

June 1858

Theory of Physical Manifestations – Second article

II

We request the reader to refer to the first article that was published about the subject. Since this is a continuation of the first article, this one is likely not to be well understood if the reader had not read the first one.

As we said before, the explanations we gave about the physical manifestations are founded on the observation of the fact and its logical deduction: we concluded in accordance with what was seen. However, how do the changes in the ethereal matter occur in order to turn it tangible and perceptible?

For starters, let the spirits whom we have questioned about the subject respond, adding our own remarks later. The answers below were given by St. Louis and are in agreement with what we were told before by other spirits.

1. How can a spirit appear with the solidity of a living body?
   The spirit combines part of the universal fluid with part of the fluid that detaches from a medium with this capability. This fluid then takes the form desired by the spirit.

2. What is the nature of such fluid?
   - Fluid. That says all.
3. Is that fluid material?
   - Semi material.
4. Is that fluid what makes the perispirit?
   - Yes, it is the bond between the spirit and matter.
5. Is this fluid the one that gives life, the vital principle?
   - It is always that fluid. I said bond.
6. Is that fluid an emanation from the Divinity?
   - No.
7. Is it a creation of Divinity?
   - Yes. Everything is created except God.
8. Has the universal fluid a relationship with the electric fluid whose effects we know?
   - Yes, it is its element.
9. Is the ethereal substance between the planets the universal fluid in question?
   - It surrounds the globes. Nothing would live without the vital principle. If a man went up beyond the fluidic covering of the globes, he would perish as his fluidic covering would withdraw to join the mass. It is this fluid that animates you. It is what you breathe.
10. Is this fluid the same in all globes?
    - It is the same principle, more or less ethereal, according to the nature of the globes. Yours is one of the most materialized.
11. Since it is this fluid that makes the perispirit, there must be a kind of condensation that, up to a certain point, approximates it to matter.
    - Yes, up to a certain degree since it does not have their properties. It is more or less condensed, according to the worlds.
12. Is it the solidified spirit who raises the table?
    - This question will not take you to the point you desire yet. When a table moves under your hands, the spirit, evoked

by your spirit, takes from the universal fluid what is needed to animate the table with a factitious life. The spirits who produce such type of effects are always inferior and are not entirely separated from their fluid or perispirit. The table thus prepared by their will (of the rapping spirits) can be attracted and moved by the spirit, under the influence of their own fluid, detached by their will. When the mass that they are willing to lift is too heavy they call for help from other spirits, who are in their identical conditions. I believe I have explained myself with enough clarity to be understood.

13. Are the spirits that are called to help you, your inferiors?
    - They are almost always equals. They frequently come by themselves.

14. We understand that the superior spirits do not bother with things that are their inferior. But we ask if, considering that they are dematerialized, they would have the power to do it, in case they wished so.
    - They have the moral strength, as the others have the physical strength. When such strength is needed, they are served by those who have it. Haven't we told you that the inferior spirits serves them as you are by workers and servants?

15. Where does Mr. Home's special power come from?
    - From his own organization.

16. What is special about that?
    - The question is not accurate.

17. We asked if it is related to his physical or moral organization.
    - I said organization.

18. Among those present, is there someone who could have the same faculty as Mr. Home?
    - They have it in a certain degree. Wasn't it one of you who made the table move?

19. When someone makes an object move, is it always with the help of a strange spirit or such an action can be exclusively done by the medium?

    - Sometimes the spirit of the medium can act alone; however, in the majority of the occasions, it is helped by the evoked spirits. This is easy to recognize.

20. How come the spirits show up wearing the outfits that they wore on Earth?

    - They frequently have only that appearance. In fact, for how many phenomena among you there is still no solution? How come the wind, which is impalpable, pulls trees off and breaks them, trees that are made of solid matter?

21. What do you mean by saying that their garment is "only an appearance"?

    - Once you touch it, there is nothing there.

22. If we understood well what you have said, the vital principle resides in the universal fluid and from that the spirit extracts the semi-material covering that makes their perispirit. It is through this fluid that the spirit acts upon the inert matter. Is that correct?

    - Yes, that is correct, the fluid animates matter by a kind of factitious life; matter is animated by the animal life. The table that moves under your hands lives and suffers like the animal; once it is intelligent, it obeys by itself. It is not the spirit who drives it like the person does with a load. When the table lifts up it is not the spirit who does that; it is the animated table that obeys the intelligent spirit.

23. Since the universal fluid is the source of life, will it be, at the same time, the source of intelligence?

    - No. The fluid only animates matter.

This theory of the physical manifestations offers several points in common with the one we gave, although it differs in certain aspects. From one as from the other a capital point sticks out: the universal fluid, in which the principle of life resides, is the main agent of those manifestations and that agent receives the impulse from the spirit, incarnated or errant. That fluid, when condensed, forms the perispirit or the semi material covering of the spirit. When incarnated, the perispirit is united to matter; it is free when the spirit is errant (see note 6).

Thus, two issues are presented here: the apparition of the spirits and the motion imposed on the solid bodies.

As for the first we shall say that the etherealized matter of the perispirit escapes the perception of our organs; only the soul can see it, be it in dreams or in somnambulistic state or even being half asleep, in one word, whenever there is partial or total suspension of the senses' activities. When incarnated, the perispirit's substance is more or less intimately attached to the body's matter; more or less adherent, if we can say so. In some people there is a kind of emanation of that fluid, as a consequence of their organization, and it is this fact that properly constitutes the mediums of physical effects. This fluid, emanated from the body, combines with that which forms the semi material covering of the spirit, according to laws that are still unknown to us. A certain reaction results form that, a kind of molecular reaction that momentarily alters its properties, to the point of making it visible and, in certain cases, tangible. This effect may be produced with or without the support of the medium's own will and this is what differentiates the natural mediums from the facultative ones. The emission of the fluid may be more or less abundant: hence, the more or less potent mediums. The occurrence is not permanent, what explains the off and on behavior of that power. Finally, if we consider the degree of affinity between the medium's fluid and this or that spirit, it is understandable that their influence may be exerted on some but not on others.

What we have just said evidently applies also to the mediumistic power, with respect to the motion of solid bodies. We now need to know how such a motion may take place.

As from the questions above, the issue is presented under an entirely different aspect. When an object is placed in motion, either taken from someone' hands or thrown in the air, it is not the spirit who grabs, pushes or lifts it, as we would do with one hand. The spirit, so to speak, saturates the object with its fluid by the combination with the medium's and, momentarily vivified, the object acts as if it were a living being, with the difference that, not having its own will, it follows the will of the spirit. This willpower can be as much the willpower of the medium as the willpower of a strange spirit or both, acting in concert, as they can be or not be sympathetic. The sympathy or lack of it that may exist between the medium and the spirits who occupy the medium with these material effects explain why not everyone is equiped to provoke them.

Considering the vital fluid, somehow driven by the spirit, gives a factious and momentary life to the inert bodies, it stands to reason that the perispirit itself is nothing less than vital fluid. It also follows that, when incarnated, it is the spirit that gives life to the body by its perispirit. The perispirit remains attached to the body while the organism is alive. When the body is no longer alive, the perispirit leaves.

Now if instead of a table, one has a piece of wood carved and shaped as a statue, and, if we act upon it, we shall have a statue that moves from its original place and will respond by movements and by raps. In this situation, a statue is momentarily animated by an artificial life. How much light such a theory sheds on a large number of inexplicable phenomena! How many allegories and wonderful phenomena it explains! It is a whole philosophy.

The Rapping Spirit
of Bergzabern

Part II

We have extracted the following text from a new German brochure, published in 1853, by Mr. Blanck, editor of the Bergzabern newspaper, about the rapping spirit that we talked about in our May issue. These extraordinary phenomena reported in the brochure, whose authenticity could not be questioned, prove that we have nothing to envy America in that regard. The meticulous care used to report the facts in the report is noticeable. One would wish that the same attention and prudence would be used in all similar cases.

It is known these days that this kind of phenomena does not result from pathological states. On the contrary, they indicate an excessive sensibility of the persons in which they manifest, always easy to stimulate. A pathological state is not an efficient cause; it can, however, be its consequence. The experimentation mania has caused grave accidents more than once in similar cases, which would have been avoided had nature been allowed to operate its course. The necessary advices to such cases are found in our "Practical guide about the spiritist manifestations".

Let us follow Mr. Blanck's report.

"The readers of our first brochure entitled "The Rapping Spirits" saw that the manifestations of Filipina Sänger have an enigmatic and extraordinary character. We reported these wonderful facts since their initiation, up to the moment when the girl was taken to the general physician of the Canton. We will now examine what happened since then.

When the girl left Mr. Bentner's house and returned to her home, the rapping and scratching restarted at Mr. Sänger's house. Up until that moment and even after her complete cure, the manifestations were sharper and changed in nature[24]. In November 1852 the spirit started to whistle; then it was followed by the sound of a wheel barrel running on a dry and rusted axle but the most extraordinary from all that, no doubt, was the knocking down of the furniture in Filipina's bedroom, a chaos that lasted fifteen days.

A brief description of the place is necessary.

The bedroom is about eighteen feet long by eight feet wide, positioned across from the living room. The door connecting both rooms is located on the right-hand side. The girl's bed was placed on the right-hand side of her room. In the middle there was a shelved closet and in the corner, on the left-hand side, is Mr. Sänger's working table where there are two circular cavities covered by two lids.

In the afternoon, when the uproar started, Mrs. Sänger and her oldest daughter were sitting in the first room, by the table where they were peeling green beans. A spindle suddenly fell on their feet, thrown from the bedroom. They were really scared, knowing that there was nobody in the room besides Filipina, who was then deeply asleep. Also, the spindle was thrown from the left hand side, although it was placed on a shelf, on the right hand side of the small armoire.

Had it been thrown from the bed then the door would have intercepted it. It was thus evident that the girl had nothing to do with the incident. While the Sänger's family was still surprised with the occurrence,

---

24 We shall have the occasion to talk about the indisposition of the child. As after her cure the same effect was produced, we have an evident proof that they did not depend on her health condition.

something fell from the table onto the floor: it was a rag of cloth which was already in a bowl of water before the occurrence. The head of a pipe was sitting by the spindle, the other half resting on the table.

What makes things even more incomprehensible is the fact that the armoire's door, where the spindle was placed, was closed before it was thrown away. Also that the water in the bowl was not stirred and not even a droplet was found on the table. Suddenly the girl, still asleep, screams from the bed: "Dad! Leave! He shoots! Everyone out! He would shoot you too." They obeyed the order but as soon as they crossed the room the head of the pipe darted across the room like a bullet, but did not break. A ruler used by Filipina in School had the same fate. The father, mother and sister looked at each other in amazement. Then, while still considering the best decision to make, Mr. Sänger had his planer and a large wooden board thrown from the carpenter's stool to the next room. The two lids on his working table were in place but the objects they were covering were also thrown away. In the same evening, the pillows were thrown onto the top of the armoire and the bed coverlet at the door.

On another occasion they had a 6 lb. pressing iron left under the girl's bed sheets. It was soon thrown to the first room; the cord had been removed, found on a sofa in the bedroom.

We witnessed chairs located 3ft away from the bed being knocked down; tightly closed windows to be opened and all this just after we turned our back to enter into the living room. On another occasion two chairs were placed on the bed, without disarranging the bed sheets.

On October 7th the window had been hermetically closed with a white cloth hanging in front of it. As soon as we left the room it was violently and repeatedly stroked to the point of scaring away street's passersby. We ran to the bedroom. The window was open, the cloth thrown on the small armoire nearby, the bed sheets and pillow on the floor, the chairs upside down and the girl still in bed, just covered by her nightgown. For fourteen days Mrs. Sänger did nothing else but to make the bed.

A harmonica had once been left on a chair. Sounds were heard. The family impetuously entered the room to find the girl in bed, as always. The instrument was on the chair but no longer playing.

One evening Mr. Sänger, after leaving the girl's room, had the cushion of a chair thrown on his back. On other occasions it was a pair of old slippers, shoes which were under the bed or clogs which would move towards him.

Many times the candles on the table would be blown off.

The raps and scratches alternated with these demonstrations of the furniture. The bed seemed to dislocate by an invisible hand. After the command of: "Swing the bed" or "Lullaby the child", the bed would noisily swing in one direction then in the other; after the word "Stop!" the bed stopped. We witnessed four men sitting on the bed, unable to stop its motion, being lifted up along with the piece of furniture.

At the end of the fourteenth day, the furniture stopped moving; the manifestations were replaced by others.

On October 26th, among other people, Mr. Luís Soëhnée, who has a bachelor's degree in law, and Captain Simon, both from Wissembourg, were in the room, as well as Mr. Sievert, from Bergzabern.

At that moment Filipina Sänger was heavily asleep in a magnetic sleep[25]. Mr. Sievert showed her a paper wrap containing a bunch of hair just to see what she would do with it. She unwrapped it without uncovering the hair; she then applied the hair onto her closed eyelids; moved the hair away as to examine it at a distance and said: "Indeed I wanted to know what was inside this wrapping. It is the hair of a lady who I don't know... If she wants to come, be it... I cannot invite her since I don't know her".

She did not answer the questions framed by Mr. Sievert but, having placed the wrapping on her open hand, she moved and turned her hand and the wrapping would remain suspended. Then she held it by the tip of her index finger and for a long time she made hand drawn semi circles, saying: "Don't fall!" and the package remained on the tip of her finger.

---

25 A somnambulist from Paris had made contact with the young Filipina and, since then, she would spontaneously fall into a somnambulistic state. On those occasions notable facts took place which we shall report another time

Later on giving the command "Fall now!" it detached from her, without any movement of the hand which could determine the fall of the package. Turning to the wall she suddenly said: "Now I want to stick you to the wall". There she placed it where it stayed stuck for about 5 or 6 minutes, having she removed it after that time. A meticulous examination of the paper and the wall could not show any cause for the adherence. It is our duty to clarify that the room was perfectly illuminated which allowed the accurate verification of the above particularities.

The following evening other objects were given to her: keys, coins, cigarette cases, watches, golden and silver rings. All, without exception, remained suspended in her hand. It was noticed that the silver adhered more easily than the other substances as it was difficult to remove the coins from her hand, and such operation caused her some pain.

One of the most curious facts of that kind was the following: Saturday, November 11th, an officer who was present gives her his spade and belt, weighing about 4lb; everything remained suspended by the finger of the medium, swinging there for a long time. What is even not less singular is the fact that all those objects, irrespective of the material, remained suspended. Such a magnetic property was communicated to the persons susceptible to the transmission of the fluid by a simple contact of the hands. We had several examples of this activity.

A captain and horse rider from Zentner, then serving in Bergzabern's regiment, witnessed these phenomena and had the idea of placing a compass near the girl, in order to observe the variations. In the first attempt the needle deviated 15° but then it remained still, although the girl held it in one of her hands, stroking it with the other. That experience proved that such phenomena could not be explained by the action of the magnetic fluid or the fact that the magnetic attraction does not happen to all bodies.

When the little somnambulist prepared to initiate the session, she would habitually call all the persons present to the room. She would only say: "Come, Come!" or even "Give, give!"

Frequently she would only calm down when all, without exception, were by her bed-side. She would then request any object, with solicitude and impatience, and as soon as she had it the object would bond to her fingers. Usually there would be ten, twelve or more people present and each would offer her several objects. She would not allow any object to be taken from her during the sessions. She seemed to prefer the watches: she skillfully opened them, examined the movements, closed and placed them nearby, to examine something else. Finally she returned to each person what was given to her. She examined the objects with her eyes closed and was never mistaken with respect to the owner. If someone reached to get an object that was not his she would send that person away. How do you explain such a spotless and multiple distributions to such a large number of people? They tried to attempt the same thing by having the girl's eyes open, but that was in vain. Once the session had finished and the strangers left, the raps and scratches that were momentarily interrupted, restarted.

Add to this the fact that the girl did not want anybody by the foot of the bed, near the armoire, where the space between the furniture was of about one foot. Whenever someone was located there, she moved him away by her gestures. If they insisted she would show great inquietude and with imperative gestures would command them to leave the place. Once she warned the audience about never occupying such a forbidden place because, she said, she did not want something unfortunate to happen to someone. This was such a peremptory warning that nobody forgot after that warning.

Following the raps and scratches, a humming sound was added, comparable to the sound of a thick bass cord; something like a whistle mixed with that sound. If someone requested a march or a dance rhythm his request was answered: the invisible musician was very accommodating.

The strangers or someone in the household were individually identified and called by scratches. Everybody easily knew to whom the appeal was directed. Once the appeal was heard, the designated person responded with a "yes" indicating acknowledgement. As a tribute to that person, a piece of music was played sometimes provoking funny situations. If another person that was not the right person responded "yes", the rapper made that clear by the use of a "no", expressing his own way that nothing was to be said to that person at that point.

These facts happened on November 10th for the first time and have continued this day.

Here is how the rapping spirit used to designate the persons:

Several nights earlier it was noticed that once requested to do this or that the spirit responded with a dry knock or a prolonged scratch. As soon as the knock was heard the rapper started to execute the order according to the audience's request. On the other hand, when there was a scratch, he would not execute to the requests. Then a doctor had the idea of taking the first noise as a "yes" and the second as a "no" and since then that interpretation has always been confirmed. It was also noticed that with a sequence of scratches, with heavy or light intensity, the spirit demanded certain things from those who were around. From the observation and giving attention to the mode by which the noise was produced, it was possible to understand the intention of the rapper. Thus, for example, the old Mr. Sänger told us that in a given morning, still at dawn, he heard certain modulated sounds.

Although, in the beginning, he had not paid attention to them, he noticed that they would not stop while he was in bed, and by that, he realized the meaning of "Wake up!" This was how, step by step, everybody got familiarized with that kind of language and that by certain signs it was possible to know who the designated persons were.

It was the anniversary of the day on which the rapping spirit manifested for the first time: many changes had taken place in the general state of Filipina Sänger. The raps, scratches and humming sounds continued but a special scream was added which sometimes was similar to a goose, other times to a parrot or any other large bird. At the same time a kind of pecking sound was heard, similar to that of a wood pecker. Over this time, Filipina used to talk a lot during her sleep and, above all, she seemed worried about a bird, similar to a parrot, located at the foot of the bed, screaming and pecking on the wall. When we wanted to hear the parrot it would produce acute noises. Several questions were framed, having screams of the same kind by answers; some persons requested the word "kakatoes" to be pronounced and the word "kakatoes" was distinctly heard, as if pronounced by the bird itself. We shall remain quiet about less relevant facts and limit ourselves to the report of those incidents that are more important, with respect to the alterations that took place in the physical state of the girl.

Some time before Christmas the manifestations returned with more energy: the knocks and scratches became more violent and lasted longer. Filipina, more agitated than normal, many times requested not to sleep in her bed but in her parent's bed; she rolled on the bed vociferating: "I cannot stay here any longer; I will suffocate; they will stick me to the wall; help!" and calm would only reestablish when she was returned to her bed. As soon as she was placed back to her bed, heavy knocks were heard as coming from the attic, as if a carpenter were hamming the roof beams. Sometimes these hits were so strong that they would shake the whole house and people would feel the floor trembling under their feet. On other occasions, similar knocks happened on the walls near the bed. The questions were again and habitually answered by raps and scratches.

The following facts, not less curious, were produced several times:

When the noise was over with the girl resting on her little bed, we often saw her stretched-out hands joined, her eyes closed, her head moving from one side to the other as if something extraordinary was catching her attention. Then she made a lovely smile. It was as if she was talking to someone. She would extend her hands indicating that she was shaking the hands of friends and acquaintances. Later she would fall back in a beseeching position, always joining her hands, moving her head until her face would touch the bed sheets, then straightening up and weeping. She would then sigh, apparently praying with ardor. On such occasions her face would change: she would look pale, having an appearance of a 24 to 25 year old woman. Sometimes this would last for about half an hour, during which period she would only say: ah! ah! Raps, scratches, humming and screams would go silent until she woke up. Then the rapper would make him heard again, trying to play joyful arias so as to dissipate the tough impression left in the audience. The girl would look greatly abated on waking up; she could only raise her arms; the objects which were shown to her could no longer remain suspended by her fingers.

She was interrogated many times by those wishing to understand what had just happened. It was only after insistent requests that she then decided to say that she had seen Christ crucified at Golgotha. The pain of the saint women at the foot of the cross and the crucifixion had produced an indescribable impression on her.

She had also seen a large number of women and virgins dressed in black, as well as little ladies wearing white dresses, following a procession through the streets of a beautiful town and, finally, that she saw herself transported to a large church where she watched a funeral.

Soon after all that Filipina Sänger's health changed to the point of causing concern. Being up and lucid, she would wander about and daydream. She would not recognize her parents, neither her sister nor any other person. She them became deaf for a period of fifteen days.

We cannot silence about what happened during this long period.

Filipina's deafness manifested between noon and three o'clock, having she declared herself that she would become deaf and ill for some time. At times she would recover her hearing for about half an hour, which was a remarkable fact that made her happy. She predicted the moment at which she would go deaf and when she would recover her hearing. One day, as on other occasions, she announced that she would start hearing again at 8:30 pm and that it would last for half an hour. In fact, at the predicted time, she heard again and it lasted until nine o'clock.

During her periods of deafness her looks changed: her face adopted an expression of stupidity, which she lost as soon as her hearing returned to normal. Nothing would then impress her. She would stay seated, staring at the audience without recognizing them. She could not understand anybody but by signs, which she would not respond to, limiting herself to fixate her eyes on the person who was talking to her. There was a time when she grabbed one person by the arm asking while pulling him: "Who are you?" She would remain in such a condition sometimes over one and a half hours, kind of immobilized in bed. She would stare at a given point then roll her eyes from right to left and stop them half open, staring at a fix point. Her whole sensitivity seemed impaired: her heart beat was hardly noticed, showing no reaction to a torch light directed to her eyes. She seemed dead.

Once, lying down and deaf, it happened that she requested a board and a piece of chalk. She then wrote: "At eleven o'clock I will say something but I demand that everybody be calm and quiet". After those words she added five signs resembling Latin writing but none of those in the room could decipher it. Someone wrote on the board that nobody understood those signs. She responded back in writing: "It is not that you cannot read!" And, further below: "It is not German. It is a foreign language". Then she turned the board and wrote on its back: "Francisca (her elder sister) will seat at the table and write what I shall dictate". Five signs similar to the previous ones followed that and the board was returned to the audience. When noticing that the signs were not understood yet she asked for the board back and wrote: "Those are particular orders".

Just before eleven o'clock she said: "Stay calm. May all be seated and pay attention!" then at eleven o'clock she fell into a magnetic sleep as usual. A few moments later she started talking for about half an hour, uninterruptedly. Among other things she declared that during the course of that year there would be facts which nobody would understand and that all attempts to explain them would be fruitless.

The pandemonium of the furniture renewed a few times during Ms. Sänger's deafness, like the inexplicable opening of the windows and the table lamp turned off. One evening two caps that were hanging in the bedroom were thrown on the table of the other room, hitting a cup and spilling the milk on the floor. The pounding on the bed was so violent that it was displaced from its original position; on other occasions the bed was noisily disassembled but the raps were not heard.

Despite the fact that the events were verified by more than one hundred witnesses who attested that the girl remained with her arms extended under the blankets during the occurrence of the phenomena, there were still skeptical people who attributed such events to a girl's prank who, in their opinion, rapped with her legs or her hands; Captain Zentner then envisaged a way of convincing the skeptical. He sent for two thick blankets from the barracks and placed one on top of the other so that both involved the bed sheets and the mattress; the blankets were very shaggy, being impossible to produce any noise on them by simple friction. Wearing a simple t-shirt and a nightgown, Filipina was placed under the blankets so that once she was covered the raps and scratches started as before, first on the bed, then on the neighboring armoire, according to what the rapper wished to express.

It frequently happens that when someone hums the sound of an aria, the rapper follows that rhythm with sounds that seem to come from two, three or even four instruments: the sounds of scratching, knocking, whistling and grunting are simultaneously heard, according to the rhythm of the chosen music. The rapper also frequently asks the audience to sing a song. He designates the person by the process we already know and when the person understands that he refers to him or her they then consult the spirit, regarding the desired song. The answer is given by "yes" or "no". When the chosen aria is sung it is then perfectly followed by the hums and whistles. After the execution of a happy song the spirit frequently requested the song *"Great God we praise you"* or the *Napoleon I* song. When asked to play this song or any other on his own, he executed them from start to finish.

The events were thus happening at the Sänger's house, in day light as well as at night, with the girl up or asleep, until March 4th 1853, when the manifestations initiated a new phase. This day was marked by a fact even more extraordinary than the preceding ones."

(To be continued in the next issue)

OBSERVATION: The readers will kindly forgive the extension given to these curious details. We thought, however, that the continuation will be read with even more interest. We want to reinforce that these facts do not come from overseas whose distance is an argument to the skeptical, despite everything else. They are not even from beyond the Rhine as they happened near our borders, almost under our eyes, only six years ago.

Filipina Sänger, as seen, was a very complex natural medium. Besides the influence she exerted on the well known phenomena of noises and motions of objects, she was an ecstatic somnambulist. She spoke with the incorporeal beings that she saw; at the same time she saw the audience and talked to them, not always responding back, which proves that at certain times she was isolated. For those who know the effect of emancipation of the soul, the visions that we have described have nothing that cannot be explained.

It is likely that during those moments of ecstasy the girl's spirit was transported to a distant place, where she watched, perhaps keeping the memory, of a religious ceremony. The memory she maintained on waking up was amazing but the fact is not remarkable on its own. It is noticeable, by the way, that the memory was fuzzy, requiring great insistence to provoke it.

If we carefully observe what happened during her deafness we shall recognize, without difficulty, a cataleptic state. As the deafness was only temporary, it is evident that no alteration was caused into her respective organs. The same happened to the obliteration of her mental faculties, which had nothing of pathological, once it all returned to normal at some point in time. This kind of apparent stupidity was due to a more complete detachment of the soul, whose excursions were undertaken with more freedom, leaving the senses with no more than the organic life.

Just imagine the disastrous effect produced by a therapeutic treatment under such conditions! Phenomena of the same kind may be produced at any time. In such cases we cannot recommend anything but circumspection. An act of imprudence may compromise the health and even the own life of the subject.

Laziness

Moral dissertation dictated by St. Louis to Ms. Ermance Dufaux
(May 5th, 1858)

I

A man left very early in the morning, going to the market place to hire workers. Well, there he saw two common men sitting down with their arms crossed. He then approached one and said: "What are you doing?" The man responded: "I have no work." The one who was looking for workers then said: "Take your tool and come to my field, by the side of the mountain, where the southern wind blows; you will cut the heathers and rotate the soil until it gets dark. The task is tough but you shall earn a good salary." The man of the people took his hoe onto his shoulder, thankful for all that, with all his heart.

Since hearing this, the other worker stood up and said, while approaching the owner: "Sir, let me go and also work in the field." Having asked both men to follow him, he marched ahead leading the way. Later, arriving at the foothill, he split the work in two and left.

As soon as the owner left, the last worker to be hired set the bushes on fire in his assigned spot on the land, turning the soil with his hoe. The sweat poured from his face under the scorching sun. The other worker imitated him, moaning in the beginning, but soon stopping, sticking the hoe on the ground, sitting by his fellow's side, watching him.

Sometime during the afternoon, the owner arrives to examine the work. Calling the hard worker he congratulated him saying: "You worked well. Here is your payment." He then sent him off, giving him a silver coin. The other man approached, demanding his payment, but then the owner said: "Lazy man, my bread will not feed your hunger as you left untouched the piece of land I entrusted you. It is not fair that the one who did nothing be paid as the one who worked well."

And then he left, not giving the man anything.

II

I tell you that neither the strength nor the intelligence of the spirit was given to man to spend his days in idleness, but to be useful to his neighbors. Well, the one whose hands are empty and the idle spirit shall be punished, having to restart his job.

Truly I tell you that when his time comes his life will be put aside as something useless. Understand this as a comparison. Who among you, having a fruitless tree in the orchard, will not tell the servant: "Take that tree down and throw it into the fire, for its branches are sterile?"

Well, as the tree will be cut down for its unfruitfulness, also the life of the lazy one will be thrown in the garbage for been sterile as for the good deeds.

Family Conversations From Beyond the Grave: Mr. Morrison, Monomaniac

Last March an English newspaper published the following story with respect to Mr. Morrison, who has died recently, leaving behind a fortune of one hundred million francs. According to the paper he was held captive of a singular obsession over the last two years of his life. He thought himself reduced to extreme poverty, having to endure manual work to earn his daily bread. Family and friends alike had acknowledged the uselessness of trying to bring him back to his senses. His conviction was this: he was poor, had not even a cent left and had to work in order to survive. Every morning he was given a hoe and sent to work in his own gardens. Later he was sought to receive his modest daily payment, which he received with pleasure. His spirit would be in peace and his mania satisfied. Had they bothered him and he would have become a really upset man.

1. We request the Almighty for the permission to communicate with the spirit of Mr. Morrison, who recently died in England, leaving a considerable fortune.
   - He is here.

2. Do you remember the state you were in over the last two years of your existence?
   - It is always the same.
3. Has your spirit resented the aberration of the faculties during your life, after your death?
   - Yes.

     St. Louis complements the answer by spontaneously saying: "Detached from the body, the spirit feels, for some time, the compression of the bonds."
4. Thus your spirit did not recover immediately its faculties in their plenitude, after death?
   - No.
5. Where are you now?
   - Behind Ermance.
6. Are you happy or unhappy?
   - Something is missing.... I don't know what... I search... Yes, I suffer.
7. Why do you suffer?
   - He suffers for the good deeds he did not do. (St. Louis' answer)
8. Why the mania of judging yourself poor when in reality you had such a great fortune?
   - I was. In reality rich is the one who has no needs.
9. Where did you take the idea from that you had to work to survive?
   - I was crazy and still am.
10. How have you come to such a crazy state?
    - Why does it matter? I had chosen such atonement.
11. What is the origin of your fortune?
    - Why is it important to you?
12. However, wasn't your invention supposed to alleviate humanity?
    - And make me rich.
13. How did you employ your fortune when you were perfectly rational?
    - With nothing. I believe I enjoyed it.

14. Why would God give you fortune since you would not make it useful to others?
    - I had chosen the trial.

15. The one who enjoys a fortune acquired by his work is not more excused to be attached to it than the other one who was born in opulence and never experienced necessity?
    - Less.
    - St Louis complements: "That one knows the suffering which he does not alleviate."

16. Do you remember the existence preceding the one you have just left?
    - Yes.

17. What were you then?
    - A worker.

18. You told us that you are unhappy. Do you see an end to the suffering?
    - No.
    - St. Louis adds: "It is too early."

19. That depends on whom?
    - On me. That is what I was told by the one who is here.

20. Do you know the one who is here?
    - You call him Louis.

21. Do you know what he was in France of the XIII century?
    - No. I only know him through you. I am thankful for what he has taught me.

22. Do you believe in another corporeal existence?
    - Yes.

23. If you have to be reborn in the corporeal life, on whom shall your future social position depend?
    - On me, I suppose. I have chosen so many times that this can only depend on me.
    - OBSERVATION: The words "chosen so many times" are characteristic. His present state proves that, despite the numerous existences, he has not progressed much and that for him it is always a restart.

24. Which social position would you choose if you could restart?
    - Low. Progress is safer. One is only in charge of oneself.
25. (To St. Louis) Wouldn't there be a feeling of selfishness in the choice of a humble position, where one only carries the burden of oneself?
    - Nowhere one has the burden of only oneself. The human being responds for all those who surround him and not only for those whose education was entrusted to him, but also for the others. The example does everything wrong.
26. (To Morrison) We thank you for your kind answers and pray that God will give you the strength to endure your trials.
    - You helped me. I learned.

OBSERVATION: The state of the spirit is easily recognized from the answers above. They are short and when not monosyllables they have something of somber and vague. A melancholic mad man would not speak differently. That persistence on the aberration of the ideas is a notable fact but which is not constant, or sometimes presents a completely diverse character. We will have the occasion of giving several other examples where the different forms of madness are studied.

Family Conversations From Beyond the Grave: The Suicide of the Samaritan Baths

The newspapers have recently published the following fact:

"Yesterday (April 7th, 1858) around 7 pm, a man about fifty years old, decently dressed, showed up at the Samaritan house, asking for a bath. A servant, worried about the customer's silence for more than two hours, decided to enter the bathroom to make sure that he was okay. He then witnessed a horrific spectacle: the unfortunate man had cut his own throat with a clasp-knife, the bath water tinted by his blood. His identity could not be established and his body was transported to the morgue."

We thought we could have a useful lesson for our own instruction on talking to the spirit of that man. We then evoked him on April 13th, just six days after his death.

1. I ask the Almighty God to give the permission to the spirit of the person who committed suicide on April 7th, 1858, in the Samaritan baths, to communicate with us.
   - Wait…. (after some time): Here he is.

OBSERVATION: In order to understand this answer it is necessary to know that in all regular sessions there is a familiar spirit, of the medium or of the family, who is always present, without the need to call him. It is him who sends for the evoked ones and, according to his more or less elevated condition, serves as a messenger or gives orders to spirits who are their inferior. When our meetings have Mrs. Ermance Dufaux as the interpreter it is always the spirit of St. Louis who voluntarily takes on that task. It was him who gave the answer above.

2. Where are you now?
   - I don't know... Tell me where I am.
3. At *Rue Valois 35 (Palais-Royal)* in a meeting of persons who occupy with spiritist studies and that are benevolent with you.
   - Tell me if I am still alive... I suffocate in the coffin.
4. Who invited you to come to us?
   - I feel relieved.
5. What made you commit suicide?
   - Am I alive? ... No! I am in my body... You don't know how much I suffer! ... I suffocate! ... May a compassionate hand come to show me the end!

OBSERVATION: His soul, although separated from his body, is still completely embedded by what we could call the maelstrom of the corporeal matter; the earthly ideas still vivid. He does not believe that he is dead.

6. Why haven't you left any identification?
   - I am abandoned. I fled the suffering to find torture.
7. You still have the same motives to remain incognito?
   - Yes, don't stick a hot spear in a bleeding wound.
8. Can you tell us your name, age, profession and address?
   - Not at all. No! ...

9. Did you have a family, a wife, and children?
   - I was abandoned. Nobody loved me.
10. What have you done for not being loved by anybody?
    - How many like me! ... A man can be abandoned at the heart of his own family when no one loves him.
11. Have you experienced any hesitation to commit suicide?
    - I was thirsty of death... I longed for the rest.
12. How come the idea of the future did not make you renounce that plan?
    - I no longer believed in the future; I was hopeless. Future is hope.
13. Which reflections you made by feeling the extinction of life?
    - I did not make any; I felt... But life did not extinguish... my soul is bonded to the body... I did not die... However, I feel the worms devouring me.
14. Which feeling did you experience once death was complete?
    - Is it complete?
15. Was it painful the moment when life extinguished?
    - Less painful than later. Then, only the body suffered.

St. Louis continued.

- A: The spirit unloaded a burden that oppressed him. He felt the ecstasy of the pain.
- Q to St. Louis: Is this state what always follows suicide?
- A: Yes. The spirit of the person who commits suicide remains attached to the body until the end of his life. Natural death is the weakening of life. Suicide suddenly interrupts it.
- Q: Will this state be the same in every accidental death which abbreviates the duration of the natural life, irrespective of one's will?
- A: No. What do you understand by suicide? The spirit can only be blamed for his actions.

OBSERVATION: We had prepared a series of questions which we proposed to address to the spirit of that man, about his new existence. Based on his answers they lost their meaning. It was evident to us that he had no consciousness of the situation. The only thing he could describe to us was his suffering.

Such doubt about death is very common among the recently dead and mainly on those who, during life, did not elevate their souls above matter. At first sight it is a bizarre phenomenon, but explained very naturally.

If we ask a person taken for the first time to somnambulism if they are asleep the answer is almost always no, and the answer is logic. It is the questioner who badly formulates the question, using an improper term. The idea of sleep, in the common language, is connected to the suspension of all sensitive faculties. Well, the somnambulist, who thinks and sees; that is aware of his moral freedom, doesn't believe that he sleeps and, with effect, he doesn't sleep in the conventional use of the term. That is why he responds that he is not asleep, until he familiarizes with this new way of understanding things. The same happens with a man that has just died. For him death was the "nothing". Well, as it happens to the somnambulist, he sees, feels and speaks. Thus, for him life continues, and he says so, until he has acquired consciousness of his new state.

Confessions of Louis

XI - Third article

Extracted from the story of his life, dictated by himself to Ms. Ermance Dufaux (see March and May issues)
The poisoning of the Duke of Guyenne

(…) then I engaged with Guyenne. Odet d'Aidies, the Lord of Lescun, who had quarreled with me, conducted the war preparations with a wonderful vivacity. It was with great effort that he fed the warlike ardor of my brother Charles, the Duke of Guyenne. He had to combat a fearful adversary in my brother's spirit: Lady Thouars, Charles' lover.

That woman was not trying anything else but to take advantage of the power she exerted over the young Duke, aiming at deviating him from the war as she did not ignore that the war's objective was her lover's wedding. Her secret enemies had affected her by praising the beauty and brilliant qualities of the bride. This was enough to persuade her that her disgrace was certain if that princess married the Duke of Guyenne. Sure about my brother's passion, she resorted to tears, prayers and to every extravagance of a woman lost in such a situation. The coward Charles gave in and communicated his new resolutions to Lescun. Lescun immediately communicated the Duke of Brittany and others also interested: they became alarmed and sent representations to my brother. That did nothing but deepen him once again in his irresolution.

The favorite, however, and not without much difficulty, was able to dissuade him of the war and marriage again. Since then all princes decided the death of the favorite.

Afraid that my brother would attribute her death to Lescun, whose antipathy towards Mrs. Thouars was known to him, they decided to conquer Jean Faure Duversois, a Benedictine monk, my brother's confessor and Abbot of Saint-Jean d'Angély. This man was one of the greatest enthusiasts of Mrs. Thouars and nobody ignored his hatred for Lescun, whose political influence he envied.

It was unlikely that my brother would attribute to him the death of his lover since that priest was one of her favorites who deserved the greatest trust. Since his thirst for greatness was the only thing that attached him to the favorite, he was easily corrupted.

For a long time I tried to seduce the Abbot but he always rejected the offers. However, he always left the impression that I would attain my goal. He easily noticed the situation he would find himself in by doing the service the princes requested from him, as he knew that it would not be difficult to them to get rid of an accomplice. On another hand he was aware of my brother's instability and was afraid of becoming his victim.

Compromising his safety with his interests, he decided to sacrifice his young master. Taking such a side he had as many chances of success as failure. To the princes, the death of the young Duke of Guyenne should be the result of an error or an unforeseen accident. Even when attributed to the Duke of Brittany and his accomplices, the favorite's death would go unnoticed, so to speak, as nobody would discover the motives that gave it real importance from a political point of view.

Admitting that they could be accused of my brother's death, they would be exposed to the greatest dangers, once it would have been my duty to severely punish them. They knew that I did not lack good will and that the people could turn against them. Then the Duke of Burgundy, not knowing what happened in Guyenne, would have been forced to become my ally, or to be accused of complicity. Even in this latest hypothesis, everything would have moved in my favor. I could have said that my brother, the reckless, was a traitor criminal, leading the Parliament to condemn him to death, by his assassination. Such condemnations, pronounced by such a high tribunal, always had great results, especially when of an incontestable legitimacy.

It is easy to see how much interest the princes had to manipulate the Abbot. On another hand, there was nothing easier than secretly eliminating him.

But with me the Abbot of Saint-Jean had more chances of impunity. His service to me was of the greatest importance, particularly at that point in time, as the formidable association which was forming, having the Duke of Guyenne at the center, should infallibly loose me. The only means of destroying it was with the death of my brother, which represented my salvation. He aspired the favors of Tristan, the hermit, thinking that by this he would be above him or, at least, he would share my good graces and my trust in him.

In fact, the princes had been imprudent enough to leave incontestable proofs of their guilt in his hands: these were multiple texts, written in very vague terms, not being difficult to replace my brother's name by his favorite, appearing between the lines. Giving me those documents he pushed away any doubt with respect to my innocence; he thus subtracted the only danger for being on the princes' side and, proving that I wasn't by any means involved in the poisoning, he would no longer be my accomplice, exempting me from any interest in killing him.

There was still the need to prove that he wasn't himself involved in all that. This was a lesser of a problem. For starters he was confidently under my protection; besides, the princes did not have proofs of his culpability and he could back fire the accusations, as slander.

Once all that was taken into account, he sent me an envoy that pretended to have spontaneously come to tell me that the Abbot of Saint-Jean was unhappy with my brother. I immediately saw the advantage I could take from such an event and fell in the trap prepared by the shrewd

Abbot. Not suspecting that he could have sent the envoy, I dispatched one of my trustworthy spies. Saint-Jean represented so well his role that my envoy was deceived. Based on his report I wrote to the Abbot in order to conquer him. He showed a lot of qualms but, although with some difficulty, I triumphed. He agreed to be in charge of the poisoning of my brother. I was so perverted that I did not hesitate in committing such a horrific crime.

Henri de la Roche, the Duke's squire, was in charge of preparing the peach that would be offered by the Abbot himself to Mrs. Thouars. While enjoying a lunch at the table with my brother, the beauty of that fruit was notable. She drew the prince's attention and shared it with him. They had just eaten when Mrs. Thouars felt excruciating pain in her stomach, soon expiring amidst terrible sufferings. My brother experienced the same symptoms but with much less violence.

It may perhaps seem strange that the Abbot had used such means to poison his master. Truly, the minor incident could spoil his plan. It was, however, the only one authorized by prudence as it admitted the possibility of a mistake. Touched by the quality of the peach, it was natural that Mrs. Thouars called the attention of his lover and offered him half. He, therefore, could not refuse eating it. Admitting that he would eat only a small piece, this would be sufficient to provoke the initial symptoms needed; then, a posterior poisoning could determine his death, as a consequence of the first one.

The princes were taken by horror as soon as they heard about the dismal poisoning of the favorite. They were not in the least suspicious of the Abbot's premeditation. They only thought of giving the young lady's death and the disease of her lover a natural appearance. None of them took the initiative of trying an antidote to the unfortunate prince, afraid of association. In fact such an attitude would indicate knowledge about the poison and, consequently, that someone was accomplice in the crime.

Thanks to his youth and strength of temper, Charles resisted longer to the poison. His physical sufferings did nothing but drive him back to his old projects with more intensity. Afraid that his illness could diminish the zeal of his officers, he wanted them to renew their oaths of fidelity. As he demanded that they should swear allegiance to him, against everything and everyone, even against me, some of them, on fearing death which seemed close, refused to obey, changing sides to my court.

OBSERVATION: In the previous issues we saw interesting details given by Louis XI with respect to his death. The fact we have just reported is not less notable from a historical point of view as well as with respect to the phenomenon of manifestations. In fact, we only had difficulty regarding the choice: the life of this King, as dictated by himself, is incontestably the most complete that we have and, we can say, the most impartial. The state of the spirit of Louis XI allows him to appreciate things in their just value today. By the three chosen fragments one can see how he passes judgment onto himself. He explains his politics better than any of his historians. He does not acquit himself for his behavior and, in his death, so sad and common to such a powerful monarch, a few hours earlier, he sees an anticipated punishment.

As for the phenomenon of manifestations, this work offers a special interest. It proves that the spiritist manifestations can enlighten us about history, as long as we know how to position ourselves in favorable conditions. We hope that the publication of Louis XI life, as well as the not less interesting of Charles VIII, equally concluded, may soon be placed side by side with that of Joan of Arc.

Henri Martin - His opinion about extra-corporeal communications

We see here certain distinguished writers shrugging their shoulders to the simple enunciation that a story was written by the spirits. They say:

- How come the beings of the other world may control our knowledge, control us, Earth's scholars? Come on! Is it possible?

Gentlemen, we do not force you to believe; not even shall we make the least effort to subtract you from such an illusion. In the interest of your future glory, we invite you to write your names with indestructible characters as footnote of this modest sentence: *All adepts of Spiritism are senseless, as only we are assigned the judgment of the extension of God's power.* This said so as posterity do not forget them. Posterity itself will see if they shall have a place side by side with those who, not long ago, were repelled by men and to whom Science and public acknowledgement now build statues.

Here you have, however, a writer whose high capacity everyone recognizes, risking himself to be taken by an empty head; He also holds the flag of the new ideas about the relationships between the physical and the extra-corporeal world. In Henri Martin's *Histoire de France*, volume 6, page 143, we read the following, regarding Joan of Arc:

"... there is in humanity an exceptional order of moral and physical facts that apparently do not comply with the ordinary laws of nature: these are the states of ecstasy and somnambulism, artificial or spontaneous, with all the admirable phenomena of perturbation of the senses, of partial or total insensitivity of the body, exaltation of the soul, of perceptions beyond all conditions of normal life. The facts that this class was judged under points of view completely in opposition. Once the common relationships of organs are disturbed, the physiologists classify the ecstatic and somnambulist states as diseases. They admit the phenomena which they can describe in the pathology but deny everything else, that is, all that seems to be outside of the laws of Physics. Disease becomes madness to their eyes when hallucinations of the senses and visions of objects only seen by the visionary are added to the alteration of the organ's actions.

"A renowned physiologist sustained with austerity that Socrates was a lunatic because he thought he could talk to his demon."

"The mystics respond by not only stating that the extraordinary phenomena of magnetic perception are real, subject about which they find numerous auxiliaries and numerous witnesses outside mysticism, but by also sustaining that the vision of the ecstatic have real objects, certainly not seen by the eyes of the body, but by those of the spirit. Ecstasy is the bridge between the visible and invisible worlds to them; the memory and the promise of a better existence, from where we fell and have to re-conquer."

"Which side should History and Philosophy take in such a debate?"

"History could not precisely determine the limits neither the extension of the phenomena, nor of the ecstatic and somnambulist faculties, but attest that they happen everywhere; that people have always given credit to them; that they have exerted a considerable action over humanity's destinies; that they have manifested not only among the contemplative but also among the most powerful geniuses and the majority of the great initiated individuals; however unreasonable the ecstatic may be, there is nothing in common between the digressions of madness and the visions of so many others; that the visions may be connected to certain laws; that the ecstatic of all times and all places have something that maybe called a common language, the language of the symbols, from which poetry is not more than a derivative, language which expresses, more or less constantly, the same idea and the same feelings through the same images."

"It might be reckless to conclude something in the name of Philosophy. Nevertheless, after acknowledging the moral importance of those phenomena, however obscure, its law and objective may be; after distinguishing them in two degrees, one inferior, which is nothing beyond a strange extension or inexplicable dislocation of the actions of the organs, and the other superior, which is a prodigious exaltation of the moral and intellectual powers, the philosopher could, as it seems to us, sustain that the illusion of the inspired one consists in considering as revelation done by exterior beings, angels, saints or genies, the interior revelations of this infinite personality, which is inside us, and that, sometimes, among the best and the greatest, manifest through latent forces which almost incommensurably go beyond the faculties of our current condition. In one word, in academic language, they are to us *facts of subjectivity*; in the language of the old mystic philosophies and of the most advanced religions, these are revelations of the *Mazdean ferouer*[26], of the good demon (of Socrates), of the guardian angel, of this other *self* which is nothing more than the eternal *self*, in full possession of itself, gliding above the *self*, immersed in the shades of life. It is the figure of the magnificent Zoroastrian symbol, represented everywhere in Persepolis and Ninive: the winged ferouer or the celestial *self*, gliding above the earthly person."

"Denying the action of the exterior beings over the inspired ones; not seeing in their pretense manifestations more than a form given to the ecstatic intuitions by the beliefs and environment of their time; looking for the solution of the problem in the depths of the human personality, it

---

26 In the avestica religion the supernatural being corresponds to the genies of the Romans or the guardian angels of the Catholic Church.

is not absolutely to doubt the Divine intervention in the great phenomena and in the great existences. The author and support of the whole life, however much essentially independent may it be from each creature and from the whole creation; the more distinct may its absolute personality be from our contingent being, it is not an exterior being, that is, strange to us, and it is not from the exterior that it speaks to us. When the soul dives into itself, it is there that it finds the Creator and, in all salutary inspiration, our freedom associates to his Providence. Here, as in everything, it is necessary to predict the double danger of incredulity and badly clarified piety: one sees nothing but illusions and purely human impulses; the other refuses to admit any portion of illusion, of ignorance or of imperfection, where it only sees the finger of God, as if God's envoys were no longer human beings, human beings of a certain time and a certain place, and as if the sublime lightning which trespasses their soul deposits in them the universal Science and the absolute perfection. In the more evidently providential inspirations, men's mistakes combine with God's truth. The infallible being communicates its infallibility to nobody."

"We hope that this digression will not be considered superfluous. We should position ourselves about the character and about the work of that inspired one who, to the highest degree of testimony of the extraordinary faculties that we mentioned above, applied them to the most brilliant mission of the modern times. It was necessary to attempt to produce an opinion adequate to the level of the category of exceptional beings to which Joan of Arc belongs."

Varieties – The magnetic banquets

On May 23rd, Mesmer's[27] birthday, two annual banquets were held with the presence of the top-notch dignitaries from Paris and foreign delegates. We have always questioned the fact that such commemorative solemnity is celebrated in two rival banquets, where each group drinks to the health of the other and where a toast to the union is unsuccessfully made.

At that point in time, one has the impression that they are about to reconcile. Why then such a rupture among people who dedicate themselves to the good of humanity and to the cult of truth? Doesn't truth show up under the same light to them? Will they have two different ways of understanding the good of humanity? Are they divided with respect to the principles of their Science? Absolutely. They have the same beliefs and the same master that is Mesmer. If that master attends their appeal, as we believe so, he must suffer with the discord among his disciples.

Fortunately, that disunion will not unleash wars like those that covered the world with blood, in the name of Christ, for the eternal shame of the ones who named themselves Christians. Nevertheless, however much

---

27 **Franz A. Mesmer** (born May 23, 1734 – died March 5, 1815) was a German physician who theorised that there was a natural energetic transference between all animated and inanimate objects that he called animal magnetism, sometimes later referred to as mesmerism (N.T.)

inoffensive it may be, this war is not less regrettable, although limited to the strikes of the pen and to the isolated drinking. We would like to see good men united by a common feeling of fraternity. With that, the magnetic Science would benefit in progress and consideration.

Once the two sides are not divided by doctrinaire divergences, what then explains their antagonism? We cannot discover the cause except in the susceptibilities inherent to our nature, from which not even superior men are exempt. The genie of disagreement has agitated its torch at all times. From the spiritist point of view, this means that the inferior spirits, envious of people's happiness, find easy access among them. Happy are those who have enough moral strength to repel their suggestions.

We were given the honor of being invited to both meetings. As they were held simultaneously, and as we are nothing more than a very much incarnated spirit, not having the gift of ubiquity, we could only satisfy one of those kind invitations.

We went to the meeting presided by Dr. Duplanty.

It is necessary to say that the adepts of Spiritism do not constitute the majority there. However, we were pleased to verify that, with the exception of some flicks given to the spirits in the verses sung by Mr. Julio Lovi and the not less amusing sung by Sr. Fortier, who had the honor of a replay, the Spiritist Doctrine did not suffer inconvenient criticism from anybody, considering the fertility of some adversaries, despite their self-praised education. Far from that, in a remarkable and deservedly applauded speech, Dr. Duplanty proclaimed, loud and clear, the respect that we must have for the sincere beliefs, even when we don't share them. Without declaring himself pro or con Spiritism, he wisely observed that the phenomena of magnetism, on revealing to us a hitherto unknown power, must make us even more circumspect with respect to the phenomena that can still reveal and that, at least, it would be imprudence to deny the ones we don't understand or have not yet attested, mainly when supported by the authority of honored people, whose lights and loyalty could not be doubted. These are wise words for which we thank Mr. Duplanty. They singularly contrast with those of certain adepts of Magnetism that inconsiderately shed ridicule onto a Doctrine which they confessedly ignore, forgetting that on other occasions they were also targeted by sarcasm; that they were sent to the hospices and attacked by the skeptical as enemies of religion and common sense. Now that Magnetism has been rehabilitated by the forces of circumstances; that one does not make fun of it; that we can fearlessly confess ourselves as magnetizers, it is not much dignified and charitable to use those reprisals against a sister Science which can only give them a beneficial support. We don't attack people, they say; we only laugh at something that seems to ridicule, while we wait for the light to be brought upon us. In our opinion, the magnetic Science, which we have professed for 35 years, should be inseparable from seriousness. It seems that there is no lack of pasture to their satirical energy in this world, not having the need to target serious things. They forget that the same language was used against them; that they themselves accused the incredulous for their lightheartedly judgment and said, as we do now, in turn: "Patience! They who laugh last laugh better!"

ERRATUM

In the No 5 issue (May, 1858), a typo disfigured a proper name that lost its meaning because of that. In the article "Family Conversations from Beyond the Grave – Mozart – Second Article", instead of Poryolise, read Pergolèse.

ALLAN KARDEC[28]

---

28 Paris, Cosson & Co. typography, Four Saint-Germain, 43

July 1858

Envy

Moral dissertation dictated by St. Louis to Mr. D...

S t. Louis had promised us a dissertation about envy, to be delivered in one of the Society's session. Mr. D... was starting to develop his mediumship, still bearing some doubts not related to the Doctrine of which he is one of the keenest followers, understanding it in its essence, that is, from a moral point of view, but with respect to his own incipient faculty, Mr. D... then evoked St. Louis, in a particular session, addressing him with the following question:

Can you clarify to me, my inquietude, with respect to my mediumship, writing through me the dissertation you promised to the Society, to be delivered on Tuesday, June 1st?

• Yes. I will gladly do it to calm you.

Then the following text was dictated. We point out the fact that Mr. D... addressed St. Louis with a sincere and pure heart, without second intentions, indispensable condition to every good communication. He was not taking a test. He just doubted himself and God allowed his wishes in order to give him means of becoming useful. Today Mr. D... is one of the most complete mediums, not only by his facilities to operate but also by his aptitude to serve as an interpreter to all spirits, even those of the highest categories, who easily and willingly express themselves. These are, above all, the qualities we should seek in the mediums and that can always be acquired with patience, resolve and exercise. Mr. D... did not need a lot of patience; he had good will and fervor, added to his natural aptitude. A few days only were needed to take his faculty to the highest degree.

Here is the text he received about envy:

"See this man. His spirit is uneasy; his earthly happiness gets to the top: he envies the gold, the luxury, the apparent or fictitious happiness of his neighbors; his heart is devastated, his soul quietly burned by the never ending struggle of pride, of unsatisfied vanity. He carries along a snake that he feeds and that incessantly suggests him the most fatal thoughts, at all times of his miserable existence: "Will I have this ecstasy, this happiness? I deserve it as much as the others; I am a man like them, why would I be disinherited?"

"He struggles in his impotence, victim of a horrible torture by envy, happy still if such dismal ideas do not drive him to the borders of the abyss. Once he takes that route he questions himself if he should not take by force everything that he judges to be owed to him; if he is not going to expose the terrible evil that devours him to the eyes of everyone."

"Had this miserable man looked only below him, he would have seen the number of those who suffer without a lament and still praise the Creator, because disgrace is a benefit utilized by God to make the poor creature advance to God's eternal throne."

"Do the good deeds of charity and submission, the only ones that can take you into God's dwelling, which are your happiness and true treasure on Earth. These good deeds will be your eternal delight and happiness."

"Envy is one of the ugliest and saddest miseries of your globe. Charity and constant demonstration of faith will eliminate all these evils which will disappear, one by one, as the good people that will come after you multiply.

Amen.

A New Photographic

Discovery

Several newspapers have reported the following:

"Mr. Badet, deceased on the last November 12th, after a three month long illness, used to be by the window of the first floor, according to the *Union Bourguignonne of Dijon*, whenever he had the needed strength, always facing the street, distracted by the passersby. A few days ago Mrs. Peltret, whose house is located just across the road to the Badet's widow, noticed on one of the glass windows Mr. Badet himself, with his cotton cap, showing his emaciated face, etc, like she had actually seen him during the period of his disease. It was a great emotion, to say the least."

"She not only called the neighbors, whose testimony could be suspicious, but also some reputable men who distinctly saw Mr. Badet's image in the glass window, where he used to be. The image was then shown to the family and they immediately got rid of the glass."

"It was demonstrated, however, that the image of the ill man was reproduced in the glass, as if daguerreotyped, phenomenon which could only be explained if on the opposite side of the window there was another one, through which the solar beams could have gotten through to Mr. Badet. But there wasn't such a window. The room has only one. This is the naked truth about this admirable case, whose explanation must be requested to the scholars."

We confess that since we read the news our first impulse was to consider it vulgar, as we do with apocryphal news. We did not give any importance to that. A few days later Mr. Jobard, from Brussels, wrote the following to us:

"On reading the following fact (the one just described), which happened in my homeland with one of my relatives, I shrugged after seeing the coverage of the newspaper referring this matter to the scientists and attested that this good family had removed the glass window, through which Badet observed the passersby. Call upon him to see what he thinks."

Such a confirmation of the fact by a man of character like Mr. Jobard, whose merits and honorability everybody knows, and the special circumstance of having one of his relatives by hero, could not leave us with any doubt with respect to the truthfulness of the event.

As a consequence of that we then evoked Mr. Badet in the session of the Parisian Society of Spiritist Studies, on Tuesday, June 15th, 1858. Here are the explanations that we obtained:

1. I request the Almighty God to allow the spirit of Mr. Badet, who died in Dijon, on the last November 11th, to may come to communicate with us.
   - I am here.
2. Is the matter related to you and that we have just recalled true?
   - Yes, it is true.
3. Could you give us your explanation?
   - There are physical agents still unknown but which later will become common. It is a very simple phenomenon, similar to a photography produced by forces that you have not discovered yet.

4. Could you precipitate such discovery through your explanations?
   - I would like to but this is the task of other spirits and human work.
5. Could you reproduce the phenomenon once again?
   - It was not I who produced it. It was the physical conditions, independent of me.
6. By whose will and with which objective the fact was produced?
   - It was produced when I was alive, independently of my will. A particular state of the atmosphere revealed it later.

A discussion was established among the audience, relatively to the likely causes of the phenomenon, having several opinions been issued, without any other question addressed to the spirit, who then spontaneously said:

"And don't you take into account electricity and galvanoplasty that also act on the perispirit?"

7. We have been told lately that the spirits have no eyes. Well, if such an image is the reproduction of the perispirit, how was it possible to reproduce the organs of sight?
   - The perispirit is not the spirit. The appearance, or perispirit, has eyes but the spirit doesn't. Indeed I told you, when talking about the perispirit, that I was alive.

OBSERVATION: While we wait until that new discovery takes place we will give it the provisional name "spontaneous photography". Everyone will regret that he glass in which the image of Mr. Badet had been reproduced was destroyed. Such a curious monument would have facilitated the research and observations for the adequate study of the subject. Perhaps they saw the art of the devil in that image. In any case, if by any means the devil is involved in this it is, no doubt, in the destruction of the glass, because he is the enemy of progress.

Considerations About Spontaneous Photography

I t results from the explanations above (previous article) that the fact on itself is neither supernatural nor miraculous. How many phenomena in similar conditions, in times of ignorance, must have shocked imagination, so much inclined towards the wonderful! It is then a purely physical effect that foresees a new step in the photographic science.

As known, the perispirit is the semi-material covering of the spirit. It is not only after death that it endows the spirit; during life it is united to the body; it is the bond between the body and the spirit. Death is only the destruction of the coarser covering; the spirit retains the second, which keeps the appearance of the first, as if preserving its image. The perispirit is generally invisible however, and under certain circumstances, condenses and combines with other fluids, becoming perceptible to the sight and sometimes even tangible. It is what is observed in the apparitions.

Whatever the subtleness and imponderability of the perispirit, it is still some sort of matter whose properties are still unknown to us. Once it is matter, it can act upon matter. Such an action is present in the magnetic phenomena. It has revealed in the inert bodies by the impression left by Mr. Badet's image in the glass. That impression was left when he was alive; it remained after his death but it was invisible. As it seems, the casual action of an unknown agent was needed, probably atmospheric, for it to become apparent.

What is so remarkable about that?

Don't we know that it is possible to make the daguerreotyped image appear and disappear?

We mentioned this as a comparison, without establishing similarity between the processes. Thus, it would have been the perispirit, coming out of Mr. Badet's body, that would slowly have exerted a true chemical action over the vitreous substance, under the scope of unknown circumstances, similar to those of light. Electricity and light must undoubtedly play a significant role in this phenomenon. The agents and circumstances are still unknown. That is what we shall likely know later and this will not be one of the least curious discoveries of modern times.

If this is a natural phenomenon, why is it the first time that it is produced, those who deny everything will ask?

We shall then ask back, why the daguerreotyped images were impressed only after Daguerre, considering that he did not invent the light, or the copper plates, neither the silver nor the chlorine. The dark chamber phenomena are known since long ago. A natural circumstance has revealed the path to the impression, followed then by the genius and step by step we arrived at the master pieces of the present times. The same will probably happen to the strange phenomenon that has just been manifested. Who knows it has already been produced, gone unnoticed by the lack of a thoughtful observer?

The reproduction of an image onto glass is a common fact, but its adherence under different conditions from those of the photography; the latent state of that image; its resurgence later, this is what should mark the archives of Science.

If we believe in the spirits, we should wait for many marvels, some of which are indicated by them. Honor, thus, to those sufficiently modest scholars who do not judge that nature has already turned its last page on them.

If that phenomenon was produced once, it can then be repeated. It is what shall likely happen when we hold its key. While we wait, here is what one of our members told us in the referred session of the Society:

"I was in Montrouge. It was summer time, the sunlight darting through the window. A flask of water rested on a straw mat on the table. Suddenly the straw was set on fire. Had nobody been there, the whole place could have been set on fire and nobody would know the cause. I have unsuccessfully tried to reproduce the phenomenon hundreds of times."

The physical cause of combustion is well known: the bottle produced the effect of a hot glass. But why the experience could not be repeated? Independently of the bottle and the water, there has been the concourse of circumstances that have acted exceptionally, concentrating the solar beams: maybe the state of the atmosphere, the vapors, the quality of the water, the electricity, etc., and all that probably in adequate proportions. This illustrates the difficulty in repeating exactly the same conditions, as well as the uselessness of the attempts to try to produce a similar effect. This is an example of a phenomenon entirely dominated by Physics, whose principle we know but which we cannot reproduce at will.

Will the most stubborn skeptical deny the fact? Certainly not! Why then the same skeptical deny the spiritist phenomena – speaking of the manifestations in general – by the fact that those cannot be manipulated at will? On not admitting that there could be new agents outside of those known to us, governed by special laws; denying such agents by the fact that they do not obey laws that we know, this is truly to give proof of little logic and to show a narrow mind.

Let us go back to the image of Mr. Badet. As with our friend of the flask, numerous fruitless trials will be carried out until a happy chance or the effort of a powerful genius may provide the key to the mystery. Then it will probably become a new art, with which industry will prosper. We can already hear many people saying: But there is a very simple way of finding that key. Why not asking the spirits?

This is then the opportunity to point out a mistake made by many who judge the Spiritist Science without knowing it. First of all let us remind the fundamental principle that all the spirits are far from knowing everything, as previously thought.

The spirits' scale gives us the measure of their capacity and morality, and experience daily confirms our observations with that respect. Thus, the spirits do not know everything and there are some that are inferior to certain people, in all aspects. This is what we cannot disregard.

The spirit of Mr. Badet, involuntary author of the phenomenon of our concern, reveals through his answers a certain elevation, but not a great superiority. He recognizes his own inability to provide a complete explanation. He says: "This is a task to other spirits and human work".

These words formulate a whole lesson. Indeed, it would be somewhat easy to have only to ask the spirits, in order to attain the most marvelous discoveries. Where would then the merit of the inventers be if a hidden hand had come to prepare the task and spare the research work? No doubt that there would not be a lack of unscrupulous persons patenting inventions in their names, not even mentioning the real inventors. Besides, such questions are always addressed with the aim of self-interest and in the hopes of easy fortune, all constituting very bad recommendations to the good spirits. Those, by the way, that never subject themselves to serve as instruments of trafficking.

Human beings must have their initiative, without which they are reduced to the condition of machine. They must perfect through work. This is one of the conditions of their Earthly existence. It is also necessary that everything comes in due time and through the means that God pleases to employ. Spirits cannot alter the paths of the Providence. Willing to force the established order is to be at the service of spirits of mockery, who praise ambition, greed and vanity only to laugh later at the disappointment they have caused. Since they are of unscrupulous nature they tell us everything we want to hear; give all the requested recipes and, if necessary, will justify them with scientific formulas, even if they hold no more value than the recipes of the charlatan.

May you, who think that the spirits would show you gold mines, be disillusioned! Their mission is more serious. "Work, endeavor! This is what you really lack", said a distinguished moralist, from whom we shall soon publish a conversation from beyond the grave.

The Spiritist Doctrine then adds to that wise statement: These are those to whom the serious spirits come to help, by the ideas they suggest or by their direct counsel and not the lazy ones who want to enjoy without having accomplished anything, neither the ambitious ones who want to have the effortless merit. Help yourself and heaven will help you.

The Rapping Spirit of

Bergzabern[29] - Part III

We continue to cite Mr. Blanck's brochure, editor of the Bergzabern newspaper.

"The facts which we will report took place between Friday 4th and Wednesday 9th, March 1853. Nothing similar happened after that period. Filipina then no longer slept in the room already known to us: her bed had been transferred to the next-door room where it is still today. The manifestations acquired such a strange character that it is impossible to admit their explanation by human intervention. In fact, these are so different from the ones observed previously that all initial hypotheses went down the drain.

It is a known fact that in the bedroom, where she slept, the chairs and other pieces of furniture were scrambled and the windows violently opened through repetitive strikes. For five weeks she had been installed in the common room where there is always light from the onset of the evening to dawn break. Anyone can perfectly see what happens in the room.

Here is what was observed on March 4th.

Filipina was not in bed yet. She was with some people talking about the rapping spirit. Suddenly a drawer from a heavy table in the middle of the room was noisily pulled and pushed back with extraordinary speed.

---

29 We owe the translation of this interesting brochure to the kindness of one of our friends, Mr. Alfred Pireaux, employee of the Post Office administration.

Those present were surprised by such a new manifestation. At the same time the table itself was set in motion, moving in all directions and then advancing towards the fireplace, close to where Filipina was sitting. She was, to say, chased by the furniture, having to leave her place and run towards the middle of the room but the table came back in that direction, stopping at fifteen centimeters from the wall. It was then put back in its normal place from where it did not move again but the boots that were under the table were thrown in the middle of the room, seen by all with great horror. One of the drawers moved back and forth on its supporting tracks, for a couple of times, in the beginning very fast but progressively slowing down. When it was wide open it would shake violently. A package of tobacco, left on the table, changed places continuously. Noises and scratches were heard from over the table. Filipina, who was then very healthy, by no means seemed uneasy by such strange things, repeatedly happening every evening since Friday.

But the events were still more remarkable on Sunday. The drawer was violently pulled in and out several times. Once settled in her former bedroom Filipina was suddenly taken by the magnetic sleep, falling on an armchair from where the scratches were heard several times. While she had her hands resting on her knees the chair would move sometimes to the right, sometimes to the left or forward and backward. When Filipina was transported to the middle of the room it was easy to observe that new phenomenon. Then, to a single command, the chair turned, advanced, backed up with a higher or smaller speed, sometimes in one direction sometimes in another. During that original dance, the girl's feet would drag on the floor, as if paralyzed; she complained of headache, moaned and placed her hands on her forehead. Then, suddenly awaken, looked around in all directions, not understanding the situation, but her sudden illness had disappeared. She lied down. Then the raps and scratches, which were heard earlier from the table, were now heard in the bed, playfully and with strength.

A few moments earlier a bell had spontaneously rung, giving some people the idea of tying her up to the bed. The bell then immediately began to swing and ring. Once the bed was raised and moved, remarkable thing, the bell remained quiet and motionless. Just about midnight all noises had ceased and the participants left.

Monday evening, May 15th, a big bell was attached to the bed. A disgusting and deafening noise was immediately heard. On the same day, in the afternoon, the windows and the bedroom door were opened, but quietly.

We have to say that the armchair used by Filipina on Friday and Saturday, taken by the old Sänger to the middle of the living room, appeared lighter than usual. It seemed that an invisible force lifted it up. If one of the presents wanted to push it, there was no resistance: the chair seemed to glide by itself on the floor.

The rapping spirit remained silent for three days during Easter Holiday: Thursday, Friday and Saturday. Only on Easter Sunday the rings of the bell restarted: rhythmical hits, composing an Aria. On April 1st, during the change of the guard, the troops that were leaving town were marching by the tune of a military music. As they were marching across from the front of Mr. Sänger's house the rapping spirit executed in the bed, on his own way, the same music that was played in the street. A few moments earlier someone's steps were heard in the bedroom and also the sound of something like sand thrown on the floor.

Worried about the facts we have just described, the Palatinate Government proposed that Mr. Sänger should take his daughter into the Frankenthal health clinic, which was accepted. We were informed that Filipina's presence produced the same prodigies of Bergazabern and that the Frankenthal doctors, as well as those in our city, cannot determine their cause. Besides, we are also informed that only the doctors have access to the girl.

Why such a measure? We ignore and cannot criticize it but if what has motivated it is not the result of any particular circumstance, we believe that not everybody should have access to the interesting girl but at least those commendable persons."

OBSERVATION: We have only received news about the published fact through Mr. Blanck's report. A fact, however, has just put us in touch with one of the persons that is more frequently shown in this case and that, with respect to the event, kindly provided us with the most interesting circumstantial documents. By evocation, we had the addition of very curious and instructive explanations about the rapping spirit, given by him. As such documents got to our hands a little bit late we will postpone its publication to the next issue of the Review.

Conversations From Beyond the Grave: The Drummer of Berezina

Some people met in our house with the objective of verifying certain manifestations; the facts below were produced in several sessions, giving rise to the reported conversation since it presents a great interest from the point of view of the study.

The spirit manifested by raps, not by knocks with the foot of the table, but inside the wood itself. The exchange of ideas between the audience and the invisible being does not leave margin to doubts with respect to the intervention of an occult intelligence. Besides the answers to several questions, sometimes by the "yes", sometimes by the "**no**", or by means of alphabetic typtology, the raps have spontaneously played a musical march; the rhythm of an aria; imitated the sounds of cannons and bayonet shots in the battlefield; the sound of the barrel or of the shoemaker; echoed with remarkable accuracy, etc. Then the motion of a table and its translation, without any contact of the hands, as the persons who were present remained at a distance. A salad bowl placed on the table slipped in a straight line, not turning, also without the contact of hands. The raps were equally heard in multiple pieces of furniture in the room; sometimes simultaneously, on other occasions as if providing answers.

The spirit seemed to have special preference for the drumbeat, as it was played every time, irrespective of a request. Instead of answering certain questions, the spirit played the General's march and the readiness tune. Once questioned about some particulars of his life he said his name was Célima, a drummer born in Paris, who died at the age of forty-five.

Besides the special medium of physical effects who produced the manifestations, there was in the audience an excellent psychographic medium that could serve as interpreter to the spirit. We have thus obtained more explicit answers. He confirmed in writing what he had said through typtology with respect to his name, place and date of birth, and date of death; the following questions were addressed to him, whose answers present several characteristic traces, confirming certain essential parts of the theory.

1 - Write anything, whatever you want to write to us.
   - Ran, plan plan, ran plan plan.
2 - Why do you write this?
   - Because I was a drummer.
3 - Did you have any instruction?
   - Yes.
4 - Where did you go to school?
   - I went to the "*Ignorantins*"[30]
5 - You seem joyful.
   - I am very much so.
6 - On a given occasion you said you liked to drink. Is that true?
   - I liked everything that was good.
7 - You were in the military?
   - Of course, since I was a drummer.
8 - Under which government did you serve?
   - Under Napoleon, the Great.
9 - Can you cite a battle in which you participated?
   - The battle of Berezina.

---

30 Name adopted by the Order of Saint-Jean-de-Dieu in France, out of humbleness.

10 - It was then that you died?

- No.

11 - Had you been to Moscow?

- No.

12 - Where did you die?

- In the snow.

13 - Which corps did you serve?

- The marines guard.

14 - Did you like Napoleon, the Great?

- Like us, everybody loved him, not knowing why!

15 - Do you know what happened after Napoleon's death?

- After my death I was only concerned with myself.

16 - Have you reincarnated?

- No, that is why I came to talk to you.

17 - Why do you manifest through raps without been evoked?

- Noise is needed to the nonbeliever's hearts. If it has not been enough, I will give you more.

18 - Have you come to rap on your own or was it another spirit that forced you?

- I gladly came on my own. There is another one who you call "Truth" that can obligate me. But I wanted to come since long time ago.

19 - Why you wanted to come?

- To communicate with you. This is what I wanted. But there was something blocking me. I was forced to do this by a familiar spirit of the household, who convinced me to become useful to the persons who would ask me questions.

Q. Then such a spirit has a lot of power, considering that he dominates the others.

R. - More than you think, and he only employs it to the good deeds.

S.

T. OBSERVATION: The familiar spirit of the house is known by the allegoric name "Truth", circumstance that was ignored by the medium.

20 - What is it that was blocking you?

- I don't know. It was something that I don't understand.

21 - Do you find life deplorable?

- No. Nothing is deplorable to me.

22 - Which one do you prefer: your current existence or the Earthly life?

- I prefer the spirit's life rather than the bodily life.

23 - Why?

- We are much better off than on Earth. Earth is a purgatory and when I was alive I always wanted to die.

24 - Do you suffer in your new condition?

- No, but I am not happy yet.

25 - Would you be glad if you had a new corporeal existence?

- Yes, because I have to improve myself.

26 - Who told you so?

- I know that well.

27 - Will you reincarnate soon?

- I don't know.

28 - Do you see other spirits around you?

- Yes, many.

29 - How do you know they are spirits?

- Among us we see each other as we are.

30 - With which appearance you see them?

- By the way the spirits can be seen but not through the eyes.

31 - And you, which appearance do you have?

- The one I had when alive, that is, of a drummer.

32 - And do you see the other spirits with the forms they had when alive?

- No. We only take an appearance when we are evoked. Besides that we see each other without a form.

33 - Do you see us clearly, as when you were alive?

- Yes, perfectly.

34 - Is it through the eyes that you see us?

- No. We have a form but we don't have the senses. Our form is nothing but appearance.

OBSERVATION: The spirits certainly have sensations, as they perceive. If not they would be inert. Their sensations, however, are not localized as when they have a body. They are inherent to their whole being.

35 - Tell us in which location you are positively here.

- Near the table, between you and the medium.

36 - When you knock, are you on the table, below it or inside the structure of the wood?

- I stay beside it. I don't get inside the wood. It is enough that I touch the table.

37 - How do you produce the noises that are heard?

- I believe it is by the concentration of our force.

38 - Could you explain how the several noises that you imitate are produced, like for example the scratching?

- I could not describe well the nature of the noises. It is difficult to explain. I know it is strange but I can't explain how I produce that noise that you call scratching.

39 - Could you produce the same noises with any other medium?

- No. There are specialties with all mediums. Not all can act like that.

40 - Do you see among us, besides the young S… (the medium of physical influence by whom the spirit manifests) someone that can help to produce the same effects?

- At the moment I see nobody. With him I am well equipped to produce them.

41 - Why with him and not someone else?

- Because I know him for some time and also because he is more capable than anyone else for that kind of manifestations.

42 - You knew him from long ago, from before the present existence?

- No. I know him from not long ago. I was somehow attracted to him, so that he would be my instrument.

43 - When the table lifts up in the air without a supporting point, who sustains it?

- Our will, which forces it to obey us, and also the fluid that we transmit to the table.

OBSERVATION: This theory supports the one we presented in the issues No 5 and 6 of this Review, about the physical manifestations.

44 - Can you do that?

- I believe so. I will try when the medium is present (at the moment he was absent).

45 - What does it depend on?

- On me as I am served by the medium as an instrument.

46 - But isn't the quality of the instrument important?

- Yes. That helps me a lot and that is why, as I said, today I could not do it with others.

OBSERVATION: During the session we unsuccessfully tried to lift the table up maybe by a lack of sufficient perseverance. There was evident effort and some motion of translation, without contact or imposition of the hands. Among the experiments there was the opening of the table that was elastic. However, as it offered too much resistance due to a constructive defect, it was left alone while the spirit was able to open and close another one.

47 - Why is it that, the other day, the motion of the table ceased every time one of us took a torch to examine it from below?

- Because I wanted to punish your curiosity.

48 - What do you do in your existence of spirit, since you certainly do not spend your time rapping?

- Several times I have missions to accomplish. We must obey superior orders, particularly when we have to do good deeds through our influence over the humans.

49 - Your earthly life, no doubt, was not exempt of faults. Do you acknowledge them now?

- Yes. I fairly expiate them, staying stationary among the inferior spirits. I cannot purify enough until I take another body.

50 - When you knocked on another piece of furniture, at the same time as on the table, was that you or another spirit?

- It was I.

51 - You were alone then?

- No, but the task of rapping was only mine.

52 - Did the other spirits who were around help you with something?

- Not with the rapping but with the talking.

53 - They were not rapping spirits then?

- The "*Truth*" only allowed me to rap.

54 - Don't the rapping spirit sometimes gather in large numbers with the objective of having more strength to produce certain phenomena?

- Yes, but for what I wanted to do I was enough.

55 - In your existence as spirit are you always on Earth?

- More frequently in space.

56 - Do you sometimes go to other worlds, say, and other globes?

- Not to the more perfect ones; only to the inferior worlds.

57 - Do you have fun sometimes on hearing what people do?

- No. However, sometimes I have pity on them.

58 - Who are the ones that you preferably seek?

- Those that in good faith want to believe.

59 - Could you read our thoughts?

- No, I cannot read the thoughts, as I am not perfect enough.

60 - However, you must know our thoughts considering that you come to us. In other words, how can you know that we believe, in good faith?

- I don't read but I understand.

> OBSERVATION: Question 58 aimed at knowing whom he would spontaneously direct his preference, if not been evoked. As a spirit that is not from much of an elevated order he can feel forced, by the evocation, to come to a place that displeases him. On the other hand, not properly reading our thoughts, he certainly could see if the audience was meeting with a serious objective. From the nature of the questions and the conversations he heard, he could judge if if individuals sincerely seeking enlightenment formed the audience.

61 - Have you met any of your military comrades in the spiritual world?

- Yes but their positions were so different that I did not recognize all of them.

62 - What made up the differences?

- The happy or unhappy situation of each one.
- What did you say in those encounters?
- I told them: We shall rise up to God that allows it.

63 - How do you understand such a rise up to God?

- Each overtaken hurdle is one step more in that direction.

64 - You said you have died in the snow. Do you mean that you died of cold?

- Of cold and hunger.

65 - Were you immediately aware of your new existence?

- No, but I was no longer cold.

66 - Have you gone back some times to the place where your body remained?

- No. It made me suffer too much.

67 - We appreciate the explanations given, with good will. They provided us with good points of observation to our own improvement in the Spiritist Science.

- I am truly yours.

OBSERVATION: As seen, this spirit is not very advanced in the spirits' hierarchy. He himself recognizes his inferiority. His knowledge is limited, but has common sense, praiseworthy feelings and benevolence. As a spirit, his mission is very insignificant, considering that he plays the role of rapping spirit to draw the nonbelievers to the faith. But, as with the play role of the theater, couldn't the humble outfit of the accomplice hide a kind heart? His answers have the simplicity of ignorance but as he does not have the elevation of the philosophical language of the superior spirits, they are not less instructive though, in the study of the spirits' customs, if we can say so. It is only through the study of all classes of that world that we will one day understand it, marking by anticipation the place where each one of us may one day occupy. Looking at the situation created by people, like us, down here, by their vices and virtues, we feel encouraged to elevate to the summit, starting from here. It is the example against the precept. It is never too much to repeat that in order to know something well, having an idea free of illusions about it, it is necessary to see it in all of its aspects, as the botanic Biologist cannot get to know the vegetal kingdom if he does not observe from the humblest *cryptogamae* under the moss of the oak tree that elevates in the air.

Imposter Spirits - False

Father Ambrose

One of the hurdles presented by the spiritist communications is that of the imposter spirits, whose identity can induce error in that, under the shelter of a respectable name, they try to pass off absurdities. Such a danger has been explained to us on many occasions; however, it represents nothing to those who scrutinize the form as well as the content of the language of the invisible beings to whom they enter into communication.

It is not possible to repeat here what we have already said with that regard. Carefully refer to what we published in this Review, in The Spirits' Book and in our Practical Instructions and one will see that there isn't anything easier than the presumption against similar frauds, however little our good will may be. We only reproduce the following comparison which we have mentioned somewhere else:

"Suppose that in the room next door to you there are unknown individuals who you cannot see, although you can perfectly hear them. Wouldn't that be easy, from their conversation, to recognize if they are ignorant or scholars, decent or evil, serious or foolish, fine or rude people?"

Let us make another comparison, without leaving our material humanity. Suppose that someone is introduced to you with a distinct scholar name. When you hear the name you will receive him with all the consideration deserved by his supposed merit, but once he expresses himself as a fool you will immediately recognize it and will send him away as an imposter.

The same applies to the spirits. They are recognized by their language. The language of the superior spirits is always dignified and in harmony with sublime thoughts. A triviality will never blemish their purity. The grossness of the rude words is a peculiarity of the inferior spirits. All qualities and imperfections of the spirits are revealed in their language. One can then rightfully apply the statement of the celebrity writer: The style is the man.

An article of the "Spiritualiste de la Nouvelle-Orléans", December 1857, suggests those considerations to us.. It is a conversation established through a medium, between two spirits, one identifying himself as Father Ambrose, the other, Clement XIV. Father Ambrose was a respectable priest, deceased in Louisiana in the last century. He was a good man, of great intelligence who left a venerable memory.

In this dialogue the ridicule competes with the ignoble, being impossible to be mistaken relative to the quality of the interlocutors. It is also necessary to acknowledge that those spirits took little precaution with their disguise. Any intellectual person would admit, even after only a minute engaged with these spirits, that Father Ambrose and Clement XIV would go down to those trivialities which are closer to an exhibition of buffoonery. Lower class comedians that imitated those two persons would not express themselves differently.

We are convinced that the New Orleans circle where the fact took place understood it as we did. It would be an insult to doubt it. We only regret the fact that upon publishing it they did not add the corrective observation, thus avoiding that superficial people take it by a model of serious style from beyond the grave. Let us quickly declare, however, that this circle does not receive communications only of that order; there are others of very different character where we find the whole sublimity of thought and expression of the superior spirits.

We thought that the evocation of the true and the false Father Ambrose could offer useful material to the observations relative to imposter spirits. That is what we did, as shown by the following interview:

1. I ask the Almighty God to allow the spirit of the true Father Ambrose, deceased in Louisiana in the last century, leaving a venerable memory, come to communicate with us.
   - I am here.
2. Could you kindly tell us if it was really you and Clement XIV who had the conversation reported in the *Spiritualiste de la Nouvelle-Orléans* which we read in our last session?
   - I am sorry for the people who fell victims of the spirits as much as I am also sorry for those.
3. Who was the spirit that took your name?
   - A tumbler.
4. Was the interlocutor really Clement XIV?
   - It was a spirit similar to the one that used my name.
5. How could you allow such things in your name? Why haven't you come to expose the imposters?
   - Because I cannot always impede that people and spirits have fun.
6. I understand you with respect to the spirits. However, with respect to the persons who received the words, they are serious people; they did not seek amusement.
   - One more reason. They should quickly think that such words could only be the language of spirits of mockery.
7. Why do the spirits not teach in New Orleans the principles perfectly identical to the ones taught here?
   - Soon the Doctrine that is dictated to you will serve them. There will be only one.
8. Since this Doctrine will be taught there later, it seems to us that if it were immediately it would accelerate the progress and avoid that some had harmful doubts.

- Gods' predetermined designs are always impenetrable. Don't other things seem incomprehensible to us, given the means that God employs to achieve His objectives? It is necessary that the human being does get used to the distinction between the true and false. Not everyone could receive light from the same beam without being obfuscated.

9. Would you kindly give us your opinion about the reincarnation?
   - The spirits are created ignorant and imperfect. One incarnation only would not suffice to learn everything. It is necessary that they reincarnate to enjoy the happiness that God reserves to them.

10. Does reincarnation take place on Earth only or in other globes?
    - Reincarnation happens according to the progress of the spirit, in worlds more or less perfect.

11. This does not answer if it can happen on Earth?
    - Yes, it can happen on Earth and if the spirit asks for it as a mission, it will have more merit than if it had asked to advance more rapidly in more perfect worlds.

12. We ask the Almighty God to allow the spirit who took the name of Father Ambrose to come to communicate with us.
    - I am here but don't you confuse me (with someone else).

13. Are you really Father Ambrose? In the name of God I conjure you to tell the truth!
    - No.

14. What do you think about what you said in his name?
    - I think the same as those who heard me also thought.

15. Why have you used a respectable name to say such foolish things?
    - Names are nothing to our eyes. The works are everything. Since they could see what I really was by what I said, I did not give importance to the substitution of the name.

16. Why don't you sustain the imposture in our presence?
    - Because my language is a keystone by which you cannot be mistaken.

OBSERVATION: We were told several times that the imposture of certain spirits is a trial to our judgmental capacity. It is a kind of temptation, allowed by God so that, as Father Ambrose said, people may get used to distinguishing the true from the false.

17. What do you think about your partner Clement XIV?
    - He is not more deserving that I am. Both need indulgence.
18. In the name of the Almighty God, I ask you that he may come.
    - I am here, since the time the false Father Ambrose had arrived.
19. Why have you abused the credulity of respectable people to give a false idea of the Spiritist Doctrine?
    - Why are we inclined to error? Why aren't we perfect?
20. Didn't you think, both of you, that one day your deception would be discovered and that the true Father Ambrose and Clement XIV would not express themselves like you?
    - The deceptions were already known and punished by the one who created us.
21. Do you belong to the same class as the rapping spirits?
    - No, since logic is still necessary to do what we did in New Orleans.
22. (to the true Father Ambrose) – Do these imposters see you here?
    - Yes and they suffer with my presence.
23. Are they errant or reincarnated?
    - Errant. They would not be sufficiently perfect to such a detachment in case they were incarnated.
24. How about you Father Ambrose, what is your state?
    - Incarnated in a happy and unknown world to you.
25. We thank you for the clarifications that you have kindly given us. Would you kindly return on other occasions, bringing us good words and leaving an essay which could show the difference between your style and of the one who stole your name?
    - I am with those who seek the good in the truth

A Lesson of Calligraphy

By a Spirit

Generally speaking the spirits are not masters of calligraphy hence the writings through the medium are not typically elegant. With respect to that, one of our mediums, Mr. D..., presented an exceptional phenomenon that was the production of a much better writing under the inspiration of the spirits than from his own capacity. His normal calligraphy is really bad (he does not brag about it saying that it is the trait of the great spirits). However he acquires a special talent, very distinct, according to the communicating spirit, and it is always the same with the same spirit, but always clearer, more legible and more correct. With some writings it has an English style, marked by some audacity. One of the members of the Society, Dr. V..., had the idea of evoking a distinct calligraphy expert, with the objective of observing the writings. He knew one expert by the name of Bertrand, deceased a couple of years back, with whom we had the following conversation in another session:

1. Following our evocation procedure, he responded:
   - I am here.
2. Where were you when we evoked you?
   - I was already near you.

3. Do you know the main reason that made us evoke you?
   - No, but I wish to know.

   OBSERVATION: The spirit of Mr. Bertrand is still under the influence of matter, as it is reasonable to suppose. It is a known fact that such spirits are less capable of reading our thoughts than those who are less materialized.

4. We would like to have you writing through the medium a calligraphic text with the characters you would use when alive. Can you do that?
   - I can.

   OBSERVATION: Since those words the medium, who does not apply the rules learned from the masters of calligraphy, assumed a correct posture, without noticing, both of the body and the hand. Everything else was written like in the attached facsimile. As a means of comparison we also reproduced the normal writing of the medium.

5. Do you remember the circumstances of your earthly life?
   - Some.
6. Could you tell us in which year did you die?
   - I died in 1856.
7. How old were you?
   - I was 56 years old.
8. In which city did you live?
   - Saint-Germain.
9. What was your life style?
   - I tried to satisfy the bodily needs.
10. Did you take care of matters related to beyond the grave?
    - Almost nothing.

11. Do you regret the fact that you no longer belong to this world?
    - I regret not having effectively used my time.
12. Are you happier than on Earth?
    - No. I suffer for the good deeds I did not do.
13. What do you think about the future that awaits you?
    - I think that I need all of God's mercy.
14. What are your relationships in the world where you are?
    - Regrettable and unhappy relationships.
15. When you come to Earth, do you go to some places preferable to others?
    - I look for the souls that have compassion for my penalties or pray for me.
16. Do you see the earthly things with the same clarity as before?
    - I don't bother seeing them. If I did it would be another cause of displeasure.
17. They say that you showed little tolerance when alive. Is that true?
    - I was much violent.
18. What do you think about the objective of our meetings?
    - I wish I could have known about them when I was alive. They would have made me better.
19. Do you see other spirits where you are?
    - Yes, but I feel confused in their presence.
20. We pray to God that He may have you in His saint mercy. The feelings you have just expressed should allow you to find grace before Him. We don't doubt that they will help in your progress.
    - I thank you. May God protect you. I praise God for that. I hope my time comes.

    OBSERVATION: The teachings provided by the spirit of Mr. Bertrand are absolutely exact and in agreement with the life style and his known character. It is only when confessing his inferiority and his mistakes that the language is more serious and elevated than what one could expect. Once more we had the proof of the difficult situation of those that are very attached to matter. It is how the inferior spirits sometimes give us, by their example, valuable moral lessons.

FACSIMILE D'ÉCRITURES

Ecriture normale du médium.

Que cette Doctrine de salut ait été
ou non revélée, peu importe ! Chacun
pourra croire à cet égard ce
qu'il voudra.

ECRITURE DE L'ESPRIT DE M: BERTRAND
par le même médium.

N° Les N°° correspondent aux questions proposées (Voyez page 196.)

4 *Il le peut*

5 *Quelques unes*

6 *Je suis mort en 1856*

7 *56 ans*

8 *St Germain*

9 *Je sachais de contenter
mon corps*

Imp. Villain, r. de Sèvres, 45, Paris.

Correspondence

Brussels, June 15th, 1858

Dear Mr. Allan Kardec,

I receive and eagerly read your Spiritist Review and recommend it to my friends, not the simple reading but an in depth study of your The Spirits' Book. I greatly regret the fact that my physical concerns do not allow me to spare the time for the metaphysic studies, although I had taken them far enough to feel how close you are to the absolute truth, particularly when I see the perfect agreement between the answers they give us – you and me. The spirits themselves who have personally given you the merit for the writings, remain astonished by the depth and logic of the texts. You have elevated yourself to the level of Socrates and Plato by the moral and esthetic philosophy. As for myself, who know the phenomenon and your loyalty, I do not doubt the accuracy of the explanations given to you and reject all ideas I have previously published about it with Mr. Babinet, when I thought that there was only physical phenomena or foolishness, unworthy of the scholars' attention. Do not feel discouraged as I do not feel discouraged in the face of indifference of your contemporaries. What is written is written; what is sowed will germinate. The idea that life is a "sharpening" of the souls, a trial and expiation, is great, consoling, progressive and natural. Those who embrace these facts are happy in all positions. Instead of lamenting the physical and moral sufferings that abate them, they must rejoice or at least withstand it all with a Christian resignation.

	(French Original)
To be happy, flee the pleasure	*Pour être heureux, fuis le plaisir:*
Is the motto of the philosopher;	*Du philosophe est la devise;*
The effort we made to enter,	*L'effort qu'on fait pour le saisir,*
Costs more than the goods;	*Coûte plus que la marchandise;*
But it comes to us sooner or later,	*Mais il vient à nous tôt ou tard,*
In a form of a surprise;	*Sous la forme d'une surprise;*
This is a lackluster game of chance,	*C'est un terne au jeu du hasard,*
Worth ten thousand times the bet.	*Qui vaut dix mille fois la mise.*

I hope to be in Paris soon where I have many friends and a lot to do but will leave it all to find you and shake your hand.

Jobard
Director of the Royal Museum of the Industry

Such clear, honest statement made by the notable Mr. Jobard is, incontestably, a precious conquest that all adepts of the Spiritist Doctrine will applaud. However, in our opinion, it is even of a greater value to publically recognize a mistake made and deny ideas already published in the past without pressure or interest, particularly when the truth has emerged. This is what one can call the true courage of opinion and more importantly when one holds a well-known name. That attitude is peculiar to the great characters that can remain above all prejudices. All people can be wrong but there is greatness in recognizing one's own mistakes, whereas there is avarice in sustaining an opinion that one knows to be false, uniquely to show to the eyes of the common ones supreme infallibility. Such prestige could not deceive posterity which relentless removes all traps of pride. It is only posterity that founds reputation; only posterity has the right to inscribe in its temple: "This one was really great by the spirit and by the heart". How many times has it not written also: "This great person was very small".

The praises contained in the letter from Mr. Jobard would have prevented us from publishing it if they were addressed to us personally. As he recognizes, however, the work is by the spirits to whom we have only been the humble interpreter, all the credit belongs to them, and our modesty has nothing to suffer with a comparison which would only prove one thing: that this book could not have been dictated by anyone else but the spirits of a higher order.

In response to Mr. Jobard, we had asked him if he would allow us to publish his letter; at the same time we were assigned by the Parisian Society of Spiritist Studies the task of offering him the title of honorary and corresponding member. Here is the answer he kindly sent us and that we are happy to reproduce:

Brussels, June 22nd, 1858.

My dear colleague,

You ask me, with spiritual circumlocutions, if I dare publicly confess my belief in spirits and perispirits, by allowing you to publish my letter, and if I accept the title of the Academy of Spiritism that you founded, which would be, as they say, to have the courage of one's opinions.

I confess to feel a little humiliated to see you employing the same formulas and the same phrases used with the fools, as you should know that my whole life has been dedicated to the support of the truth and to the testimony in its favor, whenever I found it, be it in Physics be it in Metaphysics. I know well that the role of the adept of the new ideas is not always free from inconveniences, even in the enlightened age, and that one can be ridiculed by saying that it is day light at noon, and the least risk is to be considered mad. However, as Earth rotates and noon's light will shine for all, it is very necessary that the incredulous get to the evidence. It is also natural to hear the unbelievers denying the existence of the spirits as much as those who are still deprived of their rays negate the existence of light.

Is it possible to communicate with them? That is the whole issue. See and observe.

The fool always deny what he cannot understand;
To him, wonder is a simple apparatus;
Knows nothing, wants nothing, learns nothing;
Such is the trustworthy portrait of the incredulous.

I said to myself: The human being is evidently double, as death unfolds him. When half stays here, the other half goes somewhere else and keeps its individuality. Spiritism is then in perfect agreement with the Scriptures, with the dogma and with the religion that believes in spirits so much so that she exorcices the bad ones as well as she conjures the good ones. The "*vade retro*" and the "*veni creator*" give us a proof of that. Thus evocation is a serious thing and not a devils' work or charlatanism as some think. I am curious. I deny nothing but I want to see. I did not say: bring me the phenomenon. I went after it, instead of waiting for it in my chair, according to an illogical tradition.

I made the following reasoning about magnetism, more than forty years ago: it is impossible that so honorable individuals write thousands of books to make me believe in the existence of an inexistent thing. Then I tried for long and in vain, while I did not have the faith to find what I wanted. But I was well rewarded for my perseverance, since I was able to reproduce all the phenomena I had heard about. Then I paused for 15 years. The tables had appeared and I wanted to have a clear idea. Now comes Spiritism and I act still in the same way.

Whenever something new shows up, I will rush with the same fervor that I employ to follow all modern discoveries. It is curiosity that drags me and I regret the fact that the savage are not curious, hence they remain savage. Curiosity is the mother of instruction.

I know well that this learning enthusiasm has caused me harm, and that had I remained in that respectable mediocrity which leads to honor and fortune I would have had my fair share; but long ago I told myself that I was only passing through this ordinary hostel where it is not worth to unpack. What made me painlessly withstand the adversities, the injustices and theft of which I was a privileged victim, was the idea that here there is no such a happiness or disgrace worthy of our joy or affliction.

I worked, worked, worked, and all that gave me the strength to fustigate my most bloodthirsty adversaries and imposed respect onto the others, as now I am happier and more peaceful than the persons who stole from me an inheritance of twenty million. I am sorry for them as I don't envy their position in the spiritual world. If I regret that fortune it is not for me: I have no stomach to eat twenty million, but for the good that it has prevented me from doing. Similarly to a lever in the hands of a man who could handle it, what an impulse it could have given to Science and progress! Those who have fortune frequently ignore the true enjoyment they could provide themselves.

Do you know what is missing to quickly propagate the Spiritist Science? A rich man who would dedicate his fortune to that by pure devotion, not mixing pride and selfishness; a man who would do things with greatness, without parsimony and stinginess. Such a man would make Science advance half a century. Why have I been deprived of the means of doing that?

Such a man will appear. Something tells me so. Honor him!

I saw the evocation of a living person who had syncope until the spirit returned. Evoke me to see what I am going to say. Evoke also the late Dr. Mure, who died in Cairo on June 4th. He was a great spiritist and a Homeopathic Physician. Ask him if he still believes in elves. He is certainly in Jupiter as he was a great spirit, even here on Earth; a true teaching prophet and my friend. Would he be happy with the eulogy I wrote to him?

You may say that this letter is too long but it is not so easy to have me as correspondent. I will read your latest book which I have just received. At first sight I do not doubt that you do well on destroying a lot of prejudices, hence you were able to show the serious side of the matter. The Badet case is very interesting. We shall talk about that later.

Yours truly,

Jobard.

Any comment would be superfluous. Everyone will easily appreciate the depth and sagacity that added to noble thoughts have placed the author in such a commended position among his contemporaries. We can feel honored for being crazy (according to the understanding of our adversaries) whenever we have such companions in misfortune.

To Mr. Jobard's observation: "Is it possible to communicate with the spirits? That is the whole issue. See and observe." we can add: The communications with the beings of the invisible world are neither a discovery nor a modern invention. Since the remotest antiquity they were practiced by people who were our masters in Philosophy and whose names we daily invoke as authorities. Why could this happen then and not today?

The following letter was addressed to us by one of our subscribers. As it contains an instructive part which may serve to the majority of our readers and since it is one more proof of the moral influence of the Spiritist Doctrine, we have the duty of publishing it in its totality, answering the questions it raises to everyone.

Bordeaux, June 24th, 1858.

"Dear Sir and Comrade in Spiritism,

You will certainly allow one of your subscribers and keenest readers to give you such a title, because this remarkable Doctrine must be a fraternal link among all those who understand and practice it.

In one of your previous issues you mentioned the notable drawings executed by Mr. Victorien Sardou, representing dwellings in Jupiter. Your description exacerbates in us the desire to get to know them. Can you tell us if that gentleman wishes to publish them? I have no doubt that it would be a success, considering the daily reach of the spiritist belief. It would be the necessary complement to such a seductive description given by the spirits about that happy planet.

I must say, dear sir, that about eighteen months ago we evoked, in our small and intimate circle, a former judge and our ancestor, who died in 1756, leading a life, which was the model of all virtues and a very superior spirit, although unnoticed in history. He said he was incarnated in Jupiter and gave us a moral teaching of remarkable wisdom, in total agreement with your precious The Spirits' Book. We naturally had the curiosity of requesting from him some information with respect to the state of the world that he inhabits, to which he responded with great benevolence. Now you may judge our surprise and our joy by reading in your Review a description absolutely identical of that planet, at least the outline, hence we took our questions to the same extents that you did. Everything is identical physically and morally, even relatively to the condition of the animals. Airborne dwellings were mentioned, fact not covered by you.

Considering that there were things that were difficult for us to understand, our relative added the following outstanding words: "It is not surprising that you cannot understand things that were not made for your senses, but as you advance in Science you will understand them better through your thoughts. They will no longer seem extraordinary to you. It is not far the time when you will receive more complete clarifications about this aspect. The spirits are assigned the task of instructing you about it and to give you an objective and to motivate you towards good." On reading your description and the announcement of the drawings you have mentioned, we naturally thought that the time had come.

The incredulous will, no doubt, criticize that paradise of the spirits, as they criticize everything else, even immortality and the most sanctified things. I know well that nothing materially proves the truthfulness of that description but to those who believe in the existence and revelation of the spirits, wouldn't such a coincidence bring reflection? We form an idea about countries that we have never seen by the description of the travelers, when there is coincidence among them. Why wouldn't the same apply to the spirits? Is there anything in their description about Jupiter that denies reason? No. Everything is in agreement with the idea of more perfect existences. I will say more: it is in agreement with the Scriptures, as I will one day demonstrate. It seems so logical and consoling to me that it will be painful to renounce to the hope of inhabiting a fortunate world, where there is no evil, no envy, no enemies, neither selfishness nor hypocrisy. That is why I employ all my energy to deserve to move there. When in our small circles someone seems to have too material thoughts, we say: "Be careful otherwise you won't go to Jupiter." And we are happy to think that such a future is reserved to us, if not in the next phase at least in one of the following ones. Thank you my dear brother for having opened to us that new path of hope. As you had precious revelations about that world, you may have also had about the others that form our planetary system. Do you intend to publish them? This would form a very interesting set. Looking to the planets we would rejoice on thinking about the variety of beings that inhabit them; space would seem less empty to us. How can man, who believes in the power and wisdom of God, entertain the thought that these millions of globes are inert and lifeless bodies? That we are the only ones in this miniscule grain of sand which we call Earth? I will say that it is impiety. Such an idea saddens me. If that were true, I would see myself in a desert.

With all my heart, all yours,

Marius M.

(retired)

The title that our honorable subscriber wanted to give us is very flattering so that we cannot be anything else but appreciative for his judgment by considering us worthy. Spiritism is in fact a fraternal link which must lead everyone that understands its essence to the practice of the true Christian charity, as it tends to eliminate the feelings of hatred, envy and jealousy that divide human beings. But that fraternity will not be the one of a sect; to be in perfect agreement with the Divine precepts of the Christ it should encompass the whole humanity, hence all people are children of God. If some are deviated, it commands that we feel sorry for them and prohibits that we hate them. "Love thy neighbor", said Jesus. He did not say: "Love no one but those who think like you." That is why when our adversaries throw a stone at us we should not return curses. Such principles will convert those who profess them into people of peace who will not find in chaos and in the practice of evil towards their neighbors the satisfaction of their passions.

The feelings of our honorable correspondent are impregnated by much elevation to persuade us that he understands fraternity, as it must be, in its broadest meaning.

We feel happy for the communication he promises us about Jupiter. The coincidence he indicates is not the only one, as we can see in the article about the subject. Well, whatever the opinion one might have regarding the issue, it is still a material for observation. The spiritual world is full of mysteries that need to be studied with great care. The moral consequences that our correspondent extracts from that are characterized by a logic that will not go unnoticed to anyone.

With respect to the publication of the drawings, several subscribers have indicated the same desire to us. The compilation, however, would be too extensive, as the reproduction by engraving would signify excessive thus impracticable costs. The spirits themselves had said that it was not yet time to publish them, maybe for that reason. Fortunately the difficulty has now being overcome. The drawing medium, Mr. Victorien Sardou, became an engraving medium, although he had never touched a chisel. Now he makes the drawings directly on copper, which will allow the direct reproduction without the support of any strange artist. Hence the financial issue was minimized so that we will be able to provide a remarkable proof in our next number, followed by a technical description which he will kindly write, according to the documentation provided by the spirits. There are a large number of drawings that later will form a true atlas. We know another drawing medium by which the spirits produce not less curious drawings about another world. Regarding the state of the several known globes we have general teachings about some and a few details about others. We have not yet established a convenient time for its publication.

ALLAN KARDEC[31]

---

31 Paris – Typography Cosson & Co., Rue du Four-Saint-Germain, 43

August 1858

Contradictions In the
Language of the Spirits

The contradictions so frequently found in the language of the spirits, even about essential questions, have been a cause of uncertainty to some people, with respect to the real value of their communications, circumstance of which the adversaries also take advantage. At first sight those contradictions really seem to be one of the main stopping blocks of the Spiritist Science.

Let us see if they hold the importance attributed to them.

One needs to start by analyzing how Science produced similar anomalies at the beginning of its inception. Which scholar was not confused in his investigation by facts that apparently contradicted the established rules? Doesn't Botany, Zoology, Physiology, Medicine and the language itself offer us thousands of similar examples and doesn't their bases defy any contradiction? It is by comparing the facts, observing the analogies and dissimilarities that it is possible to gradually establish the rules, the classification, and the principles: in one word, to constitute the Science.

Well, Spiritism has just germinated. Thus it is not surprising that it adjusts to the common law while its study is completed. It is only then that one will acknowledge that with this Science, as with everything else, the exception almost always confirms the rule.

As a matter of fact, the spirits have always told us that we should not be worried about such small divergences and that everything would be soon driven towards a unity of belief. In fact, such a prediction holds true every day, as we penetrate further and further into the causes of these mysterious phenomena and that the facts are better observed. Contrary to that, the dissidences manifested in the origin evidently tend to weaken. One can even say that nowadays these are nothing more than isolated personal opinions.

Although Spiritism is in nature and that it has been known and practiced since the beginning, it is a fact that it has never been as universally spread as it is today. This is due to the fact that at other times it was studied as something mysterious, where the commoners were not initiated. It was preserved by tradition so that the vicissitudes of humanity and the lack of means for its transmission weakened insensibly. The spontaneous phenomena that took place, from time to time, went unnoticed or were interpreted according to the ignorance of the day or even were exploited to the benefit of one belief or another.

It was reserved to our century, when progress receives a never-ending impulse, to bring about a Science that, so to speak, only existed in its latent state. It was only a few years ago that the phenomena were seriously observed. Spiritism is truly a new Science that step by step implants into the heart of the masses, waiting to occupy an official position.

This Science, in principle, seemed very simple. To the superficial minds it was nothing more than the art of moving tables. However, a more careful observation revealed a much more complex Science than previously thought from its ramifications and consequences. The turning tables are like Newton's apple, whose fall contains the system of the world.

It has happened to Spiritism the same that happens, in principle, to everything else: the first ones could not see it all; each one would see from their standpoint and communicate their impressions from their point of view and according to their ideas and prejudices. Well, isn't that a fact known to everyone that, depending on the environment, the same object may seem cold to some and hot to others?

Let us take another example from the ordinary things, even trivial ones, in order to make us better understood. The newspapers have published lately: "Mushrooms is one of the most bizarre foods: delicious or deadly, microscopic or showing phenomenal dimensions, constantly disorienting the Botanists. In the Doncastre tunnel there is a mushroom developing for about twelve months and, as it seems, has not yet reached its final phase of growth. It is currently fifteen feet in diameter. It showed up on a wooden log, considered the most beautiful specimen ever observed. Its classification is difficult as the opinions are divided."

Thus, here we have Science perturbed by the appearance of one mushroom that presents a new species. This fact has provoked in us the following reflection: Suppose several naturalists independently observing a variety of this vegetable. One will say that the mushroom is an edible criptogamus, appreciated by the gluttonous; the second one will say that it is poisonous; the third will say that it is invisible to the naked eye; the fourth will say that it can reach up to forty-five feet in diameter, etc. At first sight all opinions seem contradictory and not much helpful to the definition of the true nature of the mushrooms. Later a fifth observer will acknowledge the identity of the general characters and show that those diversified properties are nothing more than varieties or subdivisions of only one class. Each observer was right from their point of view; all were wrong though when concluding from the particular to the general and when they took the part by the whole.

The same happens with the spirits. They have been judged according to the nature of the relationships established with them; consequently some were made demons and other angels. Because there was rush in explaining the phenomena before everything was seen, each observer made it on their own terms and, very naturally, sought the causes where the object of their concerns were placed. The Magnetist referred everything to magnetism; the Physicist to the action of electricity and so forth. The divergence of opinions with respect to Spiritism comes then from the different aspects that are considered.

On which side is the truth?

This is what the future will demonstrate. But the general tendency will not move much. One principle evidently dominates and progressively unites the premature systems. A less exclusive observation will unite all systems in a common origin and we shall soon see that the divergence is more accessory than fundamental.

It is understandable that the individual may raise antagonistic theories about things but what can seem more original is that the spirits themselves contradict each other. This is what, since the beginning, caused a certain confusion of ideas.

The several spiritist theories have then two sources: some were born from the human brain; the spirits gave others. The former emanates from human beings that showing excessive confidence in their own judgement believe to have the key to what they seek, when most of the time they have only found a picklock. No surprise there, but the fact that among the spirits some said one thing and others something else was less conceivable. However, this is now perfectly explainable.

In the beginning an absolutely false idea was made about the nature of the spirits. They were seen as special beings, not having anything in common with matter, knowing everything. They were, according to personal opinions, malefactors or benefactors, some with every virtue others with every vice, all generally with an infinite knowledge and superior to humanity. Following the news of the recent manifestations, the first idea that came to mind to most people was that it was a means of penetrating all occult things; a new method of guess work, less subjected to doubts as with the vulgar processes.

Who could tell the number of people who dreamt of making easy fortune by the revelation of the occult treasures; by the technological or scientific discoveries which would cost the inventors no more than the work of describing what was dictated by the wise people of the other world! God knows how many failures and disillusions!

How many pseudo recommendations, each more ridicule than the next, were not given by the charlatans of the invisible world! We know someone that requested an infallible recommendation to tint the hair. A waxy formula was given which reduced the person's hair to something like a compact mass, which the poor patient had great difficulty to eliminate.

All these dreamlike hopes had to fade away while the nature of that world became clearer and the true objective of the visits we receive from its inhabitants became known. To several people, however, where was the value of those spirits who did not even have the power of providing some millions to those who did not do anything? They could not be spirits!

The short lasting fever was replaced by indifference and in some by incredulity. Oh! How many proselytes could have the spirits made if they could benefit the indolent! The devil himself would have been adored had he had agitated his wallet.

Besides the dreamers there were serious people who saw something in those phenomena beyond vulgarity. They carefully observed; probed the inside of that mysterious world and easily noticed a providential objective of an elevated order in those strange if not new facts. Everything changed in aspect once noticed that the spirits were beings who lived on Earth, to whom we will join after our death; that they left their dense covering here like the silkworm leaves its cocoon to become a moth.

We could no longer doubt when we saw our parents, friends and contemporaries coming to talk to us, providing irrefutable proofs of their presence and identity. Considering the great diversity of characters presented by humanity, under the intellectual and moral point of view, and the crowd that daily emigrates from Earth to the invisible world, it disgusts reason to admit that a stupid Samoyed, a fierce cannibal or a vile criminal suffer with death a transformation that puts them on the same spot as the scholar and the person of good deeds. One can thus understand that there should be more or less advanced spirits and from there on explain the so much diversified communications in which some elevate to the sublime and others go down to the dirt.

We understand even better when we stopped believing that our small grain of sand, lost in space, is the only inhabited among millions of similar globes, learned that it occupies an intermediary position, close to the lowest of the scale; and as consequence that there are beings more advanced than the most advanced among us and others even more basic than our savage ones.

Since then the moral and intellectual horizon have amplified, as our earthly horizon when the fourth part of the world was discovered; at the same time the power and majesty of God grew before our eyes, from the finite to the infinite. Thus, the contradictions in the language of the spirits were soon explained, as it was understood that inferior beings from all points of view could not think and express like the superior ones; consequently, they could not know everything, neither understand everything and that God should reserve only to the elected ones the knowledge of the mysteries unreachable by ignorance.

The spirits' scale, outlined by the spirits themselves and according to the observation of the facts, gives us the key to all apparent anomalies of the language of the spirits. It is necessary to get to know them by the force of habit and, so to speak, be able to deduce their class at first sight, according to the nature of their manifestations. According to the need, it is necessary to say to one that he is a liar, to another that he is a hypocrite, to this one that he is malevolent, to the other that he is rude, etc..., without being impressed by their arrogance and bragging, neither by their threats or sophisms nor even by their adulation. This is how one can keep this mob away that pullulates around us and that stays away when we know how to attract only spirits that are truly good and serious; we do the same with respect to the living ones.

Will these tiny beings be eternally dedicated to evil and ignorance? No, hence such partiality would not be in agreement with the justice, neither the goodness of the Creator who provides the existence and well being of the smallest insect. It is through a succession of existences that they elevate and approach God, while improving themselves. Those inferior spirits only know God by the name; they neither see God nor understand God, in the same way that the last peasant in the middle of his heathers does not see nor understand the sovereign of his own country.

If we carefully study the own character of each class of spirits we will easily understand that there are some incapable of providing accurate teachings regarding the state of their world. If we consider further that there are others that by nature are frivolous, liars, mockers, malevolent, and that others are still impregnated by the earthly ideas and prejudices, we will understand that in their relationship with us they can make fun of us; consciously induce error by malice; affirm something that they don't know; give us perfidious advices or even trick us in good faith, when judging things from their point of view.

Let us make a comparison.

Suppose that a colony of Earth's inhabitants, on a given day, find the means of traveling to the moon; suppose that the colony is composed of several elements of the population of our globe, since the most civilized European to the Australian savage. Moon's inhabitants would be moved and even astonished if they could obtain accurate teachings from their visitors about our planet, which some supposed inhabited but were not sure, since among them there are some that consider themselves the only inhabitants of the universe. They surround the newcomers and question them; the wise ones rush to publish the moral and physical history of Earth. How could it not be an authentic history once they have visual witnesses? One of them has a Zealander in his house who says that on Earth it is a real treat to eat men and that God allows it so as the victims are sacrificed in God's honor. In another house there is a philosopher that talks about Plato and Aristotle and says that anthropophagi is an abomination condemned by all Divine and human laws. Here a Muslim who does not eat flesh but who says that salvation is conquered by killing the highest number of Christians; in another place there is a Christian saying that Muhammed was an imposter; further down there is a Chinese who considers everyone else as barbarians and affirms that when one has too many children God allows to throw them into the river; a Bohemian paints the picture of dissolute life in the big capital cities; an Anchorite preaches abstinence and mortifications; a Hindu fakir shreds the body and to open the doors of heaven he self imposes such a suffering that, comparatively, the privations of the most devout cenobite constitute sensuality. Then comes a Scientist saying that it is Earth that turns not the Sun; a peasant says that the Scientist is a liar since he sees the

Sun rising and setting very well; a Senegalean says that it is hot; an Eskimo says that the sea is a frozen plain and that traveling can only be done by sledges. Politics is not forgotten: some praise absolutism, others the liberals; this one says that slavery is against nature and that, as children of God, all people are brothers and sisters; another one says that some races were cut for slavery and that they are much happier than in a free state, etc.

I believe the Selenites (Moon's inhabitants) would feel embarrassed to write Earth's physical, political, moral and religious history based on such documents.

"Who knows", they think, "we will find greater unity among the scholars? Let us interrogate a group of doctors."

One of them, a doctor from the Parisian Faculty, center of lights, says that every disease in principle has a contaminated blood and because of that it is necessary to renovate the blood, bleeding the patient whatever the case may be.

- You are wrong, says a wise comrade, the human being never has enough blood; if you drain it you drain life. I agree that the blood may be contaminated but what do we do when a vase is dirty? Nobody breaks it but tries to clean it; then give purgative, purgative, and purgative until it is clean.

A third one says:

- Gentlemen, with the bleeding you kill the patients and with the purgatives you poison them. Nature is wiser than all of us. Let it run its course. Let us wait.
- That is it, reply the other two, if we kill our patients you allow them to die.

Things get heated up when a fourth doctor, taking aside a Selenite, pulls him to the left saying:

- Do not listen to them. They are all ignorant. I don't even know why they belong to the Academy! Follow my reasoning: every patient is weak; thus there is a weakening of the organs. This is pure logic or I don't recognize myself anymore. One has to provide tonus but for that there is only one remedy: cold water. I stick to that.

- Do you cure every patient of yours?
- Everyone, as long as the disease is not deadly.
- With such an infallible process, do you belong to the Academy?
- I have presented my candidacy three times but would you believe that I have always been blocked by these pseudo scholars, because they know that I would pulverize them with my cold water?
- Mr. Selenite, says another person in the conversation, pulling him to the right – we live in an atmosphere of electricity which is the true principle of life; increase it when it is not enough; diminish it when in excess; neutralize the opposing fluids one by the other - that is the secret. I do wonders with my devices. Read my ads and you will see![32]

We would never come to an end if we wanted to summarize every contrary theory that was preconized, from all branches of human knowledge, including exact sciences. However, it was in the metaphysics that the field was widely open to the most contradictory doctrines.

Nevertheless, an individual of spirit and discerning capacity (why would he not be on the moon?) compare all these incoherent affirmations and comes to a very logical conclusion: there are hot and cold regions on Earth; in certain places people devour each other; in others they kill those who think differently; all for the great glory of their divinity; finally, each speaks according to their knowledge and praises things from the point of view of their passions and interests.

---

32 The reader will recognize that our criticism only addresses the exaggeration in all things. There is always a good side in everything; the error is in the exclusivism that the wise person will know how to avoid. We don't have the intention of confusing the true scholars, of whom humanity is honored in fairness, but those who exploit the ideas without discernment. These are the ones we want to talk about. Our objective is uniquely to demonstrate that the official Science is not exempt of contradictions.

Now, who is going to preferably believe?

By the language and without difficulty, he will distinguish the truly wise from the ignorant; the serious person from the frivolous; the thinker from the sophist. He will not confuse good with bad feelings, elevation with ridicule, good with evil and shall say: "I have to hear everything, understand everything, because, even from the speech of the most ignorant, I can learn; but my esteem and confidence will only be conquered by the worthy one. "If this earthly colony wants to implant their habits and customs in our world, the scholars will repel the advices that seem harmful and shall follow those that seem advanced and in which they cannot detect falsehood or lie but, on the contrary, recognize in them the sincere love for the good.

Would we proceed differently if a colony of Selenites happened to come to Earth? Then! What is presented here as a hypothesis is a reality with respect to the spirits that although don't show up in flesh and blood they are not less present because of that, in an occult way, transmitting their thoughts to us through their interpreters, which are the mediums.

When we have learned to get to know them we will judge them by their language, by their principles. Their contradictions will no longer have anything that surprises us as we will see that some know what others ignore; that some are placed much below or are still too materialized to understand and appreciate things of a more elevated order. Such is the person that at the foot of the mountain cannot see more than a few steps ahead of him while the one who is at the summit can see a boundless horizon.

The first cause of contradictions is thus the degree of intellectual and moral development of the spirits but there are others about which it is useless to draw the attention.

It should be said that one has to consider the question of the inferior spirits, since it is understandable that they can make mistakes out of ignorance. How to admit that the superior spirits may be in disagreement? How can they employ a language in one place and a different one in another place? That the same spirit, finally, is not always coherent with itself?

The answer to that question rests on the complete knowledge of the Spiritist Science and this Science cannot be taught in a few words because it is as vast as all philosophical Sciences. As all other branches of human knowledge it is only possible to acquire it by the study and observation. We cannot repeat here everything we have published with that regard; we refer the reader to that material, limiting ourselves to a simple summary. Every difficulty disappears to the one who casts an investigative eye over this question, without preventions.

Facts demonstrate that the deceiving spirits have no scruples in adopting respectable names, aiming at better enforcing their nastiness, fact that also happens among us. By the fact that a spirit presents any name it does not follow that he is really the one he declares to be. There is in the language of the serious spirit, however, a touch of distinction that could not go unnoticed. He only breathes goodness and benevolence and never denies himself. The language of the imposter spirits, on the contrary and despite the varnish that it shows, hurts the ears, as they say. It is not surprising then that under the disguise of certain names, the inferior spirits teach crazy things. It is up to the observer to know the truth, what is not difficult as long as he wishes to deeply study what we have said in the "*Practical Instruction*" (The Mediums' Book).

Those spirits flatter the taste and inclination of people whose character they know is weak and credulous enough to pay attention to them. These people become echoes of their prejudice and even of their superstitious ideas. This is due to a very simple reason: the spirits are attracted by their sympathy to the spirits of people who evoke them and listen to them with pleasure.

As for the serious spirits, according to the person they communicate with, they can also use a different language, but with a different objective. Whenever they judge convenient and to better elucidate, they express in accordance with the time, place and people, avoiding sudden confrontation with entrenched ideas. "That is why", they say, "we do not speak to a

Chinese or to a Muslim as we do to a Christian or a civilized individual, because we would not be heard. Sometimes we may seem to agree with the way people see things so as to gradually lead them to the desired teaching, whenever possible and without affecting the essential truth".

Isn't that evident that if a spirit wanted to lead a fanatic Muslim to practice the sublime teaching of the Gospel by saying: "so whatever you wish that others would do to you, do also to them…" it would have been rejected had it been said to have come from Jesus? Well, what is preferable: to leave the Muslim in his fanaticism or make him good, inducing him momentarily to think that it had come from Allah? This is a problem whose solution we will leave to the reader. As for us, it seems that making him kinder and more human he will be less fanatic and more accessible to the idea of a new belief instead of imposing it by force. There are truths that in order to be accepted cannot be carelessly thrown on people's faces.

How many bad things would people have avoided had they always behaved like that?

As seen, the spirits are very careful regarding the way they speak. In such a case, however, the divergence is apparent rather than real. It leads the individual to the good; it destroys selfishness, pride, hatred, envy, and jealousy, teaching them the practice of true Christian charity that is essential to them. The rest will come with time. They preach by example as much as by speech, since they are truly good and superior spirits. They breathe kindness and benevolence. Irritation, violence, bitterness, harsh words, or even when the spirits say good things are never a sign of true superiority. The really superior spirits are never upset or affected. If they are not heard they just leave. That is all.

There are still two causes of apparent contradiction that should not be left blank. As we already said on many occasions, the inferior spirits tell us what we want to hear, without any compromise with the truth. The superior spirits go quiet or refuse to answer whenever we ask something indiscreet or about something that they do not have permission to explain. "In such a case", they told us, "you should never insist because the frivolous spirits will respond and trick you; you may think that it was us and you will even admit that we are in contradiction. The serious spirits are never in contradiction. Their language is always the same with the same people. If some of them say contradictory things taking a common name, be certain that it is not the same spirit that speaks or, at least, that is not a good spirit. You shall recognize the good one by the principles that he teaches; hence every spirit that does not teach the good is not a good spirit. You should reject him." Wishing to say the same thing in two different places the same spirit will not literally use the same words. Thought is everything to him. Unfortunately the human being is fonder of format than meaning. It is the format that he always interprets according to his ideas and passions and that interpretation may give rise to apparent contradictions that also originate from the insufficiency of human language to express super human things. Let us study in depth, let us investigate the intimate thought and we will see that many times there is analogy where a superficial exam led us to see nonsense.

The causes of contraction in the spirits' language may thus be summarized as:

1. The degree of ignorance or wisdom of the spirits with whom we communicate;
2. The trickery of the inferior spirits who, by malice, ignorance or malevolence, on taking a borrowed name, may say things in contradiction to others that were said somewhere else by the spirit whose name they stole;
3. The personal failures of the medium who can influence the communications and alter or distort the thought of the spirits;
4. The insistence on obtaining an answer to something that the spirit refuses to say and that is answered by an inferior spirit;
5. The own will of the spirit who speaks in accordance with the moment, place and persons and may judge convenient not to say everything to everybody;

6. Insufficiency of human language to express things of the incorporeal world;

7. The interpretation that each one may give to a word or to an explanation, according to their own ideas, prejudices or the point of view that was used to analyze the issue.

There are many difficulties that can only be overcome by a long and persistent study. Also, we have never said that the Spiritist Science is easy. The serious observer that investigates everything with maturity, patience and perseverance, learns a number of delicate nuances that escapes the superficial observer. It is through these subtle details that he initiates into this Science. Experience teaches us how to get to know the spirits, as it teaches us how to get to know men.

We have just analyzed the contradictions from a generic point of view. In other articles we shall analyze specific and more important points.

Charity By the spirit of
St. Vincent of Paul

(Society of Spiritist Studies, session of June 8th, 1858)

B e good and charitable, this is the key placed in your hands. The whole eternal happiness is contained in this statement: "Love one another". The soul cannot rise to the spiritual regions unless through dedication to their neighbor; it cannot find happiness and consolation but in the ecstasy of charity. Be good, help thy brothers, and put aside this horrible ulcer of selfishness. Once this duty has been accomplished it shall open to you the paths of eternal happiness. As a matter of fact, who among you has not felt the heart beat and intimate joy expanding by the practice of one single act of charity? You should not think but in that kind of happiness provided by a good deed, with what you shall always be in the path of spiritual progress. There is no lack of examples. It is only the will power that is rare.

See the crowd of good people whose devoted memory history remembers. I can name by the thousands those whose moral had no other objective but to improve your globe. Hasn't Christ told you everything that concerns the virtues of charity and love? Why his Divine teachings are left aside? Why are the ears covered to his Divine words and the heart closed to all his sooth teachings?

I wish the reading of the Gospel were done with more personal interest. But that book is abandoned; it is transformed into empty expressions and dead words; that remarkable code is forgotten. All your evils come from the voluntary abandonment allowed to its summary of the Divine laws. Thus, read those pages of fire from Jesus' devotement and meditate about them. I feel ashamed myself for daring to promise you an essay about charity when I think that in that book you will find all teachings that should take you to the celestial regions.

Strong people, get ready; weak people, have by weapons your kindness and your faith; have more persuasion, more constancy in the propagation of your new doctrine. We only came to bring you encouragement; it is only to stimulate the zeal and virtues that God allows us to manifest to you. But, if you want, you won't need anything but God's help and your own will power. The spiritist manifestations were made but to the closed eyes and indocile hearts. There are people among you that must execute missions of love and charity: listen to them and exalt their voices; make their merits shine and you will be exalted by the disinterest and by the living faith that shall impregnate you.

Too extensive and detailed should be the advices given to you about the widening of the circle of charity; about the inclusion of all the unfortunate in this circle whose miseries are ignored; about every pain which should be sought after in their own refuge to console them in the name of this Divine virtue, charity. I see with satisfaction the number of prominent and powerful people that help in the search for that progress, which shall unite all human classes: the fortunate and the disgraced. Strange thing! All the unfortunate extend their hands and help one another in their own misery. Why do the happy ones take so long to hear the voices of the unfortunate? Why is it necessary a powerful earthly hand to promote the charitable missions? Why don't they respond with more zeal to those appeals? Why do they allow misery, as if with pleasure, blemishing the image of humanity?

Charity is the fundamental virtue that must sustain the whole edifice of the earthly virtues. Without it there is no other. Without charity, there is no faith or hope. Without charity, there is no hope of a better fate or moral interest to guide us. Without charity, there is no faith since faith is a pure light beam that enlightens a charitable soul. It is its decisive consequence.

When you allow your heart open to the first supplicating miserable whose hand reaches out to you; when you extend your hand not asking if that misery is true or if that fate has a vice by cause; when you let the whole justice in God's hands; when you pass to the Creator the punishment of all false miseries; finally when you practice charity by the pleasure it provides, without questioning its utility, then you shall be the children that God will love and embrace.

Charity is the eternal anchor of salvation in all globes; it is the purest emanation of the Creator; it is God's own virtue passed on to the creatures. How can you ignore such a supreme benevolence? With that thought, who would be the sufficiently perverse heart to suppress and repel that Divine feeling? Who would be the sufficiently evil child to rebel against such a sweet touch of charity?

I dare not mention what I have done as the spirits also have the modesty of their work. However I think that the work I have initiated is one of those that should contribute a lot to alleviate your neighbors. I frequently see spirits requesting the mission to continue my work; I see my kind and dear sisters in their devout and divine ministry; I see them practicing the virtues that I recommend to you, finding the true joy provided by their existence of devotement and sacrifices. It is a great happiness to me to see how much dignified their character is; how much appreciated and protected their mission is. Good people, people of good and strong will, unite to continue the work of amplifying the propagation of charity. You shall find the reward of such a virtue through its own exercise. There isn't a spiritual happiness that cannot be provided by that, in this existence already. Be united; love one another, according to the precepts of Christ.

Amen.

- Q. We thank St. Vincent de Paul by this beautiful and good communication just given.
- A. I wish it were beneficial to all.

- Q. Would you allow us a few complementary questions about what you have just said?
- A. Certainly, as my objective is to enlighten you. Ask whatever you want.

1. Charity can be understood in two ways: the alms properly said and the love towards humanity. When you said that we should open our hearts to the requests of the unfortunate that reaches out to us, without asking if their misery is feigned, wasn't your intention to talk about charity from the point of view of alms?
   - Yes, only in that paragraph.
2. You said we should leave it to God's justice to appreciate the false misery. However, it seems to us that giving to those that do not deserve it without discernment or that could earn their leaving through honest work is to encourage addiction and laziness. Had the lazy ones easily found their neighbors' wallet open then they would multiply to infinity, in detriment of those in real need.
   - You can identify those who can work then charity compels you to do everything to provide them with work. However, there are also miserable charlatan who know well how to simulate miseries that are not theirs. These are the ones who should be left to God's justice.
3. Someone who can only give a cent and can choose between two unfortunate persons who beg for something, has he the right to inquiry to see which one is in real need or should he give to the first to come, without examination?
   - Should give to the one who seems to suffer the most.
4. Shouldn't it be part of charity the way it is done?
   - The merit of charity is in the way it is done, above all. Benevolence is always an indication of a nice soul.

5. Which kind of merit do you recognize on those who are generally known as occasional benefactors?
   - They only do half of the good deeds. Their benefits are received but don't do them any good.

6. Jesus said: "...do not let your left hand know what your right hand is doing". Do those who give for ostentation have any merit?
   - They have only the merit of pride for which they shall be punished.

7. Christian charity, in its broadest meaning, does it not encompass kindness, benevolence and indulgence towards others' weaknesses?
   - Do as Jesus. He told you everything. Listen to him more than ever.

8. Is charity well understood when exclusive among creatures of the same opinion or from the same party?
   - No. It is the spirit of sect or party that, above all, has to be abolished. Hence, all peopel are brothers and sisters. That is the point where we concentrate our efforts.

9. Suppose a person sees two men in danger, but he can only save one. One is his friend the other his enemy. Who should he save?
   - He must save the friend as the friend could accuse him of lack of friendship. As for the other, God will take care of him.

The Rapping Spirit of Dibbelsdorf Lower Saxony

By Dr. Kerner

Translated from the German by Alfred Pireaux

The story of the rapping spirit of Dibbelsdorf, besides its humorous side, contains an instructive part, as indicated in the old documents published in 1811 by Priest Capelle.

On December 2nd, 1761 at six o'clock at night a kind of hammering sound, apparently coming from the floor, was heard from Anthony Kettelhut's room. Thinking that it was his server who wanted to have fun with the maid that was in the spinsters' room, he went out prepared to throw a bucket of water on the mischievous man's head but he found nobody outside. An hour later the noise started again and he thought that it was a rat making the noise. The next day he examined the walls, the ceiling, and the floor, but did not finding any evidence of rats.

The noise was heard again in the evening. After this, the house was considered too dangerous to live in. In addition, the servants no longer wanted to stay in the room while performing their work. Soon after the noise stopped, it reappeared again one-hundred feet away, in Louis Kettelhut's house, Anthony's brother, with increased intensity and strength. The rapping focused in one corner of the room.

The villagers then became suspicious, so much so that the burgomaster communicated what had occurred to the authorities. In the beginning the authorities did not want to get involved in a subject considered so ridiculous. However, in time and under the constant pressure from the residents, on January 6th, 1762, the burgomaster traveled to Dibbelsdorf to examine the facts. The walls and ceiling were demolished but it did not yield anything. The Kettelhut family swore that they had nothing to do with the strange phenomenon.

Up until then nobody had communicated with the "rapper" yet. One day this person from Naggam courageously asked:

- Rapping spirit, are you still there?
  A knock was heard.
- Can you tell us your name?
  Several names were said but the spirit only knocked when the name of the speaker was heard.
- How many buttons are there in my shirt?
  Thirty-six raps were heard. The buttons were counted, yielding the exact number 36.

Thereafter the story of the "rapping" spirit spread around the region and every afternoon hundreds of Brusnwick residents used to go to Dibbelsdorf, as well as some English men and curious foreigners. The crowd grew so much that the local police were incapable of containing it. The peasants had to support the guard at night and were forced to establish check-in lines to the visitors.

Such a swarm of people seemed to have motivated the spirit to produce even more extraordinary manifestations, progressing towards communications, which attested to his intelligence. He was never mistaken in his answers. People asked about the number and color of the horses that were parked in front of the house; he would respond exactly. A book would be open by chance on a given page; a finger pointed to a part of a musical piece, requesting the designated part number, sometimes unknown to the interlocutor, followed by a series of raps perfectly indicating the requested answer. The spirit would not be long; the answer would be given immediately after the question was made. He also indicated the number of persons in the room, how many were outside; designated the color of the hair, of the clothes, the position and profession of the individuals.

One day there was a man from Hettin among the curious crowd, completely unknown to the Dibbelsdorf locals; he had moved a short time ago to Brusnwick. He asked the rapping spirit about his place of birth and, wishing to induce error, he cited a large number of cities. When mentioning Hettin a rap was heard. A smart burgeon, attempting to get the "rapper" to make an error, enquired about the amount of coins he had in his pocket. The "rapper" made the exact number of raps that equaled the coins: 681. A pastry-cook was told how many cookies he had made in the morning; to a shop owner how many meters of ribbon he had sold the day before and to another one the exact amount he had received through the mail a couple of days earlier. He was playful. Whenever he was requested he played a tune with a deafening sound.

In the evenings, during meals and after *"Grace"* he would rap the Amen. That sign of devotion did not impede a sacristan to dress up with the exorcist outfit trying to expel the spirit; that plot failed.

The spirit was afraid of nobody. He was very honest in his answers to the regent, the Duke Charles, and his brother Ferdinand and other simple persons of inferior condition.

The case then became more serious. The Duke assigned a doctor and some attorneys to examine the facts. The scholars explained that the raps were due to an underground source. An eight feet deep well was excavated and water was naturally found, as Dibbelsdorf is located at the bottom of a valley. The water gushed out, inundated the room but the spirit continued to rap in the usual spot. Then scientists thought that they were victims of some sort of mystification and gave the servant the honor of changing place with that spirit who was so well informed.

His intention, they said, was to bewitch the maid. Every resident of the village was invited to stay home on a given and predetermined day; the server was kept under their vigilant eyes, as he was the culprit according to the wise men. But the spirit again answered all questions. The servant was released once his innocence was established. But justice wanted an author to the wrongdoing and accused the Kettelhut couple for the noise they were complaining about, although they were benevolent people, honest and irreproachable on all aspects and had being the first ones to seek the authorities, since the onset of the manifestations. Under threats and promises, they forced a young lady to testify against her masters. As a consequence they were arrested, despite the posterior contradiction and a formal declaration, attesting as false her first confession that was forcibly taken by the judges. Since the spirit still rapped, the Kettelhut couple stayed in prison for three months, being freed after that period without compensation, although the members of the commission summarized their report as follows: "All efforts to discover the cause of the noises rendered unsuccessful. Future will perhaps teach us about that."

- Future has not taught anything yet.

The rapping spirit continued from the beginning of December until March, when it was no longer heard. The already incriminated servant was once more thought to be the author of all those mockeries. But how could he have avoided all traps arranged by the Dukes, doctors, judges and so many others who interrogated him?"

OBSERVATION: If we pay attention to the date when such things happened and compare them to those that take place in our days, we find perfect identity in the mode of manifestation and even in the nature of the questions and answers. Neither America nor our times have discovered the rapping spirits, nor have they discovered the others, as we will demonstrate by several authentic and more or less aged facts. There is, however, between the present phenomena and the old ones a capital difference: it is the fact that the old ones were almost all spontaneous whereas ours are produced almost by the will of certain special mediums. This circumstance allowed them to be better studied and their causes better investigated. The judges' conclusion that "the future will perhaps teach us about that" would not be followed by the authors' remarks: "future has not taught anything yet". If the author were alive today he would know, on the contrary, that the future taught everything and that our modern justice, better clarified than that of a century ago, would not make the same mistakes with respect to the spiritist manifestations, mistakes that remind the Middle Ages. Our own scholars have already penetrated into the mysteries of nature so as not to play games with unknown causes. They are wise enough and do not expose themselves, like their predecessors, to be contradicted by posterity, in detriment of their own reputation. If something shows up in the horizon they no longer rush to proclaim: "This is nothing", afraid that it might be a ship. If they cannot see it, they go quiet and wait. Such is the true wisdom.

Considerations Concerning
the Jupiter's Drawings

As announced, we publish in this issue of the periodical a drawing of a Jupiter dwelling, executed and engraved by Mr. Victorien Sardou as a medium, adding the descriptive article that he kindly wrote about it. As for the authenticity of the description, whatever might be the opinion of those who accuse us of getting involved with things that happen in unknown worlds, when there is so much to be done on Earth, we beg our readers to keep our objective in perspective, as well as the subtitle of the periodical, namely that it is the study of this phenomena and, as such, should not be neglected. Well, as a fact of manifestation, these drawings are the most remarkable since the author cannot draw nor engrave and that the drawing we offer is an etching made *in a nine-hour period,* without a model or a previous test. Even supposing that the drawing is a fantasy of the spirit who drew it, the simple fact of its execution would not be a lesser important fact to notice and, under the same title, it is up to our collection to make it known, as well as the description given by the spirits about it. It is not intended to satisfy the curiosity of futile individuals but as a subject for study by the serious individuals who want to pursue more in-depth knowledge of the spiritist science.

It would be a mistake to consider that we make the revelation about the unknown worlds a capital point of the doctrine. This shall never be more than an accessory to us that we consider useful as a complementary study; the moral teaching will always be the most important to us and in the communications from beyond the grave we shall seek, above all, what can enlighten humanity and lead it to the good, the only means of ensuring happiness in this and in the other world.

Couldn't we say the same about the astronomers who examine space and ask them what is the utility to human kind of knowing how to accurately calculate the parabolic trajectory of an invisible globe?

Not all sciences have an eminently practical interest. However, nobody intends to treat them with scorn because everything that broadens the circle of the ideas contributes to progress.

The same happens to the spiritist communications, even when they surpass the narrow circle of our own personality.

Mozart's House – by Victorien Sardou (medium)

Jupiter's Dwellings

To certain people convinced of the existence of the spirits – and here I do not mention others – one must be surprised that the spirits, like us, may have their homes and cities. I was not spared of criticism: "Houses of spirits in Jupiter! ... What a joke! ..."

Joke it may be. But I have nothing to do with that. If in the likelihood of the explanations, the reader does not find sufficient proof of its truthfulness; if, as with us, he is not surprised by the perfect agreement between those revelations of the spirits and the most positive data of astronomy; if, in one word, he cannot see more than skillful mystification in the following details and in the drawing that is related to that, I invite you to explain yourself with the spirits, of whom I am a faithful echo and instrument. May Palissy or Mozart be evoked or another inhabitant of that happy world; may they be questioned; and may my assertions be controlled by theirs; may, finally, it all be discussed with them; as for myself I do no more than presenting what is given to me and repeating what I have been told; and that by an absolutely passive role, I judge myself sheltered from censorship as well as from praise.

Given that exception and admitting the trust in the spirits, if one accepts as true the only really beautiful and wise doctrine hitherto revealed by the evocation of the dead, that is, the migration of the souls from planet to planet, their successive incarnations and their never ending progress through work, then Jupiter inhabitants should no longer cause us any admiration. Since the moment when a spirit incarnates in a world like ours, subjected to a double revolution, which is the alternate days and nights and the cycle of seasons and since it has a body, this material covering, however fragile it may be, not only requires nutrition and clothing but also a shelter, or at least a resting place and, consequently, a dwelling.

This is exactly what we were told. As with us and better than us, Jupiter inhabitants have their common homes and their families, harmonious groups of sympathetic spirits, united in triumph along the way of their common struggle. Therefore the spacious homes that deserve the name of *palaces*.

Still, as happens to us, the spirits have their parties, ceremonies and public gatherings. Thus a number of edifices are especially built for that purpose. It is necessary to be prepared to find in those superior regions an active and laborious humanity as ours, also submitted to their laws, needs and duties, with the only difference that progress, which in our case reacts to our efforts, becomes an easy achievement to spirits detached from our earthly vices, like them.

I should not handle the architecture of their dwellings here. A word of explanation, however, will be useful to the understanding of the details that follow.

As good spirits only inhabits Jupiter, it does not follow that they are all on the same level of excellence: between the kindness of the simple person and that of the genius there are several nuances. The whole social organization of that superior world is based precisely on the variety of intelligences and aptitudes and, through the application of harmonious laws whose explanation would be too lengthy here, it is up to the more elevated and depurated spirits to manage the higher direction of the planet. Such supremacy does not stop there. It extends up to the inferior worlds where those spirits, by their influence, favor, and incessantly activate religious progress, are the guiders of all others. It is necessary to add that to those depurated spirits there is nothing but intellectual work as their activities take place in the domain of the mind and they have acquired enough control over matter in other not to be even slightly limited by that in the exercise of their free will.

The body of those spirits, by the way, as of all inhabitants of Jupiter, is of so low density that it can be compared to our most imponderable fluids. Somewhat taller than our body whose shape it exactly reproduces, more beautiful and purer however, it would have a vaporous shape to us – and here I regretfully use a word that designates a substance still too gross –vapor, I was saying, intangible and shiny, particularly around the borders of the face and head, hence life and intelligence irradiate from a very ardent focus. It is exactly that magnetic shine foreseen by Christian visionaries that our painters translated by the nimbus or aureole of the saints.

It is understandable that such a structure does not bring much difficulty to the extra worldly communications of those spirits, allowing them an easy and fast dislocation around their own planet. The body so easily avoids the effect of gravity and its density is so much alike the atmospheric density that it can come and go move up and down to the simple effort of the will. Thus, some characters that Palissy made me draw are represented hovering the ground or the surface of the waters or still very high up in the air, with every freedom of action and motion that we attribute to the angels. The more elevated the spirit the easier that motion, as we can easily understand. Thus, nothing in that planet is easier than the determination of the level of a given spirit, at first sight, as they move about. Two signs denounce it: the height of their flight and the more or less shiny aureole.

In Jupiter, as everywhere else, those who fly higher are infrequent. Below them there are several categories of inferior spirits, be it in virtue, be it in power, but, naturally, free to rise at a higher level one day through their acts. Leveled and classified according to their merits, they dedicate more particularly to the tasks of interest of their own planet and do not exert the influence of the others over the inferior worlds. It is true that they respond to an evocation with good and wise revelations but given the hurry to leave us, as demonstrated by their brief answers. It is promptly seen that they have a lot to do elsewhere and that they are not yet sufficiently free so as to simultaneously irradiate in two different points, far away from one another. Finally, following the less perfect of those spirits, but separated by an abyss, there are the animals that are the only servers and workers of the planet thus deserve a special reference.

If we designate the bizarre beings that occupy the inferior limits of the scale by the name of "animals" it is because the spirits themselves admitted its use, besides the fact that our language does not have a more adequate term. Such a designation significantly degrades them; however, calling them "men" would elevate them too much. These are spirits truly dedicated to the animality, maybe for a long time, maybe forever, once the spirits are not in total agreement in that regard and the solution to this issue seems to belong to worlds more elevated than Jupiter. Nevertheless, whatever their future may be there is no mistake with respect to their past: those spirits, before going to Jupiter, continuously migrated in our inferior worlds, from the body of one animal to another, through a perfectly graduated scale of progression. A careful study of our earthly animals, their customs, their individual characters, their ferocity away from men and the slow but always possible domestication, everything yields sufficient demonstration of the reality of such animal ascension.

Thus, no matter how we look at it, the Universal harmony is summarized in only one law: progress everywhere and to all, to the animal as to the plant, to the plant as to the mineral. In principle a purely material progress, in the insensitive molecules of the metal or the pebble and gradually more intelligent, as we move up in the scale of the creatures and as the individuality tends to separate from the masses, in order to stand alone and know oneself.

This thought is elevated and consoling, as never before, because it proves that nothing is sacrificed; that the reward is always proportional to the actual progress. For example: the dedication of a dog by its owner is not sterile to the spirits, as it will have its just compensation beyond this world.

That is the case with the animal spirits that inhabit Jupiter. They perfected at the same time as us, with us and with our help. The law is even more remarkable: it awards so much the devotement to the human being, as the first condition to their planetary ascension, that the wishes of a spirit in Jupiter can attract to him every animal that in one of his previous lives had given him proof of affection. Those sympathies, that in those regions form families of spirits, also aggregate around these families' entourages of dedicated animals. Consequently, our attachment to an animal in our world, our care in taming and humanizing them, everything has a reason, and everything will be rewarded: it is a good server that we prepare to a better world.

It will thus be a worker since all material work is reserved to that species, all the corporeal effort: hauling or construction, sowing or harvesting. The Supreme Intelligence has prepared a body that accomplishes all that, simultaneously participating into the advantages of animal and human. We can have an idea from a sketch of Palissy, representing some of those animals entertaining themselves in a ball game. The best comparison one could have would be with the fauns and satyrs of the Fable. The slightly hairy body stands up like ours; in some the paws disappear, giving place to certain legs which still resemble the primitive form, and also two robust arms, singularly implanted and terminated by two real hands, if we consider the position of the thumbs. Surprisingly the head is not so much advanced as the rest. Thus, the looks has something of human but the skull, the jaw and ear, above all, have nothing noticeably different from the earthy animals. It is then simple to distinguish them: this is a dog, the other a lion. Adequately dressed with outfits very similar to ours, only lack the oral word to look like some people from our planet: this is precisely what they miss and what they could not do. Skilful to understand each other through a language that has no similarity with ours, they no long misunderstand the intention of the spirits who guide them: a glance, a gesture is enough. The animal guesses and obeys, without a whisper, certain magnetic impulses whose secret is already known by our tamers of beasts and, what is more important, voluntarily since they are fascinated. That is how every heavy duty is imposed on them and that with their support everything works regularly, from one to the next extreme of the social scale: the elevated spirit thinks and deliberates; the inferior spirit acts on his own initiative and the animal executes. Thus the conception, execution and the action harmonize, bringing everything to their conclusion, swiftly and through the simplest and safest way.

I apologize for such an explanation: it was necessary to the subject that we can mention now.

While waiting for the promised maps which will greatly facilitate the study of the whole planet, we can, through the description given by the spirits, have an idea of their great city, of the city by excellence, of that focus of light and activities that they agree to call – what seems strange to us – by the Latin name *Julnius*.

"In our largest continent", says Palissy, "in a valley of seven to eight hundred leagues wide, to utilize your measurement system, a magnificent river comes down from the northern mountains and, boosted by a lot of streams and creeks, forms seven or eight lakes in its path, that the smallest would be called "sea" among you. It was by the shores of the largest of those lakes, baptized as the "Pearl", that our predecessors launched the foundations of Julnius. That primitive city still exists, guarded as a precious relic. Its architecture is very different from yours. When the time comes I will explain all that to you: know only that the modern city is just a few hundred meters away from the old one. Constrained by high mountains, the lake pours into the valley from eight huge waterfalls that form other isolated streams, dispersed in all directions. With the support of those watercourses we excavate several rivulets, canals and lakes in the plains, keeping the firm soil only for the houses and gardens. That results in a kind of amphibious city, like your Venice, where one cannot say, at first sight, if it was originally built on the ground or on the water. Today I will not say much about four sacred edifices built upstream of the falls, so that the water gushes out through their porches. Such constructions would seem incredible to you for their greatness and audacity.

"Here I describe the ground level city, somehow more material, city of the planetary occupations, the one we finally call the "*lower city*". It has its streets, or even better, its paths designed for the internal service; its public grounds, its porches and its bridges over the canals, for the come and go of the servers. But the intelligent town, the spiritual city, the true Julnius, per say, should not be sought on the ground. It is aloft.

"A firm terrain is needed to the material bodies of our animals, incapable of flying[33], but our fluidic and shiny bodies require an adequate *airborne* shelter, almost intangible and mobile, according to our wishes. Our skills solved that problem with the help of time and the conditions that the Great Architect has given us. You understand well the need for such an indispensable conquest of the air, to spirits like ours. Our day lasts five hours as also does our night but everything is relative to spirits ready to act and think like us; to spirits that understand each other by the language of their eyes and can magnetically communicate from a distance, our five hour day would be equivalent to a week of your activities. All that was still too little in our opinion. The immobility of the homes, the fixed spot of the dwellings, was a hindrance to all of our great realizations. Today, by the easy movement of those birds' nests, by the possibility of transporting ourselves to anywhere on the planet, whenever we want to, our existence has multiplied at least twice, and with that everything it can produce as useful and great.

"During certain times of the year", adds the spirit, "in certain festivities, for example, you will see somewhere the skies darkened by the cloud of houses that come from all points of the horizon. It is a curious gathering of beautiful homes, gracious, light, of all forms, colors, balanced on several levels, continuously moving from the lower to the celestial city. A few days later it is all gone, empty and all those birds gradually leave."

"Those floating homes lack nothing, not even the enchantment of the green leaves and flowers. I speak about vegetation with no similarity

---

33 Exception made, however, to certain winged animals destined to work in the air and to certain tasks that the carpenter would execute among us. It is a transformation of the bird, as the animals described above are a transformation of the quadruped.

among you, of plants and even bushes that by the nature of their organs, live, breathe, feed and reproduce themselves in the air."

The same spirit still said:

We have those bunches of huge flowers, whose forms and nuances you cannot imagine, and of such a delicate fabric which makes them almost transparent. Balanced aloft, having broadleaf supporters and tendrils like those of the vine, they assemble into a thousand shades or disperse with the wind, offering a charming spectacle to the passers-by of the lower city... Imagine the grace of those rafts of greenery, of those floating gardens that our will can make or break and that sometimes last a whole season! Long trails of vines and flowering branches are detached from those heights, down to the ground; huge clusters are agitated, exhaling perfume from the loosening petals... The spirits who travel through the air stop there: it is a place of resting and gathering and, if you will, a means of transportation to complete a journey without fatigue and in good company."

Another spirit was sitting on one of those flowers at the time I evoked him. He said:

"Now it is night time in Julnius and I am sitting at a distance, on one of those airborne flowers that only sprout under our moonshine here. The lower city sleeps at my feet; around me and just above my head and to the endless distance, there is only movement and happiness in space. We don't sleep much: our soul is much detached so that our body's needs do not tyrannize it. Night exists more to our servers than to us. It is the time of visitations, long talks, lonely strolls, daydreams and music. I only see airborne habitations resplendent of lights or rafts of flowers loaded with happy tufts... The first of our moons illuminates the lower city: it is a smooth light, comparable to your moonshines; but, the second one rises from the lake side, of greenish shines, yielding the whole river with that appearance of a vast lawn..."

It is by the right riverbank "whose water, says the spirit, would give you the impression of the consistency of a very light vaporous shape"[34]

---

34 Jupiter's density is 0.23 or about ¼ of Earth's density. Everything that the spirit says here is likely. It is understandable that everything is relative and that in such an ethereal globe everything is ethereal as well.

that Mozart's house is built, whose drawing Palissy was kind enough to make me reproduce on copper. I present here only the façade of the southern side. The great entrance is on the left, looking to the plains; to the right is the river; to the north and south the gardens. I asked Mozart who were his neighbors.

- Above and below me two spirits that you don't know, but to the left there is only a large meadow that separates me from Cervantes's garden.

The house has four faces like ours but it would be a mistake to take that by a general rule. It is built with a certain stone that the animals take from the northern mountains and whose color the spirit compares to the shades of green that sometimes mix with the celestial blue, at sunset. Regarding its strength we can have an idea by this comparison of Palissy: "it would melt so rapidly under the pressure of your fingers as the snow flake does, yet that is one of the most resistant materials of that planet!"

The spirits engraved strange arabesques on the walls that the drawing tries to reproduce. These are ornaments engraved on the stone and colored later, or incrustations produced on the rigid green stone by a process very much in use these days, that keeps the whole refinement of the contour of the vegetables, the loveliness of their tissues and the richness of their colors. "A discovery", added the spirit, "that you will have one day and that will change many things."

The large window to the right presents an example of that kind of ornament: one of its borders is nothing but a huge reed, whose leaves were preserved. The same happens to the coronation of the main window, imitating the shape of a treble clef: these are entwined and petrified plants. It is through such a process that most coronations of buildings, gates, porches, etc are obtained. Sometimes the plant is attached with its roots to the wall, free to grow. It then grows, develops, the leaves spread at random and when it achieves the full and desired development for the ornamentation of the building, the artist petrifies it on the spot. Palissy's house is almost entirely decorated by such a process.

Destined initially only to the furniture, then to the casing of doors and windows, this type of ornament gradually perfected, finally taking over the architecture as a whole. Nowadays it's not only flowers and bushes that are petrified but the whole trees themselves, from the root to the crown. The palaces, as with other buildings, have almost no other type of columns.

Similar petrification is applied to the decoration of the windows. Flowers or large leaves are skillfully stripped from its lamina. Only a bunch of fibers remain, so fine as the finest muslin. These are then crystallized and artistically arranged to make up the whole window that filters a smooth luminosity to the interior. A kind of multi-colored liquid glass that hardens in the air, transforming the leaf into a kind of stained glass, is also employed. Charming and illuminated transparent branches result from the arrangement of those leaves at the windows.

As for the dimensions of those openings and several other details that, at first sight, may surprise you, I am forced to provide an explanation: history of architecture in Jupiter would require a whole volume. I shall not talk about the furniture either, sticking to the general structure of the house.

From the preceding, the reader should have understood that the house of the continent, to the spirit, is nothing more than a kind of resting place.

The lower city is only used by the spirits of the second order, in charge of the planetary businesses, like agriculture, for example, or the exchanges and to keep the good order among the servers. Thus, every house on the ground generally has two storeys, the ground level destined to the spirits who operate under the orders of the master, also accessible to the animals; the upper level only used by the spirit that occasionally stays there. That is why we see, in several houses of Jupiter, like this one for example, as with Zoroaster's, a staircase and a ramp. Those who can fly on the surface of the water like the robins or run on top of the wheat crops without bending them can perfectly well move without stairs and ramps to get to their homes. But the inferior spirits cannot fly so easily. Those cannot rise but by irregular movements and the ramps are not always useless to them. Finally, the stairs are absolutely necessary to the animal servers that only walk like us. The former also have their pavilions which, by the way, are very elegant and are part of every large residence, but their functions constantly draw their attention to the master's house, being thus necessary to facilitate their entry and also the internal traffic. That is why such original constructions, whose bases are similar to our earthly buildings but entirely different on the upper level.

This one distinguishes itself by an originality that we could not absolutely imitate. It is a kind of arrow that swings at the top of the building, above the great window with its original coronation. That delicate and easy moving topsail is supposed to stay put, since the artist's conception, at the very place he had defined, not supported by anything, but completing the decoration. The dimension of the copper plate, regrettably, would not allow space for its representation.

As for Mozart's airborne house, it is only needed to the testimony of its existence. The limits of this article do not allow me to extend beyond the subject.

I shall not conclude, however, without an in-passing explanation about the kind of ornaments that the great artist chose for his home. The similarity with our terrestrial music is easy to identify: the treble clef is frequently repeated and – original thing – never the bass clef! In the decoration of the ground floor we find a violin bow, a kind of tiorba or bandolin, a harp and a music staff. Above there is a large window that vaguely resembles the format of an organ; the others have the appearance of large musical notes but the small ones are abundant everywhere.

It would be a mistake to conclude that Jupiter's music is comparable to ours and that it is presented by the same symbols. Mozart gave an explanation about that so as to eliminate any doubt. But, in the decoration of their homes, the spirits remember the earthly mission that gave them the merit of the incarnation in Jupiter and that magnificently summarizes the character of their intelligence. Thus, in Zoroaster's house it is the planets and the flame that constitute every decorative element.

Besides, as it seems, this symbolism has its own rules and secrecy. Those ornamental elements are not randomly arranged. They have their own logic, imagination and precise meaning but it is an art that the spirits of Jupiter refrain from leading us to understand, at least by now, and about what they do not willingly explain.

Our early architects also employed a symbolism in the decoration of their cathedrals. St. Jacques tower is a hermetic poem if we give credit to the tradition. Therefore there is no reason for surprise with respect to the originality of Jupiter's architecture. If it counters our ideas about human art it is in fact due to an abyss between an architecture that lives and speaks and an inexpressive masonry like ours. In this, as in everything else, prudence helps us to avoid such an error of relativism that intends to reduce everything else to the proportions and habits of the terrestrial man. If the inhabitants of Jupiter ate, slept, lived, and walked like us, there would be no advantage in going there. It is because that planet differs a lot from ours that we want to know it and dream about it as our future dwelling.

As for myself I believe I have not wasted my time and would be very happy for having been chosen by the spirits to be their interpreter if their drawings and their descriptions inspired in one believer only the desire to move up to Jupiter more rapidly, giving him courage to do everything in order to achieve that.

VICTORIEN SARDOU

The author of this interesting description is one of those ardent and enlightened individuals that are not afraid of confessing their beliefs loud and clear and that position themselves above the criticism of those who believe in nothing but in their own circle of ideas. Connecting their names to a new doctrine, defying sarcasm, is a courage not given to all. We congratulate Mr. V. Sardou for having done this. His work reveals a distinct author who is still young but has already conquered a place of honor in literature, allying his talent of writer to his profound knowledge of a scholar. It is one more proof that Spiritism does not recruit among fools and ignorant. We wish Mr. Sardou may complete his work as soon as possible and as brilliantly as he started. If the astronomers unveil to us, through wise researches, the mechanism of the Universe, the spirits, by their revelations, let us know its moral state and, as they say, with the objective of motivating us towards the good, to deserve a better life.

ALLAN KARDEC[35]

---

35 Paris. Typography of Cosson & Co. - Rue de Four-Saint-Germain, 43.

September 1858

Propagation of Spiritism

A worth mentioning phenomenon is taking place with respect to the propagation of Spiritism. Just resurrected a few years ago from the old beliefs, it appeared among us not as before, under the shadow of mystery, but in the open light for everyone to see.

It was an object of brief curiosity to some, an enjoyment put aside like a toy. From many people it was received by nothing but indifference; from the largest number, incredulity, despite the opinion of the philosophers whose names are frequently invoked as authorities. That is not a surprise: Has Jesus himself convinced the Jewish people about his miracles? Have the benevolence and sublimity of his doctrine conquered him any mercy before his judges? Wasn't he treated as an imposter? And, if they did not call him charlatan wasn't that because such a word of our modern civilization was unknown by then? However, serious people have seen something beyond frivolity in the phenomena that take place in our days. They studied them, investigated them, with the eyes of a conscious observer and discovered the key to a number of mysteries hitherto incomprehensible. This became a stream of light to them and behold, a Doctrine was born from those facts, a philosophy and, we can even say, a science, initially divergent according to the point of view or personal opinion of the investigator but with a gradual trend towards a unity of principles. Despite the self-serving opposition of some and systematic rejection of others who think that the light can only come from their brains, this doctrine finds many adepts as it enlightens us with respect to the present and future true interests of humanity. It corresponds to their aspiration for a future which becomes somehow tangible; finally because it simultaneously satisfies their reason and hopes and dissipates the doubts that used to degenerate into absolute incredulity.

Well, with Spiritism all materialist and pantheist philosophies fall by themselves; doubts with respect to Divinity, existence of the soul, its individuality and immortality are no longer possible; the future is presented to us like daylight and we learn that such a future, that always leaves an open door to hope, depends on our will and our efforts through the good actions.

While they could not see in Spiritism more than the material phenomena, the only interest was the spectacle that impressed the eyes. However, once it has been elevated to the category of a moral science, it has been taken seriously as it has spoken to the heart and intelligence. In addition, everybody has found in Spiritism the solution to what they were vaguely trying to find in themselves; confidence based on evidence replaces a pungent uncertainty; from such an elevated point of view where it positions us, things of this inferior world seem so small and petty that the vicissitudes of this planet are nothing more than transient incidents that we withstand with patience and resignation; the corporeal life is nothing more than a brief station in the soul's life. Using the expression of our wise and witty comrade Mr. Jobard, it is not more than an ordinary lodging-house where it is not worth to unpack. In the Spiritist Doctrine everything is defined, everything is clear, everything speaks to reason; in one word, everything is explained and those who deeply study it in its essence find such an intimate satisfaction to which they no longer renounce. That is why it has conquered so much sympathy in such a short time, sympathy not recruited in the narrow circle of a given place but around the whole world. Had the facts not been there to demonstrate, we could judge by our Review, which is only a few months old, but whose subscribers, although not counting the thousands yet, are spread all over the world. Besides those of Paris and provinces we have those in England, Scotland,

Netherlands, Belgium, Prussia, St. Petersburg, Moscow, Naples, Florence, Milan, Genoa, Turin, Geneve, Madrid, Shanghai, Batavia, Caen, Mexico, Canada, USA, etc.

We don't say this to boast but to mention a characteristic fact. In order that a recently founded and so much specialized journal be sought in so diverse and separated regions it is necessary that its major subject finds followers or they would not subscribe to it, thousands of leagues away, even if done by the best writer. It is then by its subject that it draws interest and not by its obscure editor. Its objective is therefore serious, to the eyes of the reader. Hence it is evidenced that Spiritism has roots all over the world and that, under such a point of view, twenty subscribers in twenty different countries prove more than one hundred, concentrated in one place only, hence one could not suppose this to be the works of a fraternity.

The mode by which Spiritism has propagated so far does not deserve a less accurate attention. If the press had made use of its voice in its favor by preaching it; if, in one word, the whole world had paid attention to that, one could say that it had propagated like everything else that takes place thanks to a factitious reputation and that one wishes to experiment with, even if just out of curiosity. But none of that has happened. Generally, the press had not given Spiritism any voluntary support. Press neglected it or if on rare occasions spoke about it was to ridicule it and to send its adepts to the asylums, a not very attractive thing to those who had the mere in-clination of getting initiated.

Only Mr. Home deserved the honor of some more or less serious ref-erences, while the most vulgar events are conversely widely covered. As a matter of fact it is easy to see that, by their languages, the adversaries speak about Spiritism like the blind would speak about the colors: without real knowledge of the facts; without a serious and profound examination and only through a first impression, hence their arguments are limited to a pure and simple denial, thus we cannot elevate their facetious expres-sions to the category of arguments. However witty those jokes may be they do not represent reason.

However, not everybody from the press should be accused of ill faith. Spiritism counts individually on serious experts and we know several among the most prominent people from the media.

Why then do they keep silence? The reason is the fact that, besides the problem of belief, there is that of personality that is very powerful in our days. Their belief is concealed rather than expansive, as with many others. Besides, they are forced to respond for their newspapers. As such, the journalist is afraid of losing subscribers by openly raising a flag whose color could displease some of them.

Will that situation last? No. Spiritism will soon be like magnetism that was once discussed through whispers and that now nobody is afraid of confessing.

No new idea, however right and nice it may be, implants instantaneously in the spirits of the masses, and the one that did not find opposition would be a remarkable phenomenon. Why would Spiritism be an exception to the general rule? Time is needed to mature the ideas, as with the fruits, but human levity leads us to judge them before their maturation or without the effort to analyze their intimate qualities.

This brings to mind the witty fable "The baby monkey, the adult monkey and a nut". As well known, the baby monkey picks a green nut still in the shell; bites it, making faces, amazed that others may like such a bitter thing. The adult monkey, less superficial and with a profound knowledge of its species, picks the nut, breaks it, cleans it, eats the nut and finds it delicious. A great moral teaching results from that, addressed to those who judge new things just from the outside.

Spiritism had thus to march without any strange support and behold in five or six years it spread out with an almost prodigious speed. Where has it acquired such strength if not on itself? Hence there must necessarily be something very powerful in its principle to be propagated like that, without the super exciting means of publicity. The fact is, as we mentioned above, that whoever takes the time to study it finds what was looking for, what reason would have allowed to foresee: a consoling truth and, after all, hope and true satisfaction.

Thus, the acquired convictions are serious and durable and not frivolous opinions, just born out of a breath and destroyed by another one.

Someone recently said: "I find in Spiritism such a kind hope; it gives me such a sweet and great consolation that every contrary thought would make me unhappy and I feel as if my best friend would become hateful had he tried to subtract that belief from me." When an idea has no roots it may briefly shine, like those flowers that we force to blossom; soon, however, for a lack of support, die and remains forgotten. Nevertheless, those who have a sound foundation grow and persist and become so much identified with the habits that we amaze ourselves for having gone without it for so long.

If Spiritism was not supported by the European press the same did not happen in America. This is correct up to a point. There is in America, as everywhere else for that matter, a general and a special press. The former gave Spiritism much more coverage than in our case, although less than we suppose. In fact there are some hostile institutions among them. The special press accounts for eighteen Spiritist Newspapers only in the USA, from which ten are weekly and several of large format. From that one can see that we are very late with that respect. But there, as around here, the specialized newspapers address a specific public. It is evident that a medical gazette will not have the preference of the architects or the people of law; thus, a spiritist journal, with rare exceptions, will only be read by those with knowledge of Spiritism. The large number of American newspapers that cover this subject prove one thing: they have enough readers to sustain them. No doubt that they have accomplished a lot but their influence is, generally speaking, purely local. The vast majority is unknown to the European public and our newspapers only very occasionally provide some transcriptions of their matters.

By saying that Spiritism has propagated without the support of the press, we referred to the general press, the one that addresses everybody, the one whose voice is daily heard by millions; the one that penetrates the most obscure corners; that informs the anchorite in the depth of the desert as it does with the inhabitants of the city; finally, the one that plentifully spreads ideas. Which spiritist newspaper can pride itself of echoing the claims of the world? It speaks to the persons of conviction but does not attract the attention of the indifferent.

We tell the truth by proclaiming that Spiritism has been left to its own powers and, if it has walked in such long strides by itself, how is it going to be when supported by the powerful lever of the broad publicity? While waiting for such a moment, it moves continuously, setting its landmarks; its branches will find stanchions everywhere; it will find voices whose authority will impose silence to the detractors everywhere.

The quality of the adepts of Spiritism deserves special attention. Are they recruited among the illiterate, in the inferior layers of society? No. Those are little or almost not at all concerned with Spiritism: they may have hardly heard about it. The turning tables may have found some practitioners among them. Up until now its proselytes come from the first layers of society: among the enlightened persons, among people of thought and wisdom. Furthermore, and this is a remarkable fact, the doctors who for a long time struggled against magnetism, easily adhere to this Doctrine. We count them in large numbers, both in France and abroad, which also have a large quantity of superior people, in all aspects: scientific and literary celebrities, high dignitaries, public servants, general officers, business people, ecclesiastics, magistrates, etc... all extremely serious to subscribe to a paper like ours as a pastime, considering that we do not pretend to be funny and that we are even less willing to find only fantasies in our publications.

The Parisian Society of Spiritist Studies is not any less evident proof of that truth, by the choice of persons gathered around it. Its sessions are followed with great interest, with a religious attention and, we can even say, with avidity. However, it only handles grave and serious studies, sometimes very abstract, not experiences aiming at the excitement of curiosity. We speak about what happens before our eyes; however the same can be said about other centers that occupy with Spiritism, having the same principles, hence more or less everywhere – as announced by the spirits – the period of curiosity declines.

Those phenomena allow us to penetrate in such an elevated order of things, so sublime that compared to these grave questions, a piece of furniture that moves or that raps is like a kid's toy: it is Science 101.

As a matter of fact, we now know what to give attention to with respect to the rapping spirits and, generally, to those who produce material effects. They have been called, and with justice, the jugglers of the spiritual world. That is why we associate less with them than with those that can enlighten us.

We can identify four phases or distinct periods in the propagation of Spiritism:

1° - Period of curiosity in which the rapping spirits play the main role, calling attention and preparing the way.

2° - Period of observation in which we are entering and that can also be called philosophical. Spiritism is studied in depth and depurates; tends towards a unity of Doctrine and constitute a Science.

These periods will follow:

3° - Period of admission in which Spiritism will occupy an official place among universally accepted beliefs;

4° - Period of influence over the social order. Humanity, then under the influence of these ideas, will conquer a new moral profile. That influence is, since now, individual. Later it will act upon the masses to the happiness of everyone.

Thus, on one side, we see a belief that spreads all over the world on its own, gradually and without the usual resources of the forced propaganda, and on another hand that very belief that sows roots, not in the lower layers of Society but in its more enlightened part. Shouldn't this double aspect be something very characteristic and give food for thought to those who consider Spiritism an empty dream? As opposed to many other ideas that come from below, shapeless and misleading, and that only slowly penetrate the higher echelons, where they then depurate, Spiritism starts from the top and will only reach the masses when disentangled from the false ideas, inseparable from new things.

We have to understand, however, that among many experts there exists only a latent belief. With some there is the dread of ridicule, with others the fear of personal harm by the conflict with certain susceptibilities that impede them to proclaim their opinions, out and loud. This is puerile, no doubt, and we understand that well. One cannot ask certain people something that nature has not given them: the courage to face the "what will they say about it?" but when Spiritism is present in every mouth – and that time is not far off – such courage will reach the shyest.

A remarkable change, since some time now, is already noticeable with that respect. People talk more openly; they take the risk, and this helps to open the eyes of the adversaries themselves, that inquiry if it is prudent, from the interest of their own reputation, to attack a belief that, willing or not, infiltrates everywhere and finds support on the higher social ranks.

Thus, the epithet of "mad", so much inflicted onto the adepts, starts to become ridicule. It is a common place that becomes trivial, as the mad ones will soon be in larger number than the sensible ones and more than one critic has already changed sides.

As a matter of fact, this is the fulfillment of what was announced by the spirits when they said: "The greatest adversaries of Spiritism will become its most ardent followers and promoters."

Plato And the Doctrine
of the Chosen Trials

In the interesting Celtic documents, published in the April issue of our Review, we saw that the doctrine of reincarnation was professed among the Druids, according to the principle of the ascending march of the human soul that progressed along the several degrees of our spirits' scale.

Everybody knows that the idea of reincarnation goes back to the antiquity and that Pythagoras himself learned it from the Hindus and the Egyptians. Thus it is not surprising that Plato, Socrates and others shared an opinion admitted by the most distinguished philosophers of those times. What is perhaps even more remarkable to find, since those days, is the principle of the chosen trials, taught by the spirits today, and that presupposes the reincarnation, without which it would be meaningless.

Today we shall not discuss that theory that was far from our thoughts when the spirits revealed it to us, that surprised us in a strange way because – we humbly confess – what Plato wrote about this special subject was then completely unknown to us, another proof among thousands that the communications given to us did not absolutely reflect our personal opinion. As for Plato, we only attest the central idea, leaving to each one the easy task of imagining the format under which it is presented and judge the contact points that, in some details, it can have with our current theory.

In his allegoric *"Spindle of Necessity"*, he imagines a dialogue between Socrates and Claucon and attributes to the first one the following speech, about the revelations of Er, the Armenian, a very likely fictitious character, although some take him by Zoroaster. It can be easily seen that the description is nothing but an imaginary situation, with the aim of developing the main idea: the immortality of the soul; the succession of the existences; the choice of the existences through the free will; and last but not least the happy or unhappy consequences of the choices, sometimes reckless. All those propositions are found in The Spirits' Book and confirm the numerous facts cited in this Review.

"... the story I want to tell you, Socrates tells Glaucon, is of a heartedly man, Er the son of Arminius, a Pamphylian by birth. He was slain in battle, and ten days later, when the bodies of the dead were taken up already in a state of decomposition, his body was found untouched and in good condition.

"He was then taken home to be buried and on the twelfth day, lying on the funeral pile, he returned to life and told them what he had seen in the other world."

"As soon as his soul left the body he went onto a journey with a number of souls, coming to a wonderful place where one could see two openings in the earth, close to each other, and two other openings in heaven above them. Between the regions there were judges seated. As soon as a sentenced was passed they commanded the just, after they had passed judgment on them and had bound their sentences in front of them, to ascend by the heavenly way on the right hand; accordingly the unjust were commanded by them to descend to the abyss; these also bore the symbols of their deeds stuck on their backs."

"His time came, and the judges told him that he was to report the news of the other world to people, and they ordered him to hear and see all that was to be heard and seen in that place."

"Then he noticed that the souls had gone: some gone to heaven others to Earth through the corresponding openings. And then he saw at the two other openings other souls, some rising from the earth, dusty and dirty, and some coming down from heaven pure and shiny."

"They seemed to have come from a long trip, gladly stopping in the meadow, as in a gathering place; and those who knew one another greeted and talked, the souls which came from earth curiously inquiring about the things above, and the souls which came from heaven about the things underneath. And they told each other what had happened, those from below weeping and sorrowing at the memory of the things which they had endured and seen in their journey, while those from above were describing heavenly delights and visions of the Divine beauties."

It would take too long to tell the story of the Armenian but in summary, this is what he said:

"Each soul was condemned to 10 times the suffering imposed by their wrong doings; or once in a hundred years - such being the natural length of human's life, and the penalty being thus paid ten times in a thousand years. If, for example, there were any who had been the cause of many deaths, or had betrayed or enslaved cities or armies, or been guilty of any other evil behavior, for each and all of their offences they received punishment ten times over, and the rewards of goodness and justice and holiness were in the same proportion."

"What he said concerning young children dying almost as soon as they were born deserves little attention. But to the impiety to gods and parents, and of murderers, there were cruel retributions while to the religious person and worthy children great happiness."

"He was present when one of the souls asked another, "where is Ardiaeus the Great?" Ardiaeus lived a thousand years before Er: he had been the tyrant of a city in Pamphylia, and had murdered his aged father and his older brother, and was said to have committed many other repulsive crimes. The answer of the other spirit was: "He does not come and will never come here". This was one of the dreadful sights that we ourselves witnessed. Having completed all our experiences, and were about to leave, we saw Ardiaeus and several others, most of whom tyrants like him; and there were also many individuals who had been great criminals in private situations: they tried in vain to return into the upper world, but the mouth, instead of admitting them, answered with a roar, whenever any of these incurable offenders or someone who had not been sufficiently punished tried to ascend; and then wild men of blistering aspect, who were standing by and heard the sound, seized and carried them away; and Ardiaeus and others they tied head and foot and hand, and threw them onto the ground and bashed them, and dragged them along the road through the bloody thorn bushes, repeating to the passers-by what were their crimes, and that they were being taken away to be cast in the Tartarus."

"Such a soul declared that there was nothing worse than the roar of the abyss and that it was an unspeakable happiness to leave in silence. Such were more or less the penalties of the souls, their punishments and rewards."

"Now when the spirits, which were in the meadows had waited seven days, on the eighth they were obliged to proceed with their journey, and, on the fourth day after, he said that they came to a place where they could see from above a beam of light, straight as a column, extending right through the whole heaven and through the earth, like a rainbow, but brighter and purer; and it was only another day's journey to reach the place, and there, in the midst of the light, they saw the ends of the chains of heaven: because this light is the belt of heaven, and holds together the circle of the universe. From these ends the Spindle of Necessity extends, around which all the circumferences turn."

"... and around the Spindle, at equal intervals, there is another band, three in total, each sitting upon her throne: these are the Fates, Daughters of Necessity, dressed in white robes, having chaplets upon their heads,

Lachesis and Clotho and Atropos, who follow with their voices the harmony of the sirens - Lachesis singing the past, Clotho the present, Atropos the future; Clotho from time to time assisting with a touch of her right hand the revolution of the outer circle of the spindle, and Atropos with her left hand guiding the inner ones, and Lachesis taking turns with either hand assisting the inner circles."

"Once the souls arrived, their duty was to go to Lachesis at once; but first of all a hierophant arranged them in order; then he took from the knees of Lachesis the numbers of each soul to be called as well as the multiple human conditions that were offered to their choice, and having mounted a high pulpit, spoke as follows: "Hear the word of Lachesis, the Daughter of Necessity. Mortal souls, behold a new cycle of life and mortality. Your genius will not be assigned to you, but you choose your genius; and let him who draws the first lot have the first choice, and the life that he chooses shall be his destiny. Virtue belongs to none and as a man honors or dishonors her, he shall have more or less of her; the responsibility is with the chooser - God is innocent."

"Following those words he scattered the numbers indifferently among them, each taking the lot which fell near him, all but Er himself who was not allowed. Then the interpreter placed on the ground before them the samples of lives; and there were many more kinds of lives than the souls present almost an infinite variety. There were lives of every animal and of humans in all conditions. And there were tyrannies among them, some outliving the tyrant's life, others which broke in the middle and came to an end in poverty and exile and beggary; and there were lives of famous people, some who were famous for their form and beauty as well as for their strength and success in games, or, again, for their birth and the qualities of their ancestors; and some who were the reverse of famous for the opposite qualities. There was the same variety also to the women."

"Evidently, my dear Glaucon, it is the supreme peril to humanity. May each one of us leave every other kind of knowledge and seek Science that brings happiness. Let us find a master to make us able to learn and discern between good and bad, and so to choose always and everywhere the better life as he has opportunity. He should know what is the effect of beauty when combined with poverty or wealth in a particular soul, and what are the good and bad consequences of noble and humble birth, of private and public station, of strength and weakness, of instruction and ignorance, and of all the soul, and the operation of them combined. Enlightened by consciousness, let us decide the fate of our souls. Yes, the worst destiny is the one that yields an unjust soul and the best is the one that incessantly shapes virtue. All the rest is nothing to the soul. We would forget that there isn't healthier choice after death than during life. Ah! May this sacred dogma be forever identified with our souls so as not to be fascinated by richness nor the other evils of the same sort and that ardently embracing tyranny or similar be not exposed to a large number of irrevocable evils to suffer them even more. For this is the way of happiness."

"According to the report of the messenger from the other world this was what the hierophant said at the time: "Even for the last comer, if he chooses wisely and will live diligently, there is a happy existence appointed. Let him who chooses first not be careless, and let the last not despair." And then he who was first came forward and chose the greatest tyranny of all; his mind having been darkened by imprudence and avidity, he had not thought out the whole matter before he chose, and did not notice at first sight that he was destined, among many other crimes, to devour his own children. But when he had time to reflect, and saw what was in the fate, he began to lament over his choice, forgetting the teachings of the hierophant; instead of throwing the blame of his misfortune on himself, he accused destiny and the gods, and everything but himself."[36]

---

36 In the antiquity the word "tyrant" did not have the same meaning as given today. The name was attributed to those who had the sovereign power, whatever their actions, good or bad. History cites good tyrants. However, as it happened in the majority of the cases, in order to satisfy their ambitions or to stay in power, they acted criminally and then later the word became a synonym of cruelty, applied to every person who abuses authority. By choosing the greatest tyranny, the soul mentioned by Er was not looking for cruelty but for the greatest power as the condition of their new existence. When such a choice became irrevocable the soul understood that such a power would drag her through a life of crime and regretted the decision, blaming everybody else but her. It is the story of the majority of men who are the designers of their own disgrace, but who refuse to confess it.

"He was one of the souls who came from heaven, and in a previous life had dwelt in a well-ordered State, had done the good deeds but his virtue was a matter of habit rather than philosophy. Among the souls who fell over similar mistake many came from heaven and therefore had never been tested by suffering, whereas the pilgrims who came from Earth, having themselves suffered and seen others suffer, were not in such a hurry to choose. Thus, irrespective of the classification by chance, many of the souls exchanged a good destiny for an evil or an evil for a good. For if a person over every new life on Earth had always on one's arrival dedicated oneself to sound philosophy, and had been moderately fortunate in the draw, the person might, as the messenger reported, be happy here, and also one's journey here as well as on one's return to the other world, instead of being rough and underground, would be smooth and heavenly."

"Most curious, he said, was the spectacle of the soul's choice, it was sad and laughable and strange, in most cases based on their experience of a previous life. Er saw the soul which had once been Orpheus choosing the life of a swan. He chose out of hostility towards women, hating to be born of a woman because they had been his murderers. He saw the soul of Thamyras choosing the life of a nightingale; birds, on the other hand, like the swan and other musicians, wanting to be men."

"Another soul who held the twentieth ticket chose the life of a lion, and this was the soul of Ajax the son of Telamon. He hated humanity for the judgment passed upon him about the weapons of Aquiles. Agamemnon came next, who took the life of an eagle, because, like Ajax, he hated human nature for his sufferings. Towards the middle came the lot of Atalanta; she, seeing the great honor given to an athlete, was unable to resist the temptation of being one of them. Epeu, builder of the Horse of Troy, became an industrious woman. The soul of Thersites, the jester, took the form of a monkey."

"There came also the soul of Ulysses having yet to make a choice, and his lot happened to be the last of them all. Now the recollection of former tolls had disenchanted him from ambition, and he went about for a considerable time in search of the life of a private man who had been forgotten; and when he saw it, he said that he would have chosen that even if his lot came first instead of last, and that he was delighted to have it. The animals, whatever they may be, equally change into one another and into human bodies. Those who were evil become ferocious animals and the good ones, domesticated. After all souls had chosen their lives, they approached Lachesis, in the order of their choices. Fate sent with them the genius whom they had severally chosen, to be the guardian of their lives and the fulfiller of their choices. That genius led the souls first to Clotho who drew them within the revolution of the spindle impelled by her hand, thus ratifying the destiny of each one. Then the genius carried them to Atropos, who spun the threads and made them irreversible. Next the soul and the genius passed beneath the Throne of Necessity. When they had all passed, they marched on in a blazing heat to the plain of Forgetfulness[37], which was a sterile waste destitute of trees and plants. Evening came and they camped by the river Ameles (absence of serious thoughts); there they drank the water. The reckless drank too much hence lost their memory. Now after they had gone for their sleep, about mid night, there was a thunderstorm and an earthquake. Soon the souls were dispersed in all directions towards their birth places, like shooting stars. As for himself, said Er, he was hindered from drinking the water; however, he could not say where neither when his soul had been bonded to his body. Suddenly awaking in the morning he found himself lying on the pyre."

"And thus, Glaucon, the tale has been saved and has not perished, and will save us if we are faithful to the spoken word; and we shall pass safely over the river of Forgetfulness and will keep our soul purified from every stain."

---

37 Reference to the forgetfulness that happens to the soul from one existence to the next.

A Warning From

Beyond the Grave

The following fact was reported by the *Patrie* on August 15th, 1858:
"Last Tuesday I started to tell you, maybe too recklessly, a heartbreaking story. I should have thought that there is no touching story: there is only well told stories and that the same fact described by different persons may cause the audience either to fall asleep or give them the shivers of fear. As I entertained myself with a fellow traveler on a trip from Cherbourg to Paris, Mr. B... told me a marvelous tale that if I had annotated it would have allowed me the opportunity to give you a thrill of excitement.

However, I made the mistake of trusting my terrible memory that I profoundly regret. Nonetheless, here is the adventure that proves today, August 15th, that it is really a fact.

Mr. S..., a historical name that, even these days, is surrounded by consideration, was an officer during the Directory.[38] On business or pleasure he used to travel to Italy.

In one of our central departments, he was caught by surprise by the sudden shadows of the night, feeling happy for having found shelter in a kind of suspicious cabin, where he was offered an ordinary supper and a makeshift bed in the barn.

---

38   The Directory was the government of France during the second-to-last stage of the French Revolution (N.T.)

He was used to adventures and the tough duties of war hence he ate until full and then went to bed, falling deeply asleep, without a murmur.

During the night, a terrible apparition perturbed his sleep. He saw a form rising from the shadows, heavily marching towards his bed, stopping by his head. It was a man in his fifties, whose uneasy gray hair was blemished by blood; his chest was naked and his twinkled throat was cut open, still showing the wounds. He paused for a moment, staring at the sleepy traveler with his deep black eyes; then the pale figure got animated; his pupils became shiny bright like two pieces of lit charcoal. He seemed to make a huge effort and with a trembling and muffled voice he pronounced these strange words:

- I know you! You are a soldier and like me a man of courage and incapable of faulting with his word. I come to ask you for a service that others have promised but did not deliver. I have been dead for three weeks. The owner of this house, helped by his wife, surprised me in my sleep and slit my throat. My corpse is hidden under a pile of compost, to the right, at the end of the chicken pen. Tomorrow go and seek the local authorities, bring two policemen to bury me. The owner of the house and his wife will betray each other and you will deliver them to justice. Good-bye. I count on your pity. Do not forget the request of an old brother in arms.

"Awakening, Mr. S... remembered his dream. He rested his head on his elbows while meditating. His emotion was obvious but disappeared at sunrise and like Athalie, he said:

- A dream! Should I be worried about a dream?

He betrayed his heart's message, and listening only to the voice of reason, he packed and left.

Then came the afternoon when he completed another stretch of his journey, stopping over in a boarding house to spend the night. He had just closed his eyes when the shadow appeared a second time to him, sad and almost intimidating:

- I am impressed and afflicted, said the ghost, by seeing a man like you to perjure and fail with your duties. I expected more loyalty from you. My body lies unburied and my murderers live in peace. Friend, my vengeance is in your hands. In the name of honor, I demand that you return at once.

Mr. S... spent the rest of the night under great agitation. At dawn he felt ashamed for his fear but continued his journey.

In the afternoon came a third stop and a third apparition. This time the ghost was livid and terrifying. He held a bitter smile on his white lips. He spoke with a rude voice:

- It seems that I have misjudged you; that your heart, like the others, is insensitive to the claims of the unfortunate ones. For the last time I come to invoke your help and appeal to your generosity. Go back to X... and revenge me or otherwise may you be cursed.

Mr. S... did not hesitate this time. He turned back on his feet traveling to the suspicious hostel where he had spent the first of those lugubrious nights. He went to the judge's house and requested the escort of two policemen. Just as they saw the police the guest's murderers became pale and confessed to the crime, as if a superior force had forcibly driven them to the fatal confession. The legal process was prepared swiftly and the culprits were given the death penalty.

As for the poor policeman whose cadaver was found under a pile of manure, to the right, at the end of the chicken pen, he was buried in sacred grounds, having the priests prayed for the peace of his soul.

Mission accomplished, Mr. S... was quick to leave the region towards the Alps, never looking back. The first time he stopped to rest in a bed the ghost showed up once again, no longer showing ferocious and irritated eyes but sweet and benevolent, saying:

- Thank you my brother. I wish to thank you for your service to me. You will see me again only once. I will come to warn you two hours before your death. Good-bye.

Mr. S... was then about thirty years old. For another thirty years not a single vision came to disrupt his peaceful life. But on August 14th, 182... on the eve of Napoleon's celebrations, and still faithful to Napoleon's party, he had gathered about twenty old soldiers of the Empire over dinner. The gathering was very enjoyable and happy and the host, although old, was healthy and strong. They were having coffee in the living room. Mr. S... felt like smoking his pipe and remembered that he had left the tobacco in his bedroom. Since he was used to prepare it himself he left the guests momentarily and went up to the first floor where his bedroom was located. He had not taken any light with him.

Once he got to the large hall that led to the room he had to suddenly stop and reach for the wall. The ghost of the murdered man stood across the corridor from him, at the other end. The ghost did not say a word, not even a gesture, disappearing after a few moments.

It was the promised warning.

Mr. S... who was a man of strong character, after that brief and fainting moment, recovered his courage and cold blood to proceed to his room, grab the box of snuff and return to the living room. He mingled with the others, joining the conversations, showing his joviality and customary sense of humor.

At midnight the guests left. He then sat down and spent about three quarters of an hour meditating. Then, feeling good and having organized his business, he retired to his room to go to bed.

When he opened the door, a gunshot knocked him dead, exactly two hours after the apparition of the ghost. The bullet that shattered his skull was addressed to his servant.

HENRY D'AUDIGIER

The author of the article wished to keep his promise to the newspaper about telling something touching, at any price, resorting to a story that he reports with great imagination or is the story true? We cannot guarantee. As a matter of fact, this is not important. Real or fictitious the essential here is to know if the fact is at all possible.

Then, let us not hesitate and say: yes, the warnings from beyond the grave are possible. The numerous examples attesting them are out there, whose authenticity could not be mistrusted. If the anecdote of Mr. Henry d'Audigier is then apocryphal here are plenty of the same kind that are not and we can even say that this one has nothing of extraordinary.

The apparition would have happened in his dream, which is very common. However, it is notorious that they can also visually happen in the waking state. The warning at the instant of death is not uncommon but the facts of that kind are very rare as the Providence's wisdom hides the fatal moment from us. Thus, it is only exceptionally that it is revealed to us and for unknown reasons.

The following is an example of a more recent, less dramatic analogous case, but whose accuracy we can ensure.

Mr. Watbled who was a business man and the president of the Boulogne Chamber of Commerce, died on July 12th last, under the following circumstances: His wife had died twelve years earlier and her death had brought him a permanent sorrow; she appeared to him over two consecutive nights in the beginning of July and told him: God had mercy on our souls and wants us to unite soon. She added that the encounter was scheduled for the next July 12th and, as a consequence, he should get ready. In fact, since then he went through a remarkable change: he progressively atrophied. He soon prostrated without any suffering, exhaling his final breath on the very scheduled day, in his friends' arms.

The fact is not contestable in itself. The skeptical may only discuss the cause, which they will certainly attribute to the imagination.

It is well known that similar predictions, made by future tellers, have had, not infrequently, a fatal ending. In such a case it is understandable that the organs, having the imagination excited by that idea, experience a radical alteration. More than once the fear of death has caused death. But here the circumstances are different.

Those who deeply studied the spiritist phenomena will realize the fact; as for the skeptical, those have only one argument: "I do not believe, hence this is not possible." Once questioned about this the spirits have said: "God chose that well-known man so that the event would be noticed and provided food for thought." The incredulous incessantly asks for proofs. God gives them every time through the phenomena that sprout everywhere. Nevertheless, these are the words that apply to them: "have eyes but do not see, have ears but do not hear."

The Outcries of St. Bartholomew's Night

In the *Histoire de l'Ordre du Saint-Espirit*, 1778 edition, De Saint-Foy cites the following passage from a collection of the Marquis Christophe Juvenal des Ursins, lieutenant general of Paris, written around the end of 1572 and published in 1601.

"On August 31st, 1572, eight days after St. Bartholomew's massacre, I had dined at the Louvre, in Mrs. de Fiesque's home. The whole day had been scorching hot. We sat under a small arbor by the creek, breathing fresh air. Suddenly we heard a horrible noise of tumultuous voices, mixed with groans and screams of rage and furor. We remained still, chilled by the amazement, glancing at each other from time to time, not having the courage to speak. I believe that the noise lasted for half an hour. It is certain that King Charles IX heard it too and was terrified, not being able to sleep for the rest of the night; however, he did not make any comment on the following day but his somber, thoughtful and crazy looks were noticeable. If any prodigy should not meet incredulity this is one, attested by Henry IV. In his book I, Chapter 6, page 561, d'Aubigné says: several times that prince told us, the most intimate family members and court goers – and I have living witnesses that he had never repeated it to us without showing great horror – that eight days after the Night of St. Bartholomew, he had seen a large amount of vultures landing and cawing over the Louvre's pavilion; that in the same evening Charles IX, two hours after having gone to bed, got up, sending the chamber maids to search around since he had heard a loud noise of voices and groans, very similar to the ones that were heard at the night of the massacre; that all those screams were so shocking, so much marked and distinctly articulated that Charles IX thought that the enemies of Montmorency and his followers were attacking by surprise, hence he sent a platoon of his guard to impede a new massacre. The guards informed him that Paris was quiet and that all the noise was only in the air."

OBSERVATION: The fact reported by Saint-Foy and by Juvenal des Ursins have lots of analogies with the story of the ghost that appeared to Mademoiselle Clairon, reported in our January issue, with the difference that in her case it was only one spirit to manifest during two and a half years, while after the Night of St. Bartholomew there seems to have been a large number of spirits who made the air vibrate just for a few moments. As a matter of fact, these two phenomena have obviously the same principle as the other contemporary facts of the same nature, already reported by us, not differing from them but by the detail of the form. Once questioned about the cause of such manifestation several spirits responded that it was a punishment from God, which is easy to understand.

Family Conversations

From Beyond the Grave

Mrs. Schwabenhaus –

Ecstatic Lethargy

According to the *Courrier des États-Unis*, several newspapers reported the following fact that seemed to provide interesting material for study.

The *Courrier des États-Unis* says:

"A German family from Baltimore, USA, has just been taken by great emotion due to a case of an apparent death. Mrs. Schwabenhaus who was ill for a long time had exhaled what seemed to have been her last breath overnight, from Monday to Tuesday. The persons who attended her observed every indication of death: the body went cold, the limbs rigid. The undertakers retired to their rooms after having given the corpse the final care and when everything in the mortuary chamber was ready for the funerals. Exhausted, Mr. Schwabenhaus soon followed them. Deep in his agitated sleep he was surprised by his wife's voice around 6 am. In the beginning he thought it was a dream but once he heard his name several times he could not doubt it any longer. He dashed into his wife's room and the person who was left for dead was sitting on the bed, apparently healthy and stronger than ever before.

Mrs. Schwabenhaus asked for water and later she wished to drink tea and wine. Then she asked her husband to take care of the child that was crying in the adjacent room but he was too excited for that, running to call the others from around the house. The sick lady received friends and servants with a smile; all approached her bed hesitantly. She did not seem surprised with all that mortuary apparatus that hurt her eyes. "I know you thought that I was dead", she said; "however, I was only asleep. During that period my soul was transported to celestial regions. An angel came to pick me up and in a few moments we crossed the space. The guiding angel was my little daughter that we lost last year... Oh! Soon I will reunite with her... Now that I have enjoyed the happiness of heavens I no longer wish to stay here. I asked the angel to allow me to come once more to kiss my husband and my children but she will soon come to pick me up."

At eight o'clock, after kindly having said goodbye to her husband, children and several other people who surrounded her, Mrs. Schwabenhaus definitely died, as attested by the doctors without a somber of a doubt.

That fact caused vivid commotion in Baltimore's population.

The spirit of Mrs. Schwabenhaus sustained the following conversation, when evoked in one session of the Parisian Society of Spiritist Studies, on April 27th last:

1. We want to frame a few questions with respect to your death, aiming at our own instruction.
   - How could I not answer you, now that I notice the eternal truths and know about your needs?
2. Do you remember the particular conditions that preceded your death?
   - Yes. That was the happiest moment of my Earthly existence.
3. During your apparent death did you hear what happened around you and saw the burial apparatus?
   - My soul was much concerned with its forthcoming happiness.

OBSERVATION: It is known that the lethargic generally see and hear what happens around them and keep its memory when awaken. The reported fact offers the particularity of a lethargic sleep accompanied by ecstasy, what explains the deviation in the patient's attention.

4. Were you aware that you were not dead?
   - Yes but that was painful to me.
5. Can you tell us the difference between the natural sleep and the lethargic one?
   - The natural sleep is the appeasement of the body; the lethargic is the exaltation of the soul.
6. Have you suffered during the lethargy?
   - No.
7. How did your return to life happen?
   - God allowed my return to comfort the afflicted hearts around me.
8. We wish a more material explanation.
   - What you call perispirit still animated my terrestrial covering.
9. How come you were not surprised when you woke up with all the arrangements that were going on for your funeral?
   - I knew I was going to die. I couldn't care less about all that because I had a glance at the happiness of the elected ones.
10. Returning to your alertness, where you happy to return to life?
    - Yes, to console.
11. Where have you being during your lethargic sleep?
    - I cannot describe my state of happiness. Human language cannot express these things.
12. Did you still feel on Earth or in space?
    - In the spaces.
13. When you came back to yourself you said that the daughter you had lost in the previous year came back to take you. Is that true?
    - Yes. She is a pure spirit.

OBSERVATION: From the answers of this mother, everything indicates that she is an elevated spirit. No surprise that an even more elevated spirit was united to hers out of sympathy. However, we should not take literally the expression "pure spirit" that the spirits sometimes attribute to each other. It is a fact that it refers to a more elevated order hence those that are completely dematerialized and depurated are no longer subjected to reincarnation: these are angels that enjoy eternal life. Well, those who have not yet achieved a sufficient level do not understand that supreme state. They can then employ the expression "pure spirit" to designate a relative superiority. We have numerous examples of that. Mrs. Schwabenhaus seems to be in that category. The spirits of mockery sometimes also attribute the quality of "pure spirits" to themselves in order to inspire more confidence in those who they wish to trick and that do not have sufficient perspicacity to judge their language, through which they always betray their inferiority.

14. How old was that child when she died?
    - Seven years old.
15. How did you recognize her?
    - The superior spirits recognize each other more promptly.
16. Did you recognize her under any form?
    - I only saw her as spirit.
17. What did she tell you?
    - Come and follow me to the Eternal.
18. Did you see other spirits beyond that of your daughter?
    - I saw many others but my daughter's voice and the happiness, which I had a glance at, were my only concerns.
19. Once you returned to life you said that you would soon reunite with your daughter. You were then aware of you near death?
    - It was a happy expectation.
20. How did you know?
    - Who doesn't know that one has to die? The illness told me that.

21. What was the cause of your illness?
    - The displeasures.
22. How old were you?
    - Forty-eight years old.
23. When you definitely left life, did you immediately have clear and lucid consciousness of your new condition?
    - I had it during the lethargy.
24. Did you experience the perturbation that generally follows the return to the spiritual world?
    - No. I was amazed but not perturbed.

OBSERVATION: It is well known that the perturbation that follows death is lower and shorter the more depurated the spirit is. The ecstasy that preceded this lady's death was, by the way, the first detachment of her soul from the Earthly bonds.

25. After your death have you seen your daughter again?
    - I am frequently with her.
26. Are you bonded to her for the whole eternity?
    - No, however, I know that after my previous incarnations I will be in the dwelling inhabited by the pure spirits.
27. Then your trials are not over yet?
    - No, but now they will be happy ones. I can only wait and hope. This is almost happiness.
28. Has your daughter inhabited other bodies other than that when she was your daughter?
    - Yes, many others.
29. Under which form are you among us here?
    - Under my feminine form.
30. Do you see us so distinctly as if you were alive?
    - Yes.

31. Since you are here under the form you had on Earth, do you see us through your eyes?

No. The spirit has no eyes. I only show up under my latest form to satisfy the laws that rule the spirits when evoked and obliged to return to what you call perispirit.

32. Can you read our thoughts?

-   Yes, I can. I will read them if your thoughts are good.

33. We thank you for the explanations you kindly gave us. We acknowledge by the wisdom of your answers that you are an elevated spirit and we hope that you may enjoy the happiness that you deserve.

-   I feel happy to contribute with your work. Death is happiness when one can cooperate with progress, as I have just done.

The Talismans

Cabalistic Medal

Mr. M… had bought a medal in an antique shop that seemed remarkable for its originality. It was the size of a crown of six pounds. Had a silver looks but a bit oxidized. It held several engraved markings on both sides, among them the planets, intertwined circles, a triangle, unintelligible words and some initials in common characters; then some others in bizarre characters, somehow similar to Arabic, all arranged in a cabalistic way, resembling the witchery books.

Mr. M… sought the help of a somnambulist medium, Ms. J…, who told him that it was made of seven metals; that belonged to Cazotte and that it had the power of attracting the spirits, facilitating evocations.

Mr. Caudemberg, who was the author of a series of communications that supposedly he had received from the Virgin Mary, told him that it was a malefic thing, proper to attract the demons. Ms. Guldenstube, medium, sister of Baron Guldenstube, author of a book about pneumatography or direct writing, told him that the medal had a magnetic virtue and that it could provoke somnambulism.

Unsatisfied with those contradictory answers, Mr. M… showed us that medal, requesting our opinion about it, while he also wanted us to evoke a superior spirit to inquiry about the real value of that object, regarding the influence it might have.

Here is our answer:

The spirits are attracted or repelled through thought and not through material objects that have no influence on them. The superior spirits have condemned, at all times, the use of signs and cabalistic forms and every spirit who attributes any power or that intend to give talismans that denote magic power reveal their own inferiority; acting in good faith or out of pure ignorance; driven by old Earthly prejudices that they still carry or when consciously play with peoples beliefs, as a jester spirit. The cabalistic signs, when not a mere fantasy, are symbols that remind superstitious beliefs in the virtue of certain things, like numbers, the planets and their association to the metals, beliefs born at times of ignorance and that are based on plain mistakes, to which Science has made justice, showing what is behind the seven metals, the seven planets, etc. The mystic and unintelligible format of such symbols has the objective of self-imposing onto the crowds, always inclined to consider marvelous everything that they cannot understand. Whoever has studied the nature of the spirits could not rationally admit that they would be influenced by conventional forms or substances mixed in certain proportions. It would be the same as to revisit the caldron of the witches, the black cats, black chickens and other secret plots. This is different from the effect of a magnetized object as it is a known fact that it has the power of provoking somnambulism or certain nervous phenomena on the organic structure. However, the power of such objects resides exclusively on the fluid that it is momentarily impregnated by and that thus indirectly passes on, and not in the form, color and particularly not on the signs that it may show.

A spirit may say: "Make a given signal and I will know that you call me and I will come." But in such a case the drawn signal is the expression of the thought; it is an evocation translated into a material format. Well, whatever the nature of the spirits they do not need similar means of communication. The superior spirits never utilize them. The inferior spirits may use them aiming at seducing the believers who they wish to control.

General rule: Form is nothing to the superior spirits. Thought is everything. Every spirit that gives more importance to the form than to the meaning is inferior and unworthy, even when they may say good things once in a while, as the good things are sometimes a means of seduction.

This was, generally speaking, our thoughts with respect to the talismans, as a means of entering into communication with the spirits. Unnecessary to say that it also applies to other means superstitiously employed, like avoiding diseases and accidents. Nevertheless, to the benefit of the medal owner and in order to get better knowledge into the subject, we asked the spirit of St. Louis, in the session of the Parisian Society on July 17th, 1858, who kindly communicates with us whenever there is an opportunity for instruction, to give his opinion regarding the subject. Here is his answer about the value of such a medal:

"You do well not admitting that such material object may have any power over the manifestations, be it to provoke or to impede them. Very frequently we have said that the manifestations are spontaneous and even further, that we never refuse to respond to your appeal. Why do you think we would be obliged to obey something that was manufactured by human beings?"

Q – What was the objective of fabricating such a medal?

A – It was made with the objective of calling the attention of those who could believe in such a thing. But only magnetizers could have made it with the intention of magnetizing and inducing a sensitive to sleep. The symbols are mere fantasies.

Q – Some say it belonged to Cazotte. Could we evoke him to give us some information about it?

A – It is unnecessary. Occupy yourselves with more serious things."

Moral Problems:

Suicide for Love

Seven or eight months ago Mr. Louis G..., the shoemaker, was dating the young Victorine R..., a boot stitcher with whom he was soon to marry, hence the marriage license was about to be issued. The couple considered themselves almost definitely united and to save money the shoemaker used to come to the bride's house for his meals.

As usual, he came last Wednesday to have supper at the boot stitcher's house, when a silly discussion took place over something of minor importance. Both sides were very adamant so that things heated up to a point that made Louis leave, swearing not to come back.

Nevertheless, on the very next day the very confused shoemaker came to apologize. They say that sleep is a good counselor, but the lady worker after the previous scene and maybe foreseeing what could happen when there would be no way back, refused reconciliation thus neither his protests nor his cries and desperation could win her back. Nevertheless, as several days had gone by since that regrettable incident, and expecting that his beloved one would be more manageable, in the evening before last Louis wished to try a final explanation: he knocked on the door so as to be recognized but she refused to answer. He renovated his protests and supplication through the door but his elected one remained unaltered.

"You are mean, then good bye!" said the poor man. "Good bye forever! Look for a husband that loves you as much as I do!"

Simultaneously the lady heard a muffled groan, then the noise of a falling body, as if just supported by the door, and then silence. She thought that Louis had just seated at her door step, waiting for her first coming out of the house but she promised herself that she would not step her foot outside while he was there.

A quarter of an hour had gone by when one of the residents, walking through the yard with a lamp, yelled for help. Soon other neighbors joined in and Ms. Victorine, opening the door, screamed in horror when she saw her fiancé on the ground, pale and motionless. Everybody tried to help and seek medical support but soon all noticed that it was useless since the man was gone. The unfortunate man had stabbed his own chest with a shoemaker's knife.

This fact found on the *Le Siècle* on April 7th last gave us the idea of enquiring a superior spirit about the moral consequences of such an event. Here the answers given by the spirit of St. Louis in the session of the Society, on August 10th, 1858.

1. Has the young lady, who was the involuntary cause of her boyfriend's death, any responsibility?
   - Yes, because she did not love him.
2. Should she have married him to avoid such a tragedy, even if not loving him?
   - She was looking for an occasion to separate from him; she did in the beginning of the relationship what she would have done later.
3. Thus the culpability is in the fact that she gave him hope by responding to feelings that she did not share and that was the cause of the man's death?
   - Yes. That is correct.
4. In that case her responsibility should be proportional to the fault that should not be as important as if she had premeditatedly provoked the death.
   - That is obvious.

5. Does Louis' suicide find justification in the madness that he found himself due to his obstinacy for Victorine?
    - Yes because his suicide is less unlawful to the eyes of God than that of a man that wants to get away from life by cowardliness.

OBSERVATION: By saying that the suicide is less unlawful to the eyes of God it evidently means that it is still criminal, to a lesser degree. The fault is in his weakness that he could not overcome and, no doubt, a failed trial. Well, the spirits teach us that the merit is in victoriously fighting over the trials of all kinds that are the essence of life on Earth.

The spirit of Mr. Louis C... was evoked on another day and answered the following questions:

1. What do you think about your action?
    - Victorine is ungrateful. I was wrong by killing myself for her, as she did not deserve it.
2. She did not love you then?
    - No. In the beginning she thought so but she was mistaken. The scene I created opened her eyes. Then she felt happy with that excuse to let me go.
3. And you, did you sincerely love her?
    - I was in love with her. I believe it was only that. Had I loved her with pure love I would not have wanted to hurt her.
4. Had she known that you would really kill yourself, would she have persisted on her refusal?
    - I don't know. I don't believe so since she was not mean. However, she would have been unhappy. For her it was better that way.

5. When you got to her door did you have the intention of killing yourself in case you were denied?

    -   No. I never thought of that. I did not think that she was so decided. It was only when I saw her stubbornness that I was overtaken by an unsteadiness.

6. It seems that you do not regret the suicide but only because Victorine did not deserve it. Is that your only feeling?

    -   As of now, yes. I am still perturbed. It still seems that I am at her doorstep. However, I feel something that I cannot define.

7. Will you understand later?

    -   Yes, when I am detached... what I did was bad. I should have left her in peace... I was weak and do suffer the consequences... As you see, passion leads man to blindness and to act absurdly. He only understands when it is too late.

8. You said that you suffer the consequences. What is your punishment?

    -   I was wrong abbreviating my life. I should not have done that. I should have resisted instead of prematurely ending everything. That is why I am unhappy. I suffer. It is always her that makes me suffer. I feel like I am at her doorstep. How ungrateful! Don't mention this any longer. I don't want to think any more. Good-bye.

Observation About the

Drawing of Mozart's House

One of our subscribers wrote the following lines regarding the drawing that we published in the last issue of our Review.

"The author of the article says: The treble clef is frequently repeated there and – something original – never the bass clef". It seems that the medium's eyes did not see all the details of the rich drawing executed by his hand, since a musician assured us that it is easy to recognize the bass clef direct and inverted in the decoration of the construction, whose central part shows the violin bow as in the extension of the decoration, to the left of the theorbo's tip. In the opinion of the same musician the old form of the alto clef also appears near the slabs of the stairs, on the right hand side."

OBSERVATION: We insert this observation with great satisfaction as it demonstrates how foreign the medium was to the execution of the drawing. By examining the details of the indicated parts one can effectively recognize the bass and alto clefs with which the author had inadvertently decorated his drawing. When we see him working we easily notice the absence of any premeditated conception and will. His hand, dragged by an occult power, gives the pencil or chisels the most irregular motion and, at the same time, the most contrary to the elementary precepts of art since it moves incessantly, with an incredible speed, from an end to the other of the board, unstoppable and returning to the same point a hundred times. At a first glance this results into an incoherent piece of work, only understandable when it is finished.

Such an original development is not peculiar to Mr. Sardou. We have seen all drawing mediums proceeding in the same way. We know a lady who is a skillful painter that teaches drawing skills and who is also a drawing medium. When she draws like a medium she works regardless of her own will, against all rules and by a process that would be impossible to follow when working under her own inspiration in a normal state. Her students, she said, would laugh if she taught them by the way of the spirits.

Allan Kardec[39]

---

39 Paris – Typography Cosson & Co., Rue du Four-Saint-Germain, 43

October 1858

The Obsessed and

Subjugated

A lot has been said about the dangers of Spiritism. It is remarkable; however, that those who screamed the most are exactly those who only know it from what they heard about it. We have already refuted the main arguments brought up by them – thus we shall not return to that topic. We shall only add that if we wanted to eliminate from society everything that could offer danger and give rise to abuses we wouldn't have much left, even those things of real necessity, starting from the fire, a cause of so many tragedies; then the railroads and etc. If one admits that the advantages compensate the inconvenient, the same must apply to everything else. At the same time experience indicates the precautions that need to be taken to protect us against the inevitable dangers of things.

Spiritism truly poses a real danger but it is not the danger that one supposes. It is necessary to be initiated in the principles of the Science to understand it well. We do not address those who are unaware of such principles but the individuals aware of these principals themselves, those who practice them, since these are the individuals who face danger. It is necessary that those principles be understood so as the adepts can be on guard. As they say, a known danger is a half avoided danger. We say more: to whoever is well informed about the Science such a danger does not exist; it does exist only to those who have the presumption of knowledge, that is to say, as with everything else, to those that do not have the necessary experience.

A very natural desire in everyone that starts to get involved with Spiritism is to become a medium, mainly of psychography. It is really the kind that exerts more attraction, given the facility of communications and for being the one that more easily is developed by exercise. It is understandable the satisfaction that someone must feel when, for the first time, sees their hand forming letters and later on phrases, answering to their thoughts. These automatically traced answers, without the person knowing what is going on, that frequently is outside of any personal idea, cannot leave any doubt regarding the intervention of an occult intelligence. Therefore, they show great happiness on dealing with the beings of beyond the grave, with these mysterious and invisible beings that populate the spaces: relatives and friends are no longer absent; the fact that one cannot see them does not mean that they are not present; one talks to them and is seen by them through thought; one can know if they are happy, know what they do, what they want and exchange kindness. It is clear that the separation between them is no longer eternal and that they have expectations for the moment when they can finally meet in a better world. That is not all. How much more cannot one know through the communicating spirits? Won't they lift the veil of all things? No more mysteries now: just ask to know it all. One can see antiquity shaking before the dust of times; excavate ruins; interpret symbolic scriptures and revive past centuries before one's eyes. This one is more prosaic; less worried about probing the infinite where his thought is lost, being only interested in exploiting the spirits to make fortune. The spirits, who should know and see everything, cannot deny the allowance of some hidden treasure or some marvelous secret.

Whoever takes the time to study the Spiritist Science will never fall for such beautiful dreams. They know what should be avoided with respect to the power of the spirits, of their nature and the objective of the relationships that human beings can establish with them. Let us recall, to begin with, in a few words, the main points that must never be kept off sight as they are the cornerstone that sustain the whole edifice.

1° - The spirits are not all equal nor in power, nor in knowledge or wisdom. As they are no more than human souls detached from their corporeal body, they present a variety even greater than that of people on Earth, because they come from all worlds and, among the globes, Earth is neither the most basic nor the most advanced. Thus, there are very superior spirits as there are very inferior ones; very good and bad; very wise and very ignorant; there are those of levity, malevolence, liars, astute, hypocrites, polished, sharp, jokers, etc.

2° - We are incessantly surrounded by a cloud of spirits that occupy the space around us, despite the fact that we cannot see them, watching our acts, reading our thoughts, some to do us good, others to do us harm, whether good or bad spirits, accordingly.

3° - From the physical and moral inferiority of our globe in the hierarchy of the worlds, the inferior spirits are more numerous here than the superior ones.

4° - Among those spirits that surround us there are those that attach to us; that act more particularly over our thoughts, giving us advice, and whose influence we follow unnoticeably. Good for us if we hear the voice of the good spirits only.

5° - The inferior spirits only bond to those that listen to them, that give them access and to whom they connect. If successful on dominating someone, they identify with their own spirit, fascinating them, obsessing them, subjugating them, and leading them as one does to a child.

6° - Obsession can never happen but by inferior spirits. The good spirits don't produce any kind of coercion, combat the influence of the bad spirits and stay away when they are not listened to.

7° - The degree of coercion and the nature of the effects it produces determine the difference between obsession, subjugation and fascination.

Obsession is the almost permanent action of a strange spirit that leads the person to be solicited by an incessant need to act by this way or the other and to do this or that.

Subjugation is a moral bond that paralyzes the free will of the one that suffers it, pushing the person to the most reckless attitudes, frequently most contrary to their own interest.

Fascination is a kind of illusion produced by the direct action of a strange spirit or by his cunning thoughts. Such an illusion produces an alteration in the comprehension of moral things, leading to misjudgment and to mistaken evil for good.

8° - Human beings can always disengage from the oppression of the imperfect spirits by their will power, by the choice between good and bad. If the coercion achieved the point of paralyzing the will and if the fascination is such that it obliterates reason, then the will of a third person may replace it.

The name possession was used in the past to describe the control exerted by the bad spirits, when their influence would go to the aberration of the faculties. But ignorance and prejudice have taken by possession what many times was just a pathological state. For us, possession would be a synonym of subjugation. We do not adopt that term for two reasons: first because it implies the belief in beings created and perpetually devoted to evil when in fact there is only more or less imperfect beings who can improve; second that it implies that the strange spirit takes over the body, in a kind of co-inhabitation, when in fact there is only a connection. The word subjugation gives a perfect idea. Thus for us there is no possessed in the vulgar sense, but only obsessed, subjugated and fascinated.

For the same reason we do not use the term "devil" to designate the imperfect spirits, although these are frequently not better than those called devils; it is only due to the specialty and perpetuity associated to that term. Thus, when we say that there are no devils we do not wish to say that there are only good spirits. Far from that and we know well that there are evil and much evil ones, who solicit us to evil, tricking us, not surprisingly considering that they were all human beings. We wish to say that they do not make a special class in the order of Creation and that God gives all creatures the opportunity to improve themselves.

Having said that let us go back to the mediums. For some the progress is slow, really slow; these have their patience tested sometimes. For others it is fast, and in a short time the medium begins to write with ease and eventually even more promptly than he would do under normal conditions. It is then that the medium can get carried away and it is there where the danger resides because enthusiasm leads to weakening and it is necessary to be strong with the spirits. It seems a paradox to say that enthusiasm provokes weakening but there is nothing more correct than this. Some will say that enthusiasm marches with a conviction and a confidence that overcome every obstacle, thus yielding more strength. No doubt but we become enthusiastic by the false as well as by the true. Accept the most absurd ideas of the enthusiast and you can do anything you want with him. The object of the enthusiasm is their weak spot by which they can always be dominated. The cold person, on the contrary, is impassive. He is not misled; correlates, weighs, maturely examines and does not allow seduction through subterfuge. That is his strength. The malevolent spirits who know this better than us, also know how to take advantage of the situation to subjugate those who they wish to control. The faculty of writing as medium serves them wonderfully well as it is a powerful means of captivating the medium's trust and consequently take advantage, if we are not vigilant against them. Fortunately, as we will see later, the illness also carries the remedy.

Be it out of enthusiasm, out of fascination by the spirits or the medium's self esteem, the psychographic medium in general is led to believe that the spirits that communicate with him are superior and that even more the more the spirits, by noticing the medium's inclination, ornate themselves with pompous titles, according to the necessity. Thus, pending on the circumstances, they take the names of saints, scholars, angels, of the Virgin Mary herself, and play their roles like actors, ridiculously dressing the outfits of those they represent. Remove their masks and they become what they are: ridiculous. This is what one must do both with the spirits and with human beings.

From the blind and unthoughtful belief in the superiority of the spirits to the trust in their words there is only one step, as it also happens with people. If they are able to inspire such a confidence they then feed it through sophisms and cunning reasoning, before which people normally lower their heads. The rude spirits are less dangerous: we recognize them immediately and these do not inspire but disgust. The most terrible in their world, like in ours, are the hypocrite spirits: they always speak with kindness, flatter people's inclinations; are sweet, shrewd, and plentiful of nice expressions, demonstrating dedication. It is necessary to be really strong to resist to similar seduction.

Some will ask: Where is the danger if the spirits are intangible? The danger is in the bad advices that they give, and in the ridiculous, baleful and untimely attitudes they lead us to do. We have already seen some that made certain people to walk from region to region searching for fantastic things, at the risk of their health, fortune and own life. We have seen them dictating the most banal things with a grave attitude, applying the strangest teachings.

Considering the adequacy of supplying the example side by side with the theory, we will report the case of an acquaintance of ours who had been under the dominion of a similar fascination.

Mr. F..., a highly educated young man, of kind and benevolent character, but a bit weak and indecisive, became a psychographic medium in a very short time. Obsessed by the spirit that controlled him and would not let him go, he wrote incessantly. If a pen or a pencil reached his hand he would convulsively take it, filling pages and pages out in a few minutes. In the absence of an instrument he would simulate writing with his finger, wherever he was: in the streets, on the walls, on the doors, etc. Among other things he used to write this: "Man is made up of three things: man, the bad spirit and the good spirit. All of you have your bad spirit that is connected to your body by material links. In order to expel the bad spirit it is necessary to break these links that requires the weakening of the body. When the body is sufficiently weak the link breaks and the bad spirit goes, leaving only the good spirit behind."

As a consequence of that beautiful theory they made him fast for five days in a row and wake at night. When he was worn out they told him: "Now the thing is done and the link is broken. Your bad spirit is gone: it is now only us that you must believe without reservations." And the man, persuaded that the bad spirit had fled, blindly believed in everything he was told. The subjugation had come to a point that if they asked him to jump in the waters or leave to the other side of the earth he would have done so. When asked to do something that disgusted him he felt dragged by an invisible power.

We give a small sample of their moral disposition and from there on it is possible to judge the rest:

"In order to obtain better communications it is necessary to pray first and fast for several days, some more, others less. Fasting weakens the existing links between the ego and a particular devil connected to each human being. That devil is connected to each person through the covering that unites body and soul. Such covering weakens by the lack of food, allowing the spirits to remove that devil. Then Jesus gets into the heart of the promised person, replacing the evil spirit. Such a state of having Jesus in each one is the only way one has to attain the whole truth and many other things. By successfully replacing the devil by Jesus the creature does not have the truth yet. It is necessary to believe. God does not give the truth to the doubtful: it would be like doing something useless and God does not do such things. As the majority of the new mediums doubt what they say and write, the good spirits, unwillingly, by a formal commandment of God, are obliged to lie and they have no other alternative but to lie until the medium is convinced; but as soon as they believe in one of those lies the elevated spirits rush into unveil the secrets of heavens to them: the whole truth shines up instantly over that cloud of mistakes with which they were obliged to cover their protégé. Once there, the medium has nothing else to fear. The good spirits will never leave them. However, he should not believe that he always holds the truth and only the truth.

Be it to protect him or to punish him for his past faults, be it still to punish him for selfish or curious questions, the good spirits inflict him physical and moral corrections, coming to torment him in the name of God. Sometimes those elevated spirits regret the sad mission that they accomplish: a father harasses his son for weeks in a row, from a friend to his friend, all for the happiness of the medium. Then the noble spirits say silly things, blasphemies and even nasty ones. It is necessary that the medium resist and say: you are trying me; I know that I am in the hands of caring and kind spirits; that the evil ones can no longer approach me. Good souls that torment me, you shall not impede my belief in what you have taught me and that you shall still teach. The Catholic more easily expel the devil[40] because he left instantly at the day of baptism. The Catholics are judged by Jesus, the others by God. It is better to be judged by the Christ. The Protestants are not right in not admitting that: it is necessary that you become a Catholic as soon as possible. While you don't do that, go and drink the holy water: this will be your baptism."

Later, after being cured from the obsession that victimized him, by means that we will report, we asked him to write his own story, providing us with a description of the principles that were dictated to him. He added the following text to his explanations:

"I ask myself if I am not offending God by means of writing such silly things."

We respond to that: No, you do not offend God; far from that since now you acknowledge the trap in which you fell. If I asked you for a copy of such perverse statements was to highlight them, as they deserve; unmask the hypocrites and alert whoever may receive similar thing.

One day they will make you write: "You shall die tonight". And he will answer: I feel bored in this world; let us die, if that is meant to be; I ask for no more; may I no longer suffer; this is all I wish – Then firmly sleeps at night believing that he will no longer wake up. What a surprise and disappointment in the next morning when he sees himself in his usual bed. During the day he writes: "Now that you have gone through the trial

---

40 The young medium was protestant

of death, that you firmly believed that you would die, you are like one of us, dead: we can now tell you the whole truth; you will know everything. There is nothing hidden from us; nothing hidden from you. You are one reincarnation of Shakespeare. Isn't Shakespeare your bible?

On the next day he writes:

- You are Satan.
- This a bit too much, says Mr. F...
- Haven't you done... haven't you devoured the Lost Paradise? You have read the Fille du Diable de Beranger; you knew that Satan would convert. Haven't you always believed; haven't you said that; haven't you written that? In order to convert he has reincarnated.
- I agree that I may have been some rebel angel but the king of angels...!
- Yes, you were the angel of intrepidity. You are not evil. You have a proud heart; it is that pride that you need to abate. You are the angel of pride, that people call Satan. Who cares about the name! You were the evil genie of Earth. Behold you are now humiliated... People will progress... You will see wonders. You have deceived people; you deceived the woman personified by Eve, the sinful woman. They say that Maria, the personification of the spotless woman, will crush your head. Maria will come.

A few moments later writes slow and kindly:
Maria is coming to see you. She, the one who sought you at the bottom of your kingdo3m of shadow, shall not abandon you. God is ready to extend his arms to you. Read The Prodigal Son. Good Bye.

On another day he writes:
The serpent told Eve: Your eyes shall open and you shall be like the gods. The devil told Jesus: I will give you all the power. I tell you as you

believe in our words: we love you; you will know everything... You will be king of Poland.

- Persevere in the good conditions we placed you. This lesson will give the Spiritist Science a big boost. You will see that the good spirits may say silly things and lies to make fun of the scholars. Allan Kardec has said that a way of recognizing the spirits is to make them confess Jesus in flesh. I say that only the good spirits confess Jesus in flesh, and I do it. Tell Kardec that.

However the spirit had the modesty of not advising Mr. F... to publish such beautiful statements. Had he done so and he would have published it - that would have been a perverse attitude, considering that he would have distributed it as something serious.

We would have filled a book with all that silliness dictated to him and the circumstances that followed it. Among other things they made him draw an edifice whose dimensions required an amount of sheets of paper glued on each other, which reached a height of a two-storey building.

Notice that in none of that there is something gross or banal. It is a series of sophistic thoughts, connected to give the appearance of logic. The means employed to deceive the medium demonstrates that there is indeed an evil art and, given the opportunity to report all of the manifestations, one would see to which point such astuteness was taken and with which skills such mellifluous words were employed.

The spirit that represented the main role in that business used the name Francois Dillois, when not covered by a respectable name. Later we came to know what this Dillois had been in life and then his language no longer surprised us. But in the middle of all this confusion it was easy to recognize a good fighting spirit, who from time to time would bring a word of denial to the other spirit's teachings. There was an evident struggle, but the fight was unfair. The young man was so much subjugated that the voice of reason was powerless in him. The spirit of his father notably made him write the following: "Yes, my son, courage! You are through a tough trial that will be for your benefit in the future. Unfortunately, as of now, there is nothing I can do to free you and that is hard on me. Go and see Allan Kardec; listen to him and he shall save you."

Mr. F... effectively came to see me and from start I recognized, without difficulty, the pernicious influence on him, be it by his words or by some material signs that experience helps us to identify and that cannot fool us. He came back several times. I employed all my will power to attract the good spirits through him; all my rhetoric to demonstrate that he was the victim of bad spirits; that what he was writing was meaningless, besides the fact that it was profoundly immoral. A colleague, Mr. T, seconded me... and gradually we were able to see him writing sensible things. He then created aversion to that bad influence, repelling him by his own will whenever he wanted to manifest, and then the good spirits slowly triumphed.

In order to modify his ideas he followed the spirits' advice and found himself a tough job that would not allow him time to listen to the bad suggestions.

Dillois himself ended up acknowledging defeat and manifested interest of progressing in another life. Confessed the bad things he tried to do and gave proofs of regret. The fight was long lasting and tough, offering curious particularities to the observer. Nowadays Mr. F... feels free and happy. It felt as if he had unloaded a burden. He recovered his joyfulness and is thankful to us for the service we have done.

Some people deplore the fact that there are evil spirits. Truly, it is not without certain disenchantment that we find perversity in that world, where we would like to see only perfect spirits. However, it is what it is and there is nothing we can do about it. It is our own inferiority that makes the imperfect spirits bounce around us. Things will change when we become better, as with the more advanced worlds. While we wait and find ourselves in the undergrounds of the moral universe, we are warned: it is up to us to be prepared and not accept everything that we are told without exam. Experience should make us circumspect while enlightening us. See and understand evil is a means of protecting ourselves against it. Wouldn't that be a hundred times more dangerous to have illusions with respect to the nature of the invisible beings around us? The same happens among human beings, as we are daily exposed to malevolence and perfidious suggestions; those make for many more trials that our consciousness and reason offer the means to resist. The more difficult is the struggle, the greater the merit of success. "Victory without danger is triumph without glory".

This story, that unfortunately is not the only one to our knowledge, raises a very grave question. Wouldn't that be troublesome to that young man to be a medium? Wasn't the mediumship the cause of the obsession that victimized him? In one word, isn't that a proof of the danger of the spiritist communications?

Our answer is simple and our request is that it be carefully analyzed.

The mediums have not created the spirits. They have always existed and exerted a healthy or pernicious influence on people. It is not necessary to be a medium for that to occur. The mediumistic faculty is nothing more than a means for their manifestation; in the absence of such a faculty they act in a thousand other ways. If that young man were not a medium it does not mean that he would be free from the influence of that bad spirit who, no doubt, would have made him do extravagant things that would have been attributed to any other cause. Fortunately for him, as his faculty of mediumship allowed the spirit to communicate by words through him, it was by those words that the spirit betrayed himself. The words allowed the identification of the cause of an illness that could have had dismal consequences to him and that we have destroyed, as shown, by means of very simple and rational means, and without exorcisms. The mediumistic faculty made it possible to see the enemy, if we can say so, face to face, and fight him with his own weapons. We can then say, with absolute certainty, that it was that very faculty that saved him. As for ourselves, we were only the doctors that having analyzed the cause of the illness applied the remedy.

It would be a serious mistake to think that the spirits do not exert their influence other than through verbal and written communications. Such influence is constant and those who do not believe in spirits are as much under their influence as the others and even more than the others because they do not have, as a counterpoint, the knowledge.

How many actions, unfortunately, aren't we led to and that could have been avoided had we had the means of enlightening ourselves! The most incredulous are unaware that they tell the truth when they say, with respect to someone that chooses the wrong path: "It is his bad genie that pushes him to his loss."

General rule: Whoever obtains bad spiritist communications, verbal or written, is under bad influence. Such influence is exerted on them whether they write or not, that is to say regarless if they are mediums or not. The writing provides a means of ensuring the nature of the spirits that act upon the person and to combat them, what can be done with such more success the better one knows about the reasons that make them act that way. If the medium is blind enough to not understand, others can open their eyes. As a matter of fact, is it necessary to be a medium to write an absurd? Who can tell that among these dangerous or ridiculous theories wouldn't be some whose authors are motivated by malevolent spirits? Three quarters of our bad actions and our bad thoughts are the result of such occult suggestion.

Could we have stopped the obsession if Mr. F… were not a medium? We certainly could. Only the means would have been different, according to the circumstances. But then the spirits could not have referred him to us, as they did, and the cause would have been probably neglected, since there would have been no ostensive spiritist manifestation.

Every creature of good will and who is sympathetic to the good spirits can always, with their support, paralyze a harmful influence. We say that the person should be sympathetic to the good spirits because if the person attracts the inferior ones then it is evident that it is like hunting wolves with wolves.

Summarizing, the danger is not properly in Spiritism since it can, on the contrary, serve as a control, protecting us from what we are unwillingly exposed. The danger is in the tendency of certain mediums to, very recklessly, believe that they are exclusive instruments of the superior spirits, under a kind of fascination that does not allow them to understand the fatuity to which they operate as interpreters. Even those that are not mediums can be dragged. We will finish this chapter with the following considerations:

1° - Every medium must prevent from the irresistible excitement that leads them to write incessantly, and at inadequate times; they must control themselves and only write when they want to;

2° - We cannot dominate the superior spirits, not even those who are not superior but who are kind and benevolent; however we can dominate and tame the inferior spirits.

3° - There is no other criteria to distinguish the value of the spirits but commonsense. Any formula given by the spirits with that purpose is absurd and cannot proceed from superior spirits;

4° - The spirits, like human beings, are judged by their language. Every expression, every thought, every concept, the whole moral or scientific theory that shocks commonsense or does not correspond to the idea that we have of a pure and elevated spirit, comes from a more or less inferior spirit;

5° - The superior spirits always use the same language with the same person and never contradict themselves;

6° - The superior spirits are always good and benevolent. We never find acrimony, arrogance, rudeness, pride, swagger, or silly presumption in their language. They speak with simplicity, give advice and leave when not heard;

7° - We should not judge the spirits by their material form or by the correction of their language, but probe their intimacy, scrutinize their words, cold-bloodedly analyze them, maturely and without prevention;

8° - The inferior spirits fear for their words to be analyzed, unmask their turpitude and are not attached to their sophisms. Eventually they try to resist but end up fleeing when notice that they are the weakest part;

9° - The one that always acts thinking about the good deeds elevates above human vanities, expels selfishness, pride, envy, jealousy and hatred from the heart and forgives their enemies, practicing this teaching from Jesus: "Do to others what you would have them do to you"; sympathizes with the good spirits, whereas the bad ones are fearful and stay away from them.

Following such principles we are guaranteed protection against bad communications and against the domination of impure spirits. By taking advantage of everything that the truly superior spirits teach us we will contribute, each in a particular way, to the moral progress of humanity.

Official Application of
Animal Magnetism

A letter sent from Stockholm to the *Journal des Débats*, on September 10ᵗʰ, 1858:

"Unfortunately I do not have comforting news with respect to the illness that our sovereign leader has endured for about two years. All treatments and medications prescribed by the professionals during this time have not brought any relief to King Oscar's sufferings. According to the board of medical doctors, Mr. Klugenstiern, who has some reputation as a magnetizer, has been recently called to Drottningholm Palace, where the royal family continues to live, in order to apply a periodical treatment of magnetism to the noble patient. Over here people believe that, out of a singular coincidence, the center of King Oscar's disease is located precisely at the cerebellum, which seems also to be the case of King Frederic IV of Prussia."

We wonder if only twenty-five years ago the doctors would dare to publicly prescribe such a procedure, even to a regular patient, let alone to a crowned head of state. Medical schools as well as newspapers were full of sarcasm to downplay magnetism and the people that practice it. Things have changed a lot in such a short time! Magnetism is not only not laughed at but also recognized as a therapeutic agent. What a lesson to those who laugh at new things! Will that lesson finally make them figure out the problems associated with raising issues against things that they do not understand? We have a lot of books written against magnetism by important people who did not support magnetism. Well, such books will remain as an indelible stain on their intelligences. Wouldn't they have done better by going quiet and wait? Over that time, as it happens today, the most eminent, most enlightened and conscious people manifested their contrary opinion with respect to Spiritism. Nothing disturbs their skepticism. Magnetism was nothing but mockery to their eyes, unworthy of serious people. What action could be attributed to an occult agent, controlled by thought and will, and of which a chemical analysis could not be done? We must say that the Swedish doctors were not the only ones to reconsider that narrow idea. Now, in many places, in France as abroad, the opinion has completely changed. This is so true that today, when confronted with an unexplained phenomenon, they say that it is a magnetic effect. They thus attribute to magnetism for a number of reasons that before were considered as produced by imagination, always a good explanation to those people who do not know what to say.

Will magnetism cure King Oscar? This is another matter. No doubt it has produced prodigious and unexpected cures but it has its limitations, as everything else in nature. Furthermore, it is necessary to take the following circumstance into account: people generally resort to magnetism only *in extremis*, and out of desperation, frequently when the illness has already caused irreparable devastation or when aggravated by inadequate medication. It is necessary to be really powerful to triumph over such obstacles!

If the action of the magnetic fluid is a given these days, the same does not apply to the somnambulistic faculties that still have many incredulous in the official world, particularly with respect to medical issues. Nevertheless, we have to recognize that the prejudices have waned around this subject, even among people of Science. The proof comes from the large number of medical doctors who take part in all societies of magnetism, in France as well as abroad. The facts have become so overt that willing or not it was necessary to accept the evidence and follow the mainstream. The same will soon happen to the lucid intuition as well as to the magnetic fluid.

Intimate bonds, like solidary Sciences, connect Spiritism and magnetism. However, who would believe that? Spiritism finds its most bloodthirsty adversaries among certain magnetizers that conversely do not count on the opposition of the spiritists. Spirits have always commended magnetism, be it as a means of cure, be it as the primary cause of a number of things; they defend its cause and come to support it against its enemies. The spiritist phenomena have opened the eyes of a large number of people while advocating magnetism to them. Isn't that strange to have the magnetizers so quick to forget the prejudices against them; denying the existence of their defenders and throwing against those the same darts that once were thrown at them? This is neither noble nor worthy of people to whom nature, by revealing its most sublime mysteries more than to others, subtract the right of saying the famous "nec plus ultra" (state-of-the-art). All indications are that, given the quick development of Spiritism, it will also soon be granted the status of citizenship. While waiting, it applauds with all its heart the position that magnetism has just conquered, as an uncontested sign of the progress of ideas.

Magnetism and Somnambulism Taught by the Church

We have just seen magnetism recognized by medicine. Here is another adhesion that, under a different point of view, is not of any lesser importance, since it demonstrates the weakening of the prejudices by the daily surge of more sound ideas that make them disappear: the adhesion of the Church.

We have in our hands a little book entitled *"Abrégé, en forme de caté-chisme"*, from the elemental course of Christian instruction, to be used in the catechism and in the Christian schools, written by the abbot Marotte, General Vicar of Bishop Verdun, 1853. Using the Q&A format, the work contains every principles of the Christian doctrine about the dogma, sacred history, God's commandments, sacraments, etc. In one of the chapters about the first commandment, where the sins against religion are treated, and after having taught about superstition, magic and sortileges, it states the following:

"Q – What is magnetism?"

"A – It is a reciprocal influence that sometimes take place among individuals, according to a harmony of relationships, be it by the will or by imagination, or by physical sensitivity, whose main phenomena are somnolence, sleepiness, somnambulism and the convulsive state."

"Q – What are the effects of magnetism?"

"A – Typically, as it seems, magnetism produces two main effects: 1°) A somnambulistic state, in which the magnetized person, entirely subtracted from the use of the senses, sees, speaks and answers all questions addressed to them; 2°) An intelligence and wisdom that only exist during the crisis: the person knows their state, the adequate remedies to their diseases, as well as what other people are doing, even distant ones."

"Q – Is it licit, in one's right mind, to magnetize or become magnetized?"

"A – 1°) If through the magnetic operation, diabolic means are employed or effects obtained that suppose a diabolic intervention, it will be a superstitious work and should never be allowed. 2°) The same applies to the magnetic communications that are contrary to modesty. 3°) Supposing that all care has been taken to keep the abuse away from the practice of magnetism, eliminating every danger to the faith or to the customs, every pact with the devil, it is doubtful that one may recourse to that as a natural and useful remedy."

We regret that the author had made the final exception, in contradiction to what precedes. In fact, why the use of something healthy would not be allowed, since the inconvenient that he had pointed out was removed? It is true that he does not express a formal prohibition, but a simple doubt with respect to the permission. In any event, this is not found in a scientific book, dogmatic, for the exclusive use of the theologians, but in an elemental book, for the use of catechism, that is, destined to the religious instruction of the masses. Consequently, it is not a personal opinion, but an enshrined and acknowledged truth that magnetism exists; that it produces somnambulism; that the somnambulist enjoys special faculties, like vision without the eyes, even at a distance; hearing without the ears;

providing knowledge that one does not have in the normal state; indicating medication that improves health.

The qualification of the author has great importance in this case. This is not about an obscure man speaking or a simple priest that issues his opinion: it is the teaching of a general vicar.

This is another backlash and another warning to those who judge with great hastiness.

Illness by Fear

Problem of Physiology, addressed to the spirit of St. Louis, in the Parisian Society of Spiritist Studies, session of September 14th, 1858.

The *"Moniteur"* published on November 26th, 1857:

"The following fact that confirms the influence of fear was communicated to us:"

"Yesterday Dr F... returned home after having visited some of his patients. In one of those visits he was given a bottle of excellent rum, directly imported from Jamaica. The doctor forgot the precious bottle in the car. Once he notice the fact a little bit later he went back to look for the present, telling the parking lot manager that he had left a bottle with a powerful poison in one of the carriages so that he should advise the coachmen that they should take extreme care and not make use of that mortal liquid."

"As Dr F... returned to his apartment they sent for him since three coachmen of the neighboring parking lot were under severe pain in their guts. It was with great difficulty that he was able to convince them that all they had drunk was excellent rum and that his unkindness could not bring any further punishment other than the one they already had."

1   – St. Louis could you give us a physiologic explanation about such a transformation of the properties of an otherwise harmless substance? We know that such transformation can take place by the magnetic action but in this case there was no emission of magnetic fluid: it was only the action of imagination, not the will.

- Your thought is fair with respect to imagination. But the malevolent spirits that inspired those men to commit that unkind act, have induced in their blood, in the matter, the shivers of fear that you could call magnetic fear that stretches the nerves and produces a cold feel in certain parts of the body. You know well that cold in the abdominal region may produce the cramps. It is then a means of punishment that amuses the spirits who provoked the theft, making them laugh at those who they led to misbehave. In any case it would not cause death. It was nothing more than a simple punishment to the guilty ones and enjoyment to the frivolous spirits. They act like that whenever there is an opportunity or that they even seek for their own satisfaction. I can assure you that we can avoid it by elevating ourselves to God through thoughts less material than the ones that occupied the minds of those men. The malevolent spirits like to have fun. Be careful with them! The one who judges to say something pleasant to a group of people and that entertains a society with jokes and actions is sometimes wrong and even many times wrong by thinking that it all comes from him. The frivolous spirits that surround him identify with him so much that they gradually trick him with respect to his thoughts, tricking also those who listen to him. In such a case you may think that you are dealing with a witty man when in fact he is nothing but an ignorant. Give some thought to that and you shall understand what I tell you. The superior spirits, however, are not enemies of joy. They sometimes like to laugh to become pleasant to you. But there is a time for everything.

OBSERVATION: By saying that there was no emission of magnetic fluid in the reported case, we perhaps were not precise. We venture a hypothesis. As we said, it is known that the properties of matter may alter under the influence of the magnetic fluid, led by thought. Well, wouldn't it be possible to admit that, by the thought of the doctor, who wanted to lead them to believe in the existence of a toxic substance, to give the thieves the anguish of poisoning, there could have been a kind of magnetization of the liquid, at a distance, changing its properties, fact reinforced by the moral state of the individuals, who were impressed by fear? Such a theory would not destroy St. Louis' theory about the intervention of the frivolous spirits in similar situations. We know that the spirits act physically, by physical means; they can thus be served by those that they provoke, so as to achieve certain objectives that we inadvertently provide them.

Theory of the Causes
of Our Actions

Mr. R..., corresponding member of the French Institute and one of the most eminent members of the Parisian Society of Spiritist Studies, in the session of September 14th, developed the following considerations, as a corollary of the theory just given with respect to fear, reported in the previous article.

"From all communications of the spirits that are provided to us, it is clear that they exert a direct influence over our actions, some inviting us to the good deeds, others to the evil ones. St. Louis has just told us the following:

"The malevolent spirits like to have fun. Be careful with them! The one who judges to say something pleasant to a group of people and that entertains a society with jokes and actions is sometimes wrong and even many times wrong by thinking that it all comes from him. The frivolous spirits that surround him identify with him so much that they gradually trick him with respect to his thoughts, tricking also those who listen to him."

From the above it is evident that not everything that we say comes from us; that many times, like the speaking mediums, we are nothing but interpreters of the thoughts of a strange spirit that has identified with ours. The facts confirm this theory and demonstrate that very frequently our acts are also consequence of thoughts that are suggested to us. Thus, the person who does an evil deed gives in to a suggestion, whenever weak enough not to resist, ignoring the voice of the conscience that can be either his own or of a good spirit that combats the influence of a malevolent one, through his warnings."

"According to the common sense, the human being finds all his instincts in his own physical organization for which he is not responsible or in his own nature where he can search for a cause, not been allegedly guilty for being created as such. The Spiritist Doctrine is evidently more moral. It admits human's free will in all its plenitude. By telling people that when they do a wrong deed they yield to an evil foreign suggestion, it attributes to them the full responsibility, since it acknowledges their power to resist that is evidently easier than if they had to fight against their own nature. Thus, according to the Spiritist Doctrine, there is no irresistible creeping: people can always close theirs ears to the occult voice that solicits them to bad acts, in their most inner being, as they can also ignore the material voice of someone that talks to them. They can do so their own will, asking God for the necessary strength, for which they shall beg for the assistance of the good spirits. This is what Jesus teaches us in the sublime prayer of the *Pater Noster*, when he says: "And lead us not into temptation, but deliver us from evil."

When we take the short story that we just reported as an excuse to one of our questions we would not think about the development that it would take. We feel twice as happy by the nice words it deserved from St. Louis and of those from our eminent colleague. Had we not been certain since long ago about the highest capacity of our colleague and with respect to his profound knowledge about the Spiritist Doctrine, we would be tempted to believe that such a theory came from him and that St. Louis used that to complete his teachings. We are led to add our own considerations as follows:

The theory of the exciting cause of our actions evidently sticks out from the whole teaching of the spirits. It shows not only a sublime morality but also reveals the individual to his own eyes; it shows him free to upset the obsessing oppression as he is free to close the door to the annoying ones: he is no longer like a machine, acting by impulse, irrespective of his will; he is a thoughtful being that hears, judges and freely chooses between two advices. Furthermore, despite all that, the human being is not absolutely deprived from taking the initiative; he does that on his own, since he is an incarnated spirit that preserves under his corporeal covering the qualities and defects which he had as spirit. Our faults thus have a primary source in the imperfection of our own spirit that has not yet achieved the moral superiority, which he will one day have and nevertheless he still has the free will. He is given the corporeal life in order to purge his imperfections through the endured trials, and those very imperfections are the ones that make him weaker and more accessible to the suggestions of other imperfect spirits, who take the opportunity to make him succumb in the struggles that he is going through. If he succeeds in those trials, he elevates himself. If he fails, stays the same, not better, not worse. It is a trial to restart, and this can drag on for a long time. The more one depurates, the lesser the weak points and less subjected one will be to the solicitation of evil; the moral strength shall grow in proportion to the elevation hence the bad spirits will stay away. Then, who would be those bad spirits? Would they be the ones we call demons? They are not the demons in the vulgar meaning of the word, since by demons one implies a class of beings created for evil and perpetually devoted to evil. Well, the spirits tell us that sooner or later everybody improves, according to one's free will, but while imperfect one can do bad deeds, as the dirty water can spread putrid and morbid miasmas. As long as the spirits do what is needed, they depurate while incarnated; as spirits they suffer the consequences of what they did or did not do for their improvement, consequences that they also suffer on Earth, as the vicissitudes of life are at the same time expiation and trial. All these more or less depurated spirits constitute the human species when incarnated. Since our Earth is one of the less advanced worlds, there are more bad spirits than good ones here, what explain so much perversity around us. Let us then apply every effort to not come back after this experience, so that we deserve to inhabit a better world, in one of these privileged spheres where the good reigns absolute and where we shall remember our passage through Earth as a bad dream.

The Murder of Five Children

- A Moral Problem

We read in the *Gazette de Silésie*:
"On October 20th, 1857 we got a letter from Bolkenham about a terrible crime that had just been committed by a twelve year old boy. Last Sunday the 25th three children of Mr. Hubner, the blacksmith, and later on two of Mr. Fritche, the shoemaker, were playing in the yard of the latter one. The young H..., known for his bad character, joined them, convincing all kids to get into a strongbox, inside a barn, that the shoemaker used to take his merchandise to the market. The five children could hardly fit but got stacked up with laughs, one on top of the other. As soon as they got inside the box the monster locked the chest, sat on top of it and waited for about three quarters of an hour, first listening to their screams and then to their groaning."

"When they finally went quiet so that the boy thought they were dead, he opened the box. The children were still breathing. He then closed the box again, locked it and went on to fly a kite. Once he left the garden, however, he was seen by a girl. We can only imagine the anxiety of the parents once they noticed the disappearance of the children, and their desperation when finding them inside the chest, after a long search. One of the children was still alive but did not resist and soon died as well. Denounced by the girl that saw him leaving the yard, the young H...

confessed his cold-blooded crime, not manifesting the least remorse. The five victims, a boy and four girls, between four and nine years old, were buried today."

OBSERVATION: The spirit that was questioned by us is the sister of the medium, who died twelve years ago, always showing superiority as a spirit.

1. Did you hear the text that we have just read, about the killing of the five children from Silésie, by another twelve year old child?
   - Yes, my penalty still requires that I hear abominations from Earth.
2. Which motives would make a boy at that age to commit such a barbarian crime and with such a cold blood?
   - Evilness has no age. It is natural in a child and it is thought trough in an adult.
3. The occurrence in a child, without reasoning, wouldn't that indicate the incarnation of a very inferior spirit?
   - It comes directly from the perversity of the heart: it is his own spirit that dominates him, leading him to the perversity.
4. What could have been the previous existence of such a spirit?
   - Horrible.
5. In his previous existence, was he on Earth or has he come from an inferior world?
   - I don't know well but he should have come from a world well inferior to Earth. He dared to come to Earth. He shall be doubly punished.
6. In such an age would the boy have enough consciousness about the crime he committed? The spirit shall be responsible?
   - His age was that of the consciousness. That is enough.
7. Since this spirit dared to come to Earth, too elevated for him, can he be forced to return to a world more related to his nature?

- His punishment is exactly to return; it is the very hell. Such was the punishment of Lucifer, the spiritual man that degraded to the material level; it is the veil that from now on hides God's gifts and his Divine protection from him. You must all endeavor to re-conquer those lost gifts and you shall re-conquer the paradise that Christ came to open the doors to you. It is the presumption, the pride of the person that wanted to conquer what only God could have.

OBSERVATION: An observation about the verb "dare", employed by the spirit. There are examples of spirits that were in worlds too elevated for them and were obliged to return to another one in more harmony with their nature. Someone noted that the spirits have also said that there is no decay in progress. We shall answer that indeed the spirits cannot retrograde, in the sense that it is not possible to lose what has been acquired in knowledge and morality; they can, however, decay in position. A man that usurps a superior position given his fortune and capacity may be forced to leave it and return to his natural position. Well, this cannot be called decaying as he just returns to his sphere, which he left out of pride and ambition. The same happens with respect to the spirits that want to more rapidly rise to worlds where they shall be misplaced. Superior spirits can also reincarnate in inferior worlds where they accomplish missions of progress. One cannot call this retro-gradation, as it is only devotement.

8. How is Earth superior to the world from where that spirit is originated?
   - There is a weak idea of justice. It is the beginning of progress.
9. It seems as a consequence that in worlds inferior to Earth there is no idea of justice?

- No. People live only for themselves and have no cause of action other than the satisfaction of their passions and instincts.
10. What shall be the position of that spirit in a new existence?
    - If his regret can partially or totally erase the enormity of his faults then he shall stay on Earth; if, on the contrary, he persists on what you call final impenitence then he shall go to a place where man is at the animal level.
11. Then he can find the means of expiating his faults on Earth, without been forced to return to an inferior world?
    - Repentance is sacred to God's eyes because it is like man judging himself, something rare in your planet.

Questions of Legal Spiritism

The following information was taken from the *Courrier du Palais*, published by Mr. Frederic Thomas, attorney at the Imperial Court, in the *La Presse* on August 2nd, 1858. We transcribed it textually so as to maintain the witty style of the writer. Our readers will notice the pleasant format that he knows well how to attribute to the most respectable subjects. After reporting a number of things he adds:

"We have a much more unusual case to offer our reader in a new perspective: we already see it showing up in the horizon, in the southern horizon. But where is it going to get at? Someone wrote that the sticks are burning but that is not enough for us. Here is the case:

"A Parisian read in the papers that an old castle was on sale in the Pyrenees; he then bought it and in the first beautiful days of the glorious season he moved in with his friends. They had a pleasant dinner, just going to bed after that. It was time to spend the night; a night in an old castle, lost on the mountains. On the very next day the guests got up scared, all showing frightened faces; they sought their host and addressed him with the following question, with a lugubrious and mysterious look: Haven't you seen anything last night?

The owner did not respond – he was so frightened himself! He just nodded his head."

"Then, impressions were exchanged about the previous night, all keeping their voices low: one had heard crying voices, another heard dragging chains; this one had seen displacement of the rugs and carpets, the other saw an arch waving at him; several felt gigantic bats landing on their chests. This is a castle of the White Lady. The servants stated that the ghosts had pulled their legs and that it also happened to the previous tenant. More than that! The beds moved around, the bells ringed on their own, as well as effulgent words would burst out of the old fire places."

"The castle was definitely uninhabitable. Those who were most frightened left immediately. The most courageous stayed for a second night trial. Up until midnight all went well but as soon as the clock of the northern tower rang the twelve clangs of midnight the noises and apparitions restarted. Ghosts appeared from all sides, monsters with eyes on fire and crocodile teeth, waving hairy wings. All those things were screaming, jumping, squeaking their teeth, and making hell on Earth."

"Now it was just impossible to resist to that second experience. This time everybody had left the castle and the owner is filing a law suit for losses and damage."

What a strange case wouldn't that one be! And what a triumph to the great evoker of spirits, Mr. Home! Can he be considered an expert in such a subject? Whatever happens, and since there is nothing new under the light of justice, this process that will be considered a novelty, is nothing new since there is an unsolved case that, despite being two hundred and sixty three years old, is not less interesting.

The case happened in 1595, the year of Grace, before the seneschal of Guyenne, a tenant named Jean Latapy filed a lawsuit against the owner, Robert de Vigne. Jean Latapy allegedly had to leave the house rented out by Vigne, since the old house in Bordeaux was uninhabitable. Therefore he demanded the court to void the contract.

What was the argumentation? Latapy very ingenuously presented those in his conclusions:

"The house was found infested by spirits that appeared under the form of children as well as other strange and frightening forms. They annoyed and disturbed the persons; messed the furniture around; made noises and uproar all over the place and violently knocked people down from their beds."

"Robert de Vigne, the owner, vigorously opposed the cancellation of the contract, responding to Latapy as follows: You describe my house unfairly; it is likely that you are getting what you deserve and instead of criticizing me you should, on the contrary, thank me as I help you to reach Paradise."

Next, how the owner's attorney made his case through a singular proposition:

"If the spirits come to torment Latapy and afflict him, with God's permission, he should endure the fair penalty and say with St. Jerome: *Quidquid patimur nostris peccatis meremur,*[41] and not attack the owner, who is absolutely innocent. Instead, he should be grateful to someone that provided him with the means of saving himself in this world from the punishments that, due to his demerit, wait for him in the other one."

"In order to be consistent the lawyer should have asked Latapy to pay de Vigne for his services. Shouldn't a place in paradise be worth his weight in gold? But the generous owner was happy with the refusal to call the contract off hence, before trying this, Latapy should have tried to combat and expel the spirits through means provided by God and by nature."

"Why didn't he use the laurel, argued the owner's attorney? Why didn't he use the rue or salt in the fire and the burning coal; feathers or a compounded mixture of herbs, the so called aerolus ventulus; with rhubarb; with white wine; with salt hanging at the entrance door; hyena's forehead skin; dog's gall that they say has a marvelous virtue of expelling demons? Why didn't he use Molly's herb, the same used by Mercury to expel Ulysses that used it as an antidote against Circe's charms? ..."

It is evident that Latapy, the tenant, defaulted with all his duties, by not throwing salt into the burning coal, by not using dog's gall and some feathers. However, as he would also have to find hyena's forehead skin, the seneschal of Bordeaux found that such material was not ordinary enough

---

41 Whatever we deserve to suffer for our sins (N.T.)

so that Latapy would not be excused for leaving the hyenas alone hence he determined, in a beautiful and charming way, the cancellation of the lease.

One can see from all this that neither the owner nor the tenant or the judges have any doubt about the existence of the spirits and the uproar created by them. It would then seem that over two centuries ago people were more credulous than today but we do better as far as credulity goes which is not strange: it is even necessary that civilization and progress reveal somewhere.

Leaving aside the accessories that the storyteller used to decorate the issue, such a question still has an embarrassing side, as the law has not foreseen the case in which the rapping spirits would turn a house un-inhabitable. Would it be a purposeful, malicious sale of this property? In our opinion there are pros and cons, according to the circumstances. Initially it is necessary to verify if the noise is real or simulated with any other intention, a prior question of good faith that pre-judges the others. Admitting the facts as real it is necessary to establish if they perturb peace. If, for example, things happen similarly to the events of Bergzabern42, it is then evident that the position is not sustainable. The old Mr. Sänger withstood all that because it happened in his own house and there was no escape, but there is no way that a stranger would settle in a dwelling where a deafening sound is constantly heard; where the furniture is scrambled around; where doors and windows open and close at random; where invisible hands throw things at people's heads, etc. It seems that under those circumstances there is space for complaint and that, with justice, a given contract should not bear value, had those things been hidden. Thus, generally speaking, the 1595 process seems to have been well judged, but there still remains an important question that is up to the Spiritist Science to raise and solve.

---

42 See the May, June and July issues of the Spiritist Review

We know that the spontaneous manifestations of the spirits may occur without a predetermined objective and also that they may not address this or that person; that there are places effectively haunted by rapping spirits that seem to select those places as their residence and against whom every conjuration is useless. Let us say, between brackets, that there are efficient ways for us to free from them but that such ways do not depend on the intervention of persons that knowingly produce similar phenomena since the spirits that operate through them are from a different order than those that need to be expelled. Far from keeping them away, their presence could even attract others. But we also know that in a number of cases such manifestations are addressed against certain individuals, like in the Bergzabern case. The facts demonstrated that the family, particularly the little Filipina, was their direct target, hence we are convinced that had the family left that house the new inhabitants would have nothing to fear. That family would carry their tribulations to the new address.

The question to be examined, from a legal point of view, is if the manifestations would have taken place before or only after the arrival of the new owner. In the latter case it would be evident that the owner had carried the perturbing spirits along and thus the responsibility would be totally his; if, on the contrary, the perturbations had taken place before and persisted, that is a proof that they were associated to the place and thus the responsibility would be of the owner. The owner's attorney reasoned with the first hypothesis and his argumentation did not lack logic. It is still necessary to know if the tenant had brought along those unwelcome guests, a fact which was not established in the process.

As for the ongoing pending process, we believe that a means of doing good justice would be by establishing what we have just described above. If the pre-existence of the manifestations is proven and that the fact was hidden by the owner, we face the case of a misled tenant with respect to the quality of the object of the transaction. Well, by keeping the deal under those conditions it might be a means of causing harm to the purchaser by the depreciation of the property. It is at least a cause of considerable loss, forcing him to keep something that he will have no use for, like a blind horse that he had acquired instead of a healthy one. Nevertheless, the cause in question should have grave consequences. Be it by invalidating the contract; be it by keeping the contract due to a lack of proof, the fact of the manifestations will be recognized.

By rejecting the proposition under the allegation that it is based on ridiculous reasons, one is exposed to receiving, sooner or later, the contradiction of experience, as it has many times happened to the most eminent figures, by having rushed to the negation of what they did not understand. If our parents can be censored by excess of credulity, our descendants will no doubt reproach us for the mistake of the contrary excess.

While we wait, this is what is before our eyes and that we even attest. We refer to the chronicle published by the *La Patrie*, on September 4th, 1858:

"The *Rue du Bac* is in a shambles. One can still see devilish tricks there. The house number 65 is divided in two blocks. The one facing the street has two stairwells that face each other. For the last week, at several times of the day and night, in all floors of the building, the bells ring and agitate violently. When people come to attend the door there is nobody at the entrance. In the beginning they thought it was a joke so that everybody watched, trying to catch the instigator. One of the tenants carefully sanded one glass in his kitchen to vigilantly watch. While watching with great attention his bell was shaken. He looked through the hatch and saw nobody! He then ran to the stairs, nobody! He returned to the house and removed the cord of the bell. An hour later, still feeling triumphant, the bell started to ring gallantly. He saw it ringing and became mute, depressed. On other doors the cords became twisted, entangled, like wounded serpents. An explanation is still sought and the police was called in. But what is that mystery? They still ignore it."

Phenomena of Apparitions

S ometime ago the *Constitutionel* and the *Patrie* transcribed the following fact from USA newspapers:

"The little town of Leitchfield, Kentucky, counts on numerous experts of the doctrine of magnetic spiritualism. An incredible fact that has
just happened there will certainly give a significant contribution to the
growth of that new religion. The Park's family, composed of father, mother and three children, already at the age of reason, was strongly embedded
by the spiritualist's beliefs. Yet, Ms. Harris, who was Mrs. Park's sister, did
not absolutely believe in the supernatural prodigies that they incessantly
cogitated. This was a real cause of grief among all members of the family
and more than once it broke the harmony between the two sisters. A few
days ago Mrs. Park was suddenly taken ill by something that the doctors
declared themselves incapable of handling from the beginning. The patient was a victim of hallucinations, permanently tormented by a terrible
fever. Ms. Harris spent all nights awaken by her side. On the fourth day
of the disease, Mrs. Park sat down on the bed, asked for water and started
talking to her sister. Strange enough the fever had suddenly gone. Her
pulse was regular and she spoke with ease. Ms. Harris gladly thought that
her sister was out of harm's way. After having talked about her husband
and children Mrs. Park got closer to her sister and said: Poor sister, I will
leave you. I feel death is coming closer. But at least my departure from
this world will serve to convert you. I shall die in an hour and shall be

473

buried tomorrow. Carefully avoid following my body to the cemetery, as my spirit, covered by its mortal remains, will show up to you before the coffin is covered with earth. You shall then believe in spiritualism."

"After having said those words the patient calmly lay down. However, an hour later Ms. Harris painfully verified that her sister's heart had stopped, as she had announced. Vividly moved by the incredible coincidence between what happened and the prophetic words of the deceased, she decided to follow her recommendations and on the following day she stayed home alone, while everybody else had gone to the cemetery. She locked the hatches of the mortuary chamber and sat on an armchair near the bed from where her sister's body had just left."

"Only five minutes had passed – Ms. Harris said later– I saw something like a white cloud coming out from the back of the room. The form gradually cleared up: it was a woman, kind of veiled; she moved slowly towards where I was; I heard her steps on the floor; finally I had my sister before my astounded eyes ..."

"Her face, far from showing the pale looks of death that so painfully impressed us, was radiant. Her hands, whose pressure I felt well, holding mine, maintained the warmth of life. I was like transported to a new sphere, through that marvelous apparition. Supposing that I was already in the world of the spirits, I touched my breast, my head, to ensure my own existence. But there was nothing painful in that ecstasy."

"After staying for a few minutes, just like that, in front of me, smiling but in silence, my sister seemed to have made a great effort and told me with a sweet voice:"

"It is now time for me to go. My guiding angel waits. Good-bye! I have accomplished my promise. Believe and wait!"

The *Patrie* adds: "The newspaper from where we have extracted such wonderful news did not say whether Ms. Harris had converted to the spiritualist doctrine. We admit that, however, since many people would be convinced by much less."

We add, from our own account, that the report has nothing to cause surprise to those who have studied the effects and causes of the spiritist phenomena. The authentic facts of such a kind are considerably numerous and have their explanation in what we have said on several occasions. We will have the opportunity to describe others, coming from not so far away as this one.

ALLAN KARDEC[43]

---

43 Paris. Typography of Cosson & Co. - Rue de Four-Saint-Germain, 43

November 1858

Spiritist Controversy

We have been asked many times why we do not respond, in our Review, to the attacks of several tabloids against Spiritism as a whole, against its adepts and sometimes even against us. We believe that in certain cases silence is the best answer. Furthermore, there is a kind of controversy from which we normally abstain: the one that can degenerate into personal attacks. That not only disgusts us but would also take such an amount of time that we cannot uselessly spare, besides being of little interest to our readers that subscribe to the Review for their instruction and not to be able to read more or less witty diatribes. Moreover, once we had entered into such a path it would be difficult to exit. That is why we prefer not to start. We shall never satisfy the scandal lovers.

However, there is controversy and then there is controversy. There is one before which we shall never retreat – it is the serious discussion of the principles that we profess. Nevertheless, even here there is a distinction to make. If handling only general attacks addressed to the doctrine, without a determined objective other than criticizing, and if they come from people that systematically reject everything that they cannot understand, those do not deserve our attention. The terrain daily conquered by Spiritism is a peremptory answer and should demonstrate to them that sarcasm has not granted them great results. One should also notice that the endless jests that have victimized the adepts of the Doctrine are gradually extinguishing. It is the case of asking if there are reasons to laugh at so many eminent persons for having adopted the new ideas. Some may hardly smile these days, just out of habit, while others absolutely no longer laugh and wait.

We should also notice that among the critics there are a lot of people who speak without knowing what they are talking about and that do not even make the effort to learn. In order to respond to them it would be necessary to restart the most elementary explanations and repeat what we have already written, which seems useless to us. That is different with those who studied it and did not understand all of it and those that really want to enlighten themselves, and that raise objections in good faith and with previous knowledge. We accept the controversy in such a terrain, without the presumption of resolving all questions. The Spiritist science is in its beginning and has not yet revealed all of its secrets, however great the already unveiled wonders might be. Which science does not have mysterious and inexplicable facts? Let us thus confess, without any shyness, our insufficiency about the points that we cannot explain yet. Therefore, far from repelling the objections and questions, we ask for them, as long as they are not irrelevant and do not make us uselessly waste time with frivolousness, since this is a means of our enlightenment.

That is what we call useful controversy and it will be useful whenever it takes place among serious people that are respectful enough not to lose decency. We can think differently without diminishing our mutual respect.

After all, what are we all looking for in such a thrilling and fecund question of Spiritism? Enlightenment! We look for light, before anything else, from wherever it may come, and if we express our own way of seeing things it is not a personal opinion that we intend to impose on others. We open that to discussion, prepared to renounce to them if demonstrated that we are in error.

We daily sustain such a controversy in our Review, through the answers or the collective refutations that we publish with respect to this or that article. Those who honor us with their letters will always find the answers to their questions, whenever it is not possible to respond in a particular letter, fact that is not always physically possible. Your questions and objections always constitute another group of study cases, that we personally utilize; and we feel happy to extend such a benefit to the readers, as long as facts, which are correlated to those questions, are presented.

We feel also happy to give verbal explanations to the persons that honor us with their visits and in the public conferences, characterized by a common understanding, in which we mutually clarify ourselves.

Plurality of the Existences

- First Article

From all doctrines professed by Spiritism the most controversial is undoubtedly that of reincarnation and the plurality of corporeal existences. Although this opinion is presently shared by a large number of people and that we have discussed it on several occasions, we consider our duty to examine it in more detail, given its extraordinary importance and to respond to several objections that were raised.

Before diving deep into the question we must make some observations that seem indispensable to us. The dogma of the reincarnation is not new to many people: it is resurrected from Pythagoras. We have never said that the Spiritist Doctrine is a modern invention. As a consequence of a natural law, Spiritism must have existed since the origin of times, and we always strive to demonstrate that its traces are found in the remotest antiquity. Pythagoras is not the author of the metempsychosis system, as well known. He has taken them from the Indian philosophers and the Egyptians, with whom it existed since immemorial times. Thus, the idea of the transmigration of the soul was a vulgar belief, admitted by the most eminent celebrities. Where has it come from? Has it come by revelation or intuition? We don't know. Nevertheless, however it might have been, an idea doesn't cross the ages and isn't accepted by the highest intelligences if it does not have a serious side. Therefore, its ancient character is more of a proof than an objection. However, there is an important difference between the old doctrine of metempsychosis and the modern doctrine of reincarnation, as it is also known: the spirits absolutely reject the idea of transmigration of human's soul to the animals and vice-versa.

No doubt, some contradictors say, you had such prior ideas and that is why the spirits agreed with your way of seeing things. This is a mistake that demonstrates, once more, the danger of hastily judgments, without proper examination. If, before passing judgment, those persons had their homework done and had studied what we have written about Spiritism, they would have spared themselves from the embarrassment of such a frivolous objection. We repeat what we have already said about it, that when we were taught the doctrine of the reincarnation by the spirits it was so far off from our thoughts that we had envisioned a completely different system about the antecedents of the soul. A system that is, in fact, shared by several people.

Regarding this subject the doctrine of the spirits has surprised us. We go further: it contradicted us, since it knocked our own ideas down. Hence, it is far from being a reflection of those ideas.

That is not all. We did not give in at the first clash. We fought back; defended our opinion; raised objections and only surrendered before the evidence and when we noticed the insufficiency of our system to solve all questions related to this issue.

To the eyes of some people the use of the word *evidence* may seem singular with such a subject; however it would not be improper to anyone used to analyze the spiritist phenomena. There are facts to the careful observer that, although not of absolutely material nature, they are not less truthful evidence, at least moral evidence.

This is not the place to explain those facts, only understandable through a continuous and perseverant study. Our objective was only to deny the idea that this theory is nothing but a translation of our thoughts.

We have still to make another refutation: that such a doctrine was not taught only to us; that it was vented in many places, in France as well as abroad: in Germany, in the Netherlands, in Russia, etc and all that even before the publication of The Spirits' Book.

We shall add to that the fact that since we have devoted ourselves to Spiritism we have had communications from more than fifty mediums, writing, speaking, clairvoyants etc, more or less instructed; of normal, more or less limited intelligence; some completely illiterate hence totally alien to the philosophical subjects and yet in not a single case have the spirits contradicted themselves on that point. The same applies to all circles that we are familiar with and that profess such a principle. We know that this argument is not irrefutable thus we shall not insist on anything else but the reasoning.

We will examine the question from another point of view, abstracting from any intervention of the spirits, who we will keep aside for the time being. Suppose that this theory has nothing to do with them; that we have never even considered the existence of the spirits. Thus let us momentarily position ourselves on neutral grounds, admitting the same degree of likelihood to either one of the hypotheses, that is the unity and the plurality of the corporeal existences, and let us see where our reason and own interest fall.

Some people reject the idea of reincarnation by the simple fact of inconvenience. They say that a single existence is enough and that they do not wish to restart another one. We even know some to whom the idea of reappearing on Earth infuriates them. The question is if God has taken their advice or consulted with them before creating the Universe. Well, it is one out of two possibilities: there is or there isn't reincarnation. If there is they will be upset but will have to submit to that, as God has not asked for their permission. We can even hear an ailing person saying: "I have suffered a lot for the day. I want no more suffering tomorrow." Irrespective of their mood they will not suffer less tomorrow or the day after until they are healed.

Therefore, if they have to be physically reborn they will be; they will reincarnate. There is no point in revolting like a child does, not wanting to go to school or like a person who has been sentenced that does not wish to go to prison: they will have to go. Such puerile objections do not deserve serious examination. We say, however, that the Spiritist Doctrine is not as terrible about reincarnation as they may think and had they seriously studied it they would not be so much terrified. They would know that the conditions of a new existence depend on oneself; that one will be happy or unhappy according to what one had done here on Earth; and that they can elevate so much since this existence that they should not fear a setback into the marshland.

We assume here to be talking to individuals that believe in a future after death and not to those who have the perspective of nothingness or wish to dive their souls into a universal wholeness, with no individuality, like the drop of rain into the ocean that is practically the same thing. Then, if you believe in any future, you will certainly believe that it will not be the same for everyone, otherwise what would be the utility of goodness? Why constrain oneself? Why not give rise to all passions, all desires, even if to the detriment of others, if none of that would have any meaning at all?

Do you believe that such a future will be more or less fortunate according to our deeds during this life? Do you then long for a happy as possible future, since it is for eternity? However, do you by any means have the presumption to be the most perfect person that has ever lived on Earth and thus having the right to supreme happiness of the elected ones? No. You then admit that there are persons that are more worthy then you and that have the right to a better place than you, without you being condemned for that.

Well then, place yourself, through your thoughts, in the median situation, considering that you have agreed with that, and suppose that someone tells you:

- You suffer; you are not as happy as you could be; however, you have before your eyes beings that enjoy the purest happiness. Would you like to change place with them?
- No doubt! - You will answer. What do we have to do?
- Nothing else than restart doing right what you did wrong, striving to be better.

- Would you have any doubts to accept it, even if to the expenses of several trials like existences?

Let us make a more prosaic comparison. If a man who lives in deprivation, although not in absolute misery, as a consequence of his faults, were told: "Here, there is an immense fortune; you can have it but you have to work very hard for one minute." Even if that were the laziest person on Earth he would unhesitantly say: "Let me work one minute, two, one hour, one day if needed. What is that if my whole life is going to end up in abundance?"

Well, what is the corporeal life in presence of eternity? It is less than a minute, less than a second.

We have heard the following reasoning: How can God, who is sovereignly good, force man to restart a series of miseries and tribulations? Would God find more benevolence in the condemnation of a man to a perpetual suffering as a consequence of a few moments of error than to provide him with the means of repairing his own faults?

"Two factory owners had each an employee who could aspire to become partner. As it happened one day those workers did not do their duties and deserved to lose their jobs. One employer fired his worker out right, despite his supplication. He died in misery, as he could not find another job. The other employer told his worker: You lost one day and owe me one, in compensation; by badly executing your duties you owe me amends. I allow you to restart. Go and do well and I shall keep you, and you can always aspire the superior position that I promised you."

Is it still necessary to ask which one of the two owners was more humane? Would God, who is the clemency Himself, be more inexorable than that man?

The thought that our fate is forever determined by a few years of trial, when reaching perfection on Earth has not always depended on us, has something of pungent, whereas the contrary idea is eminently consoling, for it gives us hope.

Thus, without pronouncing in favor or against the plurality of the existences; without showing preference for one hypothesis or the other, we shall say that had we been given the choice, nobody would prefer a trial without an appeal.

A philosopher has said that if God did not exist it would be necessary to invent God for the happiness of human kind. The same could be said about the plurality of the existences. However, as we mentioned, God does not ask us for permission; does not consult our taste. It is or it isn't.

Let us see on which side the probabilities fall and let us face the problem from another point of view, always making abstraction of the teachings of the spirits, considering it as a philosophical study only.

It is obvious that without reincarnation there is only one corporeal existence. If our current existence is the only one, each soul is created at birth, unless its preexistence is admitted. In such a case, one has to ask what the soul was before and if that state did not constitute an existence, in some way. There is no middle ground: Either the soul did exist or did not exist before the body. If it existed, what was its situation? Was it aware of its own existence? If not aware, it is as if it did not exist. If aware, the individuality was progressive or stationary? In either case what was its level on reaching the body? Admitting, according to the vulgar belief, that the soul is created with the body or, which is the same, that before its incarnation it only had negative faculties, we raise the following questions:

1. Why does the soul show so diverse aptitudes and independent from the ideas acquired by education?
2. Where does the supernormal aptitudes towards Science and Art, in children of early age come from, while others remain mediocre or inferior their whole life?
3. Where do the innate ideas, which some present and others don't, come from?
4. Where do premature instincts of vices or virtues; innate feelings of dignity or inferiority, in certain children come from, contrasting with the environment where they were born?

5. Abstraction made of education, why certain men are so more advanced than others?

6. Why are there savages and civilized men? If you take a tribal man in his diapers and educate him in the best colleges, will you turn him into a Laplace or Newton?

We ask what is the philosophy or theosophy that can resolve such problems. Either the souls are equal at birth or they are not, no doubt. If they are equal why do they show such diverse aptitudes? Some will say that it depends on the organism. But this will then be the most monstrous and immoral of all doctrines. The human being would be nothing but a machine and a little toy of matter; would not have the responsibility for his acts; he could attribute everything to his physical imperfections. If they are unequal it is because God so created them. But then why is such an innate superiority given to some? Would that partiality be in accordance with God's justice and to the love that God equally dedicates to all His creatures?

Let us admit, on the contrary, a series of previous progressive existences and it will all be explained. Since birth, human beings bring the intuition of what they have acquired. They are more or less advanced, pending on the number of experienced existences and how far they are from the starting point. Absolutely like a congregation of people of all ages, each will show a development that is proportional to the number of years that they have lived. The successive existences will be to the life of the soul what the years are to the life of the body.

Assemble one-day individuals from one to eighty years old. Suppose that a veil is cast over their pasts and that, out of your ignorance, you think they were all born on the same day. You shall naturally ask how come some are big and others tiny, some old and others young, some instructed and others ignorant. However, once the cloud that hides their past is withdrawn and you realize that some lived more than others, all will be explained.

In His fairness, God could not have created some souls that are more perfect than others; however, with the plurality of the existences, the inequalities that we observe will contain nothing contrary to the most rigorous justice. We see only the present and not the past. Will such an argument rest on a gratuitous system or supposition? No. We start from a patent and incontestable fact: the inequality of aptitudes and of the moral and intellectual development, fact that we find inexplicable in every existing theory, whereas its explanation is simple, natural and logic by this theory. Is it natural to prefer those that do not explain to the one that does explain?

With respect to the sixth question above some may argue that the tribal man comes from an inferior race. We then ask if he is a man or not? If he is then why has God disinherited him and his race from the privileges given to the Caucasian race? If he is not a man why are we trying to turn him into a Christian? The Spiritist Doctrine is broader than all that. To that Doctrine there isn't such a thing as different species of human beings; there are simply human beings whose spirit are more or less advanced, susceptible however to progress. Wouldn't that be in more agreement with God's justice?

We have just seen the soul in its past and its present. If we consider the soul in its future, we will find the same difficulties.

1. If our future is uniquely decided by our present existence, what is going to be the position of a savage as compared to a civilized person? Will they be on the same level or far apart in the summation of all eternal happiness?

2. An individual that has strived his whole life to become better shall be on the same level as the other who remained inferior not for his fault but because he did not have time neither the conditions to improve?

3. An individual who has done evil deeds because he did not have the possibility to enlighten himself is subjected to circumstances that did not depend on him?

4. Despite the efforts to instruct, moralize and civilize people, to each one that is enlightened there are millions that daily disappear

before the light gets to them. What is their destiny? Are they treated as outcasts? If not, what have they done to deserve the same level as the others?

5. What shall be the fate of the children that die at an early age, before they are able to do the good or evil deeds? If they find themselves among the elected ones, why such a favor, as they have not done anything to deserve that? Based on which privilege have they been released from life's tribulations?

Is there a doctrine that can solve those questions? Admit the successive existences and everything shall be explained in conformity to God's justice. What cannot be done in one existence will be done in the next. Thus, nobody will escape the law of progress and everyone will be compensated according to their real merit and nobody will be excluded from the supreme happiness, that all can aspire, whatever the obstacles found in their routes.

Those questions could be multiplied to infinity as the moral and psychological problems whose solution is found in the plurality of the existences are countless. We limited to the more general ones. Nevertheless some will perhaps say that the Church does not accept the doctrine of reincarnation; that it would be the end of religion. Our objective is not to handle such a subject at this point: it is enough to have demonstrated that that doctrine is eminently moral and rational. Later we will demonstrate that religion is closer to that than thought and that it would not suffer with this doctrine more that it had done with the discovery of the movements and geological periods of Earth that, at first sight, seemed to deny the sacred texts. The teaching of the spirits is eminently Christian. It is based on the immortality of the soul, on the future penalties and awards, on human's free-will and on Christ's moral. Thus, it is not anti-religious.

As we have said, the proposed reasoning was developed abstracting from the whole teaching of the spirits that, for some people, have no authority. If we have adopted, as many others have, the opinion of the plurality of the existences, it was not because it came from the spirits to us, but because it seemed the more logical and the only one capable of resolving problems hitherto unsolvable.

Had it come from a simple mortal and we would have adopted it, not hesitating to renounce to our own ideas. Since an error has been demonstrated the self-esteem has more to lose than to gain with the stubborn persistence on a false idea.

Accordingly, we would have repelled it, even if coming from the spirits, had it sounded contrary to reason, as we have proceeded with many others, for we know from experience that one should not blindly accept everything that come from them, or even from men.

We now have to examine the issue of the plurality of the existences from the point of view of the teaching of the spirits; how should we understand it and, finally, respond to the most serious objections that may be raised against it. This is what we shall do in a next article.

Moral Problems –

About Suicide

QUESTIONS ADDRESSED TO ST. LOUIS THROUGH MR. C..., PNEUMATOPHONY (ORAL COMMUNICATION) AND CLARVOYANT MEDIUM, IN THE SESSION OF THE PARISIAN SOCIETY OF SPIRITIST STUDIES, ON OCTOBER 12th, 1858.

1. How come a man who has the firm intention of killing himself rebels against the idea of being killed by someone else and who would defend himself against the attacks, on the very moment that he would accomplish his intents?

    - Because man always fears death. The suicidal is always super excited, his mind is disturbed, thus he accomplishes his intent without fear or courage and, so as to say, without the knowledge of his action, whereas had he been able to reason we would not see so many suicides. Human beings's instinct leads him to defend his own life and, during the elapsed time since another person approaches to kill him and the proper act he has always an instinctive repulsive reaction to death, leading him to repel that ghost, only terrifying to the guilty spirit. A person that commits suicide does not experience such a feeling since he is surrounded by spirits that push him towards that, who help him with his desires, inducing him to completely erase the memory of anything different from himself, like those of his parents, those who love him, and of another existence. At such a moment the person is only selfishness.

2. Someone that is not satisfied with life but does not wish to commit suicide and wishes that his death may serve to something, will bear the culpability if seeking death in the battlefield, defending his country?

    - Always! Man has to follow the impulse given to him. Whatever his career; whatever his lifestyle, he is always assisted by spirits that guide him, in spite of him. Thus, acting against their advice is a crime because they are there to drive us, always ready to help us whenever we want to act. However, if man wants to act by himself by leaving this life he is then abandoned. Later he shall recognize his fault when is obliged to restart in another existence.

      The human being has to be proven in order to elevate. By impeding his action and blocking his free will it would be like going against God and in this case the trials would become useless because the spirits would not make mistakes. The spirit was created simple and ignorant. In order to achieve the happy spheres it is necessary that the spirit elevates in knowledge and wisdom. It is only through adversity that he acquires an elevated heart and better understands God's greatness.

3. One of the assistants observed that a contradiction was noticed between these last words from St. Louis and the preceding ones, when he said that man can be dragged to suicide by the spirits that encourage him to do that. In such a case he would be giving in to a foreign impulse.

    - There is no contradiction. When I said that man who is impelled to suicide was surrounded by spirits that solicit him to do that I was not referring to the good spirits that make all efforts to persuade him from doing that; this should be inferred. We all know that we have a guardian angel or, a familiar guide if you like. Well, man has his free-will; if despite the good advices given to him he perseveres in that criminal intent, he so does seconded by the frivolous and impure spirits that surround him and that feel happy to see that the incarnated spirit also lacks the courage to follow the advices from his good angel, and sometimes from the spirits of dead relatives that are around him, particularly in those circumstances.

Family Conversations From Beyond the Grave: Mehemet–Ali, Second Communication

1. In the name of the Almighty God, I ask the spirit of Mehemet-Ali to come to communicate with us.
    -   Yes, I know the reason.
2. You promised to come to instruct us. Will you be kind to listen to us and answer?
    -   I don't promise, as I have not committed to doing that.
3. Let us replace the "promised us" by "you made us wait"
    -   You mean: to satisfy your curiosity. Never mind! I will make myself useful.
4. Considering that you lived in the times of the Pharaohs, can you tell us what was the reason for the construction of the pyramids?
    -   They are burial chambers. Tombs and temples. Great manifestations took place there.
5. Did they also have a scientific interest?
    -   No. The religious interest absorbed everything.

6. It was necessary that the Egyptians were well advanced in mechanical engineering so as to realize tasks that required so considerable forces. Can you give us an idea of the means they employed?

 - Masses of men moaned under the weight of those stones that crossed the centuries. The machine was man.

7. Which class of men was employed into such great work?

 - Those that you call people.

8. Were the people on a state of slavery or did they receive a salary?

 - Forced.

9. Where did the Egyptians get their taste for colossal things from, rather than the gracious ones that distinguished the Greeks, considering their common origin?

 - The Egyptian was touched by God's greatness. Wanted to equal him, overcoming his own forces. Always man!

10. Since you were a priest on those days, kindly tell us something about the Egyptian religion. What was the people's belief with respect to the Divinity?

 - Corrupted. They believed their priests. Their gods were those who kept them under the oppression.

11. What did they think about the soul after death?

 - They believed in what they were told by the priests.

12. Had the priests a more sound idea than the people about God and the soul?

 - Yes. They had the light in their hands and although hiding it from the others, they still saw it.

13. The celebrities of the state shared the priest's or the people's beliefs?

 - They were between the two.

14. What was the origin of the cult to the animals?

 - They wanted to deviate people from God by reducing them to their level, offering inferior beings as gods.

15. One can understand, up to a point, the cult to useful animals; but to dirty and harmful ones like the serpents, crocodiles, etc!
    - Human beings adore what they fears. It was a kind of oppression to the people. The priests could not believe in gods made by their hands!

16. Isn't that strange that at the same time that they adored the crocodile and reptiles they also adored the ichneumon and the ibis that destroyed them?
    - Aberration of the spirit. Human beings seek gods everywhere to hide what they actually are.

17. Why was Osiris represented with a hawk's head and Anubis with a dog's head?
    - The Egyptian liked to personify under the form of clear emblems: Anubis was good; the ruthless hawk represented the cruel Osiris.

18. How can one reconcile with the respect to the Egyptians by the dead with their disdain and horror for those who buried and mummified them?
    - The cadaver was an instrument of manifestations. According to their thoughts, the spirit would return to the body it had once animated. Since it was one of the instruments of their cult, the body was sacred and the disdain followed those who dared to violate death's sanctity.

19. Did the conservation of the body allowed for a larger number of manifestations?
    - Longer, that is, the spirit would return for longer times, since the instrument was docile.

20. Wouldn't the conservation of the body also carry an issue of salubrity, considering the floods of the Nile?
    - Yes, the bodies of the people.

21. Did the initiation into the mysteries in Egypt go through as much rigorous practices as in Greece?
    - Even more rigorous.

22. What was the aim of imposing conditions that were so much difficult to accomplish to the initiated?
    - To have only superior souls. Those who know how to understand and remain quiet.
23. Have the teachings about the mysteries had the revelation of the extra-human things as their only objective or the principles of moral and love to the neighbor were also taught?
    - All that was much corrupted. The intent of the priests was to dominate, not to instruct.

Family Conversations

From Beyond the

Grave: Dr Muhr [44]

1. Evocation.
   - I am here.
2. Would you kindly tell us where you are?
   - I am wandering.
3. Has your death occurred on June 4th of this year?
   - No, of last year.
4. Do you remember your friend, Mr. Jobard?
   - Yes, I am frequently by his side.
5. When I transmit your answer to him, he will be pleased since he speaks highly of you.
   - I know. He is one of my most sympathetic spirits.
6. What did you think about gnomes during your life?
   - I supposed they were capable of materializing and assuming fantastic forms.

---

44 He is thought to be a very elevated spirit. He was a homeopathic physician, a true spirit-ist apostle. He died on June 4th, 1857 in Cairo. He should be in Jupiter, evoked by the request of Mr. Jobard (see Spiritist Review, last July, reference made in a letter from Mr. Jobard dated June 22nd, 1858, in the section Correspondence). The difference in the writing is in the original. However, the Muhr form seems more adequate.

7. Do you still believe in that?

    - More than ever. Now I am sure. But gnome is a word too much related to magic. Now I prefer to say spirit instead of gnome.

NOTE: During his life, he believed in the spirits and their manifestations. He just called them gnomes whereas now he prefers the generic denomination of spirits.

8. Do you still believe, that the spirits, which during your life you called gnomes, can take fantastic material forms?

    - Yes, but I know this does not always happen as some people could go crazy if they saw the appearances that those can take.

9. Which appearances would that be?

    - Of animals, of devils.

10. A tangible, material appearance or just appearance, like in dreams and visions?

    - A little more material than in dreams. The apparitions that could scare us cannot be tangible. God would not allow it.

11. The apparition of the spirit of Bergzabern, under the form of man or animal, could be of such a nature?

    - Yes, it is of that kind.

NOTE: We don't know if during his life he admitted that the spirits could take a tangible form but it is evident that now he refers to the vaporous form of the intangible apparitions.

12. Do you believe that you are going to reincarnate in Jupiter?

    - I will go to a planet that is not like Jupiter yet.

13. Is it your own choice that takes you to a world inferior to Jupiter or is it because you still do not deserve to go to that planet?

    - I prefer to believe that I don't deserve it and need to accomplish a mission in a less advanced world. I know I will reach perfection and that is why I prefer modesty.

Note: This answer is a demonstration of the superiority of that spirit and it is in agreement with what Father Ambrose says: there is more merit in requesting a mission in an inferior world than to wish to advance too much in a superior world.

14. Mr. Jobard wishes to know if you were happy with the eulogy that he wrote to you.
    - Jobard gave me demonstration of sympathy by writing this eulogy. I am thankful and wish that the picture, which were somehow exaggerated, that he painted about my virtues and skills may serve as an example to those of you who follow the path of progress.

15. Considering that you were a homeopathic physician, what do you think about homeopathy now?
    - Homeopathy is the beginning of the discovery of the latent fluids. But other discoveries equally precious will happen and will form a harmonious whole that will lead your globe to perfection.

16. How do you evaluate your book *Le Medecin du Peuple (The People's Doctor)*?
    - It is the worker's stone carried to the construction yard.

    Note: The answer that the spirit gave about homeopathy supports the idea of the latent fluids, already given by the spirit of Mr. Badet about his photographed image.[45] As it seems there are fluids whose properties are unknown to us or go unnoticed, since its action is not ostensive although not less real. Humanity shall be enlightened along the way by the new knowledge of its properties, made available by the circumstances.

---

45 See Spiritist Review, July issue.

Family Conversations From

Beyond the Grave:

Madam de Stäel

O n September 28th, 1858 at the Parisian Society of Spiritist Studies, the spirit of Madam Stäel, spontaneously and without being evoked communicated through the hand of Ms. E..., psychographic medium, leaving the following words:

"Living is suffering, yes, but won't hope follow suffering? Hasn't God placed a larger dose of hope in the hearts of the unfortunate? Child, pleasure and disappointment go along with birth but hope marches before that, by saying: Move on! Happiness waits at the end. God is merciful.

Why, ask the strong spirits, why do you come to teach us a new religion, when Christ had established the basis of such charity; of such certain a happiness? We do not wish to alter what the great reformer has taught. No. We came only to strengthen consciences and increase hopes.

The more civilized the world gets the more it should have confidence and even greater the need to sustain it. We don't want to change the face of the Universe. We came to help to make it to become better. If we had not come to support human beings in this century, they would be really unhappy by the lack of confidence and hope.

Yes, we say to the wise person that reads others, seeks to know what is not important to you, and stays away from what is central to you. Open your eyes and do not despair. Don't say that nothingness can be possible, when deep in your heart you should feel otherwise. Come sit around this table and wait; you will be enlightened with respect to your future and you will be happy. Here there is bread to all. Spirit, you will improve; body, you will be fed; suffering, you will be diminished; hope, you will sprout and beautify the truth to make it supportable.

Stäel

Note: The spirit referred to the table where the mediums were sitting.

- Ask and I will respond to your questions.

1. We were not waiting for your visit that is why we don't have a prepared subject.
   - I know very well that I cannot respond to special questions. There are, however, general things that can be asked even to a woman that had some spirit and now has a lot of heart!

At that point a lady who was present at the session kind of fainted but it was only with excitement and not painful at all. It was really pleasing to her. Someone offered to magnetize her, but then the spirit of Madam de Stäel spontaneously said:

- No. Leave her alone. Allow the influence to act upon her.

Then, addressing the lady she said:

Be confident since a heart awakes by your side; she wishes to speak with you; the day will come... let us not precipitate emotions.

Then the spirit who was communicating through that lady, who was her sister, spontaneously wrote: "I will come back."

Still addressing the lady, Madam de Stäel wrote:

- A word of consolation to a heart that suffers. Why these tears from a woman for her sister? Why does she go back to the past when all your thoughts should be addressed to the future? Your heart suffers; your soul has the need to go beyond. Then, may these tears be of relief, not produced by sorrow! She who loves you and for whom you cry is happy and venturous! Wait for that day when you shall be together. You don't see her but for her there is no separation, since she can always be by your side.

2. Can you tell us what you presently think of your writings?
   - One word only will clarify you: If I could return and restart, I would modify two thirds and keep only one.
3. Could you point out what is it that you disapprove?
   - I am not very demanding; other writers will change whatever is unfair. I was too masculine for a woman.
4. What is the primary cause of such a virile character that you showed in life?
   - That depends on the phase of our existence.

In the following session, on October 12th, the questions below were addressed to her through Mr. D...., a psychographic medium:

5. The other day you came spontaneously through Ms. E... Could you tell us the reason that made you favor us with your presence, since we did not call you?
   - The sympathy that I have towards all of you. It is also a duty imposed on my current existence or even better, my transient existence, since I am called to reincarnate: that is, by the way, the destiny of all spirits.
6. Is it more pleasant to you to come spontaneously or by evocation?
   - I prefer to be evoked as it is a demonstration that you think of me, but also know that it is pleasing to a free spirit to come

to talk with the spirit of man. That is why you should not be surprised that I suddenly came to your center.

7. Would there be any advantage in evoking rather than waiting for the spirits to come, out of their own initiative?

  - By the evocation there is an objective. By allowing them to come there is a great risk of imperfect communication on several aspects, since the evil as well as the good spirits may come.

8. Have you already communicated in other centers?

  - Yes but they made me show up more than I wanted. In other words, many times they have taken my name.

9. Could you kindly come sometimes to bring us your beautiful thoughts, that we would have the pleasure to reproduce for the general instruction?

  - Gladly. I feel happy to be among those that seriously work on their instruction. My visit with you the other day is a proof of that.

The Painting Medium

From the USA

Extracted from the Spiritualist of New Orleans

Not everybody can be convinced by the same type of spiritist manifestations, thus the need for the development of mediums of many kinds. In the USA there are those who draw pictures of people who have been deceased from a long time that they had never seen before. Sensible persons who witness those paintings promptly convert, since the similarities are immediately identified. The most remarkable of those mediums is perhaps Mr. Rogers who we have already mentioned[46], a Columbus resident, tailor by profession, with no other professional habilitation.

Some educated people who have repeatedly said this about the spiritist manifestations: "Resorting to the spirits is nothing more than a hypothesis; an attentive examination demonstrates that it is not the most rational neither the likeliest", to those, above all, we offer the following summary of a translated article published on July 27th last, by Mr. Lafayette R. Gridley, from Attica, Indiana, to the editors of the Spiritual Age, who have published the integral version in their August 14th edition.

"Last May, Mr. E. Rogers from Cardington, Ohio, a well-known painting medium that makes portraits of people who are no longer in this

---

46   Vol. I, page 239 of the "Spiritualist" of New Orleans

world, came to spend a few days in my house. During his short visit he was influenced by an invisible artist that used the name Benjamin West. He painted some beautiful life-sized portraits, as well as some others of somewhat inferior quality. Here are some particularities with respect to a couple of those portraits.

Mr. Rogers painted these portraits in my house in a dark room. There was a time when, during this event, the medium was under no influence. During this break that lasted about another hour and a half, I used this time to examine his work... Then Rogers fell again in a state of trance, finalizing the paintings.

Although there had been no reference as to the individuals who were portrayed in the paintings, one of the pictures was immediately recognized as being my grandfather, Elias Gridley. My wife, my sister, Mrs. Chaney, followed by my father and my mother, all were unanimous in acknowledging the great similarity: it was a facsimile of the old man, with every detail of his vast hair, his shirt, etc.

As for the other portrait, none of us recognized it. I hung it on the wall in my store, visible to everyone, where it remained for a week without any identification. We expected that someone would tell us that it was from an old inhabitant of Greece. I had almost lost hope of identifying the person in the picture when in that afternoon, during a spiritist session that took place in my house, a spirit manifested giving me the following communication:

"My name is Horace Gridley. I have left my corporal body more than five years ago. I lived in Natchez, Mississippi, for several years, where I was the sheriff. My only daughter still lives there. I am your father's cousin. You can get more information about me from your uncle, Mr. Gridley from Brownsville, Tennessee. The portrait that you have in your store is mine, from the time I lived on Earth, short before I passed on to this other existence, more elevated, better and happier. The picture resembles me, at least as much as I was able to return to the looks of that time, since that is indispensable while we are being portrayed. We do our best to remember that appearance, according to the conditions of the moment. The portrait in question is not finished as I wished it to be. There are some slight imperfections that Mr. West says are due to the condition of the medium. In spite of that send the picture to Natchez, so as it may be examined. I do believe they will identify it."

The facts mentioned in this communication were completely ignored by me and by all inhabitants of the surroundings. Although many years ago I had once heard that my father had a relative on that side of the Mississippi, none of us knew his name, the place where he had lived; not even if he was alive. It was only several days later that I heard from my father, who lived in Delphi, forty miles from here, that it was the place of residence of his cousin, from whom he had hardly heard over the last sixty years.

We not even thought of requesting family pictures. I had just put a note, in front of the medium, with the names of about twenty former residents of Attica, from whom we wished to obtain the portraits.

Thus, any reasonable person would admit that neither the portrait, nor the communication of Horace Gridley, could be the result of our thoughts transmitted to the medium. As a matter of fact, Mr. Rogers has never known any of the persons that he portrayed and probably never heard about them, since he is an English man; he came to the USA ten years ago and has never traveled south beyond Cincinnati, while Horace Gridley, as far as I know, has never traveled north beyond Memphis, Tennessee, over the last thirty five years of his life. I ignore if he had ever visited England for one day, however this could have happened before Rogers' birth, since he is not more than twenty eight to thirty years old. Regarding my grandfather, who died about nineteen years ago, he has never left the USA and he has never had a picture taken.

After receiving the communication above I wrote to Mr. Gridley, from Brownsville. His answer came to confirm what we had heard through the communication of the spirit. I also got the name of the only descendent of Horace Gridley, Mrs. L. M. Patterson, still residing in Natchez, where her father lived for many years. He died, according to my uncle, about six years ago, in Houston, Texas.

I then wrote to Mrs. Patterson, my recently found cousin, and sent her a daguerreotyped copy of the portrait, supposedly of her father. In the letter to my uncle of Brownsville I did not say anything about the main objective of my investigation, not saying anything to Mrs. Patterson either: the reason for sending her the picture or how I had obtained it or who the portrayed person was. I just asked my cousin if she recognized the image. Her response was that she could not say for sure but assured me that it resembled her father at the time of his death. Later I wrote again saying that we also thought it had been taken from her father, not telling her however how it had been obtained. My cousin's response, in short, indicated that everybody had recognized her father in the picture, before I had told her who it actually represented. Nevertheless, she seemed really surprised that I had a picture of her father while she herself did not have any and that her father had never told her that he had a picture taken of him, from wherever. She always thought that there was no picture taken of her father and was really happy with my mail, particularly because of her children who had real veneration for the memory of their grandfather.

I then sent her the original painting, authorizing her to keep it, in case she liked it, but did not tell her how it was obtained. These are the main lines of her answer:

"I received your letter and the picture of my father which you allowed me to keep if I find that it does look like him. Truly, it is a lot like him, I will then keep this one for which I am very grateful to you, since I had never had any other image of him, although I think he was better looking when he was healthy."

Before receiving the two last letters from Mrs. Patterson, and out of pure chance, Mr. Hedges, currently living in Delphi but who was an old resident of Natchez, and Mr. Ewing, recently arriving from Vicksburg, Mississippi, saw the picture and recognized it as being of Horace Gridley, with whom both had been acquainted.

I find these facts very significant to be left unknown; therefore I considered a duty to reveal them, so as to give them publicity. I assure you that when I was writing this article I took the utmost care with its absolute accuracy."

NOTE: We already know the painting mediums. In addition to the remarkable drawings that we gave a sample of, but that represent things whose accuracy is impossible to verify, we have seen mediums, absolutely aliens to that art, executing before our eyes easily recognizable sketches of deceased persons that they had never met. But from there to a finely finished portrait, according to all rules, there is a great distance. Such a faculty is associated to a very curious phenomenon, which we are witnessing right now. We shall report that very soon.

Somnambulistic

Independence

There are many people now that accept magnetism and have for a long time contested the somnambulistic lucidity. Truly, that faculty knocked down every notion that we had with respect to the perception of the material world. However, for a long time we have had the example of the natural somnambulists who enjoyed similar faculties that, by a bizarre contradiction, had never being investigated. Today the somnambulistic clairvoyance is an established fact and if it is still contested by some people it is due to the fact that it takes long for the new ideas to ingrain, particularly when it proves necessary to abandon the old ones that we cherished for so long.

Many people believed, as some still do today with respect to the spiritist manifestations, that somnambulism could be experienced like one does with a machine, without taking into account the special conditions of the phenomenon. That is why they have concluded by the denial in the first opportunity since satisfactory results have not been achieved. Such delicate phenomena require a lengthy, frequent and perseverant observation so that the most subtle nuances can be captured. Also due to the incomplete observation of the facts certain people admit the clairvoyance of the somnambulists, but contest their independence. Their vision, they say, do not go beyond the thought of those who interrogate them. Some even say that there is no vision but simply intuition and transmission of thoughts, citing numerous examples to support these ideas.

No one doubts that the somnambulist may capture the thought, translate it and sometimes operate as its echo. No one contests the fact either that, in certain cases, thought may influence them. By only admitting that the phenomenon is limited to that, wouldn't this alone be a curious fact, worthy of observation? Thus the problem is not to determine if a somnambulist is or can be influenced by an alien thought, what in itself is not questioned, but if she is always influenced and if that results from experimental investigations. If the somnambulist only says what you already know then it is unquestionable that she only translates your thoughts. But if in certain cases she says something that you don't know; if what she says is contrary to your opinion and to the way you may see things, her independence and the fact that she follows her own impulses become evident.

For that kind of phenomenon a well characterized case would be enough to prove that the somnambulist is not absolutely subjected to someone else's thought. Well, there are thousands of examples so that we will mention two among those that we are aware of, as follows:

Mr. Marillon, a Bercy resident, Rue Charenton 43, disappeared last January 13th. Every effort to find any trace of him proved useless. None of this friends and colleagues had seen him. None of his business could be associated to such a prolonged absence. His position, character and mental state ruled out any suicide attempt. The remaining hypothesis was that he could have been a victim of a crime or an accident. In the latter case, however, he could have been easily identified and taken back home or even to the morgue. All likelihoods then indicated a crime. That idea gained support particularly considering the fact that he left home to make a payment. But where and how such a crime would have taken place? That was the question. Then, his daughter resorted to a somnambulist, Mrs. Roger, who had given demonstration of a remarkable lucidity in many other circumstances that we ourselves had the opportunity to verify.

Mrs. Roger tracked Mr. Marillon since he left his house, around three pm, up until seven pm, when he was ready to return home; she saw him walking down the Seine banks due to an imperious biological need; according to her, he then had an episode of apoplexy and fell head first on a rock, breaking his head open, falling into the waters. There was no crime or suicide. She even saw money and keys in one pocket of his jacket. She indicated the place of the accident but said that the body was no longer there as it had been dragged by the currents and would be found in another given location.

Everything happened according to her description. The man had a wound on the head, the money and keys in his pocket and besides, his clothes left no doubt as for the reason that had taken him to the river bank.

Where could one find the transmission of any thought by analyzing so many details?

Another fact where the somnambulistic independence is not less evident is given below.

The Belhomme couple, ranch owners from *Rueil* at Rue Saint-Denis 19, had saved about 800-900 francs. For security reasons, Mrs. Belhomme hid the money in a closet which was used to keep new clothes on one side as well as worn out on the other. She placed the money where the new clothes were hanging. Someone suddenly showed up forcing Mrs. Belhomme to quickly shut the closet's door. Since she needed the money later, Mrs. Belhomme went back to recover the cash, assured to have placed it among the old, worn clothes; this was her intention from the beginning, for being less tempting to an eventual thief. However she misplaced the money due to the unexpected arrival of the visitor the other day. She was so much convinced that she had the money among the shabby clothes that she did not even bother to look somewhere else. The place was empty, she had the unsolicited visit then, she thought, she had been seen hiding the money and consequently robbed; her suspicions then naturally fell onto the visitor.

Meanwhile, Mrs. Belhomme knew Ms. Marillon, the daughter of the disappeared man that we mentioned above, telling her about her unfortunate loss. Ms Marillon in turn told her the story of her father and how he had been found, advising her to seek the somnambulist's help, before taking any other action. The Belhoummes went to Mrs. Roger place, convinced that they had been robbed, hoping that they could have the thief's name confirmed; it could not be that of anyone else but the unexpected visitor. It was their only thought.

Well, after a lengthy description of the place the somnambulist said: "You were not robbed; your money remains untouched in the closet; you thought that you had it among the worn clothes; it is among the new clothes. Go home to find it." That is exactly what happened.

Reporting these two cases – and we could mention many others – our aim was to demonstrate that the somnambulistic clairvoyance is not always the reflection of a foreign thought. Hence the somnambulist can have her own lucidity, absolutely independent. This leads to consequences of paramount importance from the physiological view point. We have here the key to more than one problem that we shall examine in due course, when we will then analyze the relationships between somnambulism and Spiritism, shedding an entirely new light onto the issue.

Forgotten Night or

Manouze, the Witch

(the thousand second night of the Arabic tales
dictated by the spirit of Frédéric Soulié)
Preface by the Editor

During the year of 1856 the experiments with the spiritist manifestations held in Mr. B... house at the *Rue Lamartine* attracted a select
and large crowd of people. The communicating spirits in that circle were
more or less serious. Some have said things of remarkable wisdom, of
notable depth, as one can judge from the Spirits' Book that was initiated and in its most part accomplished there. Others were less serious:
their cheerful humor was given to jester, but fine and never inconvenient
jester. Among those was Frédéric Soulié who came on his own, unsolicited, but whose unexpected visits were always an enjoyable pastime to
everyone. His conversation was witty, fine, vivacious, opportune, having
never denied the author of the *"Mémoires du Diable"* as a matter of fact, he
never attributed importance to himself and when enquired about complex
philosophical issues he frankly confessed his insufficiency to solve them,
saying that he was still too much attached to matter and that he preferred
the funny things to the serious ones.

The medium who served him as interpreter was Ms Caroline B..., one of the daughters of the owner of the house, a medium of the exclusively passive kind, who had no consciousness about what she wrote, being able to talk and laugh her head off, what she used to do with pleasure, while her hand jotted the words on the paper. The mechanical means used for a long time was the planchettes with a pencil, described in *The Mediums' Book*. Later the medium used the direct psychography.

Some may ask what proof do we have that the communicating spirit was of Frédéric Soulié and that it was not someone else. This is not the place to discuss the subject of identity of the spirits. We shall say only that Soulié's identity was confirmed by a thousand and one details that cannot escape a careful examination. Several times a word, a gesture, a reported personal fact came to confirm that yes, it was him, and on several occasions he left his signature which was confronted with the original. One day someone asked for his picture therefore the medium that could not draw and had never seen him, made a sketch of impressive similarity.

Nobody in the session had had any relationship with him during his life. Why then would he come uninvited? The fact is that he had associated himself to one of the participants, never revealing the reason: he only showed up when that person was present; he would come and leave with that person, hence when that person was not there he would not come either and – interesting thing! – When he was there it was difficult, if not impossible, to have communications from other spirits. Even the familiar spirit of the house would yield to him, saying that he would do the honors of the house, out of pure kindness.

One day he announced that he would bring us a romance, using his marked style. Indeed, soon after he started a story that had a very promising beginning. The theme was druidic and the facts that took place in the Armorica during the Roman Empire. Unfortunately he stopped before the task was initiated, as the constant work was not his strong point; he seemed to be feeling well in his kind of lazy life. After dictating a few pages he stopped the work but said that he would write another one, less troublesome. That was when he wrote the tale whose publication we started. More than thirty people witnessed that production and can attest its origin. We do not take it as a highly philosophical piece of work but as an original sample of a hard work obtained from the spirits.

It is remarkable how everything is articulated, connected through an impressive art. The most extraordinary is the fact that the theme was resumed over five or six different occasions and sometimes after breaks of two or three weeks. Well, on every restart the subject continued as if written at once, without any obliterations, reticence or the need to recover what had been said before.

We published it as it came out from the medium's writings, without changing anything, neither the style, nor the ideas or the connection of the facts.

Some repetition of words as well as typos was observed, and then Soulié himself assigned the correction to us, saying that he would assist us in the task.

When all was finished he wanted to review everything, making occasional changes of minor importance, and then authorizing us to publish it as we wished, gladly passing the copyright to us. Nevertheless, we thought appropriate to introduce it in the Review only with the approval of the deceased friend, who held the actual rights, hence we owe him the current production from beyond the grave, for his presence and request. The title was given by the spirit of Frédéric Soulié himself.

Allan Kardec

A FORGOTTEN NIGHT

In Bagdad there was a woman from the times of Aladdin. I will tell her story.

In one of the suburbs of Bagdad, not far from the Sultan Sheherazade's palace, lived an old woman named Manouze. She was a motive of horror to the whole town as she was a witch of the most terrible kind. Scaring things happened at night in her house; so much so that after sunset nobody ventured to pass by her doorway, except some lover trying to find a potion for his rebel partner or an abandoned woman looking for some remedy for the wound inflicted by her lover, after leaving her.

One day, when the Sultan was more upset than usual and there was great desolation in town, the Sultan wanted to kill his favorite wife and following his example all husbands were unfaithful to their wives, a young man left the magnificent solar, located by the side of the favorite lady's palace. The man wore a tunic and a turban of somber colors but under the simple outfit he sustained an air of great distinction. He tried to go unnoticed along the houses, like a thief or a lover, afraid of being caught by surprise, moving towards the region where Manouze the witch's house was located. He showed great anxiety on his face, denouncing an unsettling concern. The man walked quickly but cautiously through the streets and squares.

As he arrived at her door he hesitated for a few moments, later deciding to knock. For a quarter of an hour he went through a fatal anguish since he heard noises that the human ear had never heard before: a pack of fiercely barking dogs; groaning outcries and chants from men and women after an orgy and, to illuminate all that upheaval, lights running from top to bottom of the house, like the will-o-the-wisp of all colors. Then, out of the blue, it all went quiet. The lights were out and the door opened.

II

The visitor hesitated for a moment, not knowing if he should proceed through the somber corridor extending before his eyes. After walking and groping for about thirty steps he found himself in front of a door, yielding to a room only illuminated by a cooper lamp of three tips, hanging from the ceiling, at the center of the room.

The house, which should be inhabited by a large number of people, given the noise heard from the streets, had now a deserted look. The huge room that, by its construction, should be the basis of the edifice was empty, not to mention the stuffed animals of all kinds that guarded the place.

In the middle of the room there was a small table covered by witchcraft books and across from the table, sitting on a large armchair, was an old lady only three feet tall. She was covered by her turban and scarves to the point that her face was almost completely covered. As the stranger approached, she raised her head revealing the most terrible looks that one can imagine.

- Here you are Mr. Nuredin – she said, staring at the young man with her hyena's eyes. Come! Since a few days ago my crocodile of ruby's eyes has announced your visit. Tell me if it is potion that you miss or if it is a fortune. But, what am I saying? Fortune! Wouldn't yours make the Sultan himself jealous? Aren't you the richest as you are the most handsome? It is a potion that you are likely looking for. Who is then the daring woman, so cruel to you? I should not say anything. I know nothing. I am ready to hear your whining and to give you the needed remedy, as long as my science can be useful to you. But why that look in your face and why you don't say anything? Are you afraid? Do I scare you? You now see me this way but I was beautiful once; the nicest of all women in Bagdad. It was the suffering that made me so ugly. But why bother with my sufferings? Come close, I shall hear you. I cannot give you more than ten minutes, make it fast!

Nuredin did not feel safe. However, not willing to give away his perturbation before the old lady that kept him unsettled, he stepped forward and said:

- Woman, I have come for a serious thing. My fate is in your hands. You shall decide between my happiness and my death. This is what I have to tell you:

The Sultan wants to kill Nazara and I love her. I will tell you about the origin of such love since I came here not to alleviate my pain but to save her from such an unfortunate fate, for I do not wish to see her dead. You know that my palace is next door to the Sultan's palace and that our gardens share a border line. About six moons ago I was strolling in my gardens when I heard an enchanting music following the most delicious female voice I have ever heard. I wished to figure out where it came from thus I got closer to the neighbor's garden to realize that it was coming from a green pergola, occupied by the favorite of the Sultan. Several days passed and I was absorbed by those melodious sounds. Day and night I dreamed of the unknown beauty, whose voice had seduced me for in my mind she was beautiful. Every evening I strolled through the same paths from where I had heard that enchanting harmony. For five days it was all in vain. Finally, on the sixth day I heard the music again. Then, not being able to contain myself any longer, I approached the fencing wall only to realize that I could easily escalate it. I hesitated for a few moments and took the firm decision: I then climbed the wall, passing to the neighbor's garden.

It was then when I saw, not a woman but a houri, a favorite houri of Mohammed, a true wonder! She did not show much of a surprise by seeing me but I threw myself at her feet, begging that she should not be afraid but listen to me instead. I told her that her singing had attracted me and I assured her that my attitude was profoundly respectful. She kindly listened to me. We spent the first night talking about music. I also sang and offered to accompany her. She consented so that we set up a date for the next day, at the same time.

She was more relaxed then. The Sultan was in his Council so that the vigilance was somewhat diminished. The first two or three nights were dedicated to music. But music is the voice of the lovers and from the fourth day on we were no longer strange to one another. We were in love. How beautiful she was! How beautiful was her soul too! We foresaw our escape several times. Ah! Why haven't we done that? I would not be so unhappy now and she would not be about to succumb. Such a beautiful flower would not be about to be decimated by the sickle that would have denied a ray of light to those eyes."

(Continue in the next issue)

Varieties - General Marceau

The Gazette of Cologne published the following story, sent by its correspondent in Koblenz, which nowadays is a compulsory subject of all conversations. The fact was also reported by the *Patrie* of November 10th, 1858.

"It is a known fact that below Emperor Francis' fortress, just off the road to Cologne, there is the monument to the French general Marceau, fallen in Altenkirchen, and buried in Koblenz, at Mount St. Peter, where the main part of the fortress is located. The monument to the general, a truncated pyramid, was later removed when the fortification of Koblenz started. However, by expressed order of the late King Frederic III, it was reconstructed in the place where it stands today."

"Mr. de Stramberg, who in his *Reinischen Antiquarius,* provides a very detailed biography of Marceau, saying that many people have allegedly seen the general riding his horse at night and for several times, wearing the white mantle of the French hunters."

"Since some time now the word around in Koblenz was that Marceau would leave his burial and many people have attested to have seen him. A few days ago a soldier guarding the *Petersberg* (Mount St. Peter) saw a white knight, riding a white horse. He shouted: "Who is that?" As he did not get any answer back, after three interpellations he shot the apparition and then passed out. "Hearing the shooting a patrol hurried to help and found the sentinel unconscious. He was taken to the hospital, gravely ill, where he was nevertheless able to report what he had seen. Another version says that the soldier died as a consequence of the adventure. This is the story that can be confirmed by everyone in Koblenz."

ALLAN KARDEC[47]

---

47 Paris. Typography of Cosson & Co., Rue de Four-Saint-Germain, 43

December 1858

Apparitions

The phenomena of apparitions are now presented in a kind of new aspect, shedding a powerful light over the mysteries of life beyond the grave. Before moving into the strange facts that we will report, we find it appropriate to recap the explanations given earlier and complete them.

One should keep in mind that during its life the spirit is united to the body by a semi-material substance that forms the first covering called perispirit. The spirit thus has two coverings: one dense, heavy and destructible – the body; the other, ethereal, vaporous, indestructible – the perispirit. Death is nothing but the destruction of the gross covering; it is like the worn clothes that we abandon. The semi material covering persists and constitutes, per say, a new body to the spirit.

Such ethereal matter – interesting to point out – is not the soul, absolutely; it is nothing more than its first covering. The intimate nature of that substance is not yet perfectly known to us but the observation has led us to understand some of its properties. We know that it represents a fundamental role in every spiritist phenomena; that after death it is the intermediary agent between the spirit and matter, as the body is during its life. This allows for the explanation of a large number of phenomena hitherto inexplicable. We shall see in a following article the role that it plays in the sensations of the spirits. Besides, the discovery of the perispirit, if we can say so, led the Spiritist Science into a huge step in an entirely new route.

But the perispirit, some may argue, isn't that a fantastic creation of imagination? Wouldn't that be one of those suppositions made several times to explain certain effects? No. It is not the work of imagination since it was revealed by the spirits themselves. It is not a fantastic idea since it can be verified by the senses and can be seen and touched. It does exist; we only gave it a name. We need new words to describe new things. The spirits also adopted it in the communications that we have established with them.

By nature and in its normal state the perispirit is invisible to us but it can go through changes to allow us to see it, both by a kind of condensation as well as by an alteration in its molecular structure. It is then that it can appear to us in a vaporous state. The condensation (we should not take this term formally hence we only employ it for the lack of a better one) can be such that the perispirit acquires the properties of a solid and tangible body. It can, nevertheless, instantly return to its ethereal and invisible state. We can have an idea of that effect by the vapor that can pass from the invisible to a foggy state then to liquid and then to solid and vice-versa. Those different states of the perispirit are the product of the free-will of the spirit and not of an exterior cause. When visible to us it is because the spirit gives to the perispirit the necessary property to make it visible. That property can be extended, restricted and ceased, according to their wishes.

Another property of the perispirit is its penetrability. It cannot be blocked by any matter, passing through them all, like the light passes through the transparent bodies.

The perispirit, separated from the body, takes a determined and limited form which normally is the human body, but that is not constant. The spirit can give it a variety of forms at will, including that of an animal or a flame. As a matter of fact, this capability can be easily understood. Don't we see people that make the most diverse expressions, imitating the voice and the facial looks of other people, to the point of deceiving us; pretending to be fat, disabled, etc? Who can recognize around town those actors that we only see playing a characteristic role on a stage? If man can thus give to his material and rigid body such contradictory appearances, with even more reason the spirit can do it with a covering, which is eminently flexible and can yield to all caprices.

The spirits generally appear to us showing a human form. In its normal state such a form does not have anything very characteristic, anything that markedly separate one from the others. With the good spirits that shape is, by a rule of thumb, beautiful and regular: long and fluctuating hair over their shoulders, ample mantles surrounding their bodies. But whenever they want to be identified they assume all traces by which they were known, including the outfits, if necessary. That is for example like Aesop who is not disabled as a spirit but if evoked as Aesop, considering that he had several existences prior to that, he will show up ugly and with a hunchback, as well as traditionally dressed. It is perhaps the dressing that is most intriguing; if however we consider that the dressing is also part of the semi material covering, we then understand that the spirit can give to that covering the appearance of this or that outfit as with this or that facial looks.

The spirits can appear in dreams as well as in the waking state. The apparitions in the waking state are neither rare nor new; they have happened at all times and history records them in great number. Without going back to the past, however, they are very frequent nowadays and many people have, at first, taken such visions as hallucinations.

The apparitions are particularly frequent in cases of death from individuals that come to visit relatives and friends. They do not often have a determined objective but one can generally say that the spirits that appear to us are attracted by mutual sympathy.

We know a young lady that appear many times in her house, in her bedroom, with or without light, men that would come and go, despite the fact that the door would be closed. She would feel so scared that she showed an almost ridiculous cowardice. One day she distinctly saw her brother who was alive in California, giving proof that the spirits of the living beings can cover the distances and show up in a place when the body is in another.

Once that lady was initiated into Spiritism she is no longer afraid since she is aware of the visions and she knows that the spirits that come to visit her cannot do her any harm. It is likely that her brother was asleep when he appeared to hear. If she only knew that she could have established a conversation with him, of which he could have kept a faint impression when awaken. It is also likely that he would then have thought to have dreamt of being close to his sister.

We said that the perispirit can become tangible. We spoke of that when describing the manifestations produced by Mr. Home. It is a known fact that he has made hands appear several times, hands that could be touched as if they were alive, but that would suddenly disappear as shadows, although no complete bodies had yet been seen under such a tangible form. Yet, this is also possible.

In one of our member's family, a spirit has been associated to the daughter of this family. This daughter is a ten to eleven year old child who has befriended a handsome young man of the same age. He is visible to her and willingly becomes visible or invisible to the other persons. He does all sorts of errands; he brings toys and chocolates to her; cleans the house; go to the stores for groceries and more expensive items. This is not a legend of the German mystic neither a medieval story. It is an actual fact that happens at this very moment while we write, in a French town, in the core of a very respectable family. We have even carried out interesting studies about this case which provided us with the most original and unexpected revelations. We will address this subject with our readers in a more thorough article to be published soon.

Mr. Adrien, Clairvoyant Medium

E very person that can see the spirits without the help of others is thus a clairvoyant medium. But the apparitions are generally accidental and fortuitous.

We didn't know yet anybody capable of seeing the spirits permanently and at will. That is the remarkable gift of Mr. Adrien, member of the Parisian Society of Spiritist Studies. He is simultaneously sensitive, clairvoyant, and psychographic and can also hear the spirits. Through psychography he writes what the spirits dictate but rarely in a mechanical way, like the totally passive mediums, that is, even when writing something alien to his own thoughts he is aware of what he is writing. As a hearing medium he hears occult voices that speak to him. We have in our Society two other mediums that enjoy such a faculty in its highest level and, at the same time, are psychographic mediums. Finally, as a sensitive medium, he feels the contact with the spirits and the pressure they exert on him. He even feels electric shocks that affect other people around. When he magnetizes someone he can, at will, and since that is required to the health treatment, produce the discharge of an electric battery.

A new faculty that has just manifested in him is the double vision. Not being a somnambulist and although completely awake, he can see at an unlimited distance, what happens in a given place, even overseas. He sees the persons and what they are doing; describes the places and facts with precision and confirmed accuracy.

Let us say, for starters, that Mr. Adrien is not one of those weak persons that easily yield to their imagination. On the contrary, he is a man of cold character, very calm and takes all this in the most cold-bloodedly way, but not with indifference; far from that, since he takes his faculties very seriously, considering them as a gift from Providence, given to him for the well-being of others and thus he only uses them for the serious things, never to satisfy the vain curiosity. He is a person of a distinct family, very honest, of a kind and benevolent character, whose refined education is revealed in his language and in all of his attitudes. While in the military he has already visited part of Africa, India and our colonies as a member of the Navy.

From all his faculties of medium the most remarkable and precious to us is his clairvoyance. The spirits appear to him as we have described in our previous issue regarding the apparitions. He sees them with a precision that we can figure out from the portraits given at some point later from the widow of the Malabar and from the Beautiful Weaver of Lyon.

People may ask, however, what is the proof that he sees and that he is not the victim of an illusion. The proof is that when someone that he does not know evokes a relative or a friend through him who he has never seen before, he describes that person with a remarkable accuracy, as we had the opportunity to verify. Thus, we have no doubt whatsoever with respect to that faculty that he manifests while awaken and not as a somnambulist.

What is still even more remarkable is that he does not see only the evoked spirits. He sees all those that are present, evoked or not. He sees them coming and going, listening to what we say, laughing at us or taking us seriously, according to their character. Some are grave, others show a teasing and sardonic face; from time to time one of the them approaches a person who is present, resting a hand on their shoulder or just staying behind them, while the others remain at a distance. In one word, in every gathering there is always an occult assembly, composed of spirits who are attracted by sympathy to those present and by the subjects of their interest. He sees crowds in the streets since beyond the familiar spirits that follow their protégés, there is, as among us, the masses of indifferent and idle ones. He says that he is never bored or alone at home since there is always a whole community that distracts him.

His faculty is not limited to the spirits of the dead but also of the living ones. When he sees a person he can make an abstraction of the body; then the spirit of that person shows up to him as if separated from the body and can talk to him. Hence with a child, for example, he can see the incarnated spirit, appreciate its nature and know what the spirit was before the incarnation. This faculty, elevated to such a level, can teach us more than all written communications about the nature of the spirits; it shows us what the spirit actually is, and if we don't see it with our own eyes, his description leads us to see through our thoughts.

The spirits are no longer abstract beings, becoming real creatures around us; touching us every step of the way. As we now know that their contact can be material, we understand the cause of a number of sensations that we have, without realizing it.

Therefore we place Mr. Adrien among the most remarkable mediums and in the first row of those who have provided us with the most precious elements for the understanding of the spiritual world. We locate him in the first level, particularly for his personal qualities, that are of a good man by excellence, making him eminently sympathetic to the spirits of a more elevated order, what is not always the case with the mediums of purely physical influence. No doubt that there are those among the latter that will make more sensationalism; that will better captivate public opinion, but to the observer, to someone that wishes to probe the mysteries of this wonderful world, Mr. Adrien is the most powerful support that we have ever found.

As a result, his faculty and support serve our personal instruction, be it in the intimacy, in the sessions of the Parisian Society, or even through visitations to several public places. We have been together into theaters, balls, leisurely strolls, in hospitals, in the cemeteries and churches. We were together at funerals, weddings, baptism ceremonies and sermons.

We observed the gathering of spirits in all those places. We have established conversations with some of them, questioning them and learning many things that we shall make useful to our readers considering that our objective is to help them and ourselves to penetrate into such a new world to all of us.

The microscope has revealed to us the unsuspected world of the infinitely small, although it had always been at the reach of our hands. The telescope has revealed us the infinity of the celestial worlds of which we did not suspect either. Spiritism uncovers the world of the spirits that are everywhere around us and in space, a real world that incessantly interacts with us.

A Spirit in His Own Funeral

state of the soul at the time of death

The spirits have always told us that the separation between the soul and body does not happen instantly. Sometimes it starts before real death, while the body is in agony. The detachment is not yet complete at the last heartbeat. It happens more or less slowly, according to the circumstances and up to the moment of its liberation the soul experiences a perturbation, a confusion that hinders the awareness of their actual condition. The soul is in the state of a person that wakes up with confusing ideas. Such a state is not painful to the person whose conscience is pure; not understanding completely what one sees, one is calm and fearlessly waits for the thorough wake up. It is, on the contrary, full of anguish and terror on those who fear for the future.

The duration of that perturbation, we say, is variable. It is much shorter to the one who has elevated his thoughts during his life, purifying his soul; two or three days are enough whereas to others it may take eight or ten. We have many times witnessed this solemn moment and have always seen the same thing. It is not thus a theory but the result of observation because it is the spirit who describes and paints their own situation.

Here is an example of a well characteristic and very interesting case considering that it is not related to an invisible spirit who writes through a medium but to a spirit who is seen and heard next to his own body, both at the burial chamber as well as in church, during the funeral services.

Mr. X... had just been victimized by a stroke. A few hours after his death Mr. Adrien, one of his friends, was in the mortuary chamber with the wife of the deceased. He clearly saw the spirit walking in all directions; alternatively looking to the body and to those around it, later sitting on a chair. He had the exact same appearance as he had when alive. He dressed in the same way: black overcoat and pants. He had his hands in his pockets, looking suspicious.

During that time the wife had been looking for a piece of paper on a desk. The husband looked at her and said: "Don't bother looking; you will find nothing". She did not suspect anything as Mr. X... was only visible to Mr. Adrien. On the following, day during the funeral service, Mr. Adrien saw the spirit of his friend again, wandering by the side of his coffin, but no longer wearing the clothes of the other day, now covered by a kind of tunic. The conversation below was established between the two men. Let us be clear that Mr. Adrien is not a somnambulist and that he was perfectly awake at this time as on the previous day and that the spirit appeared to him much like one of the guests of the funeral.

Q. Tell me my dear spirit: what do you feel now?
A. Comfort and suffering.

Q. I don't understand that.
A. I feel that I am living my real life, however I see my body here in this casket; I touch myself and don't feel a thing, nevertheless I feel that I am alive, that I exist. Will I then be two beings? Ah! How I want to exit this darkness, this nightmare.

Q. Will you remain like that for long?
A. Oh! No. Thank God my friend I feel that I will soon wake up. It would be horrible otherwise. My thoughts are confused; it is all obscurity; I think about the great division that has just happened... and that is what I don't understand at all.

Q. Which effect has death produced on you?

A. Death? I am not dead my son! You are mistaken. I was just standing up when suddenly I was taken by a darkness that covered my eyes; then I stood up and imagine my amazement by seeing myself, feeling alive, having my other *self* lying on the cold floor. My thoughts were confused. I unsuccessfully tried to put myself together. I saw my wife arriving at the wake, mourning for me, but I asked myself why. I offered her consolation, speaking with her but she did not reply nor understand. That was what tortured me and made my spirit even more perturbed. Only you lessened my pain as you heard me and you understand what I want. You helped me to clarify my thoughts and did me a great deal. But why don't the others do the same? That is what tortures me... My mind is smashed by that pain... I will see her. She might understand me now... So long my dear friend. Call me that I will come to see you... I will pay you a friendly visit... Will surprise you... so long.

Then Mr. Adrien saw him approaching his son, who was crying. He bent over him and remained a few moments in that position. He was not understood but he no doubt imagined that he had produced a sound. "I am convinced, says Mr. Adrien that his message got across to his son's heart. I will prove that to you. I saw him later and he was more relaxed."

OBSERVATION: This description is in agreement with everything that we had observed about the phenomenon of separation of the soul; it confirms, in very special circumstances, the following truth: the spirit is still present after death. We believe that we have only an inert body before our eyes whereas he sees and understands everything that happens around him; penetrates the thoughts of those who are present and sees that the only difference between him and them is the visibility and invisibility. The false cries of the heirs do not touch them. What a disappointment may the spirits experience in such a moment!

Phenomenon of Bi-corporeity

One member of our Society sent us a letter from one of his friends from Boulogne-sur-Mer, dated July 26th, 1856 in which one can read the following passage:

"After having magnetized my son, following an order from the spirits, he became a very rare medium; this according to the revelation he gave in a somnambulistic state, which I have induced him into from his own request, on May 14th last and on other four or five occasions."

"There is no doubt to me that, when awake, my son freely speaks with the spirits that he wishes to, through his guide who in the intimacy he calls his friend; that he transports himself wherever he wishes to, in spirit. I will report a case for which I have the written proof in my hands."

"Exactly one month ago we were both in the dining room. I was reading the course of magnetism given by Mr. Du Potet when my son took the book from me, browsing over the pages. At a given point he heard his guide saying: "Read that." It was the adventure of a doctor from America whose spirit had visited a friend who was 15 or 20 leagues away, while asleep. After reading that my son said:

- I wish I could do a similar journey.
- Then, where you want to go? Asked his guide.

- To London, to see my friends, said my son. Then he named those who he wished to visit.
- Tomorrow is Sunday. You don't need to get up early for work. You will sleep at eight and will enjoy London up until eight thirty. Next Friday you will receive a letter from your friends complaining about your very short visit with them."

"In fact, on the following day, in the morning, he fell into a deep sleep. I woke him up around eight thirty. He remembered nothing. I said nothing to him, waiting for the events."

"The following Friday I was working in one of my machines, smoking as usual since I had just had lunch. My son was observing the smoke coming out of the pipe when he said:

- Look, there is a letter in the smoke.
- How do you see a letter in the smoke?
- You will see when the mailman is here."

"In fact the mailman delivered a letter from London in which my son's friends complained about his such short a visit, of a few minutes, on the previous Sunday, from eight to eight thirty, describing a large number of details which would take long to report here, among which there was the peculiar fact of him having had breakfast with them. I have the letter in my hands, as I said before, as a proof that I am not creating things."

Once this tale was told one of those attending the meeting said that history registers several similar cases. He mentioned St. Alfonse of Liguori, who was canonized before the required time, for having simultaneously appeared in two different places, fact that was then considered a miracle.

St. Anthony of Padua was in Spain and while giving his sermon his father was about to be executed in Padua, accused of murder. At that very moment Anthony shows up, demonstrates his father's innocence and reveals who the true assassin was, who later suffered the penalties. It was verified that St. Anthony was preaching in Spain, at the same time.

St. Alfonse of Liguori was evoked so that we addressed him with the following questions:

1. The fact that justified your canonization, is that real?
   - Yes.
2. Is that phenomenon exceptional?
   - No. It can happen to every individual who is dematerialized.
3. Was it a fair reason for having you canonized?
   - Yes, since I had elevated myself to God, through my virtues. Without that I could not have been simultaneously transported to two different places.
4. Should then every individual capable of such a phenomenon be canonized?
   - No, for not all are equally virtuous.
5. Could you give us an explanation about that phenomenon?
   - Yes. When man is completely dematerialized by his own virtue; when he has elevated his soul to God, he can simultaneously appear in two places as below:
     Once he starts to feel sleepy, the incarnated spirit can ask God to take him to a given place. His spirit, or his soul, however you want to call it, leaves the body, followed by part of the perispirit, leaving the dense matter in a state that is close to death. I say close to death because the link that connects the perispirit and the soul to the body remains in the body and that link cannot be defined. The body then appears in the desired place. I believe this is all you wish to know.
6. That does not explain the visibility and tangibility of the perispirit.
   - Being detached from matter, according to his degree of elevation, the spirit can produce tangible matter.
7. Nevertheless, the tangible apparitions of hands and other parts of the body evidently come from inferior spirits.
   - The inferior spirits serve the superior ones who wish to demonstrate the fact.

8. Is the sleeping body a requirement so that the spirit may appear in other places?
   - The soul may divide itself when feeling transported to a place different from that where its body is located.
9. What would happen to a man deeply asleep, whose spirit would appear somewhere else, if that person were suddenly awakened?
   - This would not happen since if someone had the intention of waking him up, the spirit would foresee the intention and would return to the body, considering that the spirit reads the thoughts.

A similar fact is reported by Tacitus:

"During the months that Vespasian spent in Alexandria, waiting for the seasonal return of the dry winds and the time when the sea becomes favorable, several prodigies took place through which the favor of heaven and the interest that the gods seemed to have for that prince manifested... Such prodigies reinforced Vespasian wishes to visit the sacred dwelling of the god, to consult with him about the issues of the empire. He commanded that the temple be closed to everyone. Having entered the temple, his mind totally concentrated on what the oracle would say, he noticed one of the main Egyptians behind him, a man by the name of Basilide, who he knew had been sick for several days in Alexandria. He inquired the priests if Basilide had come to the temple that day; he asked around to the passers-by whether they had seen him in town; he finally sent men on horse backs to find him and certify that he was eighty miles away at that very moment. Then he no longer doubted that his vision was supernatural and that Basilide had taken the oracles' place. (Tacitus, Histories, Book IV, chap. 81 and 82, Translated by Burnouf)."

Since that fact has been communicated to us we have received several others of the same kind, from reliable sources. Among them there are some very recent ones that have occurred, say, in our environment, taking place in very interesting circumstances. Their explanations allow for a significant broadening of the psychological observations. The subject of the double men, left to the fantastic stories of the past, thus seems to have some truth in it. We shall return to this subject soon.

Spirits' Sensations

Do the spirits suffer? Which sensations do they experience? Such questions are naturally addressed to us and we try to answer them. Initially we must say that we do not limit ourselves to the answers of the spirits. We had somehow to consider the sensation as a fact, through observations.

In one of our sessions, soon after having received a beautiful essay from St. Louis regarding greed, published last February, one of our associates described the following fact with respect to that dissertation:

"We were evoking spirits in a small group of friends when suddenly and without been called, a spirit that we had known very well presented himself; he could have served as a model to the picture of the greedy one, painted by St. Louis: one of those men that live miserably surrounded by their fortunes; deprived of everything not to the benefit of others but just to accumulate more, uselessly. It was winter and we were by the fireplace. Then that spirit brought his name back to us, name that was far from our thoughts, requesting our permission to come to warm up by our fireplace, for three days, saying that he felt a horrible cold that he voluntarily endured during his life, and that he forced others to withstand, out of greed. This would be a relief, he added, if you allow me to."

That spirit was experiencing a painful sensation of cold. But how could that be? That was the difficulty. We then directed the following questions to St. Louis:

1. Could you kindly tell us how the spirit of that greedy man, who no longer had a material body, felt cold and asked for help to warm him up?

   - You can imagine the sufferings of the spirits by their moral sufferings.

2. We understand the moral sufferings like sorrow, remorse, shame, but heat, cold and the physical pain, these are not moral effects. Do the spirits experience that kind of sensation?

   - Does your soul feel cold? No, but it is aware of the sensation that it causes in the body.

3. As a consequence it seems that the spirit of the greedy did not feel real cold but he had the memory of the sensation caused by the cold he had endured and the memory that for him was like a reality, was a torture.

   - It is more or less that. Let it be very clear that there is a distinction between the moral and physical pain. One should not confuse the effect with the cause.

4. If we got it right one could explain things like this: The body is the instrument of pain. If it is not the first cause it is at least the immediate cause. The soul has the perception of that pain. That perception is the effect. The memory retained by the soul can be as painful as reality but it cannot have a physical action. Neither intense heat nor cold can disorganize its constitution. The soul cannot feel cold or heat. Don't we daily see the memory or apprehension of a physical illness producing the actual effect of reality? Even causing death? Everybody knows that amputees feel pain in the non-existent limb. That limb is certainly not the center or even the origin of the pain. The brain has kept the impression and that is all. One can thus believe that there is something analogous with the suffering of the spirits after death. Are such considerations correct?

   - Yes. Later you will understand even better. Wait for other facts that will provide you with new points of observation. You will then be able to arrive at comprehensive conclusions.

This was happening in the beginning of 1858. As a matter of fact, since then a more in depth study of the perispirit that represents a more important role in all spiritist manifestations, and that was still unnoticed, has taken place: the vaporous or tangible apparitions; the state of the spirit at the time of death; the so frequent idea in the spirits that they are still alive; the impressive portrait of the suicidal, of the executed, of those embedded in the material pleasures and so many other facts that brought light onto this question and that paved the way for explanations that we summarize below:

The perispirit is the link that unites the spirit to the material body; it is taken from the environment, from the universal fluid; it simultaneously has something of electricity, of the magnetic fluid and, up to a certain extent, of the inert matter. One could say that it is the quintessence of matter: it is the principle of the organic life, but not of the intellectual life. The intellectual life resides in the spirit. Besides, the perispirit is the agent to the exterior sensations. In the body those sensations are localized in the organs that operate as channels. Once the body is destroyed, the sensations become generic. That is why the spirits do not say that they have more pain in their head than on their feet. Furthermore it is necessary not to confuse the sensations of the perispirit, which became independent, with those of the body. The last ones have to be taken only comparatively and not as an analogy. Any excess of heat or cold may disorganize the very fabric of the body; however it cannot reach the perispirit. Once detached from the body the spirit can suffer but such a suffering is not that of the body. Nevertheless, it is not an exclusively moral suffering, like remorse, since the spirit complains about heat or cold; the spirit does not suffer more in the winter than in the summer; we have seen them going through the flames without any suffering. Thus, temperature cannot exert any impression on them. As a consequence, the pain they feel is not properly physical. It is a vague intimate feeling that the spirit himself is not always precisely aware of, since the pain is not localized and is not produced by any external agent. It is more of a memory than a reality, although it can be a really painful memory. There is, however, something else besides the memory, as we will see below.

Experience teaches us that at the time of death the perispirit detaches more or less slowly. At first the spirit is not aware of the situation; does not consider him dead; feels alive, sees the body by the side; acknowledges his own body but does not understand how it can be separated. Such a state lasts for as long as there is a bond between the body and the spirit.

Take the evocation of the person who committed suicide in the Samaritan baths described in our June issue. As everyone else, he said: "No, I am not dead." But added: "However, I feel the worms devouring me." Well, the worms cannot absolutely devour the perispirit, let alone the spirit. They only destroy the body. As the separation between the body and the perispirit was not complete, the result was a kind of moral repercussion that gave him the sensation of what was happening to the body. Repercussion might not be the correct word since it could lead to the supposition of a very material effect. It was, on the contrary, the vision of what was happening to his body, to which his perispirit was attached, that produced the illusion taken by reality. Thus, it was not a memory as he was not devoured by the worms while alive. It was an actual feeling.

From that we see the deductions that can be taken from the facts, when observed with attention. During life, the body receives exterior impressions transmitted to the spirit, through the perispirit that probably constitutes what is called nervous fluid. Once dead, the body no longer feels, as there is neither spirit nor perispirit. Once detached from the body the perispirit experiments the sensation. However, as that sensation does not arrive through a specific channel, it is then generic. Now, as in reality, there is only one transmitting agent, since it is the spirit that has consciousness, it results that if there could be a perispirit without spirit, it would not feel more than the dead body. In the same way, if the spirit had no perispirit it would be inaccessible to any painful sensation. That is what happens to the spirits who are completely depurated. We know that the more they depurate the more ethereal the essence of the perispirit becomes, from what follows that the influence of matter diminishes with the progress of the spirit, that is, as the perispirit becomes less materialized.

One would say, however, that the pleasant sensations are transmitted to the spirit through the perispirit, as well as the unpleasant ones. Thus, if the pure spirit is inaccessible to some, it must be equally to the others as well. Yes, no doubt, to those that uniquely come from the influence of the matter that we know. The sound of our instruments, the perfume of our flowers causes no impression on them. However, there are intimate sensations, of an indefinable enchantment, that we cannot have any idea about as, for that matter, we are like born blinds with respect to light. We know that it exists but through which media? Our knowledge stops here. We know that there is perception, sensation, hearing and vision; that such faculties are attributes of the whole being and not like with man, of a given part of the body. However, and once more, through which channel? That is what we ignore. The spirits themselves cannot enlighten us with that respect because our language is not capable of expressing ideas that we do not have, as a blind people would not have words to describe the effects of light, or the language of the savage would not have means of describing our arts, sciences and our philosophical doctrines.

When we say that the spirits are inaccessible to the impressions of our matter we refer to the very elevated spirits, whose ethereal covering has no analogy here on Earth. The same does not apply to those whose perispirit is denser. Those perceive our sounds, odors, but not through a limited part of their beings, as with when alive. One could say that the molecular vibrations are felt in their whole self, reaching the *sensorium commune*, which is the spirit itself, since by a different mode and even maybe with a different impression, that produces a modification in the perception. They hear the sounds of our voices but they understand us without the support of the word, through the simple transmission of our thoughts, supporting what we have said that the more dematerialized the spirit the easier that perception.

As for the vision, it is independent of light. Sight is an essential attribute of the soul. There is no darkness to the soul. Nevertheless, it is more extensive and penetrating in those that are more depurated. Thus, the soul, or spirit, has the faculty of all perceptions in itself. In the corporeal life they are obliterated by the grossness of our organs. In the extracorporeal life they are less and less obliterated, as the semi-material covering depurates.

Taken from the environment, that covering varies according to the nature of the globes. Moving from one world to the next the spirits change coverings as we change clothes from winter to summer and from the pole to the equator. When the more elevated spirits come to visit us they take by covering their terrestrial perispirit and since then their perceptions are similar to ours, common spirits. But all of them, the inferior as the superior ones, do not feel nor hear all but what they want to feel or hear. Without sensitive organs they can activate or void their perceptions at will. There is only one thing that they are obliged to hear: the advice of the good spirits.

Their vision is always active but they may become mutually invisible to one another. According to their position they can hide from those who are their inferiors but not from those who are their superiors.

Just after death their vision is always confused and perturbed. It becomes clearer as the spirit detaches and can achieve the same clearness as during life, irrespective of its penetration through the bodies that are opaque to us. As for its extension through the infinite space, towards the past as the future, it depends on the degree of purity and elevation of the spirit.

Some will say that such a theory is not very reassuring. We thought that once detached from the gross covering, instrument of our pains, we would no longer suffer. Here you are telling us that we will still suffer. Either way there will not be less suffering. Pity on us!

Yes, we can continue to suffer, and a lot, and for a long time, but we can also stop the suffering, even at the moment when we leave the corporeal life.

The Earthly sufferings are sometimes independent of us. Many, however, are consequence of our free-will. Let us go back to the source and we will see that the majority of the sufferings result from causes that we could have avoided. How many evils, how many illnesses does not the individual owe to one's own excesses, ambition, in one word, passions?

A person that had lived a sober life; that had not abused of anything; that had always been simple in one's tastes and modest in one's desires, would spare oneself of many tribulations.

The same applies to the spirit. The sufferings the spirit endures are always consequences of the way they lived on Earth. They will certainly no longer suffer from gout or rheumatism but will endure other sufferings which are not less painful. We saw that their sufferings are the result of the still existing link between them and matter; that the more separated from the influence of matter or, on another word, the more dematerialized, the less painful sensations they will have. Thus, it depends on the spirit to liberate from such influence, already in this life. The spirit has the free will and consequently the choice between doing or not doing something. Let the spirit dominate the animal passions; let there be no hatred, no envy, no jealousy or pride; let the spirit be free from selfishness; let the spirit purify its soul through the good feelings; may the spirit practice the good deeds and give to the things of this world the importance they deserve and then, even in the corporeal covering, they will already be depurated and untied from matter. On leaving such a material covering the spirit will no longer suffer its influence. The physical sufferings that he may have experimented will not leave a painful memory. There will remain no unpleasant impression because those would have affected the body, not the spirit; he will be happy for having freed himself and the calmness of his conscience will spare him from any moral suffering.

We have interrogated thousands of spirits that belonged to all echelons of society and attained all social positions; we studied them in all periods of their spiritual life, since the moment when they left the body; we followed them, step-by-step in this life beyond the grave, so as to observe the changes in their ideas and sensations. With that respect it was not the most vulgar creatures that offered us less interesting material for study. We have always seen that the sufferings depend on the conduct, whose consequences they suffer, and that this new existence is a source of ineffable happiness to those who have followed the right path, and consequently those who suffer, suffer for what they wanted and should not complain about anything but themselves, be it in this world or in the other one.

Certain critics ridicule some of our evocations, as for example of the assassin Lemaire[48], finding it strange that we get involved with such insig-

---

48 See the Spiritist Review, Volume 1.

nificant creatures, when we have so many superior spirits available to us. They forget that it is exactly because of those that we, somehow, scrutinize the nature of the fact or, better said, in their ignorance of the Spiritist Science, they don't see in such dialogues anything beyond a more or less funny conversation, whose reach is beyond them. We read somewhere that a philosopher has said, after talking to a peasant: "I learned more with this rustic man than with all scientists." It is that he could see beyond the surface. Nothing is lost to the good observer. He finds useful teachings even in the spores that grow in the manure. Does the doctor refuse to touch a horrific wound when looking for the cause of the illness?

Another word about this subject. The sufferings beyond the grave have a term. We know that the most inferior spirits can elevate and purify themselves through new trials. This can take long, very long, but it depends on the spirit to abbreviate such a painful time, because God always listen to him, as long as he submits to His will. The more dematerialized the spirit is, the ampler and lucid their perceptions; the more subjugated by the empire of matter, which entirely depends on his Earthly life style, the more limited and obscure they will be. The more one's vision extends to infinity, the more the others become restricted.

Hence the inferior spirits have only a vague, confusing, incomplete and sometimes null vision of the future. They cannot see the end of their sufferings and thus think that they will suffer for eternity, which is a penalty to them. If the position of some is afflictive, even terrible, it is not nonetheless, desperate. The position of the others, however, is eminently comforting. The choice is up to us. This is of the highest morality.

The skeptical have doubts about our fate after death. We show them exactly what happens by which we consider to be doing them a service. We have thus seen more than one retreating from their mistake or, at least, beginning to seriously consider what they only joked about before. There is nothing better than when we realize that something is possible. Had it always been like that there would not be so many incredulous people. In addition, both religion and public moral would gain insights from these facts. The religious doubt, for many people, comes from the difficulty in understanding certain things. These are positive spirits, not predisposed to blind faith, that only admit something that has a reason to them. Make these things accessible to their intelligence and they will accept them, as in the end they do not require more than that to believe. This is because skepticism to them is a more painful situation than we can imagine or they dare not confess.

There is no system or personal idea in everything that we have said. Also, it was not a group of privileged spirits that dictated such a theory to us. It is the result of studies done on individuals, corroborated and confirmed by spirits whose language would give us no doubt with respect to their superiority. We judged them by their words and not by their names or the names they have attributed to themselves.

Dissertations From
Beyond the Grave: Sleep

Poor human beings! How little you know about the most ordinary phenomena that exist in your life! You think highly of yourselves; you think that you have a vast knowledge and remain speechless before these simple questions framed by all children: "What do we do when we are asleep? What is the meaning of dreams? I don't have the pretension of making you understand what I want to explain, since there are things that your spirit cannot yet submit to, because one can only admit what one can comprehend.

Sleep entirely frees the soul from the body. When we are asleep we are momentarily in the same state that we shall definitely be after death. The spirits that have quickly detached from matter, on the occasion of their death, had intelligent dreams; those, when sleeping, meet again with the society of other beings that are superior to them; that travel, talk to them and are enlightened by them. They even work on tasks that they find finalized when they die. This, once more, must teach us that we should not fear death, as we die every day as once stated by a Saint.

All this was said with respect to the superior spirits. The large majority of people, however, who may remain in that perturbation for long hours, in that uncertainty that you were told about, those individuals go to worlds that are inferior to Earth, attracted by old affections, or to look for pleasures that are even of a lower level than those found here. They will then learn doctrines that are even more vile, ignoble and harmful than those that they profess among you. What establishes the sympathy on Earth is nothing else but the fact that we feel attracted by the heart, as we wake up, to those with whom we have just spent eight or nine hours of pleasure or happiness. What also establishes the irresistible antipathy is that, deep there in the heart, we know that those creatures have a different conscience, with respect to us; hence we know them not having ever setting our eyes on them. It is this that also explains the indifference, since we don't seek to make friends when we know that we have others that love us and wish us well. In one word, the sleep influences your lives more than you think.

Through sleep, the incarnated spirits are always in contact with the spiritual world, allowing then that the superior spirits, without much repulse, do agree to come to incarnate in your environment. God wanted that during the contact with vices they could reinforce their virtues in the source of goodness, so as not to fail, as they come to instruct others. Sleep is the door that God opened to them to meet their friends from heaven; it is the break after the work, waiting for the great liberation, the final liberation that should reintegrate them back to their real world.

A dream is the memory of what your spirit saw during the sleep. Notice, however, that you do not always dream since you do not always remember some of what you have seen or everything that you have seen. It is not your soul in its full detachment; often it is nothing more than the memory of the perturbation that follows our departure or arrival, added to the memory of what you have done or that worries you during the waking state. Without that, how can we explain those absurd dreams, of the scholars as well as of the simplest person? The evil spirits also use the dream to torment the weak and pusillanimous souls.

As a matter of fact you will soon see the development of a new kind of dreams. It is as old as the one you know but ignored by you. It is the dream of Joan of Arc, of Jacob, of the Jewish prophets and of some Indian foretellers. Such a dream represents the memory of the soul, entirely separated from the body; the memory of that second life that I was telling you about, some time ago.

For the dreams that you retain the memory try to distinguish well between those two kinds, as without it you shall fall into contradictions and cause dismal mistakes to your faith.

OBSERVATION: When required to provide his name, the spirit who dictated the communication answered: "What for? Do you think that it is only the spirits of your great individuals that come to tell you good things? Then, all of those that you don't know and that do not have a name in your world are worthless? Know this that many just use a name to satisfy you."

Dissertations From Beyond the Grave: The Flowers

OBSERVATION: This communication and the following one were obtained by Mr. F..., the same that we talked about in our October issue with respect to the obsessed and subjugated. One can see the difference regarding the nature of his communications now and those from that time. His free-will completely triumphed from the obsession that victimized him, and his bad spirit no longer showed up. These two dissertations were dictated to him by Bernard Pallissy.[49]

"Flowers were created in the world as symbols of beauty, purity and hope."

"How come the person who watches the unfolding petals every spring and the flowers fading to bear delicious fruits doesn't think that one's life, in the same way, will wither but will eventually yield eternal fruits? What does it matter to you the storms and torrents? These flowers will never perish nor the most delicate work of the Creator. Have courage then you people that fall in the streets; stand up as the lily does after the storm, purer and more radiant. As with the flowers, the winds shake you right and left from all sides; they knock you down and drag you over the mud, but when the sun is up again raise your heads as the noblest and the greatest."

---

49 See the Spiritist Review, Volume 4.

"So, love the flowers. They are the emblem of your life and do not be ashamed to be compared to them. Have them everywhere, in your gardens, in your houses, in your temples even, as they are pleasant everywhere. They always inspire poetry and elevate the soul of whoever understands them. Wasn't that in the flowers that God has manifested all of his magnificence? How would you know the sweet colors with which the Creator has brightened nature if it were not for the flowers? Before poeple had searched the entrails of Earth to find the ruby and topaz, they had the flowers before them, and the infinite variety of shades already consoled them from the monotony of Earth's surface. So love the flowers then: you will be purer and kinder; you will eventually become like children but you will be the beloved children of God, and your soul simple and spotless will be accessible to all God's love, to all joy with which He will warm up your hearts."

"Flowers wish to be treated by enlightened hands. Intelligence is necessary for their prosperity. You have been doing wrong on Earth since long ago by leaving such a care to unskillful hands that mutilated them when trying to embellish them. There is nothing sadder than those round or pointed trees in some of your gardens, pyramids of greenery that look more like a haystack. Let nature flourish on a thousand of different ways: that is the grace. Happy is the one that can appreciate the beauty of a simple branch that swings, spreading the fertilizing dust. Happy is the one who sees the infinity of grace in their brilliant colors, finesse, shades, nuances that escape and seek one another, flee and reunite. Blessed is the one that can understand the beauty of the graded shades! From the dark root that marries Earth to the blending colors of the scarlet tulips and poppies (why such harsh and weird names?). Study all this and notice the leaves that sprout from one another, like endless generations, until their complete blossom under the celestial dome."

"Doesn't it seem like the flowers germinate from Earth to launch themselves towards other worlds? Doesn't it seem like many times they painfully lower their heads for being incapable of rising even further? Don't we think that, for their beauty, the flowers are closer to God? Thus, imitate them and become greater and more beautiful."

"Your way of learning botany is defective. It is not enough to know the name of a plant. I shall call you again when you have time to work on a book of that kind. I defer to a later time the lessons I wanted to give you today. They will be most useful when we have the opportunity to apply them. Then we will talk about the kinds of culture, the places that suit them; the arrangement of the buildings for ventilation and sanitary conditions of the dwellings."

"If you publish this, remove the last paragraphs so that they are not seen as propaganda."

Dissertations From Beyond the Grave: Woman's Role

"**W**oman is more finely chiseled than man, naturally indicating a more delicate soul. That is how in a similar condition, in all worlds, the mother will be prettier than the father, for she is the first to be seen by the child. The child always turns her eyes onto the angelical figure of a young lady. It is for the mother that the child dries the tear, staring at her with those still weak and uncertain eyes. The child thus has the natural intuition of beauty.

A woman knows how to become noticed by the kindness of their thoughts, by the grace of their gestures and words. Everything that comes from her should harmonize with her being, beautifully created by God.

The long hairs, lying on the shoulders, are the actual image of kindness and the easiness with which it bends without breaking, before the trials. They reflect the lights of the suns, like the woman's soul should reflect the purest light of God. Young ladies, allow your hairs to float. God created them for that. You shall simultaneously have the most natural and ornate appearance.

A woman should dress in a simple way. She left God's hands sufficiently beautiful to spare the embellishments. White and blue should merge over your shoulders. Allow also your dresses to float. May your outfits be seen extending behind you like a long runway of gauze, like a cloud that immediately reveals your presence!

Nevertheless, what is the meaning of the ornaments, the dresses, the waving or fluctuating hairs, up or down, if that sweet smile of mothers and lovers do not shine on your lips? If your eyes do not sow goodness, charity, and hope in the tears of happiness that they allow to roll, in the lightning that shines from that brazier of unknown love?

Women! Do not be afraid of delighting men by your beauty, by your grace, by your superiority. However, men need to know that to become worthy of you, they have to be as great as you are beautiful, as wise as you are good, as instructed as you are original and simple. They need to know that they must deserve you; that you are the award of virtue and honor, but not of that honor covered by a helmet and a shield, shining on tournament jousts, holding a foot over an overthrown enemy's head; no, but God's honor.

Men! Be useful and when the poor bless your name, women shall be your equal. Then you shall form a wholesome bond: you will be the head and they will be the heart; you will be the beneficent thought, they will be the liberal hands. Therefore, unite not only for love, but also for the good deeds that you can do together. These good thoughts and good actions performed by two loving hearts are the links of these gold and diamonds chain called marriage. Then, when the links are in a large enough number, God will call you near Him and you will continue to bond new links together, links that were made of heavy and cold metal on Earth but that will be made of light and fire in heavens."

Spirits' Poetry

Note: These verses were spontaneously written through a basket, touched by a young lady and a boy. We thought that many poets would feel honored by having written them. They were sent to us by one of our subscribers.

Awakening of a Spirit

"How beautiful nature and how sweet the air is!
Lord, I say grace praising you on my knees!
May the joyful hymn of my acknowledgement,
like incense, rise to Thy supreme entitlement!
Thus, before the eyes of the sisters grieving
you sent Lazarus out of his coffin;
Distraught Jairus, his daughter, beloved,
on her deathbed by Your voice revived.
Also, mighty God! You reached me the hand of thou reign;
Stand! Thou said, You have not said in vain.
Why am I not, alas, a vile stack of mud?
I would like to praise You with the voice of a cherub;
Your work never seemed so awesome!
To the one that comes from the darkness of the tomb.
The day seems pure, and the light is shining,
the sun is more radiant and life exciting.

The air is then sweeter than milk and honey;
every sound is a word in the concerts of the holy.
The muffled voice of the wind breathes harmony
that grows in space and becomes infinity.
What the spirit conceives, or reaches the eyes,
what we can read in the book of paradise,
In the space of the seas, below the tides,
in all oceans, cliffs, and globes,
All rounds into a sphere, and we feel that in the midst
God is in the center of these converging axises.
And You, whose eyes hover the starry trails,
who are You hiding in the sky, like a King in his sails
What is Your greatness, if this vast universal face
is not but a point to Your eyes, and the submerse space

of the seas is not even a mirror of its magnificence?
What is then Your greatness, your essence?
What such a great palace have You built, Oh King!
The stars cannot separate You from us, sure thing

the sun at Your feet, immeasurable power,
like the onyx attached to the prince's slipper.
It is what I most admire in You, Oh Majesty!
Much less than greatness, Your generosity
That reveals in everything, a shining light
that hears the impotent, yielding to the prayer's might."
JODELLE

Family Conversations

From Beyond the Grave:

A Widow of Malabar

We wanted to interrogate one of those women from India, subjected to the tradition of being burnt over the cadaver of their husbands. As we did not know any of them we had asked St. Louis to send one to us, who could be capable of satisfactorily responding to our questions. He said that he would gladly do so in due course. In the Society's session on November 2nd, 1858 Mr. Adrien, clairvoyant medium, saw one woman that wanted to speak, giving us the following description of her:

"Large black eyes, with a yellow sclerotic; round face; salient and fat faces; saffron brunet skin; long eyelashes, black arched supercilious; a bit large nose, slightly flattened; large and sensual mouth; uniform, beautiful and large teeth; long wavy hair, black, abundant and greasy. She had a fat body, big and stubby. Silken outfit that left the breast somewhat uncovered. She was wearing bracelets on arms and legs."

1. Do you remember more or less over which time you have lived in India and where you were set on fire together with your husband's body?
   - She shook her head, as she did not remember. St. Louis answered, indicating that it was about one hundred years ago.

2. Do you remember your name from that time?
   - Fatima.
3. What was your religion?
   - Muslim.
4. But doesn't Islam prohibit such sacrifices?
   - I was born Muslim but my husband's religion was Brahmanism. I had to comply with the customs of the religion of the region where I lived. Women do not belong to themselves.
5. How old were you when you were killed?
   - I believe I was about twenty years old.
     OBSERVATION: Mr. Adrien explained that she seems to be between twenty-eight and thirty years old, but mentioned that women age faster in that country.
6. Did you sacrifice voluntarily?
   - I preferred to have married someone else. Think about it and you will see that all of us think like that. I followed the customs but bottom line is I would rather not have done it. I waited for another husband for several days but nobody showed up. Then I obeyed the law.
7. Which sentiment may have established such a law?
   A superstitious idea. They think that by burning us to death they please the divinity; that we redeem the faults of the one we lost and that by doing so we will help him to be happy in the other world.
8. Was your husband happy with your sacrifice?
   - I have never tried to see my husband again.
9. Are there women that do such a sacrifice in good faith?
   - There are a few: one in a thousand. The reality is that they would not wish to do it.

10. What happened to you at the time that your corporeal life was extinguished?

    - Perturbation. I felt that all went dark, and then I don't know what happened. My ideas were confused for a long time after that. I went everywhere, however, I could not see properly. Still now I do not feel completely lucid. I will have to go through many incarnations to elevate myself but I will no longer burn... I don't see the need to burn people, to thrown oneself into the flames so as to improve... particularly for faults that were not ours. Besides, I was never pleased with that... As a matter of fact, I never wanted to know about it. Would you kindly pray a little bit for me? I believe that there is nothing like the prayer to give us courage to withstand the trials that are sent to us... Ah! If I had faith!

11. You ask us to pray for you but we are Christians. How could our prayers be pleasant to you?

    - There is only one God to all people.

       OBSERVATION: The same woman was seen among the spirits present in several of the following sessions. She said that she came to be instructed. It seems that she was touched by the interest that we demonstrated towards her, as she followed us on several other meetings and even in the streets.

Family Conversations

From Beyond the Grave:

The Beautiful Weaver

News – Luísa Charly, known as Labé, also known as "The Beautiful Weaver", was born in Lyon, during the time of Francis I. She was of a perfect beauty, a finely educated lady. She knew Latin, Greek, spoke Spanish and Italian, and even wrote poetry in those languages that would not discredit the national writers. She was familiar with all kinds of physical exercises, capable of horse riding, gymnast and the handling of weapons. She had a very energetic character, distinguishing, together with her father, among the bravest fighters in 1542, during the siege of Perpignan, where she fought disguised under the cover name Captain Loys. Failed the siege, she renounced her career and returned, with her weapons, to Lyon with her father. She married a rich rope manufacturer by the name of Ennemond Perrin and soon became only known as "the beautiful weaver", name by which she was recognized in the street where she lived and where her husband's factory was located. She organized cultural gatherings in her house, for which she invited the most brilliant minds of the province. She left a collection of poetry. Her reputation as a woman and her beauty attracted to her the masculine elite, exciting the envy of the

Lyonnais ladies, who tried to revenge with calumny. Her conduct, how-ever, was always irreproachable.

She was evoked in one session of the Parisian Society of Spiritist Studies on October 26th, 1858 when we were told that she could not come yet for reasons that were not explained. On November 9th she attended our appeal and here is the description given to us by Mr. Adrien, our clairvoyant medium:

"Oval head, pale mate skin; lively, beautiful black eyes; arched eyebrows; developed and intelligent forehead; fine Greek nose; medium mouth, lips indicating goodness of spirit; beautiful, small and good looking teeth; extremely black hair, slightly curled. Noble pose of head, slender, handsome appearance. Wearing white outfit."

OBSERVATION: There is no doubt that nothing proves that such a picture, like the preceding one, is not just the result of the medium's imagination, since we cannot control it. But when he does the same with such an amount of precise details with respect to contemporary people that he had never seen, recognized by relatives and friends, we can no longer doubt his authenticity. Therefore one can conclude that if he unarguably sees some of those he can also see the others. Another circum-stance worth mentioning is that he sees the same spirit over many months and the portrait does not change. It would be necessary to assume that he has a phenomenal memory such that he was able to remember the minor details of every spirit that he had already described. This would amount to a number in the hundreds by now.

1. Evocation
   - I am here.
2. Could you kindly respond to some of our questions?
   - With pleasure.

3. Do you remember that time when you were known as "the beautiful weaver"?
   - Yes.

4. Where have you taken the virile qualities that made you embrace a career with the weapons that are, according to the natural laws, an attribute of men?
   - It was pleasing to my spirit that was eager of great things. Later it turned into another level of more serious ideas. The ideas that we bring since birth that do certainly come from previous existences. These are a reflection, however greatly modify by our own resolutions or by God's will.

5. Why haven't you persisted on those military tastes? How come they so promptly gave rise to the feminine pleasures?
   - I saw things that I wish you don't ever see.

6. You were a contemporary of Francis I and Charles V. Could you give us your opinion about those men and establish a parallel?
   - I don't wish to judge. They had imperfections that you know; their virtues were less plentiful: a few traces of generosity and that is it. Leave all that behind because their hearts could still bleed: they suffer a lot!

7. What would have been the source of such a privileged intelligence that made you capable of receiving an education superior to the women of your time?
   - Painful existences and God's will!

8. You had then accomplished a previous progress?
   - It could not have been different.

9. Has that instruction made you evolve as a spirit?
   - Yes.

10. It seems that you were happy on Earth. Are you still happy now?
    - What a question! However much one may be happy on Earth, heavens' happiness is something very different! What treasures and richness you shall one day know. Those riches that you do not even suspect or completely ignore!

11. What do you understand by heavens?
   - Heaven to me is represented by the other worlds.
12. Which world do you inhabit now?
   - I inhabit a world unknown to you but I am not much bonded to it. Matter does not attach us much there.
13. Is it Jupiter?
   - Jupiter is a happy world but do you think that among all worlds it is the only one that is favored by God? They are as plentiful as the grains of sand at the beach.
14. Have you kept the poetic vein that you had here?
   - I would respond with pleasure but I am afraid this could shock other spirits or place me below my position, what would make my answer useless, falling into the emptiness.
15. Could you tell us in which class we could place you among the spirits?
   - No answer.
16. (To St. Louis) Could St. Louis respond to that?
   - She is here. I cannot say what she does not wish to say. Don't you see that she is among the most elevated among the spirits that you ordinarily evoke? As a matter of fact, the spirits cannot precisely define the distances that separate them. They are incomprehensible to you, but those are immense.
17. (To Luisa Charly) – Under which form are you among them?
   - Adrien has just described me.
18. Why this and not another form? Finally, why in the world where you are now you don't look like you were on Earth?
   - You evoked me as a poet; I came as a poet.
19. Could you dictate some poems to us or any literary text? We would feel happy to have something from you.
   - Find my old writings. We don't like these tests, particularly in public. However, I will do that on another occasion.

OBSERVATION: Everyone knows that the spirits don't like to be submitted to tests and requests of such a nature always have more or less that character. That is no doubt why they almost never agree. Spontaneously and when we expect the least they sometimes give us surprising proofs that we would have uselessly requested. But almost always it is enough to ask them something in order not to obtain it, particularly if the request conceals a sentiment of curiosity. Thus, the spirits, and particularly the elevated ones, want to demonstrate to us that they are not at our service.

On the very next day, through the medium that had served her as interpreter, the Beautiful Weaver wrote the following:

"I will dictate what I promised. It is not poetry that I don't wish to do. In reality I don't remember what I did and you would not like that. This will be prose, of the modest kind."

"I exalted love, sweetness and good feelings on Earth; I spoke a little of what I did not know. It is no longer of love that I speak here but of a broad, austere and enlightened charity; a strong and constant charity that has only one example on Earth."

"Oh People! Consider that your happiness depends on you, as does the transformation of your world into one of the most advanced of the sky: just eliminate hatred and hostility, forget resentments and rage; lose pride and vanity. Leave all that as a burden that sooner or later is necessary to abandon. Such a burden is a treasure to you on Earth, I do know well, that is why you will have merit for abandoning it, leaving it behind; however, it is an obstacle to your happiness in heaven. So, believe me: speed up your progress. True happiness is the one that comes from God. Where will you find pleasures that are worth the joy it gives to the elected ones, the angels?"

"God loves people that seek progress in their paths. You can then count on God's support. Don't you trust God? Do you think it is perjure, that you should not give yourself entirely and without re-strictions? Unfortunately you don't want to understand or only a few among you do understand; you prefer the present day to the next one; your narrow vision limits your feelings, your heart and your soul and you suffer to move on, instead of naturally and easily walking through the good path, out of your own free will, hence suffering is the means employed by God to moralize you. Do not avoid such a safe route, but terrible to the traveler. I shall finish by exhorting you to no longer see death as a scourge, but as the door to the real life and true happiness."

LUÍSA CHARLY

Varieties - Monomania

An issue of the *Gazette de Mons* publishes the following:
"An individual afflicted by religious monomania, taken to the institution of Mr. Stuart since seven years ago, presenting himself very calm up to now, was able to deceive security and get hold of a knife. Because the guards were unable to recover the weapon the director of the institution was informed."

"Mr. Stuart then immediately approached the furious man and, armed only with his courage, attempted to unarm the man. Mr. Stuart had hardly moved a few steps when the mad man dashed like a lightning towards him, stabbing him multiple times. The murderer was dominated with great difficulty. From the seven stabbing wounds inflicted on Mr. Stuart one was mortal: the one that reached his lower belly. He succumbed as a consequence of a hemorrhage from that cavity wound on Monday, at three thirty."

What wouldn't be said if that individual had been troubled by a spirit's monomania, or if he had, in his madness, spoken of spirits? However, this would be possible considering that there are several religious monomanias and that all sciences have already given their contribution. What could rationally be concluded against Spiritism other than the fact that man, as a consequence of the fragility of his own organization, can exalt himself in that particular aspect as with others? The way by which one can prevent such exaltation is not by combating the idea, otherwise we would take the risk of seen the prodigies of Cévennes renovated. We would see Spiritism propagating remarkably had no campaign been organized against it. How to oppose a phenomenon that has neither favorite time nor place; that can happen everywhere, in all families, in the intimacy, under the most absolute secrecy, even better than in public? We have indicated the means to prevent the inconvenience in our Practical Instruction: Make Spiritism so much understood that one can see only a natural phenomenon, even with events that seem most extraordinary.

An Issue of Priority In

Matters of Spiritism

Mr. Ch. Renard, a subscriber of our Review, from Rambouillet, sent us the following letter:

"Dear Sir and dignified comrade in Spiritism.

I read, or better saying, I devour with unspeakable satisfaction your review issues, as I receive them. This is not surprising in my case since my relatives were foretellers, from generation to generation. One of my great-great-great-grandmothers was even condemned to die at the stake as contumacious in the murder of Vauldrie, and a regular of the Sabbath. She was only able to avoid the stake by hiding in one of her sister's house, an abbess of a secluded religious group. Hence I have inherited some crumbs of occult Sciences, fact that did not preclude me from going through the materialistic belief, if there is a belief there, and skepticism. Finally, exhausted, ill of negativism, then the works of the ecstatic celebrity Swedenborg brought me to the truth and good. Becoming myself an ecstatic I was convinced ad vivum about the truths that the materialized spirits of our globe cannot understand.

I had communications of all kinds: phenomena of visions, tangibility, transportation of lost objects, etc.

Would the brother kindly publish the note below in one of your next issues? It is not a question of self-love but of my condition of French man.

Sometimes the small causes lead to great effects. Around 1840 I had established a friendly relationship with Mr. Cahagnet, plumber and engraver, who had come to Ramboillet for health reasons. That high-class worker of refined intelligence was initiated by me in human magnetism. One day I told him: I am positive that a lucid somnambulist is capable of seeing the souls of the dead and establish conversation with them. He was impressed. I induced him to carry out such experiment when he could count on a lucid somnambulist. He was successful and published a first book on necromantic experiences, followed by other volumes and brochures which in the USA were translated under the title *Celestial Telegraph*. Later the ecstatic Davis published his visions or excursions through the spiritual world. About the dematerialized, Franklin did researches that achieved manifestations and communications easier than in the past. The first persons that he magnetized in the USA were the Fox widow and her two daughters. There is a remarkable coincidence between that name and mine since the English word fox means *"renard"*.[50]

Since long ago the spirits told me that it was possible to communicate with spirits of other globes, from which we would receive drawings and descriptions. I exposed the subject to Mr. Cahagnet but he did not go beyond our satellite.

I am yours.... Etc

Ch. Renard."

OBSERVATION: The issue of priority, in matters of Spiritism, is unquestionably secondary. But it is not less remarkable that since the importation

---

50 Fox in French (NT)

of the American phenomena, a number of authentic facts, ignored by the public, revealed the production of similar phenomena, both in France as well as in other European countries, in the same period or earlier.

We know that many people were involved with spiritist communications well before the turning tables were visited, and we have proofs of that we specific dates. It seems that Mr. Renard is part of that group and, according to him, his experiments would not have been different from those produced in America. We register his observation is an interesting fact to the history of Spiritism and to prove once more that this Science has roots all over the world, denying any chance of success to those who wish to impose a barrier to Spiritism. If they smother it here it will appear stronger in a hundred of other places, exactly at the time when it shall conquer a place among the common beliefs, since the doubt is no longer viable. Then, willing or not, the adversaries will have to take its position.

To the Readers of the Spiritist Review – Conclusion of 1858

The Spiritist Review has just completed its first year and we are happy to announce that its publication will continue, since its very existence is ensured by a number of subscribers that increases daily. The demonstrations of sympathy that we have received from everywhere and the support of people that are distinguished by their knowledge and social positions are signs of encouragement in the laborious task that we have initiated. May all those who have helped us with the realization of our enterprise receive our warmth gratitude!

Had we not been faced by criticism and contradictions we would be before an unprecedented fact in the chronicles of publicity, particularly considering that it is all related to such new ideas. Those are, in fact, surprisingly less frequent than the signs of support that we have been given. That is due, no doubt, much less to the merit of the writer than to the attractiveness of the analyzed subject and to the credit that it daily conquers in the highest social echelons; we owe that also – and we are completely convinced of that – to the dignified approach we have maintained before our adversaries, allowing the public to judge between moderation, from one side, and inconvenience from the other.

Spiritism marches at gigantic steps all over the world. It daily reconquers some dissidents by the force of things and if we can add some tiny bits to the scale of this inexorable movement that takes place, that will register our time as a new era, it shall not be by irritating or frontally attacking those very persons that we wish to attract, but by reasoning with them instead of telling injuries that will make us heard.

The superior spirits that assist us give the precept and example of that. It would be unworthy of a Doctrine that preaches nothing but love and benevolence to go down to the arena of personalism. We leave that task to the ones that do not understand it.

Then nothing will detour us from the line that we have been following, from the calmness and cold blood that we will always maintain in the thoughtful examination of all questions; since we know that by so doing we conquer more serious adepts to Spiritism than by discourtesy and acrimony.

In the introduction with which we opened the first issue we established the plan that we proposed to follow: cite all facts but also analyze and submit them to the scalpel of observation; appreciate them and deduce their consequences.

In the beginning all the attention was concentrated on the natural phenomena that fed public curiosity then, but which has its time; once satisfied that curiosity, we left it alone, like a child that abandons a toy. The spirits then said: "This is the first period; it will soon pass to give way to more elevated ideas. New facts shall be revealed, defining a new period, the philosophical, and the Doctrine will grow in a short time, like the child that leaves the crib. Don't be disturbed by the mockery since they will mock the mockers themselves and tomorrow you shall find zealous defenders among the strongest adversaries of today. God wishes it to be so and we are assigned with the task of executing God's will. The ill intent of some people shall not prevail against it. The pride of those who pretend to know better than God will be abated."

We are effectively far from the dancing tables that no longer amuse, since everything comes to saturation. Only those things that speak to our reason do not bore us, thus Spiritism sails full wind in its second period. Everybody understood that it is the foundation of a whole Science, a whole new order of ideas. Such a trend should be followed. More than that, it was necessary to give it our contribution; otherwise we would be soon left behind. That is why we strive to catch up, avoiding the narrow limits of an anecdotal bulletin.

Once elevated to the heights of a philosophical Doctrine, Spiritism has conquered many experts, even among those who have never witnessed a material fact. Here is why: Human beings appreciate anything that speaks to reason, anything that they can understand. They find in the Spiritist Philosophy something different from a simple amusement, something that fills up the pungent emptiness of their uncertainty. By penetrating the extracorporeal world through the observation, we wanted to introduce our readers into that, helping them to understand it. It is up to them to say if our objective has been achieved. We will proceed with our task in the year that is about to begin and that we foresee to be a plentiful one. New facts of a strange order take place now, revealing new mysteries to us. We shall carefully register them and seek the enlightenment it may provide with as much perseverance as in the past, since everything presages that Spiritism shall enter into a new phase, more grandiose and still more sublime.

ALLAN KARDEC

NOTE: The abundance of material forces us to postpone the continuation of our article about the plurality of existences as well as well as the narrative by Frédéric Soulié to the next issue.

ALLAN KARDEC

19798868R00349

Made in the USA
Middletown, DE
04 May 2015